Subjecting Verses

Subjecting Verses

LATIN LOVE ELEGY AND THE EMERGENCE OF THE REAL

Paul Allen Miller

PRINCETON UNIVERSITY PRESS
PRINCETON AND OXFORD

U.S. Library of Congress and British Library Cataloging-in-Publication Data is available
This book has been composed in Sabon
Printed on acid-free paper. ∞
www.pupress.princeton.edu
Printed in the United States of America

1 3 5 7 9 10 8 6 4 2

To Annie, *Omnia vincit amor*

CONTENTS

ACKNOWLEDGMENTS

THIS BOOK has been eight years in the making. I fear that I shall almost certainly forget to thank one of the countless people who have read drafts of various chapters. Special debts of thanks are owed Micaela Janan and Sharon Diane Nell, who read the whole manuscript from cover to cover and provided numerous comments, suggestions, and much needed criticisms. Judith Hallett as one of my readers for Princeton did me invaluable service, and the entire book has been much strengthened by her exacting and detailed criticisms. At various points during the book's composition, chapters have been read and responded to by a wide a variety of friends and colleagues: Chuck Platter, David Larmour, Ralph Johnson, Marilyn Skinner, Sharon James, Ellen Greene, Tim Moore, Douglass Parker, David Wray, Andrew Cousins, David Oberhelman, and Wayne Rebhorn. To each of you, I owe a special debt of thanks. I also most gratefully acknowledge the classics departments at the University of Texas at Austin, the University of Georgia, Boston University, the University of Chicago, Duke University, and Notre Dame University for allowing me to present the results of my ongoing research to them. Lastly, this book could not have been written without the assistance of a sabbatical leave in the spring of 1997 from Texas Tech University that allowed me to start writing in a serious fashion and a College of Liberal Arts Scholarship Support grant from the University of South Carolina in the summer of 2001 that allowed me to complete my first draft.

I owe special thanks to my teachers, Barbara Gold, Carl Rubino, and Kevin Herbert, who taught me to love this poetry and the adventure of intellectual inquiry. A debt of gratitude is also owed to my parents, Joe and Mary Miller, who have offered me unwavering support in all my endeavors, to Ann who puts up with me no matter what, and to Sam who is five-years-old today. Happy birthday, buddy!

A portion of an early draft of chapter 1 appeared in "Towards a Post-Foucauldian History of Discursive Practices," *Configurations* 7 (1999): 211–55 © The Johns Hopkins University Press and is reprinted with permission of Johns Hopkins University Press. Portions of chapter 4 were published in "The Tibullan Dream Text," *Transactions of the American Philological Association* 129 (1999), 181–224 © The Johns Hopkins University Press and are here reprinted with the permission of Johns Hopkins University Press. The first three sections of chapter 5 appeared in "Why

Propertius Is a Woman: French Feminism and Augustan Elegy," *Classical Philology* 96 (2001): 127–46. Copyright (©) 2001 by University of Chicago Press. They are reprinted here with the permission of the University of Chicago Press.

November 4, 2002
Columbia, S.C.

Subjecting Verses

TOWARD A NEW HISTORY OF GENRE: ELEGY AND THE REAL

> It seems to me rather that we have to look at failures of
> form, the impossibility of certain kinds of representation
> in a certain context, the flaws, limits, obstacles, which
> become the clue to the social truth or social meaning.
> —Jameson 1998: 361

> It can often be the emphasis on the impossibility of
> representation that gives the clue and organizes things.
> —Jameson 1998: 369

THE PURPOSE of this book is to provide a history or genealogy of the Latin love elegy. That history is problematic and demands a more comprehensive explanation in part because it is so short. Many books have already treated the form, and in recent years several have offered exciting and sophisticated readings of its rhetoric and modes of characterization (Greene 1998; Kennedy 1993; Veyne 1988), but none has offered a convincing exegesis of this subgenre's sudden flaring into existence and its just as sudden extinction. Indeed, most treatments have largely eschewed historical modes of reading, except for now outdated forays into the uncertain terrain of biographical criticism.

Latin love elegy first comes to light in the last years of Catullus's life, around 56 B.C.E. It effectively disappears with Ovid's death in exile in 17 C.E.[1] Seventy-three years may not seem short by the standards of popular culture, but it is only a blink of the eye compared with the life-spans enjoyed by genres such as epic (Ennius to Statius)[2] and verse satire (Lucilius to Juvenal)[3] in the Roman world, or the sonnet sequence (Petrarch to Shakespeare and beyond)[4] and the novel (Cervantes to the present)[5] in modern times. Nonetheless, even this rather limited chronology is overgenerous. Catullus is generally considered a precursor of elegy rather than an elegist in his own right. Ovid's exilic poetry shares with erotic elegy only meter, subject position, and allusions to the conventions defining the form. His beloved in exile is Rome, not some coy mistress. If we limit ourselves to the period between the appearance of Gallus's first book of elegies, generally considered the first complete exemplar of the genre, circa 50 B.C.E., and Ovid's publication of the definitive edition of the *Amores*, circa 7 B.C.E. to 1 C.E.,[6] the last collection of love elegy to have any observable influence on subsequent literary history, then the entire genre, as an effective and authentic form of literary expression, can be said to have bloomed and died in a mere fifty years (Lee-Stecum 1998: 16–18; Albrecht 1997: 744; Elia 1981: 74–75; Boucher 1980: 34).

Of course, this does not mean that elegies ceased to be written. We continue to have references to occasional practitioners of elegiac verse later in the imperial period, but none of them merits appearance in Quintilian's canonical list of the Roman elegists (10.1) or Diomedes the Grammarian's fifth-century compilation (1.484) or had any recognizable influence on the literature of his day (Ross 1975: 101; Boucher 1980: 164). Thus, Pliny the younger mentions a nephew of Propertius (*Epistles* 6.15.1, 9.22.1–2),[7] and Statius a certain Stella (*Silvae* 1.2),[8] but neither of them left either any substantial record of his work. The genre's moment, it seems, had passed. The extreme tensions, which I argue constitute the elegiac subject position, no longer assumed the same forms. Erotic elegy's extraordinary public dramatization of a private sphere that both engages socially constituted norms of individual conduct and insistently calls them into question—the vital contradictions at the heart of its being—were no longer able to find a place from which they could be directly spoken. Those tensions were not so much resolved as displaced. The Ovid of the *Tristia*, as we shall see in chapter 8, could only continue the discourse of elegy by speaking from the realm of the dead. What we see in him and those who come after is the specter of elegy rather than elegy proper. No longer possible is the overtly contradictory position of a Tibullus, who accepts a life of traditional martial virtue for his patron Messalla but rejects it for himself (1.1; see chapter 4); of a Propertius, who casts his love for Cynthia in terms recalling Antony's for Cleopatra while praising Caesar's victory at Actium (2.15, 2.16; see chapter 5), or of an Ovid, who simultaneously invokes the power of *ius* while proposing stratagems of adultery (*Amores* 1.4; see chapter 6). The ideological space required for this type of openly split subject is no longer available (Boucher 1980: 34–35).

Instead, we see a new model emerge in which the subject is always already absent from view, speaking from nowhere, from a place beyond the contingencies of the here and now (Newman 1989: 1501). Persius under Nero digs a grave (*scrobis*) in which to tell the truth and bury it (1.119–20).[9] Juvenal under Trajan dares only speak of (and thus effectively from) the dead (1.170–71). The position of the speaking subject has changed in a fundamental way (Auerbach 1965: 247–48; Foucault 1984: 105; Henderson 1993: 130; Edwards 1993: 32). As Shadi Bartsch demonstrates in her reading of Tacitus's *Dialogus de Oratoribus*, the place that was once the republican orator's, addressing the people *in pro-*

pria persona, could now only be occupied by the poet Maternus whose tragedy, *Cato,* by virtue of the dramatic form's remove from the first-person speaking subject, paradoxically became the heir to republican eloquence. Yet even this distance was not sufficient: for, as Tacitus intimates, Maternus paid with his life for the boldness of writing a historical drama implicitly critical of the regime (Bartsch 1994: 101–25). Only silence, it seems, could with candor address the present. Thus, the imperial period, as Pliny himself notes (*Panegyricus* 2.1–2), was one in which the seamless whole of public and private life that had constituted the arena of traditional republican *virtus*—a space whose increasingly contradictory and tense nature was the place of elegiac passion—had been definitively rent asunder (Bartsch 1994: 149–50). Propertius's nephew, Lucius Arruntius Stella, and others may have continued to produce elegies, and even to write about love, though we shall never know exactly what they said. But the subject position that constituted Roman erotic elegy, as the vital and authentic genre that is object of this study, had closed, and Ovid's *Tristia* was its obituary. This book offers not so much a chronology of names and dates related to the genre as a genealogy of that lack.

The question this study answers then is, Why? Why elegy? How can we explain both the sudden appearance and rapid disappearance of this subgenre that today constitutes one of antiquity's most widely studied forms of poetry and that exercised such a profound influence on the history of Western lyric verse?[10] Indeed, as Stapleton (1996) has recently shown, neither medieval nor renaissance love poetry is comprehensible outside the light of Ovid's *Amores,* the last and fullest flowering of the genre.[11] The Roman state lasted more than a thousand years, but one of its most conspicuous contributions to European culture survived less than fifty. What characterized this unique moment in time in which both the Roman state underwent the most profound reorganization of its recorded existence, the violent transformation from an oligarchic republic into a multinational empire, and in which one of the unique and lasting contributions to European culture was created?

To begin to answer to this question, this chapter examines two areas. First, how is genre history possible? How can we conceive of the relation between a given literary type and the world that produced it, without succumbing to the illusion that one of these terms possesses an ontological priority over the other so that either literature is an epiphenomenon of history or history the illusion projected by literature? To respond to these demands requires us to advance a theory of the relation of text to context that, while owing much to its predecessors, presents a new synthesis of Marxist, historicist, dialogic, and psychoanalytic ideas and relates them to first-century Rome. Second, why have previous studies of love elegy failed to come to terms with the history of the genre? Here, it is argued that this failure can be attributed to an inadequate conceptualization of literary history itself, thereby demonstrating the necessity of a theoretical model such as we are elaborating.

Finally, in the following chapters, we move on to a series of case studies, starting in chapter 2 with the earliest precursor of the distinctively Roman genre of first-person erotic elegy, Catullus, in whose *carmina* we find for the first time a collection of poems devoted to a single mistress (Kennedy 1993: 88–89; Hinds 1998: 29).[12] The Greek models for elegy, while important, are all partial at best. Although Antimachus's *Lyde* possessed an erotic subjective frame for a series of traditional narrative elegies, and Callimachus had presented an interventionist and opinionated narrator for the mythological tales told in the *Aitia*,[13] no precedent for Catullus 68's combination of "autobiographical" narrative and mythological exempla, nor for 76's agonized internal dialogue can be found in Hellenistic poetry. Likewise, the poet's complete subjection (*servitium amoris*) to a single mistress (*domina, era*) is unprecedented in ancient Greek poetry of any era.[14] Indeed, as I (1994) have argued before, Catullus represents the beginning of that uniquely interiorized voice that I term lyric consciousness and of which erotic elegy can be seen as a subgenre. What Hellenistic literature offered at the end of the first century B.C.E. was not a model to be slavishly copied but an alternative value system to the Roman Republic's traditional *mos maiorum* (Gutzwiller and Michelini 1991: 75).[15] Catullus and the elegists would exploit this resource, but from the unique subject positions offered by a Roman ideological system in the process of collapse and restructuration (Fredrick 1997: 179; Albrecht 1997: 751). The themes and dramatic situations exploited in the elegist's relation to his *domina* may have already been explored by the figure of comedy's *iuvenis* in his subjection to the *meretrix* and his conflict with the *senex*. Nonetheless, the unique position of the first-person speaking subject in elegy, its constitution as the site of contradiction and aporia, of temporal complexity and personal depth, remain unprecedented. What this book wants to explore is not the thematics or plot of elegy—which differs substantially from comedy with its emphasis on final reconciliation and consummation (Cutolo 1995: 93)—but the historical conditions of possibility for elegy's specific instantiation of what I (1994) call lyric consciousness.

After this second chapter, in the next four we examine the subgenre's full flowering in Tibullus and the early works of Propertius and Ovid and their elaboration of the contradictory and schizoid discourse that lies at the heart of erotic elegy. The final chapters examine the afterlife of Roman erotic elegy in Propertius's book 4 and Ovid's exilic poetry. In each case, we ask what is the nature of the elegiac subject projected in a given collection and how can we understand its relation to history in both its immediate and broadest sense. In short, we shall pose the question of what is the relation of elegy and its subject to the protean nature of the Real.

Before beginning our detailed theoretical argument, it is helpful to introduce three terms originating from Lacanian psychoanalysis but now used by a range of critics. They are the Imaginary, the Symbolic, and the Real. These terms are conventionally capitalized in English usage to indicate that they are being used in a specialized sense, although Lacan himself never followed this practice. The Imaginary is a term derived from the Freudian concept of the Imago. Although there are many subtleties to Lacan's theorization of it, on the most basic level it refers to the image of ourselves that we project upon the world. The Symbolic in contrast is the world of rules and codes. It includes language and all other shared semiotic systems. It is based on the concept of *langue* in Saussurean linguistics and represents the shared communal grid of intelligibility that defines a community. We are recognized as subjects by others only through assuming a position in the Symbolic. That position may correspond either more or less well to the vision we have formed of ourselves in the Imaginary. Poetry as a linguistic practice takes place in the Symbolic, but clearly—especially in a genre such as elegy—it always includes substantial material from the Imaginary. The Real is that which falls outside of either of the two preceding categories. It is not "reality" because it is precisely what escapes linguistic expression and Imaginary appropriation. Thus the Real cannot be the object of conscious experience. It is important to note that the Imaginary, the Symbolic, and the Real do not denote mutually exclusive realms but intepenetrating registers of existence. Our Imaginary projections are bathed in the codes and norms of the Symbolic, and the Symbolic offers rules, codes, and forms for processing the work of the Imaginary. The Real represents not so much a world outside these two as their necessary limitations.

The advantages of this triad are many. It allows us to theorize the relation of self to community without ever permitting either one to collapse into a simple opposition to the other, and without rendering one term a mere secondary reflection of the other. This triadic structure itself cannot be reduced to an essentialism, because each of the terms always relativizes and recontextualizes the others. There is no one Imaginary, no one Symbolic, but only specific examples that relate to one another in different ways. There is even no one Real. The Real marks the limits of any self-projection and any communal system of norms and codes. In doing so, it also marks the space of historical change, the space where any given ideological system or personal projection comes up against its own finitude and hence the necessity of change.

What follows in the first section is a detailed theoretical argument for the advantages of this intellectual framework when confronting problems of literary history. For those who find such abstract discussions distasteful or opaque, they may leave the theoretical subtleties aside and move directly to the more historically grounded argument that begins in the second section. There the case is made that the changes taking place in the Roman Real that led to the collapse of the republic created a crisis in the Symbolic that also led to the emergence of the subject position we recognize as that of the erotic elegists. The thumbnail definitions just offered are sufficient to grasp the arguments found there and later in the book, although a full understanding of the power of this intellectual framework and of the reasons for using it can only be had by engaging the theoretical issues on their own terms.

Representation and the Real

> When *gravitas* and *levitas*, excess and deprivation,
> equality and status distinctions cease to abut one
> another, a chasm opens, a No Man's Land out of which
> the monster and the gladiator arise. They are the mirrors
> of the absolute, inhabiting the territory at, and outside,
> the limits within which a compensatory system could be
> maintained, the territory in which the categories
> employed by Roman culture to define and create itself
> are threatened with dissolution.
> —Barton 1993: 187

> History means that there must be some unresolved
> traumatic exclusion which pushes the process forward.
> —Žižek in Hanlon 2001: 16

To begin the labor of solving the riddle of the history of elegy, we could do worse than to look to Jameson's concept of "the semantic conditions of possibility" (1981: 57), which argues that a given text's historicity is best revealed, not by inserting it

> into a genetic process in which it is understood as emerging from this or that prior moment of form or style; nor [by] "extrinsically" [relating it] to some ground or context which is at least initially given as something lying beyond it. . . . [but through] the hypothetical reconstruction of the materials which had to be given in advance in order for that particular text to be produced in its unique historic specificity. (1981: 57)

This formulation is important. It provides a way of talking about the relation of literature to history that avoids the two chief temptations awaiting any such endeavor: the reduction of literature to a mere reflection of external events; and the invocation of an evolutionist teleology[16] in which the a priori logic of the unfolding of form denies the openness of time (Morson and Emerson 1990: 47).

In this latter case, history is reduced to a logical pattern that effectively eliminates real historical change. An example of this kind of argumentation is the contention that elegy ends with Ovid's *Amores* because the genre had then reached a point of formal exhaustion allowing no possibility of further development.[17] Yet, such an explanation is not only denied by the facts—many genres continue to write variations on the same basic themes for hundreds of years without losing their vitality (e.g., epic or the love sonnet)—but it is also fundamentally ahistorical. It views the possibilities of the form as given from the outset. The evolutionist view sees genre as an ideal form whose relation to time is closed because its end is contained in its beginning (Cohen 1986b: 207; Jauss 1986: 42–49; Frow 1986: 292–93; Morson and Emerson 1990: 292–93).[18]

By contrast, the logical extension of the naive reflectionist model is the very negation of the literary. In the past, it has led to the crudest excesses of the Stalinist concept of the material base's relationship to the cultural superstructure and, in turn, to that concept's aesthetic corollary, socialist realism. More recently, this sort of reductive model has led to the censure of both the homoerotic photography of Robert Mapplethorpe and the constructivist sculpture of Richard Serra, each of whom has been criticized in the name of art's ideal correspondence to a "nature" that is at once culturally normative and untouched by the artifice of abstraction. In both cases, there is a belief that art somehow represents a world that is at once simply "out there" and yet a reflection of the viewer's understanding of and desires for that world. In the case that concerns us, this view is most fruitfully represented by Gordon Williams's (1968: 540) claim that the elegiac genre finds its termination with Ovid's *Amores* because the *lex Iulia* of 18 B.C.E. had made adultery a legally prosecutable offense, thus limiting the scope of permissible erotic intrigue to dalliances with *meretrices* as opposed to upper class *matronae*. Such a claim, however, is not only reductive, but it also ignores the ten-to-twenty year gap between the passage of the law and the final edition of the *Amores*, and it assumes against much evidence that the *dominae* or "mistresses" of the other elegists were both real women and married.[19] The task, however, is not to reduce the text to something exterior to it, to see it as a reflection of a reality that is in some sense primary, but to understand the relation of the discursive form to historical change.

Jameson's concept of the "semantic conditions of possibility" avoids these two extremes of a formalist teleology or a historical reductionism, allowing us to establish "the relative autonomy" of literature, to borrow Althusser's carefully balanced phrase (Althusser 1971a: 120–36; Jameson

1981: 23–46; Frow 1986: 110; Kang 1995: 11).[20] Through this concept, the text is tied to specific conditions of possibility, but it is never reducible to the mere expression of those conditions. It both retains a real connection to the vital mess of the world in which it is produced and consumed, a connection that cannot be reduced to the mere unfolding of formalist categories, and it remains irreducible to a theory of correspondence that inevitably is beholden, in the last analysis, to an ideology of the culturally normative. The concept of the conditions of possibility is not a causal theory, which reduces the text to some prior moment, but a way of situating a given literary form that recognizes its temporal boundedness.

What more precisely, then, is the nature of the relationship of text to world, if literature—and, more specifically, elegy—never simply reflects a reality that is somehow external to it (Bakhtin/Medvedev 1985: 18; Frow 1986: 123)? Indeed, the whole concept of externality in this context is highly problematic,[21] for, as much modernist and postmodernist philosophy, theory, and literary criticism have shown, language not only makes literature and communication possible but also constructs human reality as an intelligible, but necessarily ideological, entity.[22] Reality thus comes to us as always already socially constructed by the intersubjective world of language and its affective connotations (Parkhurst 1995: 45). In Althusser's formulation, "what is 'experienced' is always shot through with ideology" (1996b: 76). There is, thus, no neutral realm of fact or experience against which our various ideological constructions can be confidently measured,[23] no valuation that is not always already an evaluation (Morson and Emerson 1990: 134; Gardiner 1992: 85). This is a realization that, while banal in the modern languages, has only recently gained currency in the study of the ancient world and one whose implications have yet to be fully realized (Wyke 1989: 27; Joshel 1992: 12).

Another way of putting this is that fiction—in its original sense of something made or fashioned, *fictum*—makes the reality that we experience possible; for linguistic fictions ground the world's intelligibility (Eco 1976: 61–66). This observation, however, leads traditional literary study into a conundrum. If reality's existence is predicated on fictions, then on what ontological ground might it be said to be reflected by them? A mirror cannot reflect itself. This constructivist position, however, can be easily misunderstood, and we must make a distinction, if we are not to fall into the postmodernist trap of saying all is discourse (Ragland-Sullivan 1986: 98, 194, 255). Let us be clear. I am not here advocating the position that there is nothing outside the text. Rather I am contending that there is a split in our world. On the one hand, there are those necessary fictions that we have termed "reality," while, on the other, there is the world we posit beyond any historically or culturally specific construction of reality. What Nabokov called the mysterious X factor, Lacan labels the Real.[24]

Reality is a coherent system of meanings that allows us to function. It is a picture or an understanding of the world and, as such, is finite and historicizeable. Different societies and different groups within societies produce different symbolic systems, different realities (Clément 1975: 16; Ragland-Sullivan 1986: 183, 305). In Bloch's memorable aphorism, "Not all people exist in the same Now" (1977: 22). This is precisely the sense of the term "reality" that is used when we speak of friends or colleagues "not being in touch with reality"—that is, they do not share the same set of symbolic norms and interpretations that we do.[25] Anyone who has sat through a contentious university tenure and promotion meeting should understand exactly what this means. The world "they" live in is not the same as "ours." It does not mean that they have less access to the world in all its brute facticity, or that matter impinges on them less than on us. This mute realm, beyond meaning, is the Real, the silent domain that supports our various realities, the multiple nows in which we all exist (Lacan 1975: 50; Žižek 1991: 29–32).

Language is an intervention in the Real, not its reflection; nor does the efficacy of its intervention necessarily correlate with its capacity to represent the nature of things. Language is at least as performative as it is constative, as productive as it is descriptive.[26] A few quick examples make this clearer. Chinese medicine is based on a theory of entities and energies that Western thought does not recognize as existing, yet it produces visible, predictable effects within the world. Thus, the discourse of Chinese medicine produces a representational "reality," but its ability to have effects in the Real are not necessarily related to its creation of that reality. Likewise, it is now commonly acknowledged that the Romans understood sexual life in very different terms than we do. Words like *cinaedus* and *homosexual*, though covering some similar behaviors, have unique and unrepeatable resonances, and produce different effects in social life. There is, for example, very little evidence of a movement for "cinaedic" rights in Rome. Even neutral terms such as those referring to color in Latin are not directly translatable into English. Nor is there any reason to assume that the experience of *canus*, referring both to the gleaming white of the morning frost (Horace, *Odes* 1.4.4) and the gray of old age (Catullus 108.1), was identical with that of our *white*, *gray*, or something halfway in between (see Eco 1985). These terms were nonetheless very much a part of Roman reality. By the same token, the equations and mathematical formulae that constitute contemporary physics are themselves irreducible to the terms of conventional representation (e.g., a photon is both a wave and a particle), yet the effectiveness of these equations is not therefore called into question (Beer 1993).[27] Indeed, the efficacy of modern physics is founded on its move toward a pure mathematicization, that is to say, on its retreat from both the ad hoc contingencies of the Real and the conventions of representation (Julien 1990: 146). Language, thus, can have effects in the Real, without necessarily reflecting it. This does not mean that all linguistic fictions are equally effective. In science, as Lacan notes, a concept is only retained if it functions, that is, if it traces its way in the Real (Lacan 1975: 183). But language's approach to the Real is always asymptotic at best, even when it is executed through such sophisticated apparatuses as modern science, and even when it has a revolutionary and enduring impact, such as Lacan's example of Newton's Laws (Jameson 1988: 104, 108).[28]

Language and other signifying systems construct a coherent network of representations, a reality, that allows us to function within the world, but does not present the world in its prelinguistic purity.[29] All that exists outside the world of signs, and the categories of understanding they represent, can only be conceived of as a formless void of "inert presence" (Žižek 1989: 170), the literally unspeakable—what Jameson calls History, Lacan the Real, and Kant the *Ding an sich*[30] (Ragland-Sullivan 1986: 190; Jameson 1988: 104; Žižek 1989: 132). The Real is not the system of narratives, conceptual structures, and affective investments we make in the world, but rather those systems' necessary limitations, the point at which they come up short before the world (Žižek 1989: 208–9; Jameson 1988: 107). The Real is the experience of suffering, the negation of our desire—which includes our desire for knowledge (Foucault 1977a: 27–28)—as we run up against a realm of necessity for which we cannot coherently account.[31] The Real then is the beyond of the Symbolic, Lacan's term for the intersubjective realm of language and knowledge (Julien 1990: 143; Jameson 1988: 106), and it is made manifest by the incoherencies and double binds created within the Symbolic (Žižek 1989: 21; Julien 1990: 173). It is simultaneously in and beyond the Symbolic, inscribed within it as the Symbolic's external limitation.[32] As Joan Copjec writes, "the point where the *real* makes itself felt in the symbolic [is] the point at which the symbolic visibly *fails* to disambiguate itself" (1994: 176–77, emphasis in original). History, from the perspective of the Real, is not a narrative of events but a series of Symbolic systems, progressively collapsing before their own ineffable but changing beyond (Jameson 1981: 82; Žižek in Hanlon 2001: 15–16). As Ellie Ragland-Sullivan writes, "Symbolic systems build up into a state of near perfection and then decompose, as the Real and the Imaginary continually shift Symbolic order explanations and informations" (1986: 230–31). We return to the topic of the Imaginary and its role in the constitution of self-identity later in this chapter.

First, however, we must tarry a little longer with the Real, since it is the Real, as that which is unassimilable to the structures of explanation available to any given cultural formation, that makes the historical succession of cultural, linguistic, and political forms and institutions thinkable as something other than an inexplicable series of random transforma-tions.[33] For the Real marks the point at which the Symbolic meets its own systemic negation (Copjec 1994: 9, 121), its principle of finitude or limit. This moment of negation is necessary to any meaningful concept of histor-ical change, because it is precisely this moment that figures the possibility of otherness within the reigning positive system.[34] Without the negation of the Real, without this conception of the beyond of the Symbolic, the norms and systems of meaning that constitute the latter would absolutize themselves in a way that would allow no room to conceive of the radically other (Jameson 1981: 90–91; 1991: 405–6; Copjec 1994: 17, 23–24). As Derrida (1993: 68) has written, the concept of the future, of the yet-to-come (a-venir), depends on an opening within the Symbolic that cannot be reduced to the categories of either knowledge or ignorance, but must be seen as a systematic heterogeneity, an absolute otherness that exceeds the reigning positive system.

Here, however, we run into one of the cruxes of both postmodern his-torical thought and the new historicism, which trace their origins to the work of Michel Foucault: for this gesture of the reduction of the Symbolic to a pure positivity removed from the Real is recognizable in the latter's dictum that a discursive formation contains only one épistémè (Foucault 1966: 179; Laqueur 1990: 21; Macey 1993: 163; Flynn 1994: 33; Kittler 1999: 117).[35] The problem here is simple. Such a system of historical in-vestigation, as Foucault implicitly concedes,[36] while potentially quite pow-erful in its descriptive mode, is inherently unable to explain how one dis-cursive formation gives way to the next, since each moment is conceived of as a totalizing unity (Dreyfus and Rabinow 1982: 27; Macey 1993: 175). As Eve Bannet observes, Foucauldian "archeology seems to freeze history, describing discursive formations and seeking general rules which are valid for all points of time but neglecting the temporal series within these formations and reducing chronology to the point of rupture when one discursive formation is substituted for another" (1989: 108–9). In short, Foucault's analytic renders the conceptualization of historical change impossible.

This same methodological deficiency afflicts Foucault's followers as well. Thus Paul Veyne in what is in many ways a masterful book on elegy, completely avoids the question of how the genre arose or why it disap-peared, in effect severing it from any meaningful relationship with Latin literary history or with the social world in which it was formed (Miller 1998a; Kennedy 1993: 91–100; Veyne 1988: 31–32).[37] From Foucault's perspective, this isolation is the price we have to pay for preserving histori-cal specificity, for not falling into a teleological vision of history that anni-hilates difference by sublimating it into an ideological master narrative of one sort or another (e.g., the decline and fall of the Roman Empire, the rise of the West, the birth of the individual). The Lacanian position, by founding the possibility of the Symbolic in its own inherent limitation, its severance and hence inability to account for the Real (Eagleton 1983: 168), makes the negation of the Symbolic a constitutive part of any given discursive formation. Thus where the Foucauldian position must homogenize a given period's *épistémè* in the name of historical difference (Foucault 1966: 77, 103, 171; Bannet 1989: 157; Sedgwick 1990: 46–47; Macey 1993: 163), and so cut that *épistémè* off from any narrative that would explain its position in the larger historical sequence (Kremer-Marietti 1985: 49), a Lacanian stance sees the Law of the Symbolic as always opposed to and constituted by its own principle of generation and succession, a principle that escapes the Symbolic itself (Copjec 1994: 122).[38] A truly historical event, therefore, would be one that necessarily exposes the tension between the Symbolic and the Real and can never be wholly accounted for except in terms of that tension.

The collapse of the Roman Republic is a perfect illustration of this thesis: for it was not understandable in terms of the ideological categories of the traditional constitution, but only as a traumatic event that revealed the limits of those terms' applicability to the world as it existed. What could *mos maiorum* (the way of the ancestors), *libertas* (aristocratic free speech), and *res publica* (commonwealth) mean at a time of dictatorship and civil war that was not simultaneously the inverse of their normal signification? A good example of this ideological confusion can be seen in Cicero's letters to Atticus in the spring of 44 B.C.E. On the one hand, in the wake of Caesar's tyrannicide, Cicero feels obligated to reenter public life, but on the other hand he can no longer understand how he might do so. Thus on April 12, he writes:

> Nullo modo reperio quem modum possim πολιτεύεσθαι. nihil enim tam σό-λοικον quam tyrannoctonos in caelo esse, tyranni facta defendi. sed vides consules, vides reliquos magistratus, si isti magistratus, vides languorem bonorum. (14.6.2)

> I am able to find no way to enter politics. For nothing is so *hors sens* as when the tyrannicides are lauded to the skies and the deeds of the tyrant defended. But you see the consuls, you see the remaining magistriates, if magistrates they be, you see the lassitude of the noble orders.

On May 11, however, he does an about face and scolds Atticus, "Epicuri mentionem facis et audes dicere μή πολιτεύεσθαι?" (Do you bring up Epicurus and dare to tell me not to enter politics; 14.20.5). The change in tone in striking. Nonetheless, in spite of his momentary optimism ("prorsus <melius> ibat res" [at the moment things have been going better], 14.20.4),[39] Cicero has in fact still found no way to make the categories of the old world function in the new. His new attempts to save the republic meet with no greater success than did the old. Thus, we may indeed admire the courage of the later *Philippics*, but they hardly offer a way forward, a realistic political program, or an effective conceptualization of the systemic crisis gripping the Roman state.

Rather, it is precisely in Cicero's confusion, and that of others, that we see the index of real historical change, the sign of an event that exceeds the reach of the Symbolic categories available to account for it.[40] Such aporias are a symptom of the eruption of the Real and therefore the ground of effective history. In fact this tension between the Symbolic and Real guarantees for us the possibility of a nonsubjective historiography and offers the point of purchase for a historical practice that is not merely a repetition of founding assumptions and ideological truisms. "The import of the event's divulgence of the relationship between the real and the symbolic . . . proceeds from the manner in which it expedites a nonsubjective historiography. . . . Produced in the liminal space between them, the event *qua* history is therefore the effect of their differential relation" (Myers 2001: 42).

Difference, for Lacan, then, as opposed to Foucault, is not an external relation between regimes of power and knowledge but is internal to them (Copjec 1994: 9–10, 60). In this sense, the generative principle of any given discursive or ideological formation, its relation to that which exceeds it, also contains *in nuce* that formation's negation, the moment that escapes the dominant ideology's grasp and so makes change possible.[41] Every form of hegemony is always haunted by the moment of repression through which it is constituted and is thus always already internally split (Derrida 1993: 69). This internal fissure is precisely the point at which we witness the emergence of the Real. It is the space of difference that this fissure implies, the space between the Symbolic and the Real, that prevents Symbolic totalization and thus makes history possible (Žižek 1989: 135).

The relation between Foucault and Lacan, however, is more complex than this brief sketch might lead us to believe. We cannot simply demonize Foucault and exonerate Lacan. On the one hand, while Lacan's concept of the Real, in its function as the negation of the Symbolic, makes historical explanation possible, he himself is often accused of being ahistorical (Butler 1990: 29, 55, 76; Irigaray 1977c: 97). This may be an oversimplification, but he is vulnerable to the charge in part because he never treats historical verities in any depth and tends to speak as if the topics he discusses exist in an eternal present. Hence, at times, he seems to treat the current formation of the Symbolic as if it were the Symbolic *tout court*. Even though he makes it clear that the Symbolic and the subject's insertion into it are open to historical modification,[42] he never speaks in any detail about how that modification happens and the nature of its consequences. Thus his description of the Symbolic, particularly in relation to gender, can appear to be a prescription (Ragland-Sullivan 1986: 277). This is the gist of Luce Irigaray's feminist critique of her former teacher: not that his description of woman's exclusion from the Symbolic, as constituted by patriarchal reason, is inaccurate, but rather that his failure to posit an alternative to this situation implies that it is unalterable and perhaps even desirable (Irigaray 1977c: 92, 99; 1977d: 205; Weed 1994: 87, 99, 100–02).

Lacan, thus, may make historicization possible, but he does not himself historicize. Foucault, on the other hand, does historicize, but his suppression of the moment of the Real, of any effective negation of the Symbolic, makes the possibility of historicization inexplicable as anything more than the careful description of an arbitrary moment in a random series of events. What is needed is not an uncritical acceptance of either position, but a careful fusion of Foucault's practice of rigorous, nonteleological historicization, which emphasizes the radical difference between historically distinct modes of constituting the subject and power, with Lacan's ability to explain the succession of those modes. Such an amalgamation would result in the abandonment of any sort of purist Foucauldian or Lacanian position in favor of that ultimately more nuanced understanding that Jameson's concept of the "semantic conditions of possibility" demands.

Thus, the recognition that intelligible reality is only possible within a system of meaning or signification (Dowling 1984: 127) does not mean that language and fiction (i.e., the made) are all there is, or that all interpretive and linguistic positions are equally tenable (Lacan 1973: 278; Ragland-Sullivan 1986: 174). Rather, evidence of the inherent limitation of any given Symbolic regime can be seen in the fact that all literary formations are not equally possible at all times. Literary forms like people are finite. The possibility of specific fictions at specific times is historically limited (Frow 1986: 110, 114). History reveals itself precisely through this limitation, through the moment of negation inherent in any Symbolic form. Rimbaud would not only be foreign but unintelligible to a first-century Roman. The public context that made *The Countess of Pembroke's Arcadia* one of the most widely read and best-selling books in the English language throughout the seventeenth and eighteenth centuries has disappeared—few outside a trained minority find Sidney's great pastoral romance even readable. The world in which it could be produced and popularly consumed has vanished. The discursive formation that constituted its semantic conditions of possibility is no longer available, not because the structure of the sign has changed, but because the world—material, ideological, political, cultural—in which those utterances were immediately meaningful no longer exists (Eagleton 1976: 56; Jameson 1981: 148; Žižek 1991: 48; Moxey 1991: 987–88). None of this is to say that the value of the *Arcadia* was ever predicated on its ability to reflect the world that made it possible, anymore than that Vergil's *Eclogues* reflect the Augustan Real, but merely that the *Arcadia* and the *Eclogues* are not equally possible in all worlds. In addition, the fact that pastoral romance is not possible in our world, except as a curiosity, tells us that something crucial has changed in the period separating Sidney's time from our own. Likewise, the fact that love elegy was a viable genre in 30 B.C.E. but neither in 30 C.E. nor 60 B.C.E. tells us that the realm of possible meanings available to a Roman poet had changed in some fundamental fashion in the intervening period (Todorov 1984: 80; Cohen 1986a: 229–30; Morson and Emerson 1990: 277).

Literary history thus has a complex and overdetermined relation to the extraliterary. So complicated and ambivalent is this relationship that the binary opposition of literary and extraliterary that supports its conceptualization is untenable. This is true not only on the pragmatic level—elegy and the *Arcadia* are historically specific phenomena that neither necessarily reflect their worlds nor fail to transcend them as objects of consumption—but also on the more purely theoretical level of internal coherence. The opposition of literary and extraliterary, which subtends any such historical project, is based on a logic of thematics or reflection that rests ultimately on a fundamentally dualist ontology (inside-outside, literary-nonliterary), which in most accounts is never explicitly justified.[43] At the same time, this very ontological opposition, while enabling literature to be conceived of as reflecting a reality *separate* from it, also insures that the moment of re-presentation is infinitely deferred, since it is the fundamental and unbridgeable difference between the literary and the extraliterary that makes this logic of re-presentation possible. Such self-deconstructing oppositions cannot be maintained. In point of fact, inasmuch as reality, as opposed to the unreflectable Real, is linguistically constructed, no difference in primal substance exists on which such a distinction can rest. Jameson's concept of the semantic conditions of possibility avoids the theoretical impasse of the traditional ontology of reflection. By determining what made elegy possible at a given moment in Roman history and when that possibility was closed off, the history of the subgenre and its multiform relation both to other cultural forms and to the profound transformations of the Roman Real that are taking place at this time can begin to be elucidated (Cohen 1986b: 213, 216). Those changes themselves are signaled by the progressive collapse of Roman republican ideology and the vast network of formal and informal institutions set up to maintain and be maintained by it, as well as through the subsequent rise and consolidation of the imperial state with its ideological state apparatuses. Neither of these ideological formations, the republican or the imperial, nor their various and often antagonistic subformations are capable of fully representing these changes. They can only produce narratives that respond to these shifts through the deployment of strategies of appropriation and containment (Jameson 1981: 52–53). Such responses are always necessarily more concerned with power and positioning than with pure re-presentation. They are ideological and situated.

The challenge then is not only to provide a new, more accurate positive description of discursive practices but to trace within the heart of those practices their own systemic negations: to locate the emergence of the Real as a given form's simultaneous foundation and principle of finitude. Such moments of emergence will not be found within that form's structure of representation but rather in those moments of aporia and nonsense that are both constitutionally necessary and unrepresentable. Yet unlike for American deconstruction—in the hands of critics such as J. Hillis Miller (1981)—the task here is not simply to find and celebrate the undecideable but to map precisely how such moments are structured in different ways and at different places and times in the Symbolic system of a given society or societies. Different articulations of the Symbolic and its relation to the Real will produce different forms of aporia and different subject positions relative to those forms. The result of this investigation will be not the description of a unified positive system—which must by nature absolutize itself in an eternal present—but a detailed examination of the way such systems are constituted by that which they must exclude and of how this game of constitution and exclusion produces a shifting and unstable discursive field in which different Symbolic formations jockey for strategic advantage in relation both to one another and to an ever changing Real that by nature excedes their grasp.

ROMAN REALITY: IDEOLOGIES OF THE REPUBLIC AND EMPIRE

What marks the Ciceronian age is a persistent tension
between the old categories of political behavior and the
onrush of events that appeared to outstrip them.
—Gruen 1995: 49

Sed cum Lucius Domitius consulatus candidatus
palam minaretur consulum se effecturum quod
praetor nequisset adempturumque ei exercitus, Crassum
Pompeiumque in urbem provinciae suae Lucam
extractos conpulit [Caesar], ut detrudendi Domitii

> causa consulatum alterum peterent, perfecitque per
> utrumque, ut in quinquennium sibi imperium
> prorogaretur. Qua fiducia ad legiones, quas a re publica
> acceperat, alias privato sumptu addidit, unam etiam ex
> Transalpinis conscriptam, vocabulo quoque Gallico—
> Alauda enim appellabatur—quam disciplina cultuque
> Romano institutam et ornatam postea universam
> civitate donavit.[44]
> —Suetonius, *Divus Iulius* 24

The ideological nature of the responses to the fundamental shifts in the nature of the Roman Real is evident throughout the period that concerns us. As Erich Gruen in his encyclopedic *Last Generation of the Roman Republic* has demonstrated, until the moment that Caesar crossed the Rubicon in 49 B.C.E., the political class in Rome and the *populus* as well thought not in terms of impending revolution but of the traditional republican politics of competitive elites. Likewise as the passages from Cicero's letters cited earlier(14.6.2, 14.20.4–5 ad Atticum) as well as Augustus's attempts to maintain republican governmental forms even after assuming effective power (Dio Cassius 53.12.1–3, 53.16.1) show, this tension between the categories of political experience and events on the ground remained throughout the civil wars and the rise of the principate. Caesar and Pompey were less self-conscious revolutionaries in the Leninist or Jacobin mode than faction leaders seeking dominance within a system they hoped to lead, not destroy (Gruen 1995: xix).

Nonetheless, Gruen's account, while invaluable and heroic in scope, is flawed. It accepts the statements of the political actors involved at face value, even as it acknowledges their being out of phase with events on the ground. It thus abstemiously refuses to draw any larger cultural or political consequences from Symbolic patterns manifest in both those statements and their specific repressions. Indeed, in his all but Humean distaste for concepts of causality, Gruen seems to claim that the collapse of the republican constitution and the outbreak of civil war were mere accidents without antecedent causes or necessary relations, one to the other. Thus, at one point, he argues: "Transformation of the state into a monarchical regime can be laid to the charge of a devastating civil war, rather than to the putative disintegration of institutions and morale in the previous decades" (1995: xx). A short time later, he asserts, "Civil war need not be read as a token of the Republic's collapse" (1995: 5). Such statements, if not directly contradictory, border on a reduction of history to mere chronology. This positivist refusal to integrate discrete facts into larger structures of intelligibility not only smacks of what Vernant (1990: 271) refers to as the "index card" method of classical scholarship but is also unable to draw significant connections between cultural and political phenomena, and thus between statements like the following by Cicero and the emergence of the elegists:

> Quibus autem talis nulla sit causa, si despicere se dicant ea quae plerique mirentur, imperia et magistratus, iis non modo non laudi, verum etiam vitio dandum puto; quorum iudicium in eo quod gloriam contemnant et pro nihilo putent, difficile factu est non probare; sed videntur labores et molestias, tum offensionum et repulsarum quasi quamdam ignominiam timere et infamiam. Sunt enim qui in rebus contrariis parum sibi constent, voluptatem severissime contemnant, in dolore sint molliores, gloriam neglegant, frangantur infamia, atque ea quidem non satis constanter. (*De Officiis* 1.21.71)

> Those, however, for whom there is no cause (such as ill health) to say they despise those things which many others admire, power and office, I think not only ought not to be praised but be given up to vice. It is not a difficult thing to approve the judgment of such people in this matter, since they look down on glory and think it worth nothing, but in fact they seem to fear hard work and difficulties, as well as the shame and dishonor of defeats and misfortunes. For there are those who are inconsistent in contrary affairs: they severely condemn pleasure and are rather effeminate in pain, they disregard glory but are crushed by shame, and even in this they are insufficiently consistent.

The picture Cicero paints here of a seemingly principled but nonetheless effeminate (*mollis*) withdrawal from public life is almost the exact image that the elegists project for themselves. The coincidence is striking, and not least because the characterization might just as easily be applied to Cicero himself. Thus, as we saw Cicero in 44 B.C.E. is writing letters to Atticus in which he says he can neither withdraw nor abstain from politics, even as he at that moment is composing a theoretical treatise that condemns this very inconstancy. In the same period, we also begin seeing the emergence of a class of poets as well as other members of the equestrian order who publicly renounce politics and question the traditional hegemony of the senate and its ruling ideology (cf. Cicero, *Epistulae ad Atticum* 1.17.8–9). Indeed, the passage from *De Officiis* is almost a paraphrase of Propertius's position in 1.6 and Tibullus's in 1.1. At the same time, we see the republic itself crumble and the emergence of a fundamentally new kind of state that will slowly elaborate its own ideological norms and expectations. If we accept Gruen's hard positivist view, this is a mere coincidence because at no point do the actors themselves self-consciously speak of revolution but always of traditional values, their transgression and potential restoration. Yet, it is precisely the inability of the existing Symbolic categories to comprehend the profound historical changes taking place that reveals the limits of those categories and the necessary and traumatic emergence of the Real.

Indeed, as the ten years immediately preceding the outbreak of open warfare clearly show, the collapse of the republic was anything but an accident. There was both a marked increase in the recorded cases of urban violence, electoral bribery, political warfare in the courts, and extraconstitutional political maneuvering by not only the triumvirs Pompey, Caesar, and Crassus, but also Clodius, Milo, and the reactionary Catonians.[45] In each case, however, these events were presented, and presumably interpreted by the actors concerned, not as breeches of traditional republican legal principles and political norms but as actions designed to defend them (Gruen 1995: 119). Likewise, the response from the *populus* in the period was not rebellion but the continued return of the same small group of oligarchic families to office in the consular elections (Gruen 1995: ix, 158), while the senate continued to search for piecemeal and ad hoc methods of legislative reform (Gruen 1995: 506–7).

No one sought revolution, everyone restoration (Gruen 1995: xx, 153). Rather than the collapse of republican legal principles, what this period sees is their gradual hardening as the traditional governing norms of the *mos maiorum* became the object of increasingly bitter dispute. Indeed, the flurry of legislation witnessed by the last decade of the republic is not only a sign of the continuing viability of republican institutions but also a symptom of their crisis. What was once a flexible elite consensus now had to be defined contentiously and litigiously in exact legal terms (Gruen 1995: 258–59). The crisis reveals itself precisely as one of the impossibility, yet felt necessity, of consistent cultural meaning in a time of crisis. As Wallace-Hadrill argues:

> A leitmotif of the late Roman Republic is on the one hand the crucial importance of following tradition, the *mos maiorum*, if Rome is to survive and succeed, and on the other an awareness that tradition is slipping away, and needs to be painstakingly reconstructed, both at a theoretical level by redis-covery of what lost tradition was, and at a political level by its re-establish-ment and reimposition. (1997: 13).

What Gruen demonstrates, then, is not so much the accidental nature of the collapse of the republic as the inability of republican ideology to conceptualize that collapse. It is precisely the crisis of Symbolic norms in relation to a changing Real that this period reveals, as Caesar, even in crossing the Rubicon, is not only able to present himself as the savior of the republic but also able to convince others to accept that claim (*Bellum Civile* 1.85, 3.57, 3.90–91; Cicero, *Pro Ligario* 18). His belief in, or cynicism about, this ideological position is not only ultimately unknowable but also less important than the fact that all sides deployed the same narrative structure. It is precisely the aporias of that structure, its progressive inability to account for the actions of those deploying it, as revealed by their mutually contradictory claims, that provides the truest window to the historical changes taking place. What is ultimately revealed is not so much "what actually happened" as the progressive foundering of the Romans' own ability to explain the changes that were happening.

The same pattern of misrecognition continues into the early imperial period. The Augustan program of moral revival and religious reconstruction was consistently presented in terms of a return to the virtues of the past, the *mos maiorum*, and the restoration of the republic (Augustus, *Res Gestae* 8, 19–21, 34), even as it laid the ideological groundwork for consolidating what was to be the most sweeping transformation of the Roman state since the expulsion of the Etruscan kings.[46] At the same time, in spite of its self-proclaimed reactionary nature, the regime did not scruple to appropriate Egyptian concepts of sacred kingship and other ideas foreign to traditional republican political thought, where it deemed them useful (Koenen 1976: 128). Augustan imperial ideology was in fact less a coherent, theoretical edifice than an ad hoc construction designed to meet specific needs (Koenen 1977: 132; Kennedy 1993: 36–37).[47] It was more concerned with power and stability than ideological purity or revolution (Ste. Croix 1981: 360).

The republican counterprogram, to the extent that such a thing existed (Tacitus, *Annales* 1.2), offered nothing more than the myth of a return to the golden age of senatorial rule, itself based on an oligarchical system that had ceased to be truly functional since the time of the Gracchi's proposed land reforms and subsequent murder one hundred years before.[48] Despite the momentary stabilization brought about by the Sullan dictatorship and its reconstitution of the senatorial elite, the existing constitutional settlement had deteriorated to the point where civil war was a constant threat, elections had to be canceled in the face of riots, and the legions were used against the populace to quash uprisings for debt relief (Brunt 1971a: 127–32; Ste. Croix 1981: 354; Nippel 1995: 77–84).[49] The professionalization of the army, which had begun with Marius, eroded the traditional ideology that bound the soldiers to a republic in which they as landholders had a definite stake. Instead, they increasingly professed loyalty to the individual commanders, the sole authorities who had an interest in insuring that they received their just rewards, generally an allotment of land supplied by despoiling their political enemies.[50] Again Gruen offers a cautionary note, arguing that the Marian reforms merely acknowledged a state of affairs that had become increasingly the rule rather than the exception, and that many military leaders failed to establish strong bonds with their troops. This is certainly true, but it neither denies the nature of the change nor, in the cases of *imperatores* such as Caesar and Pompey, who were given commands of extraordinary length and power, that they were able as a consequence to establish power bases that were essentially beyond senatorial or popular control as demonstrated by Suetonius above (Gruen 1995: xvii, 112, 366, 377; see Shelton 1998: 244 n. 8).

In light of the changing military and political situation, the leadership of the senatorial oligarchy became beholden to the generals—Sulla, Marius, Pompey, Caesar, and eventually Octavian and Antony—to crush both their rivals and, if need be, popular resistance (Nippel 1995: 66–67, 83–84). The soldiers' alienation from the traditional instances of state power was in turn augmented by the practice of some of this senatorial elite of driving the families of these soldiers off their lands while they were away on campaign (Sallust, *Bellum Jugurthinum* 41.8; Brunt 1971b: 551–57; Ste. Croix 1981: 357). The ruling class thus became increasingly fragmented as it was forced to line up behind various warlords, like Caesar and Pompey, and the factions they represented, while constantly seeking to reassert its own *dignitas* and the values of a competitive elite in an increasingly fractious environment (Gruen 1995: 49, 66; Wallace-Hadrill 1997: 11). At the same time, certain members of the elite, such as Clodius Pulcher, who claimed to represent the interests of the *plebs urbana*, were engaging in new forms of political organizing that sought to create alternative organs of power through the mobilization of *collegia*, or guilds of tradesmen, *vici*, or neighborhood counsels, and the worshipers of nontraditional cults such as those of Isis and Bacchus.[51] Thus, at this period in Roman history, power simultaneously became more diffuse as it broke away from its traditional institutional basis, even as it also became more concentrated in the hands of the generals whose troops became the final arbiters of Roman political conflict. It is no wonder that the traditional narratives that legitimated that power became increasingly suspect.

The republican constitution in effect no longer existed. The return to it was a dead letter. The fact was that no ideological alternative as yet existed. This was the breach into which the Augustan settlement would step. But where Augustus's program camouflaged the nature of its intervention in the reorganization of the state's political and cultural apparatuses and its centralization of the powers of military command, beneath the mask of a fictional, although not necessarily insincere, return to the status quo ante (Ste. Croix 1981: 391–92), the minimal republican opposition had no solutions to propose at all (Galinsky 1996: 8). It offered only an illusory nostalgia.

Neither of these narratives, the Augustan or the republican, can be said to provide an accurate reflection of the transformations occurring in the Roman Real, nor was this even their purpose, assuming that such a thing were possible. The picture that we have pieced together here is a synthetic product drawn forth by a variety of scholars from a disparate array of materials—historical, literary, epigraphical, and archaeological—no one of which is to be taken at face value. Indeed, our mosaic offers less a coherent narrative of meaningful events than points to a series of crises in meaning whose discursive functions are symptomatic rather than expository. What does it mean to be a senator, a landholder, a soldier, at the limit, a subject in Rome? Each of these questions points to a crisis that, as we shall see throughout this book, produced conflicting ideological valuations and even violence (Barton 1993: 85, 151–52, 189). These crises in turn are registered as moments of trauma and undecidabilty in the cultural productions of the period. They produce a profound ambiguity that is most satisfying to read and most horrible to live.

For the literary historian, however, it is not a question of taking sides or of determining which valuations to believe and which to condemn but rather of studying the conflicts themselves: when they arise, when they disappear, how they are linked to other moments of conflict and stabilization, and what is the logic of their transformation. Thus, what is of utmost importance is not the content per se of the narratives produced by those who participated in these events, but the moments of ideological contradiction and aporia found therein. These are the truest barometers of the architectonic shifts occurring in the Real, that is, the profound historical movements that are reshaping the world beyond the immediate consciousness and control of its actors and participants, as well as the cultural revolution accompanying them (Jameson 1981: 82–83, 96). These are the moments that reveal the limits of ideology and that mark those junctures where we must look for the emergence of history.

SEX, LIES, AND SYMBOLIC SATISFACTIONS

Tant la confusion était grande au cours de ces années;
tant il était difficile, au moment où on réévaluait
"l'humanité," de déterminer la place que devait occuper
la folie; tant il était difficile de la situer dans un espace
social qui était en voie de restructuration.[52]
—Foucault 1972: 445

The perception of the civil wars and the monarchy
as permanently transgressing the *discrimina
ordinum* brought into play a "physics" corresponding
to René Girard's "Sacrificial Crisis: a collapse of
the *sensus communis*, a shared system of categorizing
and ordering."
—Barton 1993: 146

In *Le souci de soi*, Michel Foucault (1984: 105–6, 117) observes that the period of the late republic and early empire witnesses a profound crisis in what it means to be a subject. This crisis manifested itself in part through an increasing anxiety over matters of sexual and personal conduct.[53] The literature in and on the period is filled with anxious statements about the decline in the sexual morality of the upper classes, their increasing effeminacy, the emancipation of their women, and their progressive inability to replenish themselves (Riposati 1945: 30; Grimal 1986: 147).[54] Thus, as Maria Wyke notes, starting in the middle of the second century B.C.E., when republican Rome was at the height of its power with the end of the Third Punic War, as vast new amounts of wealth flooded into the coffers of the aristocracy, creating greater social inequality and political disruption (Sallust, *Bellum Catilinae* 9–11), a series of female scare-figures begin to appear in the literature. These are powerful and sexually liberated women who are epitomized by Sallust's portrait of Sempronia (*Bellum Catilinae* 25) and Cicero's depiction of Clodia in the *Pro Caelio*. In all cases, as Wyke (1989: 37–40) observes, the portraits of these women are embedded in larger narratives of social decay and corruption and so cannot be seen as providing independent evidence regarding the lives of real Roman women, but rather as symptoms of a crisis in the way the desiring subject constituted itself in relation to traditional republican norms. Such women are not to be found in the Real (which is not to question their "reality") but precisely at the point where the Roman Symbolic reveals its inability to conceptualize such figures as anything other than impossible monsters.[55] They are fictions of sexual and ideological aporia.

Indeed, it is precisely their status as textual constructs that allows these women to be seen as the forerunners of the elegists' own socially dubious mistresses: for such figures have become part of Rome's symbolic economy. Elegy's women are not so much revolutionary as symptomatic. The elegists refer to their beloveds as *dominae*, and hence as the mistresses of slaves, allowing elegy itself to become a tale of male subjection in which the elegiac ego assumes the position of the *servus amoris* (slave of love), in a world whose political norms have already been turned upside down. This position of dominance is doubly anomalous in that the elegists were all men of equestrian status and hence members of the Roman aristocracy. The incongruity of their position is presumably part of the fun but also serves as vivid testimony to a creeping awareness of the contingency of Symbolic norms in an environment of political disruption and social change. The *dominae*, however, are if anything more the products of textual construction than their "historical" avatars, for they are in fact lacking in the internal consistency one normally expects from literary characters, changing in manner, physical appearance, and social status from one poem to the next. There is, then, wide disagreement over who these *domi-*

nae are meant to be: courtesans; married women practicing adultery; wealthy widows; or, as has been suggested in one case, the wife of the poet himself (see chapter 4).[56] These women represent less simple identities than complex nexuses of conflicting Symbolic norms.

What they clearly do signify is a further development of the mounting anxiety over the moral and, hence, ideological fabric of the Roman state, in a period of increasing social unrest. Thus, as Wyke notes, the first century B.C.E. sees a "multiplication of discourses about . . . the female," in much the same way as Foucault has demonstrated the proliferation of discourses about sexuality in eighteenth-century Europe, also a period of widespread social reorganization and revolution (Wyke 1989: 41). Moreover, as Foucault notes in his discussion of the rise of "sexuality," that discourse—with its concerns about childhood masturbation, female hysteria, and the categorization of sexual deviants—cannot be seen as reflecting an actually existing state of affairs in Europe at the time. There is no reason, for example, to believe that children masturbated any more or less frequently at that time than they have before or since. Nor can the deployment of this discourse be seen as some sort of attempt to harness sexual power for the productive ends of the emerging bourgeoisie, a form of labor discipline; rather it represents a new articulation of the subject's relation to the body that is part of a complex response to other changes occurring simultaneously within the same material and cultural field. The rise of the discourse of sexuality is therefore a symptom of historical change, not its reflection (Foucault 1976: 137–73).

By the same token, the rise of figures like Clodia and Sempronia in the political and historical prose of the mid-first century, as well as of the elegiac *dominae* in the poetry of the next generation, is evidence of the rewriting of sexuality and gender's relation to the subject's innermost recesses and to its points of insertion in the networks of social and political power. This is the gist of Thomas Habinek's recent argument that

> the elite sectors of Roman society in the late republic and early principate underwent a transition from a sex and gender system based on the principles of honor and shame associated with peasant societies to one more closely resembling that of contemporary urban centers. The lurid accounts of sexual outrages that proliferate in the era are at least in part attempts to identify appropriate limits on behavior in an era of radical change. (1998: 143–44)

In the move from a traditional society based on implicit concepts of honor and shame controlled by a self-regulating and self-perpetuating elite to an international empire in which the claims of traditional knowledge were constantly challenged by both social disruption and a Hellenistic model of universal knowledge, sexuality according to Habinek gradually became unmoored from its position as one regulated practice among many and assumed a new position as an autonomous realm of concern. This move is testified to not only by the emergence of figures like Clodia and Sempronia, not only by the increased concern over the nature of the *mos maiorum*, but also by the appearance of Latin love elegy itself (Habinek 1997; Kaster 1997: 17; Wallace-Hadril 1997: 9–10, 20–21). Indeed, where the literature of the second century B.C.E. is dominated by narratives either commissioned by or about the ruling class, and functioned as a means of subjection and normalization, the elegists occupied a far less stable place. Theirs was an interstitial space between masculine and feminine, active and passive, for which traditional Roman discourse had no terms (Habinek 1998: 45, 121; Fantham 1996: 11; Sharrock 1995: 166). They were in short the augurs of instability.

The sexual and moral issues, which were emblematized in the figures of the elegists and their *dominae*, were profoundly linked with anxieties about the nature of the Roman class structure (Walters 1997: 30). These anxieties only deepened as the role of the traditional senatorial oligarchy in the administration of the state diminished in the final years of the republic and the early principate (Edwards 1993: 182–86). These sexual issues, moreover, formed the basis of Augustus's program of moral and religious reform. In addition to its more strictly ideological goals of establishing the *princeps* as the guardian of traditional morality, this program was also designed to repopulate the upper echelons of Roman political society, which had been depleted by a hundred years of civil conflict. Such a restoration of the equestrian and senatorial orders would provide the *princeps* with a strong political base (Grimal 1986: 157; Edwards 1993: 37–42, 57) and at the same time work to restore the ideological hegemony of the state and its elites.[57] The traditional categories of commitment to Roman political life and the public advancement of both self and household were no longer fully operative, but a complete retreat to the world of private pursuits, a realm whose existence traditional Roman ideology barely acknowledged, was not acceptable either (Nicolet 1966: 721; Veyne 1987: 95; Edwards 1993: 32; Fitzgerald 1995: 25). The categories of what constituted normative subjectivity in the Roman world are at this time in a state of flux as the verities of republican civic virtue find themselves more and more irrelevant in an increasingly administered society (Syme 1960: 508; Auerbach 1965: 247–48; Foucault 1984: 104–5; Fantham 1996: 56), whose primary claim to ideological legitimacy is that nothing has really changed. "The republic had been restored." "We have only returned to the way things really were all along." The principate's motto was "Back to the Future!":[58] for Roman ideology was profoundly conservative and unable to think of the new (*res novae*) except as the threatening (Wilkinson 1974: 168).

The Elegiac Symptom, the Roman Imaginary

> [M]asculinity, as defined through political and
> social competition, was at the end of the first century
> B.C.E. an increasingly hollow form of theater, "a
> loathsome and bitter burlesque," as Carlin Barton has
> put it. Its recuperation in elegy is therefore parodic, but
> not simply funny; for its male authors, elegy's wounds
> are ambiguous metaphors for the transformation of elite
> masculinity into text.
> —Fredrick 1997: 172–73

> [T]he imaginary is, in one sense, a thoroughly
> historicized concept.
> —Myers 2001: 37

Elegy is a symptom of this crisis in the Roman subject's self-conception. It does not so much reflect the lives and positions of a Tibullus or Propertius as it does a crisis in the categories of the Symbolic and the way the individual subject relates to them.[59] This crisis, in turn, is the point where we witness of the emergence of the Real as a moment of non-sense beyond the existing categories of understanding, the point where History becomes visible as that which exceeds the artifices of consciousness. It is, as we shall see in the coming chapters, elegy's very aporetical character[60] that is the truest marker of the historical change to which it testifies, and not the various and often self-contradictory meanings those experiencing these events attributed to those changes (Žižek 1989: 170–71; 1991: 30). That moment of emergence, I argue moreover, take place most radically within the erotic precisely because it is here that the conjugation of the private fantasmata of our Imaginary self-construction, our individually assumed self-image (Lacan 1966b: 90), and the publicly sanctioned realm of Symbolic norms, which recognize us as a subject, takes place with the greatest intensity and, hence, with the greatest possibility of conflict.[61] Augustus's moral reform legislation recognized this fact but could not fully control it. Thus elegiac discourse offers a privileged vantage point for observing the production of this split in the Roman subject of the late republican and early imperial period.[62]

In a previous study, I have argued that Latin love elegy is a subgenre of lyric and that one part of what makes lyric subjectivity possible in first-century B.C.E. Rome is a phenomenon labeled "semiotic slippage" (1994: 45–47, 131–40). Semiotic slippage in this case refers to Catullus's, and presumably the other neoterics', use of traditional Roman value terms like *fides*, *foedus*, *amicitia*, *otium*, *negotium*, and *officium* to delineate internalized realms of feeling, rather than the more traditional reciprocal communal and political obligations to which these words commonly referred (Edwards 1993: 183; Conte 1994: 137, 323).[63] *Amicitia*, for example, although often translated "friendship," is generally thought to refer to a set of conventionally accepted, mutual obligations agreed upon between two parties, a relationship sometimes closer to our notion of political alliance than to the affective bond we label friendship, although the latter is by no means excluded.[64] Thus as Sallust famously notes, "sed haec inter bonos amicitia, inter malos factio est" (but what between good men is called friendship, between the bad is called faction; *Bellum Jugurthinum* 31.15). *Amicitia* is also used of formal treaty relations between countries where it is a synonym for *foedus* or "pact" (Caesar, *Bellum Gallicum* 4.6; Sallust, *Bellum Jugurthinum* 8.2, 104.4–5; Livy 7.43). Finally, while Cicero gives an idealized image of friendship in *De Amicitia*, in *De Officiis* (2.69) he recognizes that it was often a euphemism for patronage relations between members of the upper classes. Likewise, in a letter to Trebatius, he chides the latter for trading too openly on the *beneficia* Cicero's *amicitia* has secured him from Caesar (*Ad Familiares* 7.17.1; cf. 7.5.1). An *amicitia* thus was a relationship of mutual *beneficia*[65] that could be formalized into a *foedus*, guaranteed by *fides* (*Ad Familiares* 23.16.2, 23.19.2),[66] in which each party owed the other certain *officia*[67] ranging from material and political support to simple friendship (Bowditch 2001: 17–24, 52; Helzle 1989: 22; Ste. Croix 1981: 343; Boucher 1980: 92). It could be broken off when one party or the other suffered *iniuria* and declared the other *inimicus*.

David Konstan rightly points out that the stress on reciprocal obligations in *amicitia* should not be thought automatically to exclude the affective dimension (1997: 122–48). W. Jeffrey Tatum is good on this when he notes, "Friendship and politics, while not identical, were inextricable in republican Rome" (1997: 484; see also 486–87). Tatum criticizes my stance in *Lyric Texts and Lyric Consciousness* (1994: 120–40), assimilating it to Wilamowitz's (1924: 305–10) position that Catullus's poetry is purely personal and in no way political. Unfortunately, my merit is not so great as the German philologist's, nor are our positions identical. My claim rather was that:

> [T]he lyric genre requires a society with a group of educated people who possess sufficient standing in the community to lay claim to a voice in its collective discourse but who do not, at the same time, occupy so high a rank that their interests are perceived as being identical to that of the state. . . . moreover in order for these conditions to be such as would permit the emergence of the lyric genre, this attention must be focused on the poets as individuals and artists, not as representatives of their particular group, or of society's ruling class. (1994: 125)

Such a view hardly implies a complete abstraction from the power rela-
tions that constitute a society's various political fields broadly conceived
(Tatum 1997: 482–83). Rather, as Leach (1999: 148 n.27) has recently
pointed out, this position closely corresponds to the situation in which
Cicero found himself during Caesar's dictatorship.

In Catullus's hands, *amicitia* and related terms came to designate those
aspects of his relationship with Lesbia that transcended the more purely
sexual realm denoted by the term *amor* (72.7–8, 76. 1–4, 109.6).[68]
Whether he was the first to make such use of these terms cannot be said,
but we have no record of such usage before him. What these renovated
definitions made possible was the creation of a vocabulary permitting the
discussion of issues beyond those generally recognized as admissible to
Roman public discourse, with its traditional concentration on questions
of money, power, and politics (Lyne 1980: 68; Albrecht 1997: 752). When
Augustus is presented as restoring the goddess Fides to her rightful place
at *Carmen Saeculare* 57 and *Aeneid* 1.291, it is the normative use of the
term that is being evoked, not the "faith" Catullus pledges to Lesbia (Bou-
cher 1980: 101–2). Yet, as I contended in my previous study (1994), start-
ing from the work of Carl Rubino (1975: 291–93), and as Platter (1995)
and Kennedy (1993) have argued still more forcefully, these new semantic
possibilities never simply broke free of, or replaced, the traditional mean-
ings of such words (Conte 1994: 254). Instead, they existed in a constant
and unstable dialectical tension with them. Precisely that tension made
lyric subjectivity as a publicly recognized, private consciousness possible,
with all the contradictions that such a formulation implies.

In the present work, I move beyond this earlier formulation and, with
the help of concepts borrowed from Lacanian psychoanalysis, analyze
more precisely what the nature of that semiotic slippage was, how it made
the elegiac subject possible, and how that particular kind of slippage was
ultimately stabilized and recuperated by the ideology and culture of the
imperial Roman state. I argue that the nature of these particular slippages
can best be understood as symptomatic of the opening of a new, more
radical gap between the Imaginary and Symbolic registers of language and
experience in Roman society, between the subject's sense of self and its
recognition *as a subject* in the world of codified, signifying practices. The
Imaginary represents the image with which we identify ourselves. It is how
we picture ourselves to ourselves. The Symbolic on the other hand repre-
sents the world of codes and signifying and practices wherein we are recog-
nized as subjects by the social world around us (Ragland-Sullivan 1986:
56; Žižek 1989: 109). In first-century B.C.E. Rome, certain changes in the
Real—the expansion of the empire, the civil wars, and the general collapse
of social order (Nippel 1995: 35, 77–84)—had produced a situation in
which the Symbolic's capacities for interpreting the subject no longer

meshed with that subject's own Imaginary self-identifications (Leach 1999: 148–49). This separation of the Imaginary and the Symbolic in turn permitted the emergence of new forms of self-representation and behavior. Indeed, as the gap between the Imaginary and the Symbolic, which structure all human subjectivity, became more visible, new modes of meaning and experience were possible. To take only one well-known example, Syme and Gruen have argued that Julius Caesar interpreted his political project through the paradigms of traditional patrician ideology (Syme 1960: 52–59, 68–70, 194–95; Gruen 1995: 491–92). Yet the only way he could achieve his goals in a way consistent with his own self-image or *dignitas* (Syme 1960: 13, 25, 48; Gruen 1995: 75, 496), and the demands of a state shattered by sixty years of internal conflict, was to destroy the structure that made that ideology possible, namely, the republic.[69]

Whereas *gloria* in Roman ideology represented the recognition the self receives from the instances of authority in society, and so established the subject's position in the Symbolic, *dignitas* marked for the Roman elite precisely that point where the Imaginary "provided the form of the subject's lived relation to society. Through this relation the subject was brought to accept as its own, to recognize itself in, the representations of social order" (Copjec 1994: 21).[70] *Dignitas*, as the social manifestation of the Imaginary, in fact represented the point where the ego's self-construction came directly into play with the categories of self-conception, the socially approved subject positions, offered by the Symbolic (Julien 1990: 67; Žižek 1989: 110–11; Althusser 1996c: 26; Lacan 1966b: 90–91, 95). In more traditional psychoanalytic terms, it represented the hinge point between the Imaginary ego and the ego ideal (Julien 1990: 68–69; Gunderson 1997: 215–16). Thus, whereas *pudor* represented an emotion that was ideally completely internalized, and *gloria* a recognition that could only come from the Other, *dignitas* was precisely the Imaginary self-construction we present to the Other.[71] To destroy that was to destroy Caesar. In the end, shifts on the level of the Real, such as the professionalization of the army, Sulla's proscriptions, and the Social Wars (Nippel 1995: 65–67), had produced a gap between the Imaginary and the Symbolic that could only be filled by destroying the social world that had given rise to it. *Dignitas* could only be preserved by a revolution that would shake to the roots the social categories that had made its construction and misrecognition both possible and necessary.

Elegiac subjectivity thus, I argue, is a product of this same gap between Imaginary identifications and Symbolic conceptions. It presents a schizoid personality, whose visibly split nature constitutes its ultimate, irrecuperable remainder (the excess that cannot be processed by any of the available Symbolic forms, be they republican or early Augustan). Indeed, the gap itself structures this mode of discourse and accounts for its ultimately unique, if not aberrational, nature in Roman culture. It also accounts for its bizarre status in traditional criticism: for, depending on whom one reads, elegy is either in league with the Augustan political regime (Kennedy 1993: 35–36; Newman 1997: 6) or implacably hostile to it and the traditional values it sought to promote;[72] either political allegory (Edwards 1996: 24) or an apolitical, ludic discourse that gently mocks social custom (Veyne 1988: 31–32 104–8; Kennedy 1993: 95–96; Fantham 1996: 108); either exploitative of women (Kennedy 1993: 38, 56, 73) or bent on satirizing Roman misogyny (Greene 1994). In fact, almost everyone agrees that elegy was opposed to something, but nobody can agree on what that was (Santirocco 1995: 226–28). By focusing on the split itself rather than on the pros and cons of a given binary opposition, the endless debates that have dominated elegiac criticism can be surpassed and the structure that gave rise to those debates examined.

Moreover, this shift in the relation of Imaginary to the Symbolic, which made the schizoid discourse of the elegiac genre possible can itself only be accounted for by historicizing Lacan's third term, the Real, for no change in the relations maintained between the first two registers is possible except in relation to this dialectically necessary *tertium quid*,[73] which, as Žižek (1989: 162) has shown, became the increasing focus of Lacan's later inquiries. The Real, as noted earlier, is that set of material circumstances beyond all Imaginary and Symbolic representations that makes the continued existence of both of those realms possible. The increasingly aporetical relations exemplified between the Imaginary and the Symbolic in Latin love elegy can also be seen as the momentary emergence of the Real into symptomatic visibility. Yet, that visibility exists in itself only as a moment of pure unintelligibility, a traumatic eruption that is beyond signification. As Sheri Benstock observes, "Knots or holes in language signal the Lacanian Real" (1991: 17). In modern literary practice, she notes, it is the poetry of Gertrude Stein's *Tender Buttons* that comes as close as possible to the moment in which language stumbles "up against the Lacanian Real" (1991: xxvii).

Elegy is another such stumble. It can never reflect the Real; it can only detect its seismic shifts through disruptions in the structures of signification. Latin love elegy is, on this view, made possible by certain subterranean movements of the Real, but these by nature can only be discussed through indirection. The symptoms of that movement, however, are clearly visible in the sudden emergence of this schizoid discourse during the period marking the final collapse of the Roman Republic, while the subsequent stabilization of those same architectonic forces is made visible by elegy's disappearance with the consolidation of the empire.

Chapter Two

THE CATULLAN SUBLIME, ELEGY, AND THE EMERGENCE OF THE REAL

Je suis le ténébreux,—le veuf,—inconsolé,
Le prince d'Aquitaine à la tour abolie. . . .[1]
—Nerval "El Desdichado"

Et toujours nous cherchons à nous tromper, nous nous
efforçons d'accéder à la perspective de la continuité,
qui suppose la limite franchie, sans sortir des limites
de cette vie discontinue. Nous voulons accéder
à l'*au-delà* sans franchir le pas, nous maintenant
sagement *en deça*. Nous ne pouvons rien concevoir, rien
imaginer, sinon dans les limites de notre vie, au delà
desquelles il nous semble que tout s'efface.[2]
—Bataille 1957: 155–56

CATULLUS IS A PROBLEM. No matter the narrative, he never quite fits. He is a lyric poet who almost never writes in lyric meters. He is a young rebel who invokes traditional values. He is a spontaneous and passionate poet who composes complex learned poetry. He is an elegist, but not quite (Albrecht 1997: 324, 355–56). Most scholars of Latin poetry see a profound kinship between Catullus and the later Latin love elegists. Indeed, it is not uncommon for him to be listed as either the first of the elegists or the prototype from which elegy sprang.[3] What has proven far more vexing is to define the basis for assigning Catullus this position. The identification, however strong its intuitive basis, has never been given an adequate theoretical foundation. This chapter argues that the anomalous nature of his poetry is in no way accidental but rather central to his identity as an elegiac precursor.

On a formal level, the correspondences between Catullus and the elegists are not that numerous. The majority of Catullus's production in elegiac meter is either of the short epigrammatic variety or, as in the case of poems 65–67, not about love at all. Moreover, many of the most important Lesbia poems for Catullus's Augustan successors are not in elegiac meter but rather in the melic and iambic forms found in the polymetrics (Ross 1975: 16; Quinn 1969: 57). Luck, who cites Catullus as the first of the elegists, identifies only one text as truly anticipating the work of the later poets, 68: a long, erudite poem on love that manifests the mythological learning and the complexity of structure generally associated with Propertius, Tibullus, and Ovid (Luck 1960: 48–50; Grimal 1987: 253; Hubbard 1984: 41).[4] One poem, however, is a thin reed on which to base the founding of an entire subgenre, especially given the fact that many of the most important passages in the corpus, those which resonate longest through the later tradition and create the implicit narrative structure of the Lesbia affair, are not found within this poem. Only an approach that links 68 to those elements that most clearly anticipate the elegists' work could establish the centrality of this text. Moreover, Luck (1960: 58) himself recognizes differences between Catullus's use of mythology in 68 and that found in the later poets, particularly Propertius.[5] Thus 68's form alone can hardly account for the creation of the genre.

Correspondences on the level of content are no more satisfying. The observation that Catullus and the elegists write about love is banal. If we try to be more specific, in the manner of Lyne (1980: 1–81), and claim that what Catullus initiates is a specific treatment of love, one that seeks to unite sexual passion with emotional rapport in a fashion atypical of Roman marriage practices, there are a number of difficulties. First, a substantial portion of the Catullan corpus has nothing to do with love, although most scholarship has tended to focus on the Lesbia poems. Second, Lyne presumes a level of sincerity in Latin love poetry that is impossible to judge on a purely textual basis. This objection is not merely epistemological but also pragmatic: for the assumption of elegiac sincerity is at variance with most contemporary readings of Propertius, Ovid, and Tibullus. Indeed, Veyne's (1988: 12, 34–36) influential account of the elegiac genre argues that Catullus's is the only erotic poetry of the time that was meant to be read as sincere, and therefore he concludes that the *carmina* should not be seen as part of elegy, which wears its artificiality as a badge of honor.[6] Third, Lyne's account postulates a consistent treatment of love on the part of these poets, ignoring the fact that the pictures of the affairs presented in the elegists are often inconsistent and self-contradictory.

If Luck's formal analysis and Lyne's concept of "whole love" will not stand up to critical scrutiny, what could unite the elegists and Catullus as participants in a single enterprise or as the producers of related works? In short, why do most critics, myself included, see them as engaged in a related if not common enterprise? My argument is that the most significant relation tying Catullus to the elegists is prediscursive and can best be described in terms of the speaking subject's self-constitution in relation to the three fundamental realms of Lacanian thought, the Imaginary, the Symbolic—and the Real. More specifically, I want to argue that Catullus bequeaths to the elegists the poetic precedent of a subject position constituted by a profound dissociation of the Imaginary and the Symbolic, that is to say, by a fundamental conflict between the subject's baseline self-identification in the world of Imaginary reflection and its recognition *as a subject* in the world of codified, signifying practices. The result of this conflict is a split subject whose own discourse is self-undermining and recognizably double, and whose position vis-à-vis communal, ideological norms is therefore profoundly ambivalent. The fact of this radical split, I would contend, has led different commentators to see the same elegist, and often even the same passages, as both profoundly subversive of the existing Roman moral and political order and as strictly conventional. Thus has this poetry produced the irresolvably conflicting claims that these poets are either rebels, traditionalists, or apolitical practitioners of ludic semiosis. In all these cases, critics have tried to reduce a complex schizoid discourse to a univocal phenomenon that directly reflects an ex-tratextual political position, even if—as in the case of Veyne—it is one of a sophisticated agnosticism.

Such a split or schizoid discourse will be the least mystified when it is most aporetical (Lacan 1975: 86). In these undecidable passages, the gap between the Imaginary and the Symbolic is most clearly revealed, and the resulting moments of opacity constitute the symptomatic emergence of the Real—that is, the world beyond signification, the realm of what can-not be assimilated to language and thought (Lacan 1973: 276; Jameson 1981: 56–57; Moi 1985: 94; Žižek 1989: 21). As noted in the previous chapter, the moment of emergence takes place most forcefully within the erotic because here the conjugation of the private fantasmata of the Imagi-nary and the publicly sanctioned realm of Symbolic norms takes place with greatest intensity, and hence with the greatest possibility of conflict. Because Catullan erotic discourse offers a privileged vantage point for observing the initial production of the elegiac subject, it is a crucial ba-rometer for measuring the kinds of architectonic shifts that are restructur-ing the Roman ideological landscape, the profound historical movements that are reshaping the world beyond the immediate consciousness and control of its individual actors and participants (Jameson 1981: 82–83).

Precisely in the realm of Catullan desire we witness the encounter with the Real that underwrites the poetic invention of the Roman "erotic sub-lime." Far from Lyne's domesticated image of "whole love"—a longed-for realm of bourgeois contentment—the Catullan erotic sublime presents a shattering moment that shakes the subject to its roots. It is embodied less in the need for emotional reciprocity between two fully constituted subjects than in that shearing of the self that Catullus articulates in the narratives of Attis and Ariadne, or in his own "odi et amo."[7] This is a kind of obscene sublime. It articulates a gap at the heart of being, a gap that will later be constitutive of the Propertian obsession with erotic

death, the dreamlike quality of Tibullus, and that will finally be sharpened
and reduced to self-subverting irony in Ovid's *Amores*. The Catullan
erotic sublime finds its most striking emblem in the figure of Ariadne
standing at the edge of the sea, scanning the waves for the lost Theseus.
As her vestments trail in the water swirling round her feet, she embodies
a simultaneous moment of death and desire, an alienation of the self that
is both destructive and erotic.

> prospicit et magnis curarum fluctuat undis,
> non flavo retinens subtilem vertice mitram,
> non contecta levi velatum pectus amictu,
> non tereti strophio lactentis vincta papillas,
> omnia quae toto delapsa e corpore passim
> ipsius ante pedes fluctus salis alludebant. (64.62–67)

> She looks out and is battered by vast waves of grief,
> her blonde hair no longer bound by the thin net,
> her veiled bosom no longer covered by the light cloak,
> her milky breasts no longer bound by their smooth girdle.
> All the clothes that had slipped from her whole body
> the salt waves played with, here and there round her feet.

This passage is obscene, not because it is erotic, but because it violates
the integrity of the subject. It rips away that which is most intimate and
re-presents it as alienated from an integral self, in the same way that por-
nography separates the sexual from the illusion of coherent subjective
experience. In the moment of Ariadne's grief, we are invited to linger over
her smooth breasts, the swirling waters around her feet. As Bataille notes,
"The obscene signifies a disturbance that troubles that condition of bodies
that would conform to self-possession, to the possession of a durable and
assured sense of self" (1957: 22).[8] The alienation of either the flesh or
experience from the self, its specularization *ob scaenam* (for the stage) is
the essence of the obscene (cf. Varro, *De Lingua latina*, 7.96, cited in
Barton 1993: 142n.173).[9]

This same moment of radical alienation, as Kant first recognized, is
integral to the experience of the sublime. In the sublime, the subject en-
counters that which exceeds—in terms of magnitude or power—the cate-
gories of individual understanding, so that he or she encounters his or her
own limits. The sublime is a ripping or tearing of the self. It is an experi-
ence of excess that does "violence to the imagination; and yet is judged
only to be the more sublime" (Kant 1951: 83). The Kantian sublime is a
moment of simultaneous "pain" and "pleasure" (Kant 1951: 96).
Through it, the subject suffers a moment of self-division while yielding to
the desire to comprehend or incorporate what exceeds it. "The mind feels

itself moved in the representation of the sublime. . . . The movement may (especially in its beginnings) be compared to a vibration, i.e. to a quickly alternating attraction toward, and repulsion from, the same object. The transcendent (toward which the imagination is impelled in its apprehension) is for the imagination like an abyss in which it fears to lose itself" (Kant 1951: 97). The sublime, as opposed to the harmony of faculties designated by the beautiful, presents a site where the subject experiences ontological rupture (Steele 1997: 159), a hole or gap in being that is the symptomatic irruption of the Real onto the stage of experience (Žižek 1989: 135). But whereas for Kant the experience of the sublime is always to be recuperated by a renewed respect for the powers of objective reason in the face of the subjectively unthinkable, for later writers and theorists, beginning with the romantics, this moment of regrounding the subject is far less assured. In Dequincey, Baudelaire, Sartre, and the modernists, the sublime names an experience that fractures the subject, and thus presents a desire for wholeness in the very moment of death, mutilation, or violation (Black 1991: 50–51, 68–73, 98, 109; Žižek 1989: 204–5; 1991: 169; Stoekl 1992: 85–92). This dialectical tension between wholeness and dissolution, between sexuality and death, as Bataille (1957: 65) notes, is the essence of erotic experience.[10] It is the momentary opening of the closed world of the subject to the radically other (Bell 1998: 135–36),[11] the experience of the violation of the subject's own bounds (Black 1991: 205). "The whole process of the erotic has as its end the attainment of being at its most intimate, at the point where the heart experiences a lack. The movement from the normal state to that of erotic desire presupposes in us the relative dissolution of that being which is constituted in the order of discontinuity or individuality" (Bataille 1957: 22).[12] It is precisely this realm of the erotic sublime, a form of experience at odds with traditional republican notions of *gravitas* and *dignitas*, that Catullus distills in poem 68, a poem whose form and whose deep internal splits mark it as the beginning of the elegiac genre. The formalization of this sublimely aporetical subject position is what Catullus bequeaths the elegists of the early empire.[13]

    I begin to outline the case for this revision of the relation between Catullus and the elegists in a reading of Catullus 68 that focuses on just such moments of aporia. In particular, I shall examine the way in which poem 68 destabilizes Catullus's subject position in the Symbolic through a close reading of the interlocked similes in lines 51–66 and their relation both to the Laudamia and Protesilaus simile, which occupies the center of the poem (72–134), and a second analogous set of interlocking similes framing the second half of the poem (119–34). In each case, we can see how these similes run aground in their attempt to simulate the unassimilable, to represent a gap in the structures of representation. My exposition is perforce nonlinear since the poem, while possessing a discernible rhetorical structure, proceeds by an associative logic in which one term becomes identified with another in such a fashion as to prohibit a strict demarcation of discrete passages, themes, or images without falsifying the nature of the text itself. As Micaela Janan writes, "The poem realizes, paradoxically, the two tendencies of desire at once: the preservation and the abolition of difference. . . . But . . . the two antinomies refuse to collapse into one another; rather, they are the basis for endless substitutions. Their suspension in mutual relation constitutes the basis of creation in c. 68" (1994: 141).

THE PROBLEM OF THE REFERENT

Allius's aid has the paradoxical quality of being both an opening of exterior space (v. 67 *is clausum lato patefecit limite campum*) and a closure of interior space (v. 68 *domum nobis, isque dedit dominae*). This duality is characteristic of language, which both encloses the signified and at the same time explodes it into a broad field of disseminated significations.
—Hubbard 1984: 34

The elegy is a eucharistikon—a *gratiarum actio* which begins with an included recusatio: and as with other recusationes the refusal is a means whereby what is refused is indirectly granted.
—Cairns 1979a: 164

The expanded Homeric similes in Catullus 68 have long represented one of the cruxes of the poem's interpretation. As Gordon Williams has observed, "double similes of this extent are without precedent in poetry before Catullus, either Greek or Latin" (1980: 52). Their strangeness cannot be removed by any appeal to tradition (Feeney 1992: 38). Moreover, as Janan (1994: 124) notes, the analogical relations governing the similes do not strictly scan. The resulting confusion is not simply a consequence of Homeric expansion run amok; these are self-consuming artifacts that consistently subvert their own status as illustrative figures through the deployment of complex, interlocking patterns of mutual reflection. In them, one set of terms of comparison is constantly being identified with or substituted for another. In the process, these similes obscure both the boundaries between themselves and between their referents. They call into question the very relation between figure and ground upon which any meaningful distinction between the representative and the represented rests. Indeed, these similes—whose express purpose is to illustrate A by comparing it to B—ultimately serve to undermine the very function of difference itself in the conceptual world of the Symbolic, that is, the creation of a realm of differentiated signifiers that can be ascribed unique and specifiable signifieds. As such, they nullify that division of the phenomenal world into discrete entities that makes meaning and comparison possible: for saying A is like B is only meaningful as long as A and B can each be distinguished from all other entities and an agreed-upon basis of comparison can be found.[14] Thus, what begins as a well-attested piece of the poetic inheritance, the expanded Homeric simile, finishes by calling into question the very concept of difference on which language and hence the Symbolic are founded, producing an all but omnivorous set of Imaginary identifications that are strictly at variance with the elaborate and well-demarcated rhetorical structure in which they are found. As Denis Feeney remarks, "this dense and bizarre barrage of analogy leaves one with the sensation that similes are no added ornament to the poem, something additional to what the poem is saying. They *are* the poem, they *are* what the poem is saying" (1992: 35, emphasis in original).

Indeed, it is widely debated whether the initial set of similes in lines 51–66 contains one, two, or three examples of the figure. What is at stake in how we answer this question is not only the understanding of the rhetorical construction of this particular passage but also a reading of the poem's structure as a whole. The implications of this seemingly simple textual problem are not limited to purely formal considerations, for the way the reader understands the structure of the similes and their relation to the poem ultimately determines the identification of the similes' referents: do they point back to Catullus's *cura* (51), forward to Allius's *auxilium* (66), or somehow encompass both (Feeney 1992: 38)? What began as a question of simple rhetorical divisions—where does one simile end and the next begin?—quickly comes to pose problems relative to the poem's internal structure and its external reference, so that each becomes implicated in the other. Thus, the problem of the text's internal structure is generally formulated in terms of a question concerning whether 68 has an identifiable ring composition or proceeds by a process of metonymic association that eludes the rational ordering of a strict rhetorical partitioning. The first option assumes that the various sections of the poem, including its similes, can be clearly identified and demarcated from one another, thereby allowing the reader to see correspondences between individual passages separated by as much as one hundred lines. These correspondences in turn render a pattern of symmetrical ring composition clearly visible. The second option assumes that each passage contains imagistic and verbal links to that which immediately proceeds and follows it, making a strict demarcation of elementary textual units impossible as each term in the series becomes identified with and displaced by those that surround it. These options—that is, ring composition versus metonymic association or, following Bright (1976: 103), hypotaxis versus parataxis—would seem to be mutually exclusive. In addition, the problem of the similes' referents bears on the fundamental question of whether poem 68 posits the existence of discrete, individual subjects, whose lives continue separately from the speaker's life or is he trapped in a world of narcissistic Imaginary identification, in which Allius (or Lesbia, or his brother) ceases to exist apart from Catullus and his desire. Again, these would seem to be mutually exclusive options. Yet, the logical opposition of identity and difference is consistently undermined within this poem and its relation to the surrounding corpus. This is true on the rhetorical, referential, and ultimately ontological levels.

Indeed, the difficulties faced by even the most elementary concepts of discrete personal identity when dealing with the complexities of poem 68 are made clear by such well-known textual cruxes as the slippage from Mallius to Allius as the name of the addressee of 68a (lines 1–40) versus 68b (lines 41–160); the fact that 68b appears to be the same poem that Catullus tells Mallius he is incapable of writing in 68a; and the verbatim repetition of the passage identifying Catullus's brother's death with that of his entire family (*domus*) in both texts. Indeed, whether by accident or design, we may never know if 68a and 68b are addressed to the same person, and consequently if they are two parts of the same poem (Bright 1976: 89). The arguments for and against taking the switch from Mallius (or Manius or Manlius) to Allius have remained inconclusive and no consensus has been reached.[15] What is not in doubt, however, is that each text repeats the same basic themes (Cairns 1979a: 164–65; Williams 1980: 9; Edwards 1991: 80–81)—the shipwrecked sailors (lines 1–4, 63–66), the debt owed a friend (11–12, 68–69), the *domus* (passim), and the death of the poet's brother (20–24, 92–96)—while each retains an independent structure and a differently named addressee. As such, 68a's relation to 68b is one of both identity and difference. Poem 68a is the letter that proclaims the poet's inability to write 68b, but 68b exists nonetheless (Hubbard 1984: 42).[16] In fact, 68a and 68b have the same essential relationship to one another as 65 and 66: 65 being the cover letter that announces the poet's inability, due to the death of his brother, to write a poem promised to a friend; 66 being the translation of Callimachus that stands in its stead.[17] The relationship between the two pairs of poems does not stop there. Poem 66 combines the same motifs of romantic love and the loss of a brother that feature prominently in 68 (Janan 1994: 127–28; Miller 1994: 113–14; King 1988: 387–88). Indeed, all that is missing is the darker theme of amorous infidelity. This lacuna however is filled by poem 67's modified paraclausithyron (Copley 1956: 35–36), which provides the bridge between the lighter treatment of the themes of fraternal and romantic love found in 66 and their darker portrayal in 68 (Wiseman 1969: 24; King 1988: 388; Miller 1994: 114; Fitzgerald 1995: 202–3).[18] Thus, the dialectic of identity and difference that characterizes the referents and structure of the similes in poem 68 is in fact characteristic of the whole of Catullus's longer elegiac production. Poem 68 represents a summation of these efforts on both the formal and the thematic levels.[19]

These two sets of problems outlined here—the structure of the text in terms of ring composition or metonymic association and the problem of the identity of the similes and their referents—are not unrelated. In each case, the crux is the opposition between boundless identity and structured difference, and this tension as we noted earlier is at the center of the Catullan erotic sublime. The answer to these problems in every instance, as we shall see, is that both options, although contradictory on the logical level, are true: for one of the bewildering yet fascinating things about this poem, which has allowed critics to see it as both an aesthetic failure and triumph (Janan 1994: 151–52n.25), is its foregrounding of the presence of parallel, but noncoincident, registers of meaning, which, following Lacan, we label the Imaginary and the Symbolic.[20] It is moreover precisely at the point where these two registers become incommensurable that we witness the emergence of the Real, of that which cannot be assimilated to a structure of meaning. Alternatively, to return to our revised Kantian terminology, it is this point of incommensurability that both denies to the poem the stabler category of the beautiful and yet constitutes its claim to the negative moment of the sublime.

THIS SIMILE WHICH IS NOT ONE

Let us begin our reading of the poem by examining more closely lines 51–66:

> nam, mihi quam dederit duplex Amathusia curam,
>   scitis, et in quo me torruerit genere,
> cum tantum arderem quantum Trinacria rupes
>   lymphaque in Oetaeis Malia Thermopylis,
> maesta neque assiduo tabescere lumina fletu
>   cessarent tristique imbre madere genae.
> qualis in aerii perlucens vertice montis
>   rivus muscoso prosilit e lapide,
> qui cum de prona praeceps est valle volutus,
>   per medium densi transit iter populi,
> dulce viatori lasso in sudore levamen,
>   cum gravis exustos aestus hiulcat agros,

hic [21] velut in nigro iactatis turbine nautis
   lenius aspirans aura secunda venit
iam prece Pollucis, iam Castoris implorata,
   tale fuit nobis Allius auxlium.

For you know what anxiety the duplicitous Amathusian
   has given me, how she burned me alive,
when I boiled like the lava of Sicily's Mount Aetna
   and the Malian pools of Oeta at Thermopylae;
my sad eyes never stopped melting in constant weeping
   nor my cheeks to be awash in a stream of tears,
as a silvery cascade on a high mountain's peak
   bursts forth from the moss-covered stone,
which when it crashes in the steep ravine below
   and washes across the way where men come and go,
serves as sweet solace to the sweat-covered traveler
   when the heavy summer heat splits the burnt up soil.
Then, just as a gentle favoring breeze comes
   to sailors tossed by the black storm
(when they have offered prayers to Castor and Pollux),
   so was Allius's aid to me.[22]

Again, the crucial questions are: how many similes do we have; and to what do they refer? Neither of these questions can be answered successfully without making prior assumptions as to how we would answer the other: for we can only establish the boundaries between similes by referencing that which lies outside them and which they purport to represent; and we can only establish those points of reference once the boundaries of the similes themselves have been established. As such, these questions are strictly undecidable and should alert us to the presence of structures that are unassimilable to the logic of noncontradiction that rules the Symbolic (Janan 1994: 35, 79). For if we assume two similes, that requires us to assimilate the cool stream of 57–62 to Catullus's hot tears in 51–56 and not to Allius's aid. Such an assumption, however, is arbitrary in that it requires us to reject the obvious parallel between the solace provided by the stream to weary travelers and the assistance Allius gave in providing a home in which Catullus and Lesbia could slake their passion (Dollar 1997: 37–39). On the logical, and hence Symbolic (Kristeva 1982: 15), level, lines 57–62 would seem to have more in common with the favoring wind that rescues sailors caught in a storm than with tears of searing grief. On the associative level of the Imaginary, however, the stream of Catullus's tears cannot be rigorously distinguished from the spring that provides comfort to the traveler drenched in summer sweat (Jameson 1988: 97–100).

The correlatives *qualis* (57) and *talis* (66), whose status as markers of syntactical and rhetorical subordination situates them firmly within the Symbolic at its purest—the realm of "quantitative and purely formal reasoning"—are of little help (Butler 1990: 82–83). The passage introduced by *qualis* can be read in at least two different ways. On the stylistic level, as Fordyce (1978: ad loc.) points out, when Catullus introduces similes elsewhere with *qualis*, they refer to what precedes them, not to what follows. The most persuasive piece of evidence he adduces to make this case is the Hercules simile in lines 105–16 of this very poem:

> quo tibi tum casu, pulcerrima Laudamia,
> > ereptum est vita dulcius atque anima
> coniugium: tanto te absorbens vertice amoris
> > aestus in abruptum detulerat barathrum,
> *quale* ferunt Grai Pheneum prope Cyllenaeum
> > siccare emulsa pingue palude solum,
> quod quondam caesis montis fodisse medullis
> > audit falsiparens Amphitryoniades,
> tempore quo certa Stymphalia monstra sagitta
> > perculit imperio deterioris eri
> pluribus ut caeli tereretur ianua divis,
> > Hebe nec longa virginitate foret.

> This then was your downfall, beautiful Laudamia,
> > your marriage, sweeter than life or breath,
> was torn away.
> > > With so great a maelstrom,
> > > > boiling
> all-consuming love swept you into a steep chasm
> *as deep as* the one the Greeks say drained the marsh
> > and fertile soil near Cyllenian Pheneum,
> the one the so-called son of Amphitryon is said
> > to have dug, mining the mountain's marrow,
> while with a sure arrow he slew the monsters of Stymphalus,
> > on the order of an inferior master,
> so that the threshold of heaven might be worn smooth by more gods,
> > nor Hebe remain long a virgin.

Here *qualis* certainly refers back to the chasm into which Laudamia is swept. Thus usage within the poem seems to confirm Fordyce's observation that *qualis* in Catullus refers back to that which preceded it and so *qualis* in line 57 would indicate that the simile of the refreshing mountain stream refers back to Catullus's *cura* rather than forward to Allius's *auxilium*.

The testimony of the Hercules simile, however, may be less univocal than first appears to be the case, since it contains both deep associative links with the two similes that follow and is part of the larger Laudamia and Protesilaus simile that occupies the center of the poem. Thus, as Bright points out, the *Stymphalia monstra* of line 113 anticipate both the *volturius* of line 124's simile of the newborn grandson, and the *columbus* of line 125's simile of the passionate dove, so that a second parallel set of imagistically interlocked comparisons echoes that found at the poem's beginning.[23] In the second set, birds serve as the identifying metonym, as water did in the first. The observation of imagistic continuity between these similes, as well as the fact that this continuity parallels that seen in the initial set, makes clear distinctions between the various subject positions outlined in this later passage—for example, *pulcerrima Laudamia* (most beautiful Laudamia, 105), *Hebe nec longa virginitate* (Hebe not long a virgin, 116), the *una nata* (only daughter, 120), and the *multivola mulier* (much desiring woman/wife,[24] 128)—hard to maintain (Bright 1976: 98, 102–3; cf. Feeney 1992: 40–41). Laudamia's beauty, Hebe's virginity, the only daughter's birth of a grandson, and the woman or wife's consuming passion not only succeed one another, but also substitute for one another in a series that creates a space of neither logical equivalence nor imaginary identity. Moreover, this entire second set of similes refers not to any extratextual reality but is part of the Laudamia simile itself, a complex rhetorical structure that, as we shall see, insistently subverts its own referential value within the poem. In fact, the double movement of the text as a whole can be illustrated by the relationship of this second set of similes to the first: for, while an emphasis on the parallels between them draws attention to the ring structure of the text, and hence the clear distinctions that underwrite a strict rhetorical partitioning, the subordination of the second set to the Laudamia simile erases these boundaries, making those distinctions impossible. As such, the Hercules simile's value as an index of logical and/or rhetorical clarity is difficult to maintain.

Nonetheless Fordyce's claim that *qualis* refers back to Catullus's *cura* does find support in the poem's associative logic of images: for *qualis*, because of its position immediately following the description of the tears streaming down Catullus's cheeks, would seem most naturally to introduce a comparison between them and the cool mountain spring described in the clause that follows, water being a common element in both (Quinn 1973: ad loc.).[25] These initial observations on Catullus's usage of *qualis* and the associative link between tears and a mountain stream find confirmation in Jane E. Philips's argument that lines 51–62 represent a coherent artistic and imagistic sequence that conforms to the more general aesthetic model of ring composition governing the poem as a whole (Philips 1976). That sequence begins in line 52 where the notion of dry, searing heat is introduced with the verb *torruerit*. The evocation is carried forward into the next line with, *arderem*, which modulates into a comparison to Sicily's Mount Aetna through the use of the quantifying correlatives *tantum* and *quantum* that anticipate the qualifying correlatives *talis* and *qualis*. The poet makes a great show of the logical and rhetorical exactitude of his comparisons. Volcanic heat, however, rather than bringing to mind the dry, baking warmth of *torruerit*, has connotations of liquidity. Not only does lava represent a form of liquefaction, but also hot springs are often found in regions of volcanic activity. The gradual movement from dry heat to its opposite, the cool water of the stream, is then further advanced by the mention of the hot springs round Thermopylae in line 54, which are in turn metamorphosed into warm tears in line 55, as the poet's eyes melt in a volcanic eruption. Tears are, of course, cooler than volcanic springs, and when in line 56 they are compared to rain, the transition from dry heat to watery coolness has been all but completed. We are ready, then, for line 57's comparison, introduced by the word *qualis*, of the falling tears to a cascading mountain spring that provides welcome relief to weary travelers who are covered in sweat (line 61). This last detail recalls the warm tears with which the comparison began and initiates the regression to dry heat that is rapidly completed with the evocation of the heavy summer sun cracking open the parched fields in line 62.

Thus, we have come full circle. Lines 52–62 represent ring composition in miniature, a structure that in turn echoes the form of the poem as whole, which as virtually all agree is constructed in concentric rings around the *omphalos* evoking the death of Catullus's brother.[26] In sum, the coherence of the imagistic pattern, its consonance with the aesthetic principles of the poem as a whole, and the evidence of Catullan usage seem all but explicitly to mandate that *qualis* introduce a comparison referring back to Catullus's tears, rather than forward to Allius's aid. Yet, each one of these points can be answered by an equal and opposite argument pointing in the other direction. Indeed, the crucial center of the passage in question, the *qualis*, which functions as the *omphalos* in lines 52–62's ring composition, comes to represent not a moment of either logical or rhetorical congruity, let alone an imagistic evocation of Imaginary plenitude, but rather, as the point of articulation between what we for convenience term the first and second similes, it denotes a moment of absolute lack or absence. It, like the death of Catullus's brother—which serves as the *omphalos* for the poem as whole—represents the hollow center, the switching point between registers of meaning that mark their finitude, the gap, the irredeemable absence that our Imaginary identifications and

Symbolic constructions strive to fill. It marks the sublime encounter with the Real (Copjec 1994: 35).

With these considerations in mind, it is time to look at the arguments for taking *qualis* as introducing a simile pointing forward to Allius's *auxilium* rather than back to Catullus's *cura*. In terms of the coherence of the imagistic pattern, the first thing to be noticed is that this argument cuts both ways: for the water imagery begun in line 54 is continued in lines 63–65's picture of sailors tossed about by a storm on the sea. Likewise, the sad rain of tears that covers Catullus's cheeks in 56 is evoked in 63–65's figure of the storm. Nor is the connection purely imagistic, for Allius's aid is the gentle wind that blows away the storm and sends the sailors safely home to port in 63–65, and it is that same aid that, at least temporarily, dries Catullus's rain of tears. Thus, each figurative storm is calmed by the same gentle breeze, leading the reader inevitably to presume a deeper connection than their mutual association with water. Indeed, on the level of imagistic identification, Catullus's anxiety and Allius's aid are indistinguishable. And if the similes' referents are no longer completely separable, then determining which terms are modified by which similes and where the boundaries between those similes are located becomes highly problematic if not impossible. Consequently, the notion that the simile contained in lines 57–62 refers back to 51–56 but not forward to 63–66 is untenable.

The relation between 57–62 and 63–66 becomes all the stronger when we take into account the provenance of the similes. K.M.W. Shipton (1985: 56) has noted that this same collocation of the spring providing solace to weary travelers and of sailors saved from the storm can be found in Clytemnestra's speech welcoming Agamemnon in Aeschylus's tragedy by the same name (lines 899–901). The figures there are far less elaborate than they are in Catullus, and certainly are sufficiently common to be found in many other places than Aeschylus, but their immediate succession, one after another, is, as far as I know, unparalleled elsewhere in ancient literature. Moreover, the verbal and imagistic correspondences are redoubled on the dramatic level, for Clytemnestra makes her speech just before Agamemnon's entrance into their house. Likewise, in Catullus the similes occur just before his description of Lesbia's shining entrance into the house Allius provided (Shipton, 1983: 56–58). Of course, in Aeschylus, the passage is a prelude to Agamemnon's murder at the hands of Clytemnestra and no such fate awaits Lesbia from Catullus. But while on one level Clytemnestra and Catullus are clearly demarcated figures that occupy different Symbolic categories in terms of their genders, social stations, and respective relations to the action portrayed in the literary works under discussion, on another, true to the metonymic logic of the similes in which these lines are embedded, those differences are slowly effaced as we consider the remainder of the poem and Catullus's own ambivalent self-portrayal throughout the corpus.

First, gender inversion—a rhetorical transvestism—is far from uncommon in Catullus (Miller 1994: 71, 110–17; Martin 1992: 44; Gantar 1976: 119; Rubino 1975: 294). Indeed, one of the most famous passages relating to this topic occurs within this very poem when Catullus compares his need to overlook Lesbia's occasional infidelities (*rara furta*, line 136) to Juno's having to forgive Jupiter's nonstop philandering (*plurima furta*, line 140). In so doing, Catullus comes to occupy the feminine position—in terms both of his personal identification with Juno and of Roman sexual ideology, which permitted masculine peccadilloes but strictly sanctioned feminine promiscuity. Consequently, from the perspective of the poem, there is no prima facie reason why, with regard to gender, Catullus could not also occupy the position of Clytemnestra. Moreover, this inversion of gender values is one of Catullus's most concrete legacies to the later elegists (Hallett 1974: 212; Wyke 1989: 36; Gold 1993: 85–86; Albrecht 1997: 343): a poetic cross-dressing, that as Marjorie Garber (1992: 18) notes, is symptomatic of a category crisis in the society as whole.[27] On a general level, then, we can say that this consistent inversion of normative gender categories indicates that the Symbolic codes of masculine ideology no longer were completely adequate to the Imaginary identifications that structured the elegiac poet's experience. Whether these identifications with the figure of the feminine are sincere, ironic, or even mocking and manipulative is, on this level of analysis, less important than the evidence they yield of a fundamental slippage occurring between Roman masculinist ideological categories and Imaginary experience. Here, in this moment of contradiction, the emergence of the Real as a manifestation of historical change is most clearly felt, and in the creation of this poetic subject position, which allows Catullus and Clytemnestra momentarily to become one, we see one of the elegists' greatest debts to Catullus (Hallett 1973: 111; Gold 1993: 85).

Second, while Lesbia may not be killed by Catullus, death and tragedy, both in terms of the metonymic progression of the poem and the "chronology" of the affair itself, do ensue from her entrance into the house Allius provided. On the one hand, immediately following Catullus's description of Lesbia's entrance as the *candida diva* (line 70), a simile begins formally comparing her with Laudamia. This is the longest of the poem, stretching from lines 73 to 134 and containing within it the second set of interlocking similes (119–34) that most commentators see as mirroring those in 57–72 and thereby functioning as part of poem 68's overall ring structure. The simile itself recounts the story of Laudamia's ill-fated love for Protesilaus who is doomed to be the first to die at Troy shortly after they are married because of a failure on his part to perform the requisite sacrifices when he began building their new home ("domum / inceptam frustra," 74–75). The use of this particular mythological exemplum to describe the ostensibly happy occasion of Lesbia's entrance, which marks the beginning of the affair itself, into the *domus* (68) that Allius provides cannot help but strike the reader as odd: for, if the simile is not a mere arbitrary assertion of resemblance without any authentic relation to the poem's themes or structure, a bit of Alexandrian puffery, then it must imply that, as in the case of Laudamia and Protesilaus, the result of Lesbia's crossing the threshold will be tragedy and death. Consequently, her entrance would also recall that of Agamemnon and thus make the Laudamia simile central to the understanding of the allusions to the *Agamemnon* just discussed. This potential parallelism is given added credence by the fact that Lesbia herself is often portrayed in a phallic and hence masculinist fashion, most notably in the famous simile of the flower and the plow at the end of poem 11 (Fitzgerald 1995: 180–81; Putnam 1974: 79–80; Ferguson 1985: ad loc.). Of course, neither Catullus nor Lesbia dies in the poem, but his—at least figurative—demise at her hands is clearly evoked in the larger collection where his relationship to Lesbia is portrayed as a disease (*morbum*, 76.25), a casualty of her thoughtless violence (11.21–24), and a form of mental torture comparable with being hung on a cross (*excrucior*, 85.2). She is the death of him. All of these characterizations and the betrayals on which they rest are the temporal consequences of Allius's act. Without his kindness, the tragedy of Catullus and Lesbia's love would have never been played. Thus, in terms of the consequences of his actions as well the imagistic way in which they are portrayed, the distinction between Allius's *auxilium* and Catullus's *cura* becomes increasingly difficult to maintain.

Likewise, in terms of the metonymic progression of the poem itself, Lesbia's entrance and her comparison to Laudamia lead directly into the central panel's mourning for the death of his brother, the *omphalos* of the poem's ring composition. This too evokes a figurative demise of the poet. As Catullus tells us, his brother's passing effectively means the death of the whole family, "tecum una tota est nostra sepulta domus" [our whole household is buried together with you]; (l.94). Thus within twenty-six lines the house provided by Allius for the poet and Lesbia's initial assignation becomes first the doomed house of Laudamia and Protesilaus, and then the entombed household of the *gens Valerii*, the figurative death of Catullus and his kin with the loss of his brother (Sarkissian 1983: 24). Catullus in turn becomes identified with each of these subject positions in a series of mutually exclusive but imagistically equivalent moments of projection onto the other and consequent reflection of the self. Hence in poem 68, through a process of metonymic progression and Imaginary identification,[28] the distinct loci of subjectivity that make the Symbolic possible are consistently undermined, leaving Catullus himself no recognizable place in which he can stand, even as the very womb of Imaginary identification and reflection, the family, has become nothing more than a tomb, now metonymically identified with one of the greatest icons of the ancient Symbolic, Troy itself.

The loss of his brother, moreover, puts Catullus in the position of one who has lost his or her beloved. Likewise, as later sections of the poem make clear, he is the one abandoned by Lesbia's infidelities, rather than the other way around. His losses thus are double,[29] and it is he who most closely resembles Laudamia, not Lesbia (MacCleod 1974: 83–86; Bright 1976: 99; Johnson 1982 161; Sarkissian 1983: 22; Hubbard 1984: 34; Feeney 1992: 37). As Williams writes:

> [I]t instantly becomes clear that Laudamia is more truly a figure for Catullus than for Lesbia, and that Catullus's relationship with his brother was in some ways analogous to Laudamia's with Protesilaus. This is mirrored in the love-language the poet uses to describe his affection for his brother. . . . The agony of the poet over his brother's death is certainly self-contained and needs no external justification. Nevertheless it seems to have a resonance which extends beyond itself, for the simple reason that, as Laudamia figures Catullus, so Protesilaus is a figure not only for the poet's brother but also for Lesbia. Hence the agony of Catullus over his brother's death seems to foreshadow the loss (in a sense analogous to, but not necessarily identical with the death) of Lesbia. The poet's extremity of desperation in these lines, the only direct expression of emotion in the poem, seems to move in the direction of Laudamia's suicide[30] (84: she could not go on living after the destruction of her marriage), as if he were foreshadowing his own death also. (1980: 59–60, see also 55)

This realization that it is Catullus who most clearly resembles Laudamia and not Lesbia has a ripple effect throughout the poem: for, if Catullus, who was in the position of Clytemnestra welcoming Agamemnon home, switches places with Lesbia to become Laudamia, then, Lesbia, adopting Catullus's former position, turns into Clytemnestra, thus causing Catullus to metamorphose into the figure of Agamemnon struck down by Lesbia/Clytemnestra's infidelities. Consequently, the initial gender inversion that led Catullus to be identified with Clytemnestra is set aright by a second shift in which Catullus comes to occupy the position formerly possessed by Lesbia (Shipton 1985: 69–70). Thus the slippage that allows Catullus to assume the feminine position in relation to the Laudamia and Protesilaus simile is also what makes the masculine position relative to the Aeschylean subtext possible. Consequently, neither gender position can ever be stable since the intertextual figure (i.e., Agamemnon) and intratextual figure (i.e., Laudamia) stand in contradictory relation to one another. Catullus can only be a man in one by being a woman in the other.[31] Conversely, the same must hold true for Lesbia as well.

Catullus and Lesbia are doomed to alternate between the same set of subject positions, each changing places with the other in a dance that constantly reasserts their sexual and subjective differences in the Symbolic even as it affirms their Imaginary identification. The categories of normative subject and personal identity are out of sync. The persuasiveness of this reading is enhanced when we recall that Aeschylus's text is itself characterized by a certain gender instability. Thus Clytemnestra at the beginning of the *Agamemnon* is said to be a woman who acts like a man (line 11), making her a figure open to appropriation by both an effeminizing Catullus and the ever-phallic Lesbia (cf. poem 11). Finally, the subversion of the analogical relations governing the simile—through the possibility of substituting Catullus for Lesbia within the structure of the figure itself—echoes the confusion we saw in lines 51–66 as to whether 56–62 refers back to Catullus's tears or forward to Allius's *auxilium* (Feeney 1992: 39–40). Catullus throughout this poem erects a rigid structure of formal similes, learned literary allusions, and complex ring composition in a homage to the Apollonian forces of the Symbolic only to undermine them through a series of Imaginary identifications whose Dionysian contempt for the world of boundaries refuses to allow him (or Allius or Lesbia or his brother) any single, stable position.

This is not to say that there is no potential for mediation. The Aeschylean subtext points to such a possibility in the figure of Aegisthus. As Shipton (1985: 68–69) observes, in terms of the narrative dimension of poem 68, as opposed to the imagistic sequences established by its multiple and interpenetrating similes, Catullus's position is not that of the lawful husband but rather of the adulterous lover.[32] In Aeschlyus's version of the story, Aegisthus plays the contradictory figure of the passive male. He is thus the complement of Clytemnestra's phallic female. As a figure of sexual ambiguity who lies outside the normal binary oppositions of ancient gender, he is a monster who must be destroyed according to the sacrificial logic of the *Oresteia*. For Catullus, however, he represents the possibility of a momentary stasis in the alternation of gender and subject positions with Lesbia, but one that can only be purchased through either the sacrifice of the norms of the Roman sexual Symbolic, and hence of Catullus's claims to recognition as a subject, or by the death of Catullus. This is the same position in which the poet finds himself in poem 76, where he invokes the traditional Roman ethical and political norms of *fides* and *pietas* to sanction his behavior in an adulterous relationship that represents their antithesis and a violation of the lawfully constituted *domus* that is one of poem 68's central concerns.[33] The intertextual role of Aegisthus represents an impossible position that can only function as a moment of synthesis to the extent that it reveals the poetic subject as irredeemably split.[34]

The allusions to the *Agamemnon*, then, are an integral part of the structure of the poem, as Shipton himself has argued. Consequently, we must assume that the collocation of those allusions in lines 57–66 is not arbitrary and that they are meant to be read together. This interpretation, in turn, would argue for taking the image of the refreshing stream with Allius's *auxilium* rather than Catullus's *cura*, since the last two similes (to the extent that they can be separated)—those of the stream and the storm—both derive from the same source, whereas the first (the volcanic spring of Catullan tears) has no such provenance. In sum, the coherence of the intertextual references and their consonance with the structure of the poem as a whole, both in terms of the formal pattern of ring composition and the subtler but consistent undermining of those same patterns, seems to be at least as cogent as the arguments advanced earlier for taking 57–62 with 51–56, based on the coherence of the imagistic pattern found in 51–62 and its recapitulation of the ring structure of the poem as a whole. A third image drawn from Clytemnestra's speech can be found in the poem, that of "the pleasure given by the appearance of an only child" (Shipton 1985: 59, citing line 898, the one just before that describing the sailors saved from the storm). This image is paralleled in 68.119–24, the first of a pair of similes generally thought to mirror those in 57–72, where the initial allusions to the *Agamemnon* are found. This passage, however, is often thought to derive from Pindar's *Olympian* 10, but the consonance with the earlier pattern of allusions to the *Agamemnon* would argue for at least a double derivation.

The final line of argument for taking lines 57–62 with 51–56 rather than 57–62 was Fordyce's claim that similes introduced with *qualis* in Catullus always refer back to that which preceded them rather than forward to what follows. However, most of the cases Fordyce cites are not parallel. They do not possess a corresponding *talis* clause (65.13, 64.89, 68.109–16) or, in those other cases in the corpus where *talis* and *qualis* are used correlatively (61.221, 64.200, 64.247, 64.336), *qualis* does not introduce a simile and the clause in which *talis* appears is brief and to the point. Here alone, however, in the Catullan corpus does *talis* introduce a simile after one introduced by *qualis*. Thus Fordyce's interdiction does not necessarily apply, and given the correlative nature of the two adjectives, and the fact that their respective similes employ water imagery and speak of relief from distress, it is hard not to take the two similes together. There is, however, at least one case in Catullus where *qualis* and *talis* appear within five lines of each other and manifestly do not possess a correlative relationship (64.265–69).

In short, the arguments on each side of the question cancel each other out. Any attempt to short-circuit the process of reading and reduce the complexities of this text, whether through emendation or interpretive ingenuity, can only be in the service of satisfying some preexisting desire, some ideology. Indeed, the argument can be made on imagistic grounds, as pointed out before, that Catullus's tears anticipate the very storm from which Allius's aid saved him.[35] Likewise, although Allius's aid on one level saved Catullus from his tears, the result of that aid was the tragedy of the affair itself. Hence, cause and effect, subject and object, anxiety and aid are not rigorously distinguishable in either their imagistic portrayal or their concrete, narrative manifestations. Poem 68 presents us with a crisis of the normative Roman subject as envisioned by the legal, political, and sexual ideology of the republic. All efforts to locate a stable responsible agent whose consciousness or subject position can account for both these enunciations and the acts named therein quickly runs aground on the same rhetorical shoals as the attempt to locate a stable referent for the similes in lines 51 through 66.

THE APORIAS OF PERSONA THEORY: BEYOND DECONSTRUCTION

Such a reading of the similes argues for a third possibility, that of taking them as a poetic unity. One version of such a thesis has already been advanced by David Bright. He contends that, while 51–56 need to be separated from 57–72 for a variety of logical and formal reasons, the persistence of the water motif introduced in 51–56 cannot be ignored and finds a parallel in the repeated bird images in the set of three similes that begin the second half of the poem (Bright 1976: 99–100, 112). They begin with 113's *stymphalia monstra* and continue through the vulture-like kin of the heirless old man and the passionate doves whose love pales in comparison with Laudamia's for Protesilaus (lines 119–28). His explanation of the phenomenon, however, remains purely formal, noting merely the presence of a paratactic mode of composition in the poem without recognizing the contradictory nature of such a compositional style when combined with the elaborate subordinations, and hence the hypotactic style, necessary on the formal level to produce the complex ring structure on which his interpretation ultimately rests (Bright 1976: 103).

Another version of this reading has been offered by John Sarkissian, who writes, "The first impression is that Catullus's tears of line [*sic*] 55–56 are being compared to a mountain cascade, but as the relief that the stream brings a weary traveler is brought into focus, it appears that this simile, along with the ensuing one (63–65), describes rather the assistance Allius gave to Catullus. . . . In fact, the simile describes both Catullus's tears and Allius's *auxilium*" (1983: 15). Sarkissian, however, does not elaborate on the possible significance of this structural anomaly either for the poem itself, the subject position from which it is enunciated, or the society whose Symbolic structures make it possible. Rather, he proposes to solve all such interpretive cruxes by positing a separation between poet and persona that allows hermeneutic difficulties to be attributed to the persona and moments of poetic felicity to the poet. In this manner, each aporetical moment in the poem is able to be seen as part of a rhetorical strategy designed to illustrate the shortcomings of the persona, who also happens to be a poet (3–4, 16). Such an approach, however, is too all encompassing. Any text, by anyone, at any period, according to this logic, no matter how inconsistent, no matter how aporetical, can be seen as an exercise in sublime irony on the part of an omniscient author. Persona theory, rather than offering an interpretation, is an ideological and rhetorical strategy that allows the critic to continue the New Critical quest for seamless aesthetic unity while retaining biographical criticism's reassuring belief in a centered subject who always controls his or her discursive position and is never controlled by it (Zajko 1997: 68–69; Braund 1997 40). I am reminded of a lecture I attended in which all the speaker's slides were upside down. When this was pointed out, three-quarters of the way through the talk, he responded, "I knew that." Persona theory is a closed system allowing no moments of otherness to emerge from the text. It always already "knew that."[36]

More satisfying is the model offered by Thomas Hubbard (1984: 31–32), who argues that poem 68 is "most authentic" in precisely those moments of contradiction and inconsistency that previous generations have spent so "much energy rationalizing and smoothing over." Hubbard (1984: 34–37) contends that 68 is, in fact, constituted by an unresolved dialectic between a "mystified" and "demystified" self, neither of which gains final primacy over the other, so that each undermines the other in an endless cycle of de Manian deconstruction. Yet while this position has the virtue of allowing the text's moments of aporia to stand, rather than be sublimated into the image of an all-controlling poetic subjectivity, it is also in the final analysis ahistorical, since Hubbard affirms, "Any subjective literary work must enact the conflict of these mutually deconstructing rhetorical stances" (1984: 46n.25). Thus, in a move typical of the kind of deconstructive criticism practiced in America in the 1980s, at the moment in which the critic is about to offer us his greatest insight, there is a retreat into a formalism that is incapable of differentiating Catullus 68 from Sappho 31, or a Shakespearean sonnet from a poem by Sylvia Plath.[37]

The crucial question, then, is, How can the formal recognition of these moments of aporia be maintained without history, and thus the possibility of asking the question what is the relation of Catullus to the elegists, being erased? The answer, as I argued in chapter 1, can be found in the Lacanian concepts of the Imaginary, the Symbolic, and the Real. Through the use of these registers we are able to posit a discursive position that is by nature internally divided but also in which the content, intensity, and visibility of that division can vary dramatically, depending on the historical context. In addition, these registers still situate that position within the world of a material history (i.e., the Real) that both determines that position and is determined by it, without ever the one signifying the other. We may live in the Real, but we experience a reality constructed by the Imaginary and the Symbolic's interpretations of it. It is precisely the fracturing of the unity constituted by these two constructions that poem 68 stages in a form that can neither be recuperated by an all-knowing subject prior to the moment of enunciation (persona theory) nor mapped onto the positive ideological coordinates of other periods or genres (formalism).

IMAGINARY DOMICILES, SYMBOLIC DOMINATIONS

> In light of the increasing fragility of aristocratic political
> and social relations in the closing years of the Republic
> as Rome heads toward civil war, the Catullan Lover's
> irrational dedication to an irreplaceable beloved
> is also a fantasy of absolute commitment possible
> only in some other world.
> —Fitzgerald 1995: 134

> Belonging to a period between two dictatorships,
> [Catullus] took his stand in a space characterized by
> unresolved tensions, equally distant from two centers
> of gravity. Politically, there was a condition of
> "suspension of gravity."
> —Albrecht 1997: 335

To illustrate more precisely the historical specificity of the Catullan sublime, let us return to the theme of the house Allius provided and show how the slippages embodied in its usage within the poem can be traced out into the larger corpus and its complex engagement with the norms of Roman ideology. The word *domus* itself serves as an aporetical metonym that simultaneously charts the progression of the poem and establishes verbal links between the similes evoking Allius's aid, the story of Laudamia and Protesilaus, and the death of Catullus's brother (Whitaker 1983: 61). The interpretive problem posed by this word stems from the fact that these contexts, which the poem invites us to compare with one another, are not commensurable with one another. Not only are these different houses (Allius's in Rome, Laudamia's in Greece, Catullus's in Verona but buried at Troy), they mean different things. The *domus* Allius provides is strictly a physical building where Catullus and Lesbia can meet to make love. That of Laudamia and Protesilaus is both the household they would have established and the building that would never be completed due to Protesilaus's early death (Janan 1994: 121). Finally, the *domus* of the Valerii Catulli is the least substantial of all since it refers not to Catullus's ancestral seat but rather to the ideal family unit for which the house stands as synecdoche. Thus there is a clear progression from the merely physical to the abstract and ideal,[38] but that process of rarefaction is in turn associated with death, as each step beyond the initial threshold leads closer to the grave.

Indeed the final *domus* of this initial series seems to defy any placement in space and comes to figure a pure displacement since it must be conceived as existing simultaneously in Verona, the actual home of the Valerii, and Asia Minor, the site of Catullus's brother's grave. This latter location is in turn assimilated within the poem to the mythical territory of Troy (lines 89–92), a place outside of space and time that joins Catullus's loss of his brother to Laudamia's loss of her husband (lines 83–88):

> Troia nefas! commune sepulchrum Asiae Europaeque
>   Troia virum et virtutum omnium acerba cinis,
> quaene etiam nostro letum miserabile fratri
>   attulit. Ei misero frater adempte mihi,
> ei misero fratri iucundum lumen ademptum,
>   tecum una tota est nostra sepulta *domus*,
> omnia tecum una perierunt gaudia nostra,
>   quae tuus in vita dulcis alebat amor.
> quem nunc tam longe non inter nota sepulcra
>   nec prope cognatos compositum cineres,
> sed Troia obscena, Troia infelice sepultum
>   detinet extremo terra aliena solo.
> ad quam tum properans fertur lecta undique pubes
>   Graeca penetralis deseruisse focos
> ne Paris abducta gavisus libera moecha
>   otia pacato degeret in thalamo.
> (89–104)

> Unspeakable Troy,
>   Europe and Asia's common grave,
> Troy,
>   the bitter ash of men and valor
> Troy which bore foul death even for my brother.
> O brother torn from wretched me!

> O joyous light torn from my wretched brother!
> Our entire *household* lies buried with you.
> All our joys perished with you!
>   joys which your sweet love
>   nourished
>   while still in life
> who now, so far away amidst unknown graves,
>   lie distant from your ancestors' ashes.
> But obscene Troy, cursed Troy, holds him buried
>   in the earth's far corner, beneath an alien land.
> Hurrying from everywhere, the chosen bands of Greece
>   have left their households' hearths,
> lest Paris rejoice in his stolen whore,
>   and lie in a peaceable bed.

The losses of Catullus and those of Laudamia in their common relation to Troy are here joined together, at the end of the poet's apostrophe to his brother's grave, by the evocation of the adultery of Paris with Helen, a violation of a lawfully constituted *domus*, which, as many scholars note, echoes Catullus's adulterous affair with Lesbia (Janan 1994: 131; Edwards 1991: 76; Williams 1976: 59; Bright 1980: 98). In this fashion, Catullus directly associates the death of his brother with his own adulterous behavior, while his identification with the position of Laudamia allows the loss of Protesilaus also to be assimilated to Catullus's "loss of Lesbia" through *her* infidelity to him. This whole complex of metonymic identifications is, in turn, folded back into the structure of the poem as a whole in the succeeding image of passion's whirlpool that both sweeps away Laudamia (lines 105–8) and recalls from our initial set of similes the image of sailors caught in a storm at sea (lines 63–66). That simile of course referred to Allius's ill-fated aid and the *domus* he lent Catullus, a *domus* that is now both verbally and imagistically tied to that of the Valerii and their burial in Troy (Janan 1994: 132; Edwards 1991: 78–79). Thus Allius's *auxilium* and Catullus's *cura* once more become one. The two images of shipwreck, in turn, recall a third found in poem 68a, where Mallius is portrayed as drowning in a sea of heartbreak at the very beginning of the poem (lines 1–4) (Janan 1994: 132; Edwards 1991: 78–79).[39]

Moreover, the first and last usages of *domus* just examined are both accompanied by a shadow or afterimage that expresses a desire for what could have been. In line 68, when Allius's *domus* is first introduced, Catullus writes, "isque domum nobis isque dedit dominae" (he gave the house both to me and my mistress). The word *domina* here is much debated. Many see it as the first example of the later elegiac usage in which the mistress is portrayed as the dominant partner in the relationship, as opposed to the poet's role as *servus amoris*. This reading is strengthened by Catullus's use of the word *era* (slave mistress) to describe Lesbia later in the same poem (68.136). Such a reading is also consistent with the poet's anticipation of the elegist's inversion of normative sexual roles discussed earlier.[40] Others follow the manuscript tradition and read *dominam*, as opposed to Froelich's emendation to *dominae*. They see a reference to a housemistress or chaperon proffered by Allius in order to provide cover for Catullus and Lesbia's adulterous affair.[41] In either case, however, there is an etymological play on the relation between *domus* and *domina* that necessarily recalls the more normative use of the word *domina*, the mistress of a lawfully constituted household (Lyne 1980: 6–7), a *domus non incepta frustra*, for which the poet can wish, but which, as he admits in the second half of the poem he can never have:

> quae tamen etsi uno non est contenta Catullo,
> > rara verecundae furta feremus erae,
> ne nimium simus stultorum more molesti.
> > saepe etiam Juno, maxima caelicolum,
> coniugis in culpa flagrantem concoquit iram
> > noscens omnivoli plurima furta Iovis
> atqui nec divis homines componier aequum est,[42]
> > ingratum tremuli tolle parentis onus.
> nec tamen illa mihi dextra deducta paterna
> > fragrantem Assyrio venit odore *domum*,
> sed furtiva dedit mira munuscula nocte,
> > ipsius ex ipso dempta viri gremio.
> (135–46)

And if Catullus alone cannot satisfy her,
> we shall bear the rare infidelities of a chaste mistress,
so as not to be petty and act like a fool.
> Often even Juno, queen of heaven,
must mollify her anger at the faults of her husband
> knowing the infidelities of all-desiring Jove.
But it is not right to compare men to gods,
> nor play the role of aged parent.
She was not led to me by the hand of her father,
> nor came to a *house* suffused with Syrian perfume.
Yet one wondrous night she gave me her dear gifts,
> stolen from the lap of her husband himself.

A number of commentators have noted the paradox of terming Lesbia *verecunda* (chaste), especially in the context of acknowledging her infidelities (Hubbard 1984: 47n.34; Sarkissian 1983: 31–32; Williams 1980:

58). *Verecunda* denotes an almost religious awe. This is what a true Roman *domina* (as opposed to an elegiac one) would be expected to display before the sexual norms implicit in the creation of a lawfully constituted *domus*. Hence the word *domina* itself displays the slippages that constitute the Catullan subject position both in this poem and throughout the corpus: slippages between the normative sexual ideology of the Roman Symbolic (the *matrona* as *verecunda domina* or *era* of a lawfully constituted *domus*); Catullus's Imaginary self-identification (the projection of such values onto his relationship with Lesbia); and the Real (the impossibility of these two realms ever coinciding). Moreover, as the complex and overdetermined use of the word *domus*—with its fusing of the themes of adultery, family, marriage, and death—indicates, poem 68 displays a profound disagregation of the relation between the poet's constitution of his personal identity through Imaginary experience and the Symbolic categories that Roman life offered to make sense of it.[43] The result is a gap or absence at the subject's center, a kind of death, that reveals the hidden world of terror we call the Real (Stoekl 1992: 166–67).

This gap, with its complex ideological articulations around traditional concepts of household, marriage, and their simultaneous sanctity and nullification, is evident throughout the poem. Thus, in the Hercules simile, not only is Laudamia's passion compared to a whirlpool (*vertex*) in an abyss (*barathrum*)—itself an image of death and the tomb[44]—but the posthumous marriage of Hercules to Hebe is also evoked. In this passage, death, marriage, and passion, the normative and the transgressive, serve as a series of metonymic substitutions, that neither stand for one another nor stand apart from each other (Sarkissian 1983: 27). The erotic becomes a sublime field of thought and feeling, unable to be comprehended either by the rule-based norms of the Symbolic or the seamless identifications of the Imaginary. It posits a beyond that can only be imagined as absence or death. The sequence of thought is strikingly emblematic. We move from the *sepulta domus* of the *gens Valerii* (line 94) to the *domus* violated by the illicit love of Paris and his *moecha* (103), then to the passion of Laudamia's *domus incepta frustra* imagined as an abyss or tomb (107–8), and finally to a vision of the divine *domus* of Hercules and Hebe beyond the grave (116). This last image, in which Hercules is envisioned as wearing down the threshold of the gods ("pluribus ut caeli tereretur ianua divis," 115), in turn, recalls that of Lesbia's entrance into the *domus* provided by Allius (71–72), which not only marks the beginning of the Laudamia simile but also marks the union of Catullus and Lesbia as a kind of marriage (Sarkissian 1983: 27–28; Wiseman 1985: 161–62; Lieberg 1962: 251). Yet Lesbia's foot creaks on the threshold marking the constitution of this *domus* as ill-omened from the start (Williams 1980: 54; Sarkissian 1983: 17), a fact confirmed by Catullus's later admission

that Lesbia's father had not led her to his *domus* and that this marriage
was in fact adultery (Lyne 1980: 59). At each stage in the progression,
there is a simultaneous evocation of the normative vision of the Roman
household so dear to Catullus from the marriage hymns, 61 and 62, and
so ironically subverted in poems 64 and 67 (Feeney 1992: 33–34; Wil-
liams 1980: 56; Wiseman 1969: 20–23). The passage ends with an asser-
tion that Laudamia's love was in fact deeper than the *barathrum* of Her-
cules, "sed tuus altus amor barathro fuit altior illo, / qui tamen indomitam
ferre iugum docuit" (but your love was deeper than that abyss, / which
nonetheless taught you, though untamed, to bear the yoke, 117–18):

> Here it is asserted that her love was deeper than the *barathrum* of Hercules;
> previously (109) only equivalence was asserted. The reference in the word
> "untamed" is to virginity (the taming being thought of as done by a husband),
> and "bear the yoke" is another clear allusion to Roman marriage ideals of
> obedience and faithfulness (in the wife). The poetic strategy of this whole
> section is to use Laudamia's love (emphasising its strength and depth) to draw
> in Hercules as the vehicle for ideas of adultery on the one hand, and of happy
> marriage on the other: then to use Laudamia's love again (relying metonymi-
> cally on *barathrum*) to identify ideals of marriage in the behaviour of this
> particular wife, and so to analyse the nature of Laudamia's love more directly.
> (Williams 1980: 56)

This double movement of the establishment and violation of the *domus*,
the heart as Cicero argued of the *res publica* (*De Officiis* 1.53–58), is
then repeated in the two following similes that continue the bird motif
established in the figure of Hercules. In the first (lines 119–24), Lauda-
mia's love is compared to that of a grandfather for the birth of a grandson
from his only daughter. This simile is based on the emotional bonds en-
tailed in the establishment of a lawful household and its intergenerational
continuity in Rome. Such a *domus* is both the ideal Catullus articulates for
Manlius Torquatus in the first wedding hymn (61.204–23)[45] and precisely
what is denied the poet through both the death of his brother and the
adulterous nature of his relationship with Lesbia (Fitzgerald 1995: 118).
The simile's shift in genders, from the feminine Laudamia to the masculine
grandfather, continues a theme we have seen throughout the poem, while
the comparison of exogamous heterosexual passion to endogamous, male
homosocial bonds, anticipates poem 72's comparison of Catullus's love
for Lesbia with that of a father for his sons and sons-in-law (Williams
1980: 60–61; Albrecht 1997: 343). Here too the *domus* invoked is one
already violated ("nunc te cognovi: quare etsi impensius uror, / multo mi
tamen es vilior et levior [now I know you: and though my passion burns
more intensely / nonetheless you are to me a far cheaper and more trivial
thing]).[46] In poem 72, the bonds of *amor* and *amicitia* that constitute the

ideal fusion of the domestic and the communal, the endogamous and the exogamous, the heterosexual and the homosocial, the Imaginary and the Symbolic, have split apart to create a schizophrenic text in which passion and a mutual regard founded on social law cannot coincide, nor can the Catullan subject imagine himself whole when they are apart (Rubino 1975: 293). The normative language of homosocial aristocratic obligation as embodied in the alliances of family and friendship that Catullus mobilizes here and throughout the epigrams—*pietas, officium, amicitia, fides*, and the like—is a measure of his deviance from that very norm, an index of the split that defines his world (Fitzgerald 1995: 117–18; Albrecht 1997: 350).[47] By the same token, the *domus* of the grandfather in poem 68 is one likewise under siege, as a greedy kinsman circles round his head like a vulture in hopes that that death will leave him a fortune. The continuity of this *domus* is tenuous at best, and it too is as much threatened from within as without (Hubbard 1984: 35). The bonds that unite it are those that tear it asunder.

The image of the vulture modulates in the next line into that of the dove, joining death and passion, lawful constitution and violation into a single complex of images. The dove is traditionally an image of faithful love (Propertius 2.15.27–28; Pliny, *Historia Naturalis* 10.104), but the comparison of its wantonness to the *multivola mulier*—a phrase that anticipates both Lesbia's *furta* and the comparison to *omnivolus* Jupiter—inevitably invokes the opposite of what the simile ostensibly meant to convey (Williams 1980: 57–58; Hubbard 1984: 35). This duality of purpose is ultimately distilled into a single image at the end of the Laudamia simile. Using a cinematic technique, Catullus pans back to Lesbia, right where he left her, crossing the threshold of the *domus* Allius lent him:

> aut nihil aut paulo cui tum concedere digna
>   lux mea se nostrum contulit in gremium,
> quam circumcursans hinc illinc saepe Cupido
>   fulgebat crocina candidus in tunica. (131–34)

> Worthy then of conceding nothing or very little to her [Laudamia]
>   my light bore herself into my lap,
> as Cupid often circling here and there
>   shone brightly in his saffron tunic

Cupid here is dressed as Hymen, traditionally imagined as accompanying the bride in the *deductio* from her father's house to that of her new husband. The irony is not to be lost. What masquerades as marriage and the constitution of a lawful *domus* is precisely the force that insures its violation (Williams 1980: 58; Sarkissian 1983: 31). The lawful separation of relations into officially approved and unapproved categories, signified by

Hymen, is here transformed into the very force that breaks down these categories, Desire, that universal and strange attractor.[48]

In the end, the *domus* theme and its slippages, reveal a longing for a lawful household with a lawful *domina* that Catullus cannot acquire. This semiotic slippage and the inversion of values it creates are parallel to the slippage and longing for lawfully constituted relationships in poem 76. Yet in that poem, as here, the invocation of traditional values such as *pietas*, *fides*, and reciprocal *benefacta*, cannot manufacture a return to a vanished ideal of Roman normality, but instead produces images of transgression, splitting, and death. The slippage with regard to *domus* reveals a gap between the Imaginary and the Symbolic, as each Symbolic marker is emptied of meaning by a subsequent identification with a different version of the same term. In the same way, each attempt to specify the logical limitations of the similes in lines 51 through 66 is undermined by a subsequent imagistic, intertextual and/or thematic displacement. This insistent pattern of metonymic identification let us see the emergence of the Real as the space between, and hence that which supports, each of these successive moments (Žižek 1991: 29, 120; Lacan 1975: 108).

Catullus bequeaths this deeply divided subjectivity to the elegists, one in which the recognized structures of the Symbolic are no longer adequate to containing the forces of the Imaginary. Such a schizoid subject can only be symptomatic of profound disturbances at the level of the Real, disturbances that by nature cannot be reflected thematically, but can only emerge in the disarticulation of the two primary registers of signification. It is the moment of an obscene sublime in which the subject cries out "nec bene velle queat tibi, si optima fias, / nec desistere amare, omnia facias" (neither is it possible to wish you well if you became the best of women, / nor to cease to love you, no matter what you would do, 75.3–4), even as its own division becomes specularized *ob scaenam*.

Chapter Three

CYNTHIA AS SYMPTOM: PROPERTIUS, GALLUS, AND THE BOYS

> Ce qui signifie que la possibilité de notre socialité, de
> notre culture, revient à un monopole hommo-sexuel? La
> loi qui ordonne notre société, c'est la valorisation
> exclusive des besoins-désirs des hommes, et des échanges
> entre eux. Ce que l'anthropologue désigne comme le
> passage de la nature à la culture revient donc à
> l'instauration de l'empire de l'hom(m)osexualité. Non
> dans une pratique "immédiate," mais dans sa médiation
> "sociale." . . . Partout regnante, mais interdite dans
> son usage, l'hom(m)osexualité se joue à travers
> les corps des femmes, matière ou signe, et
> l'hétérosexualité n'est jusqu'à présent qu'un alibi
> à la bonne marche de rapports de l'homme à lui-même,
> des rapports entre hommes.[1]
> —Irigaray 1977a: 168

> Lacan accounted for the effects of foreclosure with the
> following formulation: "what is foreclosed in the
> Symbolic returns in the Real.". . . . Thus Woman
> returns, persistently and repetitively from the Real, as
> the effect of a central foreclosure in the Symbolic and the
> symptom, equally, of Man.
> —Janan 1994: 31

WHERE LESBIA is an important and certainly the most memorable feature of Catullus's poetry, Cynthia in Propertius's *Monobiblos* is a dominating figure unlike any seen before in extant Roman poetry (King 1975–76: 108). She is the first word of the first poem and the topic of every text in the book except the last three and 1.16. Where Lesbia appears in less than a third of Catullus's poetry, Cynthia is the subject of the vast majority of Propertius's poems in books 1–3. As Boucher (1980: 240) notes, Cynthia and the implied narrative of Propertius's affair with her is the animating force of Propertius's poetry. Without Cynthia, the *Monobiblos* would not exist. Yet, although there is wide agreement on Cynthia's importance, stating who or what Cynthia is is far more problematic. Moreover, Cynthia is inextricably linked to Propertius's relationship with his male interlocutors throughout book 1, with particular reference to Gallus. The present chapter therefore examines three related areas: who is Cynthia, who is Gallus, and how does their interrelation structure the homosocial order of the *Monobiblos* as a symptomatic text? In the first section, I look at the way in which Cynthia's very indefinability is related to her function in the book on both a thematic and a structural level and how that function is related to the figure of Gallus in poems 1.20–22. In the second section, I examine the historical Gallus, his impact on Propertius's poetry, and his semiotic function in the *Monobiblos*. In the third section, I undertake a close reading of poem 1.1's relation to poems 1.4, and 1.5, with particular attention to these poems' pederastic Catullan intertexts, and to how Cynthia relates to these poems' "hom(m)osexual" desire.

Who Is Cynthia?

The question of Cynthia's status has long been at the center of Propertian studies. Is she a person and if so of what status: *matrona* or *meretrix*, free or slave? Is she a fictive construct and if so to what purpose: a character in a drama, a literary allegory, the symbolic representation of the author's nonconformist poetic and political agenda? All of these positions have been argued, and each has merit. Boucher advances the strongest argument for Cynthia being a *matrona*. He notes that her life-style and travels as depicted throughout the corpus indicate a personal freedom and wealth incommensurate with that of a freedwoman or slave. In Juvenal's *Satire* 6's list of *uxores* (normally translated "wives" but able to be used figuratively of longtime companions), she appears next to Lesbia. She is also directly compared with Lesbia in Propertius 2.32.45. Lesbia as the wife and later widow of the consul Metellus was an adulterous *matrona*.[2] Cynthia, Boucher (1980: 447, 455–59) argues, can therefore be attributed the same status. Gordon Williams (1968: 529–30, 534) makes the identical argument. He advances the additional contention that poem 2.23, which celebrates the easy access of common prostitutes as opposed to a woman such as Cynthia who is kept under the guard of a *custos*, only makes sense if the *vir* mentioned is Cynthia's "husband" (again a common, but not necessary translation)[3]. Finally, to the counterargument that no Roman husband would ever allow his wife to engage in the adulterous behavior portrayed throughout the corpus, and therefore Cynthia must either be a *meretrix* or intended to represent one, Williams responds not only with the example of Clodia Metelli, who is generally believed to be Catullus's Lesbia, but with other similarly notorious *matronae* (e.g., Sulla's daughter

Fausta, and Cato's half sister Servilia). He and Grimal also allege such examples as *Amores* 2.19 in which Ovid urges a *maritus* to keep better watch over his *uxor*, Augustus's law against *lenocinium* or the pimping of one's own wife (19 B.C.E.), and the charge that the *Ars Amatoria* aimed to promote adultery and hence was grounds for Ovid's exile (Williams 1968: 540–41; Grimal 1986: 147). All of these, they argue, show that adultery was perceived to be a real problem and merited not only poetic treatment but also legislation.

Nonetheless, the identification of Cynthia as a *matrona*, is far from sure and in many ways unsatisfying. The corpus presents substantial evidence contradicting this view. If Cynthia were intended to represent an adulterous *matrona*, why in 4.3 does she have a *lena* (procuress), and why in 1.3 is a drunken Propertius able to stumble into her house and contemplate molesting her only to have her wake up and berate him? Would the husband not have awakened? Would a wealthy libertine widow like Lesbia or Clodia Metelli, in spite of Cicero's assertions to the contrary, really sleep in a house unguarded by servants and open to casual drunks?[4] Moreover, if Cynthia were wealthy and free, then why would Propertius fear rich rivals (see, e.g., 2.16 on the Illyrian *praetor*)? Catullus never does. As Sharon James points out, the whole scenario of the *dives amator* (wealthy lover, see chapter 4) only really makes sense if we assume that Cynthia was dependent upon her lovers' largesse for her financial well-being and hence was a *meretrix* (2003; see also Konstan 1995: 151–52, 158; Cairns 1979b: 189). Moreover, Cynthia's being a *meretrix* would far better explain Propertius's claim in 2.7 that he would have been forced to marry another if Augustus's law had not been withdrawn (for a complete review of the controversies surrounding this poem and the law mentioned in it, see chapter 5). A man of equestrian status was forbidden to marry a *meretrix* under the later marriage laws, and we may assume that similar restrictions were found in the law referred to in 2.7, whatever its provenance. Moreover, later legislative efforts reflected presumed social norms, however loosely constructed and enforced they may have been, and whatever the resistance they generated. In fact, given the ease of divorce in the first century B.C.E., it would have probably been easier to marry Cynthia if she *were* a *matrona* than if she were a *meretrix*, as Augustus's marriage to Livia demonstrates (Hallett 1973: 106–7).

How are we to reconcile these contradictory images? The fact is that in some poems Cynthia is portrayed in ways that indicate a courtesan and in others an adulterous *matrona* (Stahl 1985: 143–44; Fedeli 1983: 1866). An either/or solution to this problem is simply not available without mutilating the text. Propertius, in fact, pays little attention to dramatic or even characterological consistency from one poem to the next. Thus in 1.3 Cynthia chastises the poet saying that she had stayed up late awaiting his return from a night of drunken carousing, putting off sleep with her weaving ("fallebam stamine somnum"). This last phrase is recognized to be an allusion to Penelope putting off the suitors with her trick of weaving and unweaving Laertes's shroud. Cynthia in this passage is cast in the role of the faithful wife waiting at home for the return of her wandering husband. Few would argue from this that Cynthia and Propertius were to be thought of as married, but the portrait of faithful domesticity is wildly at odds with that found in 2.32 in which Cynthia is kept under lock and key by her *vir*'s *custos*.

Indeed, as Maria Wyke (1989: 28–34) contends, not only have attempts to establish Cynthia's social standing come to naught, but so has describing her physical appearance. It seems there are as many Cynthias as there are poems. As Veyne notes, "From one page to the next . . . Cynthia may be a courtesan, an adulterous wife, a free woman" (1988: 7, see also 89). Propertius sums up the pregnant ambiguity of her position in the final couplet of 2.6, "nos uxor numquam, numquam seducet amica: / semper amica mihi, semper et uxor eris" (Never will a wife, never will a mistress seduce us / ever will you be my mistress and ever my wife). Cynthia is to be *matrona* and *meretrix* in one, and consequently from the perspective of traditional Roman ideology she can be nothing at all since these categories are mutually exclusive. She is less a person than a function. Her role within Propertius's poetry is more that of a narratological "actant" (an agent construction necessary for narrative progression) than of a fully developed character or "actor" capable of synthesizing and thematizing a variety of "actantial functions" (Greimas 1987: 106–20). On a discursive level, she allows Propertius's poetry to get things done. As Joy Connolly has recently observed of all the elegiac mistresses, "Even when they offer a name, the lovers manifest such vagueness and variance of character that the names appear to be nothing more than labels, convenient merely for the purposes of ease of recognition, minor plot development, or meter" (2000: 87).

A third strand of interpretation has developed precisely on the basis of the recognition that Cynthia is a literary construct. It argues that Cynthia is an allegory for poetry itself. The most obvious level on which this is true is that, inasmuch as *Cynthia* is the first word of the first poem, she would have served as the title of the *Monobiblos* according to ancient poetic practice. Propertius, thus, later speaks of his *Cynthia* being read all over town (2.24.2), meaning the *Monobiblos*. By the same token, when the poet says he wins fame through Cynthia, the statement is humorously double-edged, meaning both his poetry and the love affair he professes to recount therein (Kennedy 1993: 50–51; Gold 1993: 88; Veyne 1988: 3). On this level, Cynthia's infidelity, her passing from hand to hand, becomes a metaphor of the successful poet's fame. Thus what is most a cause for the character Propertius's shame—his being betrayed by his mistress—is the sign of the poet Propertius's glory (Fear 2000: 228–29).

The literary allegory, however, goes deeper still. The name Cynthia carries with it poetic implications that link it to the elegiac tradition and the poetry of Cornelius Gallus. It is then a metonym for the genre. As Maria Wyke notes: "On entry into the Propertian corpus, the epithet *Cynthia* brings with it a history as the marker of a poetic programme. Mount Cynthius on Delos had been linked with Apollo as the mouthpiece of a poetic creed by the Hellenistic poet Callimachus. That association was reproduced by Vergil's sixth *Eclogue* where the god directing Vergilian discourse away from epic material was given the cult title *Cynthius*" (1989: 33). The sixth *Eclogue* features a lengthy digression on Gallus, by general agreement the first of the actual elegists, and the name of the addressee of five poems in the *Monobiblos* (1.5, 1.10, 1.13, 1.20, 1.21). *Eclogue* 6 is a programmatic statement about the nature of Gallan poetry that seems to indicate a movement from amorous elegy to more learned etiological poetry in the Hesiodic mode, or at least to the composition of a poem on the origin of the Grynean grove:[5]

> tum canit errantem Permessi ad flumina Gallum
> Aonas in montis ut duxerit una sororum,
> utque viro Phoebi chorus adsurrexerit omnis;
> ut Linus haec illi divino carmine pastor
> floribus atque apio crinis ornatus amaro
> dixerit: "hos tibi dant calamos, en accipe, Musae,
> Ascraeo quos ante seni, quibus ille solebat
> cantando rigidas deducere montibus ornos.
> his tibi Grynei nemoris dicatur origo,
> ne quis sit lucus, quo se plus iactet Apollo."
> (6.64–73)

Then Silenus sang Gallus wandering along the banks of the river Permessus[6] in the hills round Helicon where one of the Muses led him and where the whole chorus of Phoebus rose up to greet the man; where the shepherd Linus, his hair wreathed in flowers and bitter parsley said these things to him in divine song: "Accept these pipes the Muses give to you, which before belonged to the old man of Ascrea[7] and with which he was accustomed to call down the mighty mountain ashes with his singing. With these let the origin of the Grynean grove be said, so that Apollo will not boast more of any other grove on earth."

The name Cynthia/Cynthius, then, in the context of elegy could not help but evoke this image of the poetic initiation of Propertius's predecessor. The identity of the Gallus or Galluses addressed in Propertius's first book is a problem that will occupy us shortly. But it is generally agreed that Propertius imitates the genre's founder at several points throughout his poetry, and he explicitly mentions him in his catalog of predecessors at the end of poem 2.34 where Cynthia is also specifically named as the poet's means to achieving lasting poetic fame (2.34.87–94).

The equation of *Cynthia* with *Cynthius* is thus rich in literary allusions. There is no room in the present chapter to explore exhaustively the full range of this vast and complex intertextual web. For now, however, let us merely note that poem 1.18[8] in the *Monobiblos* has an explicit allusion to both Gallus and his portrait in Vergil's tenth *Eclogue*, thus recalling the evocation of Cynthia/Cynthius in the sixth *Eclogue*. The passage from 1.18 features the image of Propertius scratching Cynthia's name on the bark of various trees, a direct imitation of Vergil's *Eclogue* 10.52–54 (Ross 1975: 88–89n.2; King 1980b: 219, 222–23; Courtney 1993: 270):

> vos eritis testes, si quos habet arbor amores,
>> fagus et Arcadio pinus amica deo.
> a quotiens teneras resonant mea verba sub umbras,
>> scribitur et vestris Cynthia corticibus.
> (Propertius 1.18.19–22)

You also will be witnesses, if trees have any loves,[9] beech and pine, friend[10] of Arcadian Pan! Oh how many times my words echo in your tender shade and Cynthia is written on your bark.

Eclogue 10, according to Servius, the later Vergilian commentator, is a translation or pastiche of Gallus (Courtney 1993: 269).[11] Duncan Kennedy has argued that the passage from Propertius 1.18, in turn, contains an elaborate pun equating the inscription of Cynthia's name in tree bark with the composing of poetry in her name: "The verb *scribere* can signify both 'to scratch' and 'to write,' and *cortex* signifies the 'the outer bark of a tree,' corresponding to *liber*, the 'inner bark,' *liber* can in turn signify 'book': according to the ancient Virgilian commentator Servius (on *Aeneid* 11.554), books were originally made from bark" (Kennedy 1993: 51). Thus, when Propertius writes Cynthia's name on the bark of a tree, he also inscribes a poetry book, written in the manner of Gallus's as instructed by Apollo Cynthius, with the title *Cynthia*.

This literary allegory, however, is not a self-enclosed, hermetic system, sealed off from the poems' erotic content. Rather, as we shall see, the intertextual switching of genders signified by the change of *Cynthius* to *Cynthia* is part of a larger pattern linking Cynthia, Gallus, gender inversion, and poetic composition to one another throughout the *Monobiblos*. It is no accident in this regard that the one poem in the *Monobiblos* that seems most clearly to be an imitation of Gallus's manner, poem 1.20 on

Hercules and Hylas, substitutes a pederastic beloved for Cynthia or Gal-
lus's Lycoris. In this regard, it is instructive to remember that *Eclogue* 6,
which first entered our discussion for its use of *Cynthius* to refer to Apollo
and for its evocation of Gallus, also has Silenus sing of the Argonauts'
sorrow over Hercules' loss of this same Hylas *(Eclogue* 6.43–44), thus
tying Cynthia, Gallus, gender inversion, and poetic composition into a
complex but well-defined inter- and intratextual weave.

Yet as tempting and productive as the reading of Cynthia as poetry can
be, it too has its limitations. Many passages in the corpus cannot be read
as allegories of reading. When Propertius admonishes Cynthia in 1.2.1–
8 to eschew fine ornaments and cosmetics in favor of *nudus Amor* (a
hilarious pun), it would be ludicrous to read this as signifying his advo-
cacy of the plain style.[12] Likewise, the notion that when the drunken Pro-
pertius of 1.3 attempts to steal kisses from the sleeping Cynthia he is
actually puckering up to a papyrus roll is almost as comical as the poem
itself. Cynthia is in fact both an allegory for poetry and, like Propertius
himself, a character in a fragmented, nonlinear, comic drama. At times
those roles converge, at others they are mutually inconsistent, but both
levels of reading coexist and interpenetrate, often within the same poem
(Sharrock 2000: 276; Ross 1975: 58–59).

The poetry of the *Monobiblos* is inconceivable without Cynthia. She is
what allows the work to function and the semiotic game to be played. Yet
she herself never comes into focus, rather she is like the vanishing point
in a painting that allows the other more defined shapes around it to have
their form and intercourse with one another (Nell 2000; Lacan 1973: 92–
103). Thus, as Ellen Greene (1998: 40) notes, while Cynthia is the first
word of the first poem, her name is never again mentioned in 1.1, nor
does the reader receive any more concrete information about her. In fact,
the first poem opens with an imitation of a pederastic poem by Meleager
(1–4), and then modulates into an address of Propertius's young patron
Tullus at the beginning of an extended mythological exemplum generally
thought to be derived from Gallus (Albrecht 1997: 745). The collection,
in turn, concludes with a three-poem coda in which Cynthia is never
brought up: 1.20, addressed to Gallus on his pederastic beloved; 1.21, an
address to a passerby in which another Gallus explains his death at the
hands of brigands after having escaped the slaughter at Perusia; and 1.22,
in which Propertius makes clear to Tullus that the Gallus of the preceding
poem was his relative and that his family had suffered grievous losses in
the Perusine War.[13] The *Monobiblos*, thus, is framed by Gallus (or Gal-
luses) and Tullus as surely as it begins with Cynthia (Sharrock 2000: 267;
Putnam 1976: 115; King 1975–76: 116; Courtney 1968: 254). Moreover,
Gallus and Tullus appear throughout the book as the addressees of a vari-

ety of poems in contexts that often relate them both to one another and to Cynthia.[14]

In fact, if one examines the structure of the book 1, it quickly becomes apparent that the affair with Cynthia is played out against the background of—or, better, serves as the medium for—relations between Propertius and a series of male friends, rivals, and patrons.[15] Thus 1.1 is addressed to Tullus, but simultaneously imitates Gallus. Poem 1.4 is addressed to Bassus, 1.5 again to Gallus, 1.6 to Tullus, and 1.7 to Ponticus. Poem 1.8 is another imitation of Gallus (Fantham 1996: 58–59), and 1.9 is addressed to Ponticus while 1.10 and 1.13 are addressed to Gallus. Poem 1.14 is written to Tullus, while 1.18 is another Gallan imitation. Poems 1.20, 1.21, and 1.22 have already been discussed. In each of these poems, with the exception of the final coda, Cynthia figures explicitly or implicitly. Thus in 1.4 Bassus tries to lure the poet away from Cynthia by praising other beauties. In 1.5 Gallus directly competes for Cynthia's affections. In 1.6, Tullus proposes that Propertius leave Cynthia and join him on his uncle's proconsular mission to the East, and in 1.7 Ponticus's epic poetry is shown to be useless in love compared with Propertian elegy. As Joy King has argued, each of these masculine addressees represents a fundamentally different position within the Roman ideological and literary firmament: Bassus is an iambic poet, Gallus a rival lover and love poet, Tullus the representative of traditional aristocratic values, and Ponticus their literary defender, the epic poet (King 1980b: 220).

On the surface, then, these men share little beyond Cynthia herself and the love she represents. She functions as the medium of their exchange, the currency of their intercourse.[16] As Allison Sharrock concludes at the end of her reading of poems 1.4 and 1.5, "a relationship with Cynthia is a shared relationship between men" (2000: 270). Cynthia is thus impossible to define in her own terms because she is both the point around which the relationships between Propertius and Gallus, Tullus, Ponticus, and Bassus are articulated and that which separates the poet from his friends in their competition for her favors. She is the symptom of their discontent, the embodiment of their desires, and the medium of their exchange (Irigaray 1977b: 184). Moreover, insofar as Cynthia herself or her analogues (cf. the *doctae puellae* of 1.7.11) are imagined as the objects of desire in these poems, then each man's desire is presented as the mirror of the other's and the essence of their relationship is, in Irigaray's terms, "hom(m)o-sexuel" (Oliensis 1997: 160; Janan 2001: 43).[17] Even, in those cases where their desires are initially presented as heteronomous, as with Propertius and Tullus in 1.6, there is always an attempt to reinstitute their fundamentally "homo"-erotic basis on another level, so that the affective and often erotically charged ties between men, which were the emotive basis of such Roman aristocratic ideals as *fides* and *amicitia*, might be maintained even as they were increasingly problematized in the unstable and changing environment of the early principate.[18] Thus, while in 1.6 Tullus is preparing to accompany his uncle on a proconsular mission to the East, Propertius, who cannot go because Cynthia would make too great a scene, responds with the language of *militia amoris* so as to create a rough equivalence between the lover and the soldier (Kennedy 1993: 54–55; Wyke 1989: 36–37). In fact, he claims that his lot is *durus* (1.6.35) while that of Tullus is *mollis* (1.6.31), thus humorously inverting the values normally associated with the poet's and the soldier's life as well as their associated gender valences (Kennedy 1993: 31–34). Cynthia, here, functions as the medium for negotiating between their conflicting ideologies and desires, the means to effect symbolic exchanges between otherwise incommensurable use values (Irigaray 1977a: 167, 184). As such, she is also necessarily a symptom of the fundamental rift in the fabric of Roman masculinist life, the hole in the Symbolic, that has made this renegotiation necessary (Lacan 1982: 168; Janan 1994: 31).

The nature of this hole can in part be seen in the figure of Gallus himself: for like Cynthia he too is both central to the book and yet not quite whole. His parts do not cohere. There are nine poems in the *Monobiblos* in which a Gallus is either named, discussed, or imitated (1.1, 1.5, 1.8, 1.10, 1.13, 1.18, 1.20, 1.21, 1.22). They represent almost half the book.[19] It has long been agreed that these men cannot all be the same Gallus. One of them is a relative of Propertius who died shortly after the battle of Perusia in 41 B.C.E. (cf. 1.21) and another is the poet and politician Cornelius Gallus who fell out of favor with Augustus and committed suicide in 27 B.C.E., at least a year after the publication of the *Monobiblos* in 29 or 28 (Sullivan 1976: 3; Hubbard 1974: 44).[20] Some would argue for other Galluses still, on the grounds that the person addressed in 1.5, 1.10, 1.13, and 1.20 can neither be Cornelius Gallus nor Propertius's kinsman.[21] The details of these arguments are examined later. What is important for the moment is to recognize both the centrality of Gallus to the *Monobiblos* and the inability to define a stable identity for him. As Janan has persuasively demonstrated, the Gallus poems "refuse to hang together or hang separately" (2001: 33–34). Instead, she argues, they thematize the very tenuous nature of identity in general and the specific challenges it faced in the early Augustan period (2001: 36). Thus, the Galluses of 1.20 and 1.21 cannot be the same man, and yet, as Sharrock notes, the poems' immediate juxtaposition suggests at least the possibility of their identification (2000: 268n.13). Indeed, as Nicholson (1998–99: 146–47) observes, the reader is quite deliberately brought up short and made to rein in the natural impulse to assume that two poems in the same book, featuring the same name, one after another, would refer to the same person. Extending the line of argumentation begun by Nicholson, Sharrock, and Janan, I

argue in the remainder of this chapter that the double nature of Gallus—
as both one and not-one, as both rival poet and dying soldier—signifies
a traumatic eruption of the Real, of the literally unspeakable, and that
Cynthia functions as its symptom:[22] the visible sign of a traumatic exclu-
sion, of what cannot, indeed must not, appear.[23] The simultaneous impos-
sibility of identifying the Gallus of 1.20 with that of 1.21 and the necessity
of perceiving a common link between them creates a moment of unintelli-
gibility or aporia that retroactively structures the whole of book 1, even as
it calls to mind the simultaneous impossibility of defining Cynthia herself.

The level of suggested identity between the two Galluses, however, goes
much deeper than what has been outlined thus far. As noted earlier, the
final three poems of the *Monobiblos* constitute a coda that separates them
from the rest of the book. None of them concerns Cynthia and all three
are addressed to or allude to a Gallus. The last of the poems is addressed
to Tullus, who is also the addressee of 1.1, a poem in which Propertius is
generally thought to imitate Gallus the poet in the Milanion exemplum.
The pairing of Gallus and Tullus, as already observed, opens and closes
the book, but they cannot be the same Gallus and yet if they are not, then
why are they paired with Tullus. More intriguing still, is the observation
made first by Davis (1971: 213) and echoed by Nethercut that the "Mila-
nion, who groans wounded on the rocks for his love" in 1.1 "is echoed
by Gallus in the penultimate elegy 1.21, who lies wounded outside Perusia
and groans aloud to a passerby" (1983: 1825). In addition, as Davis ar-
gued, there are specific thematic reflections of the earlier erotic poems
in the collection's final poems, "The last two poems of the *Monobiblos*
summarize the erotic themes of the earlier book in a non-erotic setting.
The loss of Cynthia's love, which the poet depicts in book 1, finds its
literary analogue in the loss of this *propinquus*, Gallus, in the poet's more
distant past" (1971: 212).[24] Davis's intuition has recently been refined
and made more specific by Nicholson's methodical reading of the ways
in which the themes of watching, being watched, and death, which are
central to 1.10 and 1.13, are reflected in 1.20, 1.21, and 1.22. Nicholson
(1998–99: 144–45, 150–56) observes that on a semiotic level this encour-
ages us to identify the Gallus of 1.21 and 1.22 with that in the earlier
poems, even as on a mimetic or historical level that identification is ac-
knowledged to be impossible.

The coda then is not quite as separate as it first appears. Poems 1.21
and 1.22, as noted earlier, oddly mirror the love poems that come before
them. Thus, Janan argues that where Cynthia allows Gallus and Pro-
pertius to identify with one another, even as they compete for the objects of
their desire, poems 1.21–22 reflect the fundamental breach in the Roman
Symbolic that makes the moment of identification and completion always
fall short. Propertius, she argues, uses the Gallus poems to show the im-

possibility of ever achieving the stable identity that the full possession of the object of desire, on both the personal and the political level, represents (Janan 2001: 45).

Poems 1.21 and 1.22 introduce the political into the realm of love. More specifically they introduce History as the realm of the incomprehensible Real in the traumatic image of the massacre at Perusia. This battle, as Judith Hallett (1977) has shown, was a contest between what the Antonian forces portrayed as an effeminized Octavian and what Octavian's troops as well as the young triumvir's own later poetry portrayed as a transsexual Fulvia, Antony's preternaturally phallic wife (cf. Martial 11.20; Plutarch, *Antony* 10.3). The discourse surrounding Perusia thus anticipates the very inversion of gender values that we have already seen in Cynthia/Cynthius and that we shall be exploring further in our examination of Propertius's use of pederastic intertexts in the *Monobiblos*. The Perusine War was among the most savage fought during the period of civil turmoil that marked the early life of Propertius. Ostensibly a conflict over where to settle the veterans of Octavian and Mark Antony's victory over Caesar's assassins, the Perusine War represents an early round in the political maneuvering that would culminate in the battle of Actium. While Mark Antony regulated affairs in the East after the battle of Philippi (42 B.C.E.), his brother, Lucius, served as Octavian's colleague in the consulship for 41 B.C.E. When the Northern Italian landowners protested against Octavian's plan to seize land for the veterans, Lucius, working in consultation with Fulvia, took the opportunity to portray his brother as the landowners' champion. Riots broke out in Rome, and both sides assembled their troops. After some initial victories, Lucius was cornered by Octavian in the town of Perusia, where a siege was laid. Relief from other legions loyal to the Antonian cause never materialized due to factional infighting and an unwillingness on the part of the soldiers to fight against a plan whose purpose was to insure their own rewards. In the end, Octavian, although allowing Lucius to surrender and return to Rome, put to death the entire town council of Perusia as well as three hundred senators and equestrians who had accompanied Lucius's army. It was a massacre that sent a chilling message, but one that Octavian, once he became Augustus, preferred to forget.

Poems 1.21–22 present the disturbing image of a Gallus who escaped Caesar's swords at Perusia only to die at the hands of unknown brigands, and of a Propertius who identifies himself to Tullus as one whose close relative lies unburied near the "Perusina . . . sepulcra" (1.22.3). These poems are among the most moving in the Propertian corpus. They are also among the most puzzling. They are like jagged wounds that disturb the narrative framework of the *Monobiblos*, piercing it from another direction entirely. They evade full comprehension in its terms even as they recapitulate its motifs (Janan 2001: 34; Nicholson 1998–99: 144). As Fedeli (1983: 1916–17) notes, Heinsius preferred to see them as fragments because he was unable to make sense of them on their own.[25] Their aporetical nature continues to be reflected in the divisions of received critical opinion. To some, they express a profound alienation from the Augustan settlement (Heiden 1995: 167). Others have argued that these poems are deliberately apolitical and present a purely personal perspective on the suffering of the civil wars since no one is directly blamed and Gallus is said to have escaped Caesar's army (Newman 1997: 6; Tränkle 1983: 158; Boucher 1980: 105–6; Alfonsi 1974: 6–8, 37).

Nonetheless, it is hard to see how any statement about the wars and particularly about incidents such as Perusia, in which there were widespread civilian casualties, could be without political implications. These topics were not brought up in public discourse. Propertius is the only Augustan poet to mention Perusia (Nethercut 1963: 23–25), and where Horace speaks warmly of Augustus as the "ultor Caesaris" (Caesar's avenger; Odes 1.2.44), Propertius more ominously evokes "Caesaris ensis" (Caesar's swords, 1.21.7) (Stahl 1985: 103–4; Nethercut 1971: 465–66).[26] Still, these poems are not political programs or orations designed to rally the opposition (Nethercut 1971: 469–70n.14). They express a fundamental alienation, a horror before an incomprehensible social rift that has opened up in the Roman Symbolic. Tullus asks Propertius, "Qualis et unde genus, qui sint mihi, Tulle, Penates / quaeris pro nostra semper amicitia" (On account of our friendship, Tullus, you are always[27] asking of what sort and from where is my family, and who are my household gods, 1.22.1–2). Propertius can only reply:

> si Perusina tibi patriae sunt nota sepulcra,
> Italiae duris funera temporibus,
> . . . .
> proxima supposito contingens Umbria campo
> me genuit terris fertilis uberibus.
> (1.22.3–4. 9–10)

If the Perusine graves of the fatherland are known to you, as well as the deaths of Italy from that hard time . . . fertile Umbria, right next door, touching the field below, gave birth to me in her rich land.

The nature of their amicitia rests on Propertius's answers to Tullus's questions, but all he can do is mention the graves of Perusia and his Umbrian birth.[28] There is an unbridgeable chasm between Propertius's world and Tullus', between the world of traditional Roman politics represented by Tullus (1.6) and his proconsular uncle and the world of elegy, between an ideal of seamless masculine self-reflection (amicitia) and the world of

Cynthia (*amor*) (Gold 1987: 152; Putnam 1976: 116; King 1975–76: 122). Indeed, the final poem in the poet's first collection, the *sphragis* with which he seals the work, never even supplies his name (Nicholson 1999: 155). The answer to who he is is silence coupled with the image of an unburied body, "sic mihi praecipue, pulvis Etrusca, dolor, / tu proiecta mei perpessa es membra propinqui, / tu nullo miseri contegis ossa solo" (for this reason, you are especially painful to me, Etruscan dust, that allowed the bones of my kinsman to be scattered, that covered them with no soil, 1.22.6–8). This body is generally believed to be the Gallus of 1.21, whose bones were scattered across the Etruscan hills (1.21.9–10; Nethercut 1971: 464). The answer to "Who am I?" is a mute image of trauma and civil slaughter.

Poem 1.22, however, has intratextual links with the other Gallus poem of the final coda. Poem 1.20 on Gallus the poet's affair with Hylas begins "hoc pro continuo te, Galle, monemus amore." This line, which is echoed in 1.22.2's "pro nostra semper amicitia" (Rothstein 1979: ad loc.; Enk 1946: ad loc.), may be translated two ways: either "we give you this warning in order that your love affair may be uninterrupted"; or "we give you this warning in order that our love be uninterrupted," (Richardson 1977: ad loc.). In the one case, Propertius plays *praeceptor amoris*, having now become Gallus's teacher, and will show him through the story of Hercules and Hylas how he may keep possession of his pederastic beloved. In the other, he offers Gallus amatory advice as a means of insuring their continued friendship or mutual affection. In this one line, then, and its echo in 1.22.2, *amor* and *amicitia* become, if not synonymous, then at least substitutable. An ideal world of masculine mutual affection and friendship becomes visible in the same moment as the death of Gallus, the horror of Perusia, an unburied corpse, and Propertius's pregnant silence before the inquiries of Tullus is recalled. All of these elements become metonymically linked in these last poems, even as *amor* and *amicitia* are identified with one another and yet estranged (Oliensis 1997: 161).

Nonetheless, if 1.21 and 1.22 represent the mirror of history and *Roma* that reflects back on the elegiac world of *amor*, then poem 1.20 represents the hinge between the body of the *Monobiblos* and this final coda (Nicholson 1998–99: 143; Davis 1971: 212): for, while it may be concerned with *amor*, it is not concerned with Cynthia, but Hylas. This conjunction between pederasty and the eruption of the Real is far from fortuitous. It is part of a pattern that can be traced throughout book 1, as Cynthia serves as the medium for the renegotiation of a lost hom(m)osexuality, a homosocial world of ideal aristocratic relations torn asunder by the civil wars and by the gaping wounds of events such as Perusia that had alienated men like Propertius from the emerging Augustan regime (Fedeli 1983: 1914–15). The pattern can be traced throughout book I as Cynthia serves not only as a means of exchange but also as medium for the discussion of ideological conflict and displacement, a kind of substitute for this lost world, an *homme manqué*.[29] At the same time, there is a consistent system of allusions to and imitation of homosocial and pederastic subtexts and situations, such as the substitution of *Cynthia* for *Cynthius*, which echo the charges and the countercharges in the propaganda surrounding the battle of Perusia itself. Before we examine that system, however, one question must be asked.

WHO IS GALLUS?

> Cornelio Gallo è l'ultimo poeta di rilevo che finisca
> prefetto; gli altri passano da un esperienza giovanile
> di partecipazione politica e militare al solo impegno
> poetico; Properzio, Ovidio, et tanti altri si dedicano
> direttamente e solo alla poesia.[30]
> —Elia 1981: 72

> Gallus epitomizes the geographic and social
> displacements that Italy suffered in the years just before
> the principate. A *novus homo* from Gallia Narbonensis,
> he nonetheless secures his own advancement by
> becoming a *vir militaris* useful to Octavian the Triumvir.
> One of Gallus's early magistracies (41 B.C.E.) involved
> a role in the confiscation of lands and redistribution to
> veterans. He apparently did not divide land himself, but
> only exacted money from towns whose lands remained
> intact; nonetheless he participated in a process that . . .
> unsettled the geographic bases of Roman identity.
> —Janan 2001: 51

Gallus is the *eminence grise* behind Augustan elegy. Acknowledged by Propertius (2.34.85–94) and Ovid (*Amores* 1.15.27–30, 3.9.61–64; *Ars Amatoria* 3.533–34, 3.535–58; *Remedia Amoris* 763–66; *Tristia* 2.427–48, 4.10.51–54, 5.1.15–18) as an influential predecessor, he is listed by Quintilian (10.1.93) as the first of the elegists. Yet we possess but ten lines, nine of which were discovered in Egypt this past quarter century. Gallus is "the uncaused cause" of elegy, the poet to whom all can be attributed since nothing is known (Verducci 1984: 119–20). Indeed, the case of Gallus is almost the exact opposite of all the other poets we are examining in this book. Whereas for Catullus, Propertius, and Tibullus we know virtually nothing about their lives but have their complete poetic output, in the case of Gallus we know a great deal about his life but very little about his poetry. Lack of knowledge, however, has never stood in the way of philological speculation, and many are the reconstructions of Gallus's oeuvre based for the most part on the meager remains and references in other poets.

The nature of our knowledge of Gallus, in fact, testifies to the unique qualities of his status. As Salvatore d'Elia has argued, Gallus's career represents a turning point in the history of Roman literature. Whereas in the period before the principate, literature was often the extension of a public political career, most noticeably in the case of Caesar, but also in that of Cicero and even Catullus—with his invective against Caesar, Pompey and Memmius—after the consolidation of the Augustan regime literature became the province of equestrian order, which eschewed direct participation in politics (Elia 1981: 70–73; Tatum 1997).[31] Gallus is the last figure of any note to attempt to combine an independent political career with serious literary achievement until the age of Nero, by which time the relationship between the individual subject and political power had been radically transformed. Even then, the major talents of the age, Seneca, Petronius, and Lucan all died at their own hand. This fate, of course, as Dio Casssius tells us, awaited Gallus, an ambitious member of the provincial nobility who through loyal service climbed the ranks of Julius Caesar's allies and became a valued assistant to Octavian. The latter appointed him prefect of Egypt. When Gallus attempted to use the prefecture as an independent political base, setting up pharaonic statues of himself and having his own achievements memorialized on the pyramids, Augustus excluded him from his friendship. A feeding frenzy soon began and those attempting to curry favor with the *princeps* had Gallus brought up on charges. He was sentenced to exile and the loss of his estates. To prevent the loss of his family's property and to avoid public humiliation, Gallus took his own life (Dio Cassius 53.23.5–53.24.2; Koenen 1976: 133–34). No formal book burning or proscription took place afterward, but there is anecdotal evidence that Vergil may have removed a section of the *Georgics* devoted to praising Gallus, and it is small wonder that little of the latter's poetic oeuvre survives (Albrecht 1997: 744–45; White 1993: 145–47; Nisbet in Anderson et al. 1979: 155).[32]

Gallus's poetry, though the literary ancestor of elegy and perhaps even establishing many of its fundamental motifs (Fantham 1996: 107; Courtney 1993: 267; Veyne 1988: 103; Philips 1980: 274–75; Cairns 1979a: 227), was ultimately probably something rather different from what we find in Propertius, Tibullus, and even Vergil—another self-avowed Gallan disciple (Merriam 1990: 452; Ross 1975: 48–49, 53). As R.G.M. Nisbet (in Anderson et al. 1979: 155) observed, where the later elegists speak of the hardship of campaigns, the conflicts of duty and passion, and the prospect of despoiling the Parthians, these were immediate possibilities

for Gallus, not mere themes to be exploited. And yet, perhaps, these possi-
bilities were not quite as immediate as they may have appeared both to
Gallus and to his modern commentators. As Gallus's ultimate fate demon-
strates, Propertius, Tibullus, and Vergil may have drawn the lessons to be
learned from Perusia and the proscriptions more acutely than he did. The
restoration of the republic did not mean the return to republican culture,
but the gradual and piecemeal evolution of a new imperial Symbolic (see
chapters 6–8) that had little place for the previous era's Imaginary projec-
tions of individual *dignitas* and political ambition. Augustus's natural al-
lies were the equestrian landholders and financiers of the Italian country-
side, who had little interest in aristocratic self-aggrandizement[33] and every
reason to support peace and stability. Literature under the new regime
was less a means of self-assertion than a complex negotiation of new
Imaginary and Symbolic categories of what *Romanitas* and *nobilitas*
meant in a world of public subordination to a single central authority
(Fear 2000: 236–37; Habinek 1998: 121; Wallace-Hadrill 1997: 22;
Conte 1994: 251; Elia 1981: 69). The moments of aporia and symptom-
atic eruption that we find in a Propertius are precisely the evidence of
what needed to be negotiated, of the intractable problems of creating a
stable and workable identity in a situation where all the known parame-
ters have changed, where the old affective bonds binding one citizen to
the other have proven inoperable and no new forms of self-formation
have grown in their place (Janan 2001: 49).[34]

This process of negotiation is perhaps nowhere better seen than in the
elegists' later reworkings of Gallus himself. Nine lines of continuous verse
survive. They are printed in four-line stanzas with gaps and odd *h* shaped
punctuation marks between the stanzas. These marks and spacing pat-
terns are unprecedented and difficult to interpret (Parsons in Anderson et
al. 1979: 129). The generally accepted reconstruction of the text reads as
follows:

tristia nequit[ia . . . .]a, Lycori, tua.

fata mihi, Caesar, tum erunt mea dulcia quom tu
    maxima Romanae pars eris historiae,
postque tuum reditum multorum templa deorum
    fixa legam spolieis deivitiora tueis.

]. . . . . tandem fecerunt c[ar]mina Musae
quae possem domina deicere digna mea
    ].atur idem tibi, non ego, Visce,
    ]. . . . . . . .l . Kato, iudice te uereor.

Sorrows caused by your infidelity Lycoris . . .

Caesar, the fates to me will be kind when you will be the crowning glory of
Roman history, after your return I shall read the temples of many gods decor-
ated more richly with your spoils.

Finally, the Muses have made songs that I can call worthy of my mistress . . .
the same thing for you, I do not fear even if you, Viscus, [or] you, Cato, are
the judge.

Many problems are raised by these lines, but some things can be said with
reasonable certainty. The consensus is that the Caesar mentioned in line
2 is Julius Caesar and that the pending campaign was that against the
Parthians on which the dictator was about to depart when he was assassi-
nated (Courtney 1993: 265; Merriam 1990: 447; Nisbet in Anderson et
al. 1979: 152). This view is reinforced by recognizing the parallels be-
tween the second quatrain and Propertius 3.4 addressed to Augustus
when he too was considering a campaign against the Parthians (see chap-
ter 5). In the latter poem Propertius says that he will read to Cynthia the
names of captured towns from the banners that would be mounted on
the floats representing them in Augustus's triumphal parade ("et titulis
oppida capta legam," 3.4.16).[35] This imitation provides key information
as to how *legam* should be read in line 5 of the Gallus fragment: for
while some have argued that it refers to Gallus's reading about Caesar's
triumphs in later historical accounts, it seems clearly to refer to his stand-
ing before the trophies of Caesar's victory when they were displayed in the
god's temples and reading the attached labels or inscriptions. *Historiae* in
line 3 does not refer either to historiography per se or to the acts them-
selves but to the representation of those acts in the codified cultural dis-
plays that legitimated the Roman political elite (Courtney 1993: 266; Ver-
ducci 1984: 133–34; Putnam 1980: 52–53; Parsons and Nisbet in
Anderson et al. 1979: 141, 152).

Florence Verducci (1984: 132–34) has argued that what the second
quatrain represents is a *recusatio* in which the poet says he will read of
Caesar's triumph, but he will not write about it. The textual support for
this position, however, is thin, nor does it have any historical basis in what
we know of Gallus's involvement in Caesarian and triumviral politics.
Gallus and the Propertius of 2.1 or the Horace of *Odes* 1.6 do not occupy
symmetrical positions in relation to the exercise of political and military
power. The provisional separation of the poetic from the political that the
recusatio normally seeks to enact would be an absurd pose for an active
military man and politician to adopt. Rather what we seem to have is a
contrast between the *nequitia* of Lycoris at the end of the first quatrain
and the *fata dulcia* that Caesar's triumph will grant at the beginning of
the second. This continuity indicates that the fragments form part of a
single continuous text. Even Parsons admits that they read in a more inter-

esting manner if interpreted in this fashion, but he argues that the unprece-
dented punctuation and spacing between the stanzas seems to indicate a
high degree of separation between the quatrains (Anderson et al. 1979:
129). Yet this argument cuts both ways. The lack of any parallel for this
punctuation and spacing makes it impossible to use it as the basis of any
positive argument. There is a separation between the quatrains but of
what kind? Moreover, the fact that the passages are written as uniform
quatrains tells against Courtney's (1993: 264) view that the papyrus is a
fragment from a more or less random anthology of Gallan verse. If that
were the case, why should all the selections be of equal length? The next
column in the papyrus, although unreadable, indicates that the same pat-
tern of division, four-line strophes, and punctuation continues. That an
entire anthology would deliberately only choose four line excerpts seems
unlikely.

Janet Fairweather has proposed a preliminary answer to these interpre-
tive problems. She argues that the fragments are best read as an exchange
of amoebean verse. Such a reading has the advantage of giving a reasoned
account of the punctuation as well as of the thematic and prosodic conti-
nuities between fragments noted by Nisbet (Anderson et al. 1979: 148–
49). Fairweather (1984: 167–71) underlines the parallel case of Theocri-
tus's *Idyll* 8 where shifts in speaker are marked only by dashes between
the stanzas:

> Let us surmise that the fragmentary epigram ending with our line 1 and the
> first complete quatrain (lines 2–5) were a matched pair, the former taking as
> its theme "happiness destroyed by misfortune in love," the latter answering it
> with "happiness brought about by good fortune in war." Both poems feature
> apostrophe (to Lycoris/ to Caesar); *tristia* (line 1) is picked up by *dulcia* (line
> 2); *tua* (line 1 fin.) by *tueis* (line 5 fin.). The antithesis between love and war
> is, of course, a favorite theme of the Latin love elegists; *triste* is used as the
> opposite of *dulce* in the amoebaean verses of Verg. *Ecl.* 3. 80–4; *tua* and *tueis*
> represent a type of formal correspondence between the corresponding lines
> which one expects in a pair of amoebaean quatrains; note that both these
> possessive adjectives agree with ablative nouns (*nequitia/spolieis*), both of
> which in turn bear a similar relation to neuter plurals in —*a* (*tristia/fixa*) at
> the beginning of their lines. (1984: 168)

Our final quatrain would be a capping gesture where the poet of unhappi-
ness in love would claim poetic superiority over the celebrator of Caesar's
martial valor. This is a move that while related to the *recusatio* in its
claim of superiority for elegiac love poetry over encomiastic verse does
not require the Gallan narrator to adopt a subject position at odds with
what the audience would know of his extraliterary persona. More im-
portant for our purposes, however, Propertius makes the same gesture in

poem 1.7 addressed to the epic poet Ponticus. Here Propertius notes that although he was forced to serve a harsh mistress, "haec mea fama est / hinc cupio nomen carminis ire mei" (this is my fame / I desire the renown of my poetry to come from this; 1.7.9–10). This same poem is preceded by 1.6 in which Propertius turns down Tullus's invitation to join him in a life of action and political achievement, not unlike that of the historical Gallus, and 1.5 where the Propertian Gallus tries to steal Cynthia. In Propertius's poetic dialogue the subject position of the speaker of the second quatrain in the Gallan fragment would be occupied by Tullus and Ponticus, while he and the Gallus of 1.5 would vie for who would occupy that of the first and third. The real Gallus, however, could articulate both positions, an option that Propertius and the later elegists can no longer envision.

Confirmation of Fairweather's reading of the fragments as amoebean verse has been offered by James O'Hara's interpretation of Propertius 1.10. In this poem, where Propertius professes to have observed Gallus in the arms of his girlfriend, readers have long seen references not to the poet's practice of voyeurism[36] but to his reading of Gallus's poetry (Sharrock 2000: 271–72; Commager 1974: 12n.23). The double entendre is of course consonant with Cynthia's function as an allegory of Propertius's poetic practice. And if the Gallus of 1.10 were Gallus the poet, then, Propertius the young elegist would quite naturally be reading his predecessor's work with a mixture of admiration, wonder, and envy. Such a reading is reinforced if we recall that 1.9 is addressed to the epic poet Ponticus. As we have already seen in the sequence 1.5, 1.6, and 1.7, Propertius positions himself as Gallus's competitor in the pursuit of Cynthia or elegy in opposition to Tullus and Ponticus who represent the life of action and its associated poetic genre. Poem 1.10 in turn looks back to poem 1.5 and ahead to 1.13, a second Gallus poem in which Propertius plays the voyeur. Poem 1.14, addressed to Tullus, follows it in turn (Richardson 1977: ad loc.; Rothstein 1979: 1.141). Thus, the opening sequence of poems (1.1 to 1.14) not only introduces us to Cynthia but also to a patterned alternation of poems in which Propertius counterposes his love for Cynthia— both as poetic achievement and a love story—with the rival claims of public virtue, epic poetry, and his predecessor in elegy. This pattern only makes sense, however, if we assume that the Gallus of 1.5 and 1.10, like the Ponticus of 1.9 is a fellow poet (Ross 1975: 83–84; Benjamin 1965). Such a reading is reinforced when we recognize that 1.4 is addressed to yet another known poet, Bassus, a practitioner of the rival genre of iambic.[37] Indeed, all the characters addressed in the body of the *Monobiblos* are historical characters with the exception of Cynthia. It would be odd if Gallus broke the mold (Janan 2001: 36–37; Cairns 1983a).

The passage on which O'Hara bases his reading is the following.

> O iucunda quies, primo cum testis amori
> affueram vestris conscius in lacrimis!
> o noctem meminisse mihi iucunda voluptas,
> o quotiens votis illa vocanda meis,
> cum te complexa morientem, Galle, puella
> vidimus et longa ducere verba mora!
> quamvis labentis premeret mihi somnus ocellos
> et mediis caelo Luna ruberet equis,
> non tamen a uestro potui secedere lusu:
> tantus in alternis uocibus ardor erat.
> (1.10.1–10)

O joyous night, when I had been a witness to the beginning of your love, an accomplice in your tears! O joyous pleasure to me to remember that night! O how many times must it be called back by my vows, when we saw you, dying in your girl's embrace and uttering words after a long delay! Although sleep pressed my drooping eyes and the moon turned red with its horses in mid heaven, nonetheless I was not able to tear myself away from your game: so great was the passion in your alternating voices.

Particular emphasis should be laid on three terms: *verba*, *lusus*, and *alternis vocibus*. What fascinates the watching Propertius is not the sexual act but Gallus's words, *verba*. Thus when the poet says he is an accomplice (*conscius*) in the poet's tears, he casts himself as the reader of elegy, which is always presented as a genre of lamentation (e.g., *Heroides* 15.7). The pleasure (*voluptas*) of tears may be mildly paradoxical, but the pleasures of vicariously experiencing the sufferings of others (particularly in love) are well known to any connoiseur of Italian opera, and every reader-listener is an accomplice in those tears. *Lusus*, while often used for sexual play is also used by Catullus for erotic verse, most notably in poem 50 where the poet is sleepless after an afternoon of trading verse with Licinius Calvus. It has long been recognized that Catullus in this poem mixes the vocabulary of sexual attraction with that of literary admiration to create an image of ideal homosocial, homoerotic bonding between two poets. Lastly, what actually kept Propertius up all night, sleepless like Catullus, was the passion of Gallus and his puella's *alternis vocibus* or "alternating voices." If we are correct in reading the poem itself as a literary allegory that alludes to Catullus 50, then "alternating voices" would necessarily mean "alternating verses" as in the case of Catullus and Calvus (Janan 2001: 37; King 1980b: 225; Thomas 1979: 204–5). This recognition, as O'Hara (1989) observes, in turn provides confirmation of Fairweather's reading of the Gallus fragment as amoebean verse,[38] since that would be the form most logically alluded to here.[39]

Gallus's verse, then, would, at least on the level of idealizing nostalgia, represent a lost wholeness to Propertius—a possibility of fusing the twin voices of *virtus* and *lusus* found in the fragments. The fissure between the voices is marked in the *Monobiblos* by the division between the erotic Gallus of 1.5, 1.10, 1.13, and 1.20 and the dying Gallus *militaris* of 1.21. Cynthia as the medium of the younger poet's competitive emulation of his older rival, then, becomes precisely the symptom of that split. She is the ground of their relationship and thus the space that articulates their difference. She represents the return and the occultation of the Real in the realm of *amor* from which the horrors of *Roma* had been banished. The split itself, in turn, only truly becomes visible at the moment when the world of *amor* shifts focus from Cynthia to Hylas, from the world of mediated homosociality to the evocation of a lost ideal of immediate masculine mirroring[40] and homoerotic desire in the closed world of the Argonauts. Yet, as poem 1.20 makes clear, even that world was always already fallen, always able only to give the illusion of wholeness, not its reality: for Hylas is ultimately lost to the nymphs.

The main objection to this reading is the contention by some that the Gallus of 1.5, 1.10, 1.13, and 1.20 cannot be Cornelius Gallus.[41] This is now a minority position,[42] but its advocates are worthy of respect and the evidence needs to be examined. The objections to the identification are essentially three. First, Propertius treats Gallus as a friend and contemporary, when Cornelius Gallus would have been almost twenty years Propertius's senior. Second, Gallus is portrayed in 1.20 as having a pederastic beloved when that is mentioned nowhere else in the literature on Cornelius Gallus. Third, Cornelius Gallus was a *novus homo* from a provincial family, but the Gallus of 1.5 is said to be a member of the *nobilitas* and possibly to have had ancestors of consular rank. Only the last of these poses serious difficulties. First, Propertius never mentions Gallus's age, and if we accept the literary reading of 1.10, there is no need to assume a real personal encounter. These poems are sophisticated poetic artifacts, not historical documents. Indeed, the age objection is based wholly upon the biographical fallacy and can be summarily dismissed.[43] Second, the pederastic objection is based on a conception of exclusive sexual identity, according to which one is either homosexual or heterosexual. If Gallus had a mistress, Lycoris, he couldn't possibly have had a boyfriend. But such assumptions of heteronormativity have been repeatedly shown to be inoperative in the ancient world.[44] In fact, as Crowther observes, Vergil attributes to Gallus in *Eclogue* 10.35 the desire "to sing like the shepherds of the love of the boy Amyntas" (1983: 1638). Likewise, if the extant corpus of Catullus and Tibullus were in the same state as that of Gallus and we had to rely primarily on the ancient testimonia, we would not now know of the Juventius and Marathus poems either. Nonetheless, as Catullus's marriage hymn shows, the assumption of the attractiveness of boys was the ancient norm (61.119–37).[45] Ovid is the odd man out when he declares his clear preference for female sexual partners, although he acknowledges boys as desirable (*Ars Amatoria* 2.684).[46] Finally, it is recognized by even those who object to the identification of the Gallus addressed in 1.5, 1.10, 1.13, and 1.20 with Cornelius Gallus that Propertius in 1.20 is writing on a subject that Gallus the poet had dealt with in his elegiac poetry and that 1.20 echoes a passage in 1.18 generally thought to be derived from Gallus (Fedeli 1983: 1910–11; Hubbard 1974: 37; Rothstein 1979: 1.191; Enk 1946: 180–81).[47] This leaves the objectors in the paradoxical position of claiming that the ancient reader would recognize the intertext but not connect it with the name of the person addressed.

The third objection is not so easily dismissed: for it is based on textual evidence that appears to indicate that the Gallus addressed by Propertius in 1.5—who all agree must be the Gallus addressed in 1.10 and 1.13— was a *nobilis* with consular ancestors. In the final section of this chapter we give independent reasons for believing that the Gallus addressed in 1.5 is meant to be seen as an elegiac poet, and thus logically the reader would be led to think of Cornelius Gallus, but the lines in question at the moment are the following, "nec tibi nobilitas poterit succurrere amanti /: nescit Amor priscis cedere imaginibus" (And high social status will not be able to help you as a lover: love does not yield to the likenesses of ancient ancestors; 1.5.23–24). Strictly, a *nobilis* was a member of a family that had included at least one consul. Cornelius Gallus, as a *novus homo* from the provinces, did not meet this definition. But we know that the adjective *nobilis* was capable of a wider, more metaphorical usage referring generally to character and high social standing. Cicero, for example, uses it of prominent equestrians (e.g., *Pro Cluentio* 109; *Ad Familiares* 6.6.3–9). By the late thirties or very early twenties when this poem was being composed, Gallus was a prominent government official, with vast personal wealth accrued from his connections with Julius and Octavian Caesar, and therefore certainly a *nobilis* in the broader sense (Edwards 1993: 14; Crowther 1983: 1638; Cairns 1983a: 86–87; Thomas 1979: 204n.84; Alfonsi 1943: 54).[48]

Nor does 1.5 itself encourage a literal reading. As King and others have noted, the poem as a whole contains numerous examples of etymological play on the root meaning of *nobilis* as *notabilis* or "known": *nosse* (line 4), *ignotos* (5), *notam* (16), *nosse* (18), and *nomen* (26). *Nobilitas*, then, rather than having a single monovalent sociological meaning in the poem is in fact part of a complex system of textual play (Cairns 1983a: 85; King

1980b: 213–14). Thus line 23 on it own hardly excludes Cornelius Gallus from consideration.

The *priscae imagines* of the second line of the couplet are somewhat more problematic. It is universally agreed that these represent the wax masks of prominent, normally consular ancestors that were displayed in the entry hall of a Roman aristocratic house. A number of solutions have been offered to this problem. It is noted that the provincial Cornelii Galli probably acquired their name when they were sponsored for citizenship by a member of the aristocratic Galli of Rome and that, as happened with other families after the devastations of the proscriptions, they or their supporters might have laid claim to their adopted pedigree as their own (Cairns 1983a: 86–87). It is also noted that there is no direct syntactical link between lines 23 and 24 so that line 24 may be read as a general statement rather than one directly connected with Gallus (Cairns 1983a: 85). The first of these arguments has merit, but is unprovable and the second is tenuous since Propertius is fond of asyndeton and often eschews subordination in favor of a more compact style. A third line of argument offers more promise. Tränkle noted that 1.5.24, "nescit Amor priscis cedere imaginibus," is a direct calque of 1.14.8 "nescit Amor magnis cedere divitiis." This would indicate that both lines derive from a single common source that Tränkle argues must be Gallus (1960: 23; see Cairns 1983a: 87–88). Janan has recently confirmed this observation by noting:

> Propertius's allusion unmistakably looks to elements of the tenth *Eclogue*. Vergil has Gallus yield to Love's cruel intransigence: "omnia vincit Amor: et nos cedamus Amori"—"Love conquers all things; let us, too, surrender to love" (10.69, Gallus's final line). Propertius's repeated collocation of *Amor* and *cedere* echoes Gallus's portrait in the tenth *Eclogue*, and both his and Vergil's poem may well look to a passage or line from Gallus's poetry itself. (2001: 40)

Of course, if line 24 alludes either to a passage from Gallus, or at least to a well-known and influential portrait of him, then it is no longer necessary that his family literally possess *priscae imagines*. Rather the joke would be in Propertius's citing this line in a poem where he is trying to dissuade Gallus from seducing Cynthia.

Moreover, we know, as observed earlier, that Propertius also imitated Gallus in 1.1, 1.8, 1.18, and 1.20. In 2.34, he explicitly laid claim to being Gallus's successor in the elegiac genre (Newman 1997: 17; Stahl 1985: 186–87). In this context, it is hard to imagine that the name Cornelius Gallus would not have come to the reader's mind when presented with 1.5, 1.10, 1.13, and 1.20. As Janan has pointed out, however, a literal reading of the *priscae imagines* may well have given the same reader pause. She argues that this uncertainty is a function of a broader problematization of identity in the *Monobiblos* (Janan 2001: 35, 40). Such a reading is consonant with my own understanding of Gallus's representing a lost illusion of wholeness whose image is preserved in the pairing of the two voices of the fragment's amoebean verse. The split, however, is evident both in the need to partition the papyrus's competing *alternae voces* of amorous and political fulfillment—and this is true whether one reads the passage as a continuous poem or as a series of discontinuous epigrams or excerpts—as well as in the *Monobiblos*'s move from the erotic Gallus of 1.20 to the dying Gallus of 1.21. The reality of that split is ultimately confirmed by the fate of the republic's last poet-politician, Cornelius Gallus, almost immediately after the publication of the *Monobiblos*.

WHERE THE BOYS ARE: SHARING THE JOY

> "O iucunda quies!" the poet exclaims at the beginning
> of the poem. "Quies" here is often glossed as equivalent
> to night but with no justification. The word means
> serenity, rest, or by extension sleep, which often occurs
> at night but is certainly not happening on this particular
> night. Since the poet is exclaiming, we assume that
> it is he who is experiencing the feeling. "Iucunda,"
> however suggests pleasure of an erotic kind. So Gallus is
> making love but Propertius feels "jucunditas" as well.
> From the beginning, a strange bond has been established
> between Gallus and Propertius.
> —Hodge and Buttimore 1977: 139

τόν με Πόθοις ἄτρωτον ὑπὸ στέρνοισι Μυΐσκος
ὄμμασι τοξεύσας τοῦτ' ἐβόησεν ἔπος·
"τὸν θρασὺν εἷλον ἐγώ· τὸ δ' ἐπ' ὀφρύσι κεῖνο φρύαγμα
σκηπτροφόρου σοφίας ἠνίδε ποσσὶ πατῶ."
τῷ δ' ὅσον ἀμπνεύσας τόδ' ἔφην "φίλε κουρε, τί θαμβεῖς;
καὐτὸν ἀπ' Οὐλύμπου Ζῆνα καθεῖλεν Ἐρως."[49]
(Meleager 103, Page 1975)

In poems, 1.10 and 1.13, Propertius and Gallus enjoy a sexual experience. Gallus is the performer, and Propertius a voyeur. The scene is charged with the very shared eroticism that defines Irigaray's concept of *hom(m)o-sexualité*. The imagery at times borders on the graphic. Propertius in 1.13 uses the exemplum of Neptune assuming the body of the river god Enipeus so as to make love to Tyro. Here the two men's bodies become one, each penetrating the other in order to have intercourse with the woman who is the medium of their union (Hodge and Buttimore 1977: 158;

Rothstein 1979: ad loc.). This exemplum, in turn, modulates directly into that of Hercules and Hebe, which, while in itself heteroerotic, looks forward to the only other mention of Hercules in the *Monobiblos* in the next and last of the erotic Gallus poems, 1.20 on Hylas (Rothstein 1979: ad loc.):

> non ego complexus potui diducere vestros:
> tantus erat demens inter utrosque furor.
> non sic Haemonio Salmonida *mixtus* Enipeo
> Taenarius facili presset amore deus,
> non sic caelestem flagrans amor Herculis Heben
> sensit in Oetaeis gaudia prima iugis.
> (1.13.19–24)

> I was not able to divide your embraces: so great was the mad frenzy between you two. Not thus did the Taenarian[50] god embrace Tyro in easy love when he had *mingled* with Enipeus, nor thus did the burning love of Hercules feel heavenly Hebe in the first joys of Mount Oetae.

Lest there be any doubt about the erotic implications of Poseidon mingling with Enipeus, as the waters of the sea swirl into those of the river, the word that describes this action, *mixtus,* is a common euphemism for intercourse (Adams 1982: 180–81). This is not the only such instance of shared bodies in these poems. Ellen Oliensis has noted that the opening of 1.10 casts Propertius as Gallus's *testis*, meaning his "witness" but also punningly his "testicle" (Oliensis 1997: 160).[51]

There has been debate about whether the girl in Gallus's embrace should be seen as Cynthia. On one level she has to be.[52] For, insofar as Cynthia is a metonym for elegy and insofar as these poems can be read as allegories of the younger poet's fascination with and envy of the older poet's work, then Cynthia has always already been shared with Gallus. Moreover, just as in the example of Catullus 50, examined earlier, where the depiction of homoerotic attraction is a metaphor for poetic emulation—but where poetry is also a medium of erotic exchange between men—so here Cynthia is a medium for this same kind of complex literary, erotic, and ideological exchange.

This pattern of erotic substitution and literary as well as ideological intercourse is pervasive throughout book 1. I shall finish this chapter by examining three poems that illustrate this thesis, 1.1, 1.4, and 1.5, as well as the inter- and intratextual relations that govern them. What will emerge from this examination is a complex yet consistent system of relations that on the manifest level substitute heteroerotic relations for homoerotic ones, while maintaining the affective and erotic valorizations of the homoerotic subtexts. These patterns of polarities and substitutions, in turn, consistently center on problems of poetic composition and political commitment. Elegy in general, then, and Cynthia in particular, are the medium through which a longed for wholeness exemplified by an ideal community of affectively bonded men can be reconstituted, even as it serves as the symptom of its dissolution.

We begin with poem 1.1 and its intertexts. Our second headnote for this section is a pederastic epigram of Meleager. It is the recognized model for the opening of Propertius's first poem:

> Cynthia prima suis miserum me cepit ocellis,
>   contactum nullis ante cupidinibus.
> tum mihi constantis deiecit lumina fastus
>   et caput impositis pressit Amor pedibus. . . .

Cynthia was the first to capture me with her eyes, I who was stricken before by no desires. Then Love cast down my face of unceasing pride and pressed upon my head with his feet.

As Fedeli notes the relationship between Propertius 1.1.1–4 and Meleager's epigram is so close as to indicate clear programmatic intent. Why else would Propertius begin the first poem of his first book with such a quotation? He notes that Catullus 1 had begun with a similar evocation of Meleager and argues that Propertius here is indicating his adherence to principles of Alexandrian composition while tipping his hat to one of its earliest advocates in Rome and his acknowledged predecessor in the realm of erotic verse (Fedeli 1980: 62; 1983: 1865–66). This reading is certainly credible given what we have already seen of Propertius's reworking of Catullus 50. The imitation of Meleager, however, contains ironies that have not been noted. Cynthia is *prima*, but the announcement of her firstness is a quotation and hence already *secunda*. If we recall the literary significance of Cynthia being the first (*prima*) word of the poem, then the programmatic nature of this statement becomes clear. It also indicates that the poetry that follows will be organized around polarities and inversions such that the surface meaning is often at odds with that contained in the subtext. Cynthia may be first, but only in a way that announces her as second. The poem itself, rather than having a stable center, functions as the locus for a series of tensions between a set of analogous polarities and their inversions (Maleuvre 1998: 56; Hodge and Buttimore 1977: 71). The citation of Meleager is programmatic but in a more complex way than Fedeli recognizes.

One of the most obvious ways in which Propertius's poem differs from Meleager's is that the gender of the beloveds has been switched. Everybody knows this, but no one has remarked upon its significance. This is no doubt because much Hellenistic poetry is pederastic in nature and so it is not unusual to find intertexts that have masculine in place of feminine objects of desire. The genders would appear to be commutable. Roman poets just substitute girls for boys and go on their way. And yet it is precisely the supposed impossibility of that substitution that has led critics to claim that the Gallus of 1.20 could not be Cornelius Gallus since we have no independent evidence that he wrote pederastic verse. Why should the wall between the genders be so permeable in the one case and so impermeable in the other? Moreover, if there is such a neat equivalence between the two that no notice need be taken of the gender of the beloved, then why is Roman elegy predominantly addressed to the poet's *puellae* in spite of the manifest existence of *pueri*, even in the poetry itself? I would argue that this inversion of genders is part of a larger pattern of the use of pederastic intertexts to frame the relation of Propertius to Tullus, Gallus, and Bassus in 1.1, 1. 4, and 1.5, with Cynthia as the common link between them. It is perhaps good at this time also to recall that Cynthia's name was itself derived from Apollo Cynthius, and that the battle of Perusia was depicted even by its combatants as a contest between a masculinized Fulvia and an effeminate Octavian (Hallett 1977: 152–60). Thus, Propertius, Tullus, Bassus, and both the erotic Gallus as well as the Gallus *militaris* are situated by the *Monobiblos* in a complex semiotic field in which ideological, gender, sexual, and political instability are all inter-implicated. Cynthia, in this context, becomes a means of articulating the possibility of reconstructing an Imaginary *hom(m)osexuel* relation between these men that has been torn asunder by the collapse of the traditional homosocial bonds that were ideally conceived of as binding together the Roman aristocracy in the republic. Within Propertius book 1, she is the medium both of their exchange and of their potential mutual identification and self-reflection.

In this regard, it should be remembered not only that poem 1.1 is addressed to Tullus and features an imitation of Gallus, but also that the collection closes with three poems concerning first the erotic and then the dying Gallus, the last of which is addressed to Tullus. The first poem of this coda, in turn, is the only one that makes the homoerotic subtext explicit. If the quotation of Meleager at the beginning of 1.1 marks it as a programmatic passage for the book as a whole, then any convincing exegesis has to explain how it relates both to the Gallus imitation and the address to Tullus in 1.1 as well as to the corresponding gestures at the end of the book, including 1.20 (Gold 1987: 146).

In fact, the Meleager epigram has been recast in heteroerotic terms on only the most superficial level. Cynthia ceases to be the subject of the finite verbs in lines 3 and 4 (Hodge and Buttimore 1977: 63–64). Amor who is male replaces her. This metonymic evocation of a homoerotic context is made more explicit when it is recognized that in Meleager's poem no such substitution takes place, but rather Muiskos, who is not just notionally but actually male, remains the subject throughout. He is the one who treads upon the head of the recalcitrant Meleager. Thus, the intertext makes clear what is only alluded to in 1.1 itself: the *hom(m)osexuel* nature of Propertius's desire.

Finally, there is a pun in the midst of this very substitution of Amor for Cynthia contained in the words "impositis . . . pedibus." It can mean either "with his feet placed on my head" (Meleager's sense) or "with meter imposed" (Commager 1974: 24). Thus, *Cynthia prima* both as love object and as poetry functions as a substitute for a direct relation between men that is, in turn, ideally reconstituted through poetic composition (Sharrock 2000: 267–68).

Within the first four lines, the boundaries between *prima* and *secunda*, primary and secondary, masculine and feminine, poetry and experience have been called into question. This process of decentering and ideological inversion unfolds systematically throughout the poem. Indeed, as Duncan Kennedy notes, the very image of love placing his feet upon the poet's head is a reprise of the gesture of triumph found in Roman depictions of single combat. The poet is therefore portrayed as subjected and effeminized at the very moment where his text effects a double gender substitution of Cynthia for Muiskos and Amor for Cynthia (Kennedy 1993: 48). Subject and object, masculine and feminine, then, are in very fluid relation to one another. The pattern of reverse polarities continues in the next couplet, "donec me docuit castas odisse puellas / improbus, et nullo vivere consilio" (then the lascivious one taught me to hate chaste girls and to live by no counsel). This is an inversion of normative values. The prudent Roman young man married a *casta puella* and heeded the advice of his elders. What is not obvious is whether Cynthia is to be considered a *casta puella* or not. If so,[53] then how are we to explain the evidence cited at the beginning of this chapter that she is a *meretrix* or an adulterous *matrona*?[54] If not, then why would Propertius hate chaste young women? Cynthia is not one, and she is the one subjecting him. Perhaps it is because chaste girls don't grant their favors to poets. But Cynthia is by no normal definition of the term *casta*, except toward Propertius. Thus Butler and Barber (1969: ad loc.) as well as Camps (1961: ad loc.) reach an aporia over whether the couplet means Cynthia is *incesta* and thus Propertius no longer loves women who are *castae* or if it means he is frustrated with Cynthia and no longer loves women like her who are *castae*. In short the couplet establishes a polarity of values that inverts the normative stance, and then proceeds to undo the opposition itself in a fashion precisely homologous with the gender shell game seen in the first four lines (Hodge and Buttimore 1977: 64–65). In each case, Cynthia is the means of establishing the initial opposition, its subsequent inversion, and its final deconstruction through a process of systematic exchange between the poles.

Fedeli proposes to do away with this deconstructive tangle of competing interpretations: he appeals to the Atalanta exemplum to demonstrate that Cynthia, like the untamed virgin, must be *casta* (1983: 1866; see also Stahl 1985: 39). But this move is unconvincing since Propertius himself admits that the exemplum is not apposite, "in me tardus Amor non ullas cogitat artis, / nec meminit notas, ut prius, ire vias" (in my case slow love does not recognize any arts / nor does he remember to go along known paths as before, 1.1.17–18); (Hodge and Buttimore 1977: 66). What the exemplum does do, however, is testify simultaneously to the poet's Alexandrian learning (in making Atalanta's suitor Milanion rather than the more familiar Hippomenes) and address both Tullus and Gallus in a context rich with images of gender substitution that recall those found in the opening couplet:

> et mihi iam toto furor hic non deficit anno,
>   cum tamen adversos cogor habere deos.
> Milanion nullos fugiendo, Tulle, labores
>   saevitiam durae contudit Iasidos.
> nam modo Partheniis amens errabat in antris,
>   ibat et hirsutas ille videre feras;
> ille etiam Hylaei percussus vulnere rami
>   saucius Arcadiis rupibus ingemuit.
> ergo velocem potuit domuisse puellam:
>   tantum in amore preces et bene facta valent.
> (1.1.7–16)

And now this madness has not left me for a year, though I am, nonetheless, forced to consider the gods opposed to it. Milanion, Tullus, by fleeing no labors struck down the harshness of Iasus's daughter. For nearly mad he wandered in the caves of Mount Parthenius and went to see shaggy beasts. Stricken with a wound from the club of Hylaeus, injured he moaned among the Arcadian cliffs. Therefore, he was able to tame the swift girl: so much are prayers and good deeds worth in love.

As Hodge and Buttimore (1977: 65) note, the introduction of Tullus is peculiarly unmotivated. Why at this point introduce the one addressee who throughout the *Monobiblos* most clearly stands for traditional Roman *virtus* as instantiated in public accomplishment (1.6) and its material remuneration (1.14) (Gold 1987: 147)? Tullus and Milanion are hardly parallel figures. As Sharrock observes, "The abstruse telling of this exotic myth stands at one extreme of the spectrum . . . but, in a sense the artificial, mythic Milanion is a kind of foil to the real-life Tullus as well as an exemplum for Propertius. Here is another man invited into the poem, invited to join the manly business of looking at Cynthia . . . and looking at *domuisse puellam*" (2000: 268–69). Tullus and Milanion, like Tullus and Propertius, and Tullus and Gallus, represent polar opposites who nonetheless meet in the figure of Cynthia and in the possibility of illustrating her character through that of Atlanta. Yet where Atalanta is tamed, Cynthia is not. Cynthia as a figure of Propertian discourse remains a symptom, a return of the Real into the very masculinist Symbolic system that depends on her exclusion.

How exactly does Milanion "tame" Atalanta? "Tame," of course, implies to marry and take her virginity, as the Greek verb *damazō* means both to wed and to break a wild horse (Calame 1977: 333, 340, 413). In the traditional version of the story, Hippomenes conquers Atalanta in a footrace by tossing golden apples to distract her. While Propertius alludes to this version of the myth with the epithet *velox*, he concentrates on a lesser-known version according to which the young maiden was accosted by the centaurs Hylaeus and Rhoeteus while hunting in the Arcadian hills. In Apollodorus (3.9.3) and Aelian (*Varia Historia* 13.1) she slays them herself. In Propertius, Milanion apparently comes to her aid and is wounded by Hylaeus's club. Thus, Milanion paradoxically beats down (*contudit*) Atalanta's *saevitiam* by being stricken by another man. Propertius here uses a verb (*contudere*) that is a frequent metaphor for sexual penetration (cf. *pertundo*, Catullus 32.11; Adams 1982: 145–49). She then slays the centaurs while he lies moaning in the Arcadian cliffs. Moreover, Ovid, in a passage from the *Ars* (2.185–88) that makes clear reference to our own poem, pictures Milanion as carrying her hunting nets, a servile activity that Tibullus in 1.4.49–50 recommends as a means of winning the favors of your pederastic beloved. Hunting was a traditionally male activity and virgins were in religious and medical discourse considered preternaturally masculine, so that Diana is both the goddess of maidens and the hunt (Dean-Jones 1993: 81; Lefkowitz 1981: 18). Thus Milanion conquers through subjection and takes the girl by treating her like a boy.

Of course, as was pointed out earlier, the figure of Milanion moaning among the rocks looks forward to that of the dying Gallus in 1.21: Tullus and Gallus, figured implicitly and explicitly in the description of Milanion's distress, anticipate their reassociation in book 1's coda, 1.20–22— the poems where pederasty first explicitly appears in this book. It is now generally agreed that the Milanion exemplum derives from Gallus's work or at least Vergil's representation of it.[55] Propertius, thus, uses this exemplum both to acknowledge his literary debt and to establish his own originality (Ross 1975: 65). He is a poet in the line of Gallus, but Gallus himself is problematized throughout Propertius's corpus. Indeed, collocating Gallus and Tullus presages the articulation of the conflictual relation between traditional Roman ideology and the elegiac genre: poems 1–14 articulate this in the alternating sequence of elegies dedicated to Tullus, Gallus, Ponticus, and Bassus. By the same token, the values for which Tullus is the metonym and Ponticus the poetic representative are traditionally depicted as *durus* and gendered masculine, while elegy is *mollis* and effeminate. Nonetheless, in each case elegy is shown to be the master genre that either subjects its competitors or establishes a homology with them through the deployment of topoi such as *militia amoris*.

Poems 1.4 and 1.5 follow the pattern already outlined in 1.1. On the one hand, they articulate a relation between competing male values and their associated poetic genres through the figure of Cynthia (Sharrock 2000: 270). On the other, they deploy this discourse within a complex weave of inter- and intratextual homoerotic relations and inverted gender polarities. Poem 1.4 is addressed to Bassus, an iambic poet. Iambic, as exemplified in the works of Archilochus, Hipponax, Catullus's polymetrics, and Horace's *Epodes*, was an invective genre that dealt with the seamier side of life. As one of the lower forms, it was associated with elegy, and in Greek practice it was spoken or chanted, like elegy, as opposed to the sung poetry of lyric (Nagy 1990: 19–26, 29, 53–55, 363; Cairns 1983a: 81–82; Hodge and Buttimore 1977: 103). Thus, when Propertius presents Bassus trying to lure him away from Cynthia by praising the beauty of women of easy virtue (Enk 1946: 49; Rothstein 1979: 1.85), this is a recognizable iambic pose that can be read as Bassus claiming the superiority of his own poetic genre to elegy/Cynthia (Hodge and Buttimore 1977: 100–101). Propertius responds by telling Bassus that he should cease and desist or Cynthia will so blacken his name that he will be welcome at no girl's door. Cynthia will be transformed into an iambist whose invective will reduce Bassus to the archetypal position of the elegiac lover, the *exclusus amator*, and elegy will show that it can beat iambic at its own game (Fedeli 1983: 1876; Hodge and Buttimore 1977: 103; Suits 1976: 88–90; Rothstein 1979: 1.88).

Poem 1.5 is widely recognized as the companion piece to 1.4 (Fedeli 1983: 1878; Hodge and Buttimore 1977: 100; Richardson 1977: 158; Courtney 1968: 251–52). Francis Cairns (1983a: 62–77) has demonstrated exhaustively that the two poems correspond to one another in numerous ways both thematically and structurally, as well as through direct echoes. In fact, there seems to have been a deliberate conflation between the addressees. Poem 1.5's topos would be appropriate to Bassus and to Propertius's warnings to him—Callimachus in his *Iamboi* had already treated the topic of the friendly rival for one's beloved. Nor does Propertius immediately inform the reader that he has switched addressees—the name Gallus is deferred to the last line of poem 1.5. Likewise, *invidia*, the rival's motivation as given in the first word of the first line, was a common topic of iambic poetry (Fedeli 1983: 1878; Cairns

1983a: 81, 96). Thus, the poems as well as their addressees are cast as mirror images. As Cairns has argued, these parallels only make sense insofar as we see the Gallus of 1.5 as a rival poet like Bassus: but the Gallus of 1.5 (like Propertius) desires only Cynthia, where Bassus has urged Propertius to play the field. The symmetry of Gallus's desire with Propertius's, and its contrast with Bassus's, implies that Gallus is also an elegist. Therefore the pairing of 1.4 and 1.5 presents independent confirmation that the erotic Gallus of the *Monobiblos* was intended to evoke Cornelius Gallus in the reader's mind (Cairns 1983a: 84). Where 1.4 presents the triumph of Cynthia over her rivals, 1.5 presents Propertius's competition for the possession of the crown of elegy with Gallus himself (Oliensis 1997: 159; King 1980b: 219).

We have seen this theme of friendly erotic rivalry with a poetic subtext in 1.10 and 1.13's reworking of Catullus 50, and the same intertextual relation has been noted in 1.5 (Oliensis 1997: 159). Here too the homosocial bond becomes almost explicitly *hom(m)osexuel* as the two lovers are pictured in a mutual embrace sharing the same beloved and trading "tears" or elegiac poems with one another: "sed pariter miseri socio cogemur amore / alter in alterius mutua flere sinu" (but equally miserable we shall be forced by a common love to each weep on the breast of the other; 1.5.29–30). The metathesis whereby Propertius has been substituted for Cynthia in Gallus's embrace is striking (Hodge and Buttimore 1977: 108–9). Butler and Barber (1969: ad loc.), moreover, note the presence of an important intertext, epigram 92 of Meleager, that recapitulates the very same scenario envisioned from an explicitly homoerotic angle. This use of Meleager corresponds to that found in the opening of 1.1.

One last parallel between 1.4 and 1.5 needs to be discussed: their common Catullan intertexts. First, on a thematic level, Fedeli notes that both poems examine the topic of *fides* betrayed in the context of failed *amicitia* and amorous betrayal. He cites specific parallels with epigrams 77 against Rufus and 91 against Gellius (1983: 1876). However, the Catullan subtext goes much deeper and is more specific. The phrase "non impune feres" (you will not get away with it) at 1.4.17 is a direct quote from Catullus 78b.3.[56] The phrase is admittedly not uncommon as Richardson (1977: ad loc.) observes—while nonetheless noting the parallel—but it is unexampled elsewhere in elegiac couplets, let alone in couplets written with clear iambic intent:

> sed nunc id doleo, quod purae pura puellae
>   suavia comminxit spurca saliva tua.
> verum id non impune feres, nam te omnia saecla
>   noscent et, qui sis, fama loquetur anus.
> (78b.1–4)

But now I am pained at this, that your foul spit has polluted the pure kisses
of a pure girl. But you won't get away with it: for all the ages will know you
and old lady fame will say what you are.

The Catullan and Propertian contexts here are identical. Propertius
threatens Bassus the iambist with everlasting infamy from Cynthia's in-
vective, while Catullus actually performs the invective and forecasts the
same fate for the target of his abuse. The most interesting point for our
argument, however, is the distinct possibility that Catullus's target is also
either named Gallus or poetically associated with a Gallus.

Many modern editions print 78b as a separate fragment from poem 78
(Pöschl 1983; Quinn: 1973; Mynors 1958), but the relation between the
two is uncertain. There may simply be a lacuna. Poem 78 is an invective
elegy addressed to a Gallus accused of arranging a sexual liaison between
one of his brother's wives and another's son.[57] Poem 78b is also an invec-
tive on sexual impropriety, and so it is entirely possible that we are dealing
with a later part of the same poem. If 78b is also addressed to Gallus, the
numerous parallels between 1.4 and 1.5 already remarked are augmented
by this intertextual resonance. But even if 78b is not addressed to Gallus,
then it like Propertius 1.4 is an iambicizing poem written in elegiac cou-
plets immediately next to a poem addressed to a Gallus. Propertius 1.5 is
a poem addressed to Gallus immediately following an iambicizing poem
written in elegiac couplets.[58]

Verbal echoes match the structural mirroring between the two corpora:
1.5 ends with the phrase, "non *impune* illa rogata venit" (that girl when
asked does not come without you paying the price). Cairns (1983a: 77)
has noted the parallel with 1.4.17. Camps (ad loc.) and Rothstein (ad
loc.), however, give another Catullan parallel as well, 99.3, "verum id
non impune tuli" (but I did not get away with it). Again the context is
that of kisses and sexual misconduct, but this is a pederastic poem on
Catullus stealing kisses from Juventius. Thus once more—as throughout
the Gallus poems—we have Propertius substituting a heteroerotic context
for a homoerotic one, but with both inscriptions of the palimpsest still
visible to the discerning reader.

To sum up, what we have is two poems in Propertius, 1.4 and 1.5, that
constitute a pair. Each of them portrays recognizably Catullan themes on
the importance of *fides* in the context of *amor* and *amicitia*. The first is
an elegiac poem on iambic themes and the second a poem that, while
recalling iambic themes, addresses itself to the question of elegiac rivalry
with Gallus. That second poem has strong homoerotic overtones and
shows itself in part to be a reworking of Catullus 50, an important in-
tertext for the later Gallus poems. The couplet that most clearly recalls
Catullus 50 also imitates a homoerotic epigram by Meleager, now used

to describe the relationship between Propertius and Gallus in relation to Cynthia. The opening of Propertius 1.1 featured a similar use of an epigram by Meleager in a context that also recalled Catullus. Finally, poem 1.4 contains an allusion to a Catullus poem that is either about someone named Gallus or directly next to a poem on someone named Gallus. The line containing this allusion is echoed in poem 1.5 in the couplet (1.5.31–32) immediately following the evocation of Catullus 50 and the pederastic epigram of Meleager (1.5.29–30). This is the first time Gallus is named in the poem or the collection. The same passage to which poem 1.4 alludes and that 1.5 recalls has a further echo in the Catullan corpus at 99.3 where the kisses of the pure girl that the *spurca saliva* pollutes in 78b become those stolen by Catullus from Juventius, who in turn seeks to wash off the *spurca saliva* of the poet (99.10). The systematic responsion of names, themes, and intertexts between the poems is too great and too finely woven to have occurred by chance. Moreover, it is at one with the pattern of pederastic substitution and *hom(m)osexuel* longing that we have seen throughout the *Monobiblos*.

CONCLUSION

The graves of Perusia haunt the *Monobiblos*. They and the poems on them are so distant from Cynthia's erotic world that scholars have either seen poems 1.21–22 as the late additions of an overzealous editor or as a final coda completely separate from the main body of the work. This chapter, however, has shown an intimate relation between Cynthia and those graves. This is not to deny that these final poems come as something of a non sequitur, but rather to see that non sequitur, that moment of nonsense, as ultimately related to the figure of Cynthia: for, it is in the space between the erotic world of Cynthia and the dead of Perusia that the figure of pederasty emerges. Pederasty, in turn, is associated with Gallus, but the Gallus of the *Monobiblos* is irremediably divided between the erotic Gallus of poems 1.1–20 and the dying Gallus of 1.21–22. The moment of their suture, the hinge point between the erotic Gallus and the Gallus *militaris*, is precisely marked by poem 1.20, the one poem that almost all agree is directly derived from and alludes to Gallus the poet, and the one poem in which the homoerotic intertexts of 1.1, 1.4, 1.5, 1.10, and 1.13 become explicit in the figure of Hylas. It is also the sole erotic elegy in the collection not to feature Cynthia.

These two Galluses, split along the fault lines marked by the graves of Perusia, are in turn doubled by the competing figures of Gallus and Tullus within the body of the *Monobiblos*. They, in turn, also recall the lost Gallus of the papyrus fragments, a figure alluded to in the Milanion simile of 1.1, itself addressed to Tullus. This historical Gallus is retrospectively transformed into an ideal image capable of uniting the political and the poetic, the masculine and the feminine, the Imaginary and the Symbolic sides of Roman manhood (*virtus*) into a lost image of wholeness—a moment of captivating mirroring such as that experienced by Hylas just before the nymphs drag him beneath the water. Gallus and Tullus, thus, frame the *Monobiblos*, appearing in its first and last poems and defining the homosocial space in which the anomalous figure of Cynthia circulates.

Cynthia, in turn, represents the return of the Real, the indefinable moment whose very inconsistencies signify both the split within the Propertian poetic subject and that between it and the larger Symbolic community. She is also the moment that covers over that split, that allows exchange to occur. Thus, Cynthia's essence is precisely her circulation between men, and the space within which she circulates is the gap between the old and the new orders marked by the bleaching bones on the hills outside Perusia. She is both a substitute for Hylas and one of the nymphs who take him away. She figures elegy as both an alienated desire, a symptom, and a potential means of communication.

Chapter Four

"HE DO THE POLICE IN DIFFERENT VOICES": THE TIBULLAN DREAM TEXT

Das ländliche Existenz ist bisher nur ein Teil seines
Daseins, sie stellt das Element einer Spaltung dar. Sie ist
nicht in seinen vollen Lebenskreis "integriert."[1]
—Wimmel 1976: 33

Il motivo principale del canto si annunzia da principio
in una forma generale, che è come il preludio della
sinfonia; poi si perde nell'ondeggiare dei pensieri e dei
sentimenti, delle immagini e delle visioni nuove.[2]
—Riposati 1945: 169

THIS CHAPTER argues that Tibullus's poems are best read as complex, multivoiced, dream texts that construct a world at once idyllic and nightmarish. It is a world that modulates, at times almost imperceptibly, between images of the poet-subject now as humble farmer, now urbane poet, now *exclusus amator*, now fever-wracked soldier, now loyal *cliens*, now moralizing social critic, now *praeceptor amoris*, now pederast spurned (Fineberg 1991: 24). Nor is this polyphonic quality of Tibullan verse simply a function of the variety of poems found in the corpus, for even within a single poem the poet often seems not a unified subject but rather, in W. R. Johnson's words, "a sheer discontinuum, fragmentations of self and work and love, [a series of] multiple and mutually exacerbating conflicts" (1990: 108). This inconstant quality of Tibullan verse and the Tibullan subject has presented many problems for the poet's modern readers and can be seen as one factor in his relatively low standing vis-à-vis his better loved peers, Ovid and Propertius (Fineberg 1991: 156). As we shall see, however, from the perspective of the dream text—as defined by Freud and Lacan—the conflicts that arise between such competing voices are to be treated neither as problems to be solved by sublimating them to a higher level of hermeneutic abstraction on which their seeming oppositions can be conjured away,[3] nor as mere aesthetic blemishes (Cairns 1979a: 1–5) to be castigated or removed by the blunt instrument of textual criticism.[4] Rather, such moments of contradiction in the text of Tibullus are best treated as symptoms that point to the traumatic irruption of the "Real" into the ordered realm of language and the Symbolic (Jameson 1981; Miller 1995). In Micaela Janan's terms, "Traumas are of the Real: they give rise to significations in symptoms, dreams, parapraxes, and so on, but are not themselves signifiable" (Janan 1994: 17, as well as 44; and Žižek 1991: 30, 36, 104–5). From such a perspective, I argue that interpretive dilemmas on the level of the text, when there is no evidence of manuscript corruption—for example, metrical irregularities, contradictory readings among otherwise reliable texts, or linguistic impossibilities—are most productively read as indexes of conflict in the mute world beyond its borders. Thus, by examining Tibullus's texts from the combined perspectives of its complex interplay of conflicting poetic voices; the Freudian interpretation of dreams; Lacan's concepts of the Imaginary, Symbolic, and Real; and the context of the unsettled world of the early principate, we shall see how the poet creates a multileveled text that defies linear interpretation even as it manifests what Jameson would term the Augustan "political unconscious."

POUND, ELIOT, AND TIBULLUS

My title for this chapter comes from the original appellation Eliot gave the *Wasteland*, before it was pared down to its present angular and asymmetrical form by the modernist representative of "those who prefer Propertius," Ezra Pound.[5] It was Pound's view that "Eliot's style throve on terseness, twists, ellipses, and died in explicitness," and he pursued his editing with this in mind (Bedient 1986: 158). The comparison of Eliot's poem to Tibullus's corpus is apt on several counts. First, in the original version of the *Wasteland*, Eliot like Tibullus allows images and voices to succeed one another in an often baffling fashion that eschews clearly delineated transitions. The texts of both poets contain less a narrative of discrete acts than a series of intertwined associations, images, and echoes (Veyne 1988: 36; Fineberg 1991: 155–56). In both texts, multiple voices and intonations arise within a poem, each of which is imagined as emanating from, or referring to, a single but hardly unified psyche that both is and is not the poet. Thus in Eliot all the speaking parts are held together by the fiction that the voice is that of Tiresias, the unifying consciousness, or unconscious, that holds this hallucinatory internal dialogue together. By the same token, as Lyne notes, for Tibullus "the poem's unity (if that is the word) is" not dramatic, thematic, or modal, but "psychological."[6]

Eliot's title is taken from a line in Dickens's *Our Mutual Friend* (bk. 1, ch. 16) that refers to the talent of a rustic boy named Sloppy for doing dramatic readings of the newspaper. Its intertextual status serves two functions. On the one hand, it points to a preexisting literary tradition that, at least in Eliot's and Pound's eyes, can only be recalled through nostalgia, since in the avant-garde literary salons of the early twentieth century its Dickensian realism would have seemed rustic and quaint. On the other, Eliot's use of this literary allusion reveals a sophisticated self-consciousness of literary tradition quite at odds with the apparent homeliness of Dickens's style.

Tibullus too engages in this mixture of nostalgia and high literary sophistication. On the one hand, he expresses a consistent desire to return to the simple world of the traditional Roman farmer with his homely deities and quaint rites. He wishes to become a *rusticus* (1.1.8), a country bumpkin—the embodiment of everything opposed to neoteric *urbanitas*[7]—a self-identified boor unwelcome in the sophisticated world of Messalla's literary salon (Lyne 1980: 153; Lee 1974: 107; Bright 1978: 193). On the other, he expresses this wish in an impeccable Hellenistic style (Putnam 1973: 9; Cairns 1979a: 6), with an exemplary command of the metrical nuances of the elegiac couplet (Riposati 1945: 183–88), and numerous knowing, but veiled, allusions to Horace (Lee 1974: 98, 101–2; Wimmel 1976: 23; Leach 1978), Vergil (Lee 1974: 100–101; Bright 1978: 11; Leach 1978), and the Alexandrian personification of literary sophistication, Callimachus (Bright 1978: 70, 229, 239; Luck 1960: 86–87, 91). Indeed, the entire desire for rustic poverty can itself be read as a Hellenistic literary topos, signifying the refined or "slender style" of composition favored by the Alexandrians, as opposed to what they saw as the grand and often "flatulent style of epic" (Cairns 1979a: 20–21). Tibullan *rusticitas* is, then, a form of *urbanitas*. Like Eliot's use of Dickens, it represents sophistication raised to the second power.

Telling in this regard are Slavoj Žižek's remarks on Dickens's depiction of the poor, which apply equally to the Roman mythologization of the farmer in the first century B.C.E. It is to this myth that Tibullus alludes and to which most Augustan writers, with the notable exceptions of Propertius and Ovid, pay homage.

> At the opposite extreme [from Charlie Chaplin] we find the Dickensian admiration of the "good common people," the Imaginary identification with their poor but happy, close, unspoiled world, free of the cruel struggle for power and money. But (and therein lies the falsity of Dickens) from where is the Dickensian gaze peering at "the good common people' so that they appear likable; from where if not from the point of view of the corrupted world of power and money? We perceive the same gap in the Brueghel's [sic] late idyllic paintings. . . . Their gaze is . . . the external gaze of the aristocracy on the peasant's idyll, not the gaze of the peasants upon themselves. (Žižek 1989: 107)

Tibullus, through his ironic embedding of the aristocratic vision of the agricultural past in both an elaborate Hellenistic poetic structure and a series of topoi that we shall be examining later (e.g., wealth, warfare, love in the city, Messalla's political achievements), deconstructs, if not actively demystifies, the power of that patrician gaze. Similarly, Eliot's invocation of Dickens both recalls and offers a critique of the great Victorian's empathetic condescension.

At the same time, Eliot's use of the third person in the original title creates a distance between the speaker and the poet against which his use of the first-person singular in the text of the poem mitigates. An analogous modus operandi is found in Tibullus, who, while he does not indicate a separate speaker from himself, maintains an ironic distance from the ego of the poems that, as Veyne (1988: 37) notes, is consistently underlined by the subtle humor that marks so much of book 1. The stage on which the Tibullan ego performs is, in fact, an absurdist theater of the soul that precludes complete identification between poet and speaker because of the latter's studied incoherence of self-presentation.

Finally, Eliot's notion of the "police" effectively introduces the realm of politics and ideological coercion into what might otherwise be construed as a liberal, pluralist consciousness. The police signify not only the boundaries of law that place a limit on our desires but the power through which those boundaries are guaranteed. The fundamental conflict between an unfulfilled desire for cultural, personal, and/or amorous plenitude and the realm of limit and necessity is in fact a constitutive principle in both of these texts. Indeed, what I want to contend is that it is the intersection between these various, incompatible voices that constitutes the space of Tibullan consciousness and, ultimately, points to that necessary realm of the Real, which is by nature beyond all signifying processes and so can only be indicated by a breakdown in signification. The difficulty in determining the relation between these voices in any single poem by Tibullus is great. That difficulty is compounded when the reader moves to the collection as a whole. Questions of order and unity then loom larger. Should each poem's series of associations be interpreted as a unified whole that only relates to other poems in the collection as one totality to another, or can groups of images or verbal themes (e.g., the golden age, Messalla, the journey, farming, the lover at the door) be detached from their immediate contexts and directly compared to one another? This is not a simple question.

Take the example of wealth, one of the more prominent motifs in the collection. *Divitiae* is the first word of the first poem and thus following ancient practice could have served as the title of the book. As a theme in poem 1.1, it is systematically contrasted with an agricultural poverty (*paupertas* 1.1.5) that recalls the traditional values of the Roman farmer and is replete with references to the homely rituals of the countryside (Bright 1978: 9). Wealth is also identified with the notion of martial conquest and the terrors of war (1.1.3–4). Thus in 1.1, *divitiae*, on a first reading, seems to function more as a moral than a purely pragmatic value. The issue is what wealth means, given its association with violence and conquest (*militia*)—the source of most of the great fortunes of the first and second centuries B.C.E. —rather than what wealth can do (Gaisser 1983: 66–67).

At first 1.1's concern with the topic of wealth seems an isolated instance in the corpus. The terms *divitiae, dives*, or *munus* do not occur in poems 1.2, and 1.3, which do, however, continue the first poem's examination of the relationship between love and soldiery. Yet the topic of wealth does recur. In poem 1.4, the ability of *divitiae* to buy love through the offering of presents is a central concern.[8] Priapus, the poem's main speaker, says that wealth gives the *dives amator* (wealthy lover) an unfair advantage over the poor poet:

> heu male nunc artes miseras haec saecula tractant:
> iam tener adsueuit munera velle puer.
> at tua, qui venerem docuisti vendere primus,
> quisquis es, infelix urgeat ossa lapis.
> (1.4.57–60)

> Oh now these times vilely traffic in wretched arts:
> now the tender boy is accustomed to want gifts.
> But you who first taught them to sell love, whoever you are,
> may an unlucky gravestone press upon on your bones.

In this poem, although the curse lends the passage a moralizing tone, the real issue is practical: rich guys get all the boys. Thus 1.4's treatment of wealth seems at odds with 1.1's and could lead the reader to suspect another, less rarefied, agenda beneath the first poem's moralizing posture. However, there are difficulties with such a neat reversal. It takes into account neither the structural integrity of poem 1 and the complex set of relations in which wealth finds itself embedded in that text, nor the nature of 1.4. Rather it reads thematically across the corpus without regard to the specific contexts of these themes' enunciations and the dialogic relations that ensue.

Poem 1.4 is in many ways atypical of the Tibullan collection to this point. First, the speaker is not Tibullus himself but Priapus. Second, Tibullus's love object has hitherto been Delia, but in 1.4, his desire has shifted into a pederastic mode, and he is "tortured" by his love for Marathus (1.4.81). The unique status of the poem is widely granted: in studies of the arrangement of book 1, poem 1.4 is generally identified as one of two "genre" poems (the other being 1.7) that serve to mark the major divisions in the two series of love poems, those devoted to Delia (1.1, 1.2, 1.3, 1.5, and 1.6) and those to Marathus (1.8 and 1.9).[9] Hence, by virtue of its very eccentricity, 1.4 does not directly call into question the authenticity of 1.1's opposition to wealth on moral grounds. The two poems' structures are so heterogeneous that neither one by itself is capable of fully undercutting the other. But, insofar as we accept the fact that 1.4 plays a key role in dividing the major sequences of the first book into smaller, more coherent units, then the poem's status as a mediating link between 1.3 and 1.5 becomes all the more important (Leach 1978: 83).[10] Consequently, it cannot be insignificant that although wealth is not discussed in poems 1.2 and 1.3, in 1.5, immediately after Priapus has introduced the theme of gifts, Tibullus is unable to gain access to his beloved because she is locked inside her house with her *dives amator* (1.5.47). Her door, he confesses, is to be struck only by one whose hand is full of money (1.5.68).

As in 1.4, money is necessary if love is to be found. One may hate money in 1.4 and 1.5, but the reasons are a good deal less high-minded than those in 1.1. Poem 1.5, as a Delia poem, moreover, is less eccentric to the concerns of 1.1 than 1.4, and so has greater power to subvert its ethical valorization of poverty. The question is complicated further when this same link between money and access to love is taken up in 1.9, but now the moral objection is married to the practical so that the poet declares, this time in relation to Marathus, "divitiis captus siquis violavit amorem" (anyone captured by riches has trampled on love; 1.9.19) (Wimmel 1976: 3). The line can be read two ways, either as a cynical manipulation of the moral topos for the purpose of trying to persuade Marathus that he should leave his own *dives amator*, or as a genuine expression of the desire for an emotional, or at least erotic, relationship that transcends the demands of mere exchange. Finally, the return to the moral realm in which wealth is condemned because of its relation to violence, to *militia*, is completed in 1.10.29, "*alius* sit fortis in armis" (Let *another* be brave in arms), which, as Wimmel (1976: 3) sees, is an analog to 1.1.1's "Divitias *alius* fulvo sibi congerat auro" (Let *another* pile up riches in tawny gold).

How, then, are we to interpret the intersection of the seemingly incompatible voices in Tibullus's poems? And, more specifically, how does the treatment of wealth in the later poems of book 1 affect our understanding of it in 1.1? I would suggest a middle course. Recurrent images, when they appear in a collection, can be related to one another and can be seen as arising from a single (un)consciousness. Their specific meanings, however, are only ascertainable with reference to the actual contexts in which each of them appears. The hermeneutic relationship between individual examples of recurring thematic elements such as wealth is thus overdetermined by the material context of those elements' poetic form, that is, their appearance in a planned collection (Bakhtin 1986: 92). The Tibullan collection thus engenders a dialectic between the particular and the general that creates ever more complex sets of relations both within and between individual poems, interweaving the political, the personal, the ideological, and the poetic into a dream text in which the irrational whole is always more than the sum of its sensible parts. The concept of the dream is particularly important here, since, as Freud explains, dreams constitute fantasy wish fulfillments in which personal and political contradictions are temporarily overcome, or at least elided.

On a more concrete level, this means that the moral objections to wealth voiced in poem 1.1, even after the reader has seen 1.4, 1.5, and 1.9, cannot be read simply as mere rationalizations, projections of the poet's erotic *ressentiment* onto the realm of the ethical (Jameson 1981: 200–205). Rather what we must elucidate is the intersection of the cynical reduction of the moral to the material with the continuing existence of the moral even so: for, in addition to the structural integrity of 1.1 itself, and the consequent way in which wealth and other terms are woven into its specific structures of signification and thereby acquire contextually bound connotations, the objections to wealth in 1.1 and the poem's espousal of the traditions of the countryside are firmly rooted in the Roman ideology of the period. It is impossible to read this opening poem and not be reminded of both the traditional mythology of Rome—the city of small farmers whose greatness was bound to their simple piety (Cairns 1979a: 13–14; Edwards 1993: 149)—and of Augustus's attempt to appropriate this imagery for his own project of religious and ideological reconstruction (Edwards 1996: 49–50), an undertaking whose reflection and impetus can be seen in Vergil and Horace (Lee 1974: 101; Murgatroyd 1991: 49–50; Boyd 1984a: 274). As Lyne notes, Tibullus is in fact "re-deploying against the Roman establishment's thinking" its "own moral mythology" (1980: 155). Thus, although on one level Tibullus will tell us in 1.4, 1.5, and 1.9 that contempt for money and desire for the return of the old ways represents merely the *ressentiment* of those who wish to occupy the position of the wealthy—and, within the world of elegy, therefore to possess the boy or girl of their dreams—on another, he is articulating a genuine desire for a world before exchange, a dream of the time before *ressentiment*, the golden age. The cynical reading is fostered by a narrative strategy that develops and complicates various themes as the collection progresses, while constantly referring back to previous, more naive enunciations of them.[11] The reader is thus encouraged to practice a form of backward scanning even as she moves forward: from the perspective of poems 1.4, 1.5, and 1.9, 1.1's protestations smell of bad faith. However, within 1.1 itself this is not the case, and the one reading does not preclude the other. Indeed, one of the characteristics of Tibullus's poetry is the way the individual, idyllic passage transcends its ironic frame. Thus 1.5's dream of Delia as the mistress on Tibullus's farm serving Messalla the finest fruits of their labor is admitted to be a fantasy, and yet it is one of the most powerful and lasting images of the poem.

Tibullus therefore, like Eliot, forces us to deal both with the individual passage on its own terms and in its relation to the often dissident passages surrounding it. His is a poetry of aporia and contradiction in which logical and communal norms are often at odds with his Imaginary self-conceptions, with the way the poet envisions himself (Kennedy 1993: 20; Bright 1978: 140–41). In some poems, such as 1.2, even the setting is self-contradictory, the position of the speaking subject impossible to determine. When the poem opens, the poet is calling for more wine and seems to be in a private or sympotic setting (Lyne 1980: 180; Bright 1978: 137; Ponchont 1967: 15). Later in the same poem, he appears to be portrayed as the *exclusus amator* standing before his lover's door.[12] From a logical point of view, both cannot obtain. He must be either in the bar or at the door. Consequently, the partisans of each view line up the reasons why their opponents' reading could not be true and why the imagery of either the symposium or the paraclausithyron must be an illusion. Yet clearly the question is not which context is correct, but what does it mean for Tibullus to create poetry consistently capable of being read in such contradictory ways (Kennedy 1993: 18; Konstan 1995: 179; Lee-Stecum 1998: 72–73). Why does he go to such lengths to subvert his own dreams, producing self-canceling images of desire whose consummation can never be realized? Elder sums up the significance of this pattern of self-subversion nicely when he writes:

> The instinct to "undercut" his idyll must originate in large part from life at Rome as he found it. That life drove him to his dreams, and that same life made him masochistically snap the dream-thread. Both instincts reflect the urge he must have felt somehow to try to come to a conscious definition of what he was and should be in his actual circumstances, that is, these instincts are intimately connected with the necessity he felt for making judgements upon himself in terms of the reality of life in Rome. To say that he did not succeed is virtually to say that we have his poems about his unresolved problem. (Elder 1962: 84–85)

In cases such as this, to insist on univocal meaning is to apply a standard of rationality as alien to Tibullus's text and its time as it would be to Eliot's and his.

My reasons for beginning with an analogical and comparative approach to Tibullus's poetry via Eliot, however, go well beyond the merely illustrative and heuristic value that a recognition of parallels between the texts implies and aims directly at the rehabilitation of Tibullus's poetry in the eyes of modern scholarship. The poetry of Propertius today enjoys a prestige that far surpasses that of his contemporary, Tibullus, although just the opposite was true in Rome (Cairns 1979a: 1–5; Fineberg 1991: 3). Indeed, Tibullus continued to be the favorite until the early decades of the twentieth century. The fact that the change in the relative estimation of these two poets coincides with the beginning of modernism is not, I would submit, an accident. As the aesthetic paradigms that were dominant in western Europe and the United States shifted, so did the paradigms through which ancient poetry was read. Symptomatic of this shift is the interest shown by Ezra Pound in the poetry of Propertius. Other artists and critics followed his lead, resulting in a body of scholarship including but not limited to J. P. Sullivan's book on Pound's *Homage to Sextus Propertius*, D. Thomas Benediktson's work, *Propertius: Modernist Poet of Antiquity* (which uses Pound's aesthetic categories to read Propertius), and more indirectly to W. R. Johnson's frequent use of the term "modernist" to discuss a variety of poetry written under the Augustan regime. The perceived analogy between the poetry of Propertius and the modernist work of Pound has had a significant positive impact on the way that Propertius is read and has resulted in a consequent devaluation of Tibullus (Fineberg 1991: ii). The ability, therefore, to offer similar analogies for Tibullus offers the hopes of being able to perform a comparable act of rehabilitation for him as well.

The new light postmodernism has shed on modernism itself also motivates my pursuit of this analogical level of analysis. The work of critics like Žižek has permitted us to pursue much more rigorous and analytical understandings of both modernism and postmodernism. Žižek argues that modernism differs from postmodernism not so much in form or content per se—let alone sheer chronological positioning—but in its strategy for addressing the *aporiai* that lie at the heart of each discourse. Žižek's contention is that modernism and postmodernism, as I would argue for Latin love elegy, both represent essentially schizoid modes of discourse that focus on the unbridgeable gap between the personal identifications of Lacan's Imaginary and the more social (and therefore rule-based norms) of the Symbolic. Each, moreover, makes the consciousness of that gap the site of the emergence of the poetic subject per se (Žižek 1991: 167–68; Janan 1994: 19, 35; Fineberg 1991: 9–10). From this perspective the voice of the poet, precisely in its often paradoxical and schizoid nature, functions as "the making present in the Real, the objectivization, the incarnation of the fact that, on the symbolizing level, something 'has not worked out,' in short, the objectivation-positivation of a *failed* symbolization" (Žižek 1991: 104, emphasis in original). The poetic voice is the voice of a gap and hence symptomatic of a shift in the Real as it relates to the Imaginary and the Symbolic. To that extent, it is the voice of History, as the inarticulate process of change that moves the earth beneath our feet.

The strategies of modernism and postmodernism (or of Propertius and Tibullus) for dealing with this absurd emergence of the Real at the heart of their respective discourses are, however, precisely opposite. Whereas modernism presents a lack at the heart of things and pursues a fragmentary or elliptical style (like Pound's or Eliot's in the revised *Wasteland*), designed to reveal that lack, postmodernism focuses on the positive presence of the nonsensical, on repetition. The repetitions and barely perceptible transitions of Philip Glass's or Steve Reich's minimalist music, for example, carry listeners effortlessly along until suddenly they realize they are some place very different from where they began, as opposed to Webern's or Schoenberg's modernist compositions that combine dissonance, an alien twelve-tone scale, and a closed formal structure. In a similar vein, one can contrast Tibullus's use of anaphora and the proverbial smoothness of his transitions,[13] to which the symphonic analogy has often been applied, and his diversity of themes,[14] with Propertius's notoriously elliptical style, syntactical irregularity, and unified construction (Lee 1974: 103; Cairns 1979a: 107; Elder 1962: 71–72). Rather than examining the lack at the heart of signification, according to Žižek, postmodernism as an artistic style looks at the abundance of the unintelligible. Modernism and postmodernism are not so much two different historical stages as two different views of the same phenomenon, two strategies of the schizoid (Myers 2001: 36). Žižek's postmodernism then, might be more properly termed the modernism of abundance and repetition, as opposed to the high modernism of concision and ellipsis. It is this latter style of modernism that, as Žižek correctly sees, provided the clearest stylistic precedents for the properly postmodern culture that would follow in its wake. Thus, whereas Pound may be taken as emblematic of the modernist, Žižek lists Kafka as his archetype for the "postmodernist"; I would add Eliot in his pre-Poundian mode (Žižek 1991: 145–46). Similarly, whereas Propertius is a modernist, Tibullus, whose dreamlike continuities are often much maligned, stands as the Kafkaesque or early-Eliotic "postmodernist." As such, the Tibullan style may well be more congenial to today's tastes than it was to the high, Poundian modernism that dominated the first three quarters of the twentieth century.

THE DREAM TEXT AS A FORMAL CONCEPT

With these observations in mind, I would argue that Tibullus's poems are best examined in the terms Freud proposes for the interpretation of dreams, rather than as dramatic narratives or the recountings of actual events (Lyne 1980: 178–79; Cairns 1979a: 24). Indeed, one of the commonplaces of Tibullan criticism is the dreamlike quality of his text, a view that normally goes hand in hand with the devaluation of his poetry as overly smooth or soft, and lacking the formal integrity, imaginative leaps, and sharp juxtapositions that characterize Propertius (Fineberg 1991: 59, 155–56; Veyne 1988: 36; Lyne 1980: 178; Dunlop 1972: 44–49). One commentator, as Bright notes, has gone so far as attributing Tibullus's style to a brain abnormality (1978: 9–10, citing J. van Wageningen, "Tibulls sogennante Träumereien," *NJA* [1913]: 350–55). Even the poet's supporters often damn him with faint praise. Thus Smith writes, "He is not man of brilliant passages" (1964: 68), while Putnam and Lyne characterize his poetry as "smooth" and "drifting" (Putnam 1973: 6–7, 11–12; Lyne 1980: 181–83). The fact is that all agree, whether friend or foe, that Tibullus's poetry is highly internalized, nonlinear,[15] and often seems to move from one topic to the next "through the mere associations of ideas and words" (Veyne 1988: 36). Thus Johnson speaks of the corpus as "a fever's dream," an "achronological, spiritual, autobiographical collection" (1990: 102–3), while Veyne writes that "Tibullus's transitions, unpredictable by nature of their intended banality and, sometimes, incongruity, prohibit the reader from assuming that the poem has a subject. . . . this theater is a dream theater" (1988: 41–43). Likewise, Kennedy observes that in Tibullus, fantasy not only cannot be separated from reality but also actively constitutes it. He continues, "These poems have often been dismissed as disorganized concatenations of motifs, and, although this is a view which has become increasingly difficult to defend, they are tantalizingly elusive" (1993: 13–17). Bright argues, "The distinction between past, present and future, as between reality and fantasy, is never clear in Tibullus" (1978: 59; cf. Riposati 1945: 93–94). Indeed, one finds in Tibullus's poems no terra firma, no Archimedean point from which to distinguish subject from object, reality from whim, or margin from center. Leach notes that Tibullus's "lack of a single emotional obsession for a common theme has convinced readers" that the collection is "no more than a random grouping of the poet's favorite pieces" without any overarching unity (1980a: 80). Likewise, Van Nortwick sees this same indefiniteness of theme as evidence of Tibullus's awareness "of the fragility of his dream, and of the paradoxes that lay at the center of that dream" (1990: 122–23).

This last observation is acute. It implies that the traditional image of Tibullus, the dreamy dilettante, may be made to yield a more fertile hermeneutic model if the insight on which it is based—the oneiric quality of Tibullan verse—can be purged of its ideological and historical limitations. The model of the dream, rather than signifying merely the lack of a clear outline, or a lazy drifting from topic to topic, may instead be read as a measure of the profound emotional complexity of these poems, the subtle and multiple levels of determination that shape their content, and their continuing engagement with the contradictory, the marginal, and the non-linear. They are indeed wish fulfillments whose multiple and mutually exclusive determinants, such as poem 1.1's unprecedented—and logically impossible—combination of the rural idyll with the urban paraclausithyron (Van Nortwick 1990: 121; Gaisser 1983: 72; Leach 1980a: 86; Cairns 1979a: 23), both undercut each other's claims to an authentic existence outside the dream world, while each reinforces the other's status as the object of an impossible desire. These texts are less a series of coherent rhetorical arguments in the manner of Ovid[16] (Luck 1960: 74; Riposati 1945: 168), than complex tissues of related, interwoven, and sometimes contradictory themes.

The Freudian model of interpretation is appropriate in part because it begins by allowing us to see condensation and displacement, or metaphor and metonymy in Lacan's linguistic reading of Freud (Janan 1994: 43; Fineberg 1991: 14–15, 118–19, 158; Barthes 1967: 88), as the fundamental axes along which texts are constituted. By refusing what Kennedy has labeled the "rhetoric of realism," the Freudian model can approach these artifacts on their own terms, as structures of signification rather than as documents whose meanings must conform to an ideology of univocal reference and "human" experience (at least so long as the latter is regarded as a self-evident and unproblematic term). From the perspective of the interpretation of dreams, recurring analogous images and terms are progressively regrouped into ever larger paradigms of substitution (i.e., metaphor), where lion stands for Achilles or cigar for phallus. One signifier can be substituted for another, and hence in Freud's terms an operation of condensation has taken place, as one signifier now stands for two. Naturally this operation can be, and is, extended to encompass more than two terms at a time. Given the right context, its scope is theoretically infinite. At the same time, these signifiers are also made to add ever new levels of individual signification as they are scattered across the discursive field delimited by the corpus (i.e., metonymy). They are thus moved from their "original" contexts to new positions in the text. In each new position, they acquire new connotations even as they bring with them the marks of their previous contexts. They are then, in Freud's terms, displaced (Miller 1995: 228).

The work of dream interpretation itself consists in discovering the mediating links (both metaphoric and metonymic) that allow often disparate, latent thoughts to be associated with a single set of manifest materials: contradictions from this perspective are not to be resolved but exfoliated (Freud 1952: 27–38). As we shall see in the case of Tibullus, images such as the city, the countryside, and military life and words such as *iners* and *decus* are susceptible to multiple and often contradictory interpretations that defy any univocal resolution by traditional philological means. The matrix out of which these conflicts arise can be provisionally sketched by examining the intersection of the following recurring motifs with special reference to their occurrence in 1.1: *amor, militia, rura*, Messalla, the golden age as an evocation of the Lacanian Imaginary, the world of property and exchange as an evocation of the Symbolic, and the castration of Uranus as the mythic point in time that marks the birth of Venus, and hence of the subject of desire.[17] Such an investigation, however, must ultimately lead beyond 1.1 to both book 1 and the Tibullan corpus as a whole.

MILITIA AND RURA: WHEN OPPOSITES ATTRACT

Julia Haig Gaisser (1983: 59) has shown that poem 1.1 consists of two separate sections. The first half of the poem is devoted to the contrast between *militia* and *rura* and the second to that between *militia* and *amor*. Similar analyses by Leach (1980a) and Boyd (1984a) have noted how this basic set of contrasts structures the collection as a whole. Their analyses diverge, though, when they try to decide when and if these oppositions are resolved. Where Leach and Boyd argue for their eventual resolution in 1.10, Gaisser (1983: 70–72) rejects this thesis. We shall return to the analysis of 1.10 at the end of this chapter. The problem, however, is in some ways a false one, because a close examination of the sections in which these terms are first introduced shows that the oppositions are in large part self-undermining, and the relations maintained between them are revealed as highly unstable (Lee-Stecum 1998: 33–34, 66–69). Consequently, the relationship of their individual elements to one another (*militia* versus *rura* and *militia* versus *amor*) can only be clarified by references to terms outside their initial binary oppositions.

To understand how this works in the case of *rura* and *militia*, we can begin by reading closely 1.1.1–6:

> Divitias alius *fulvo* sibi congerat *auro*
>   et teneat culti iugera multa soli,
> quem labor *adsiduus* vicino terreat hoste,
>   Martia cui somnos classica pulsa fugent:
> me mea *paupertas* vita traducat inerti,
>   dum meus *adsiduo luceat igne* focus.

> Let another pile up *riches* in *tawny gold*
>   and let another possess many acres of tilled soil
> whom *constant* struggle terrifies with the enemy nearby,
>   whose sleep Mars's trumpet blasts sets to flight:
> let my *modest means* lead me over to a life of inactivity,
>   while my hearth *shines with a constant fire*.

The first thing to be noted about this passage is that the opposition between *divitiae* and *paupertas*, which is initially set up on the logical or rhetorical level, is undermined on that of image and diction. As Putnam (1973: 50) notes, *divitiae* is itself cognate with the Greek *dios* and so anticipates *fulvus* and *aurum* later in the line. The luster of riches and gold is on one level, then, contrasted with the poet's avowed modesty of means in line 5, but at the same time made to reflect the gleaming (*luceat*) fire of line 6. This same combination of contrast and reflection can, in turn, be seen in the poet's use of the word *adsiduus*. In line 4, it modifies *labor* and is therefore part of the soldier's world of *militia*. In line 6, it modifies *ignis*, and so is part of the poet's world of ideal agricultural poverty. Moreover, as Cairns (1979a: 16–17) notes, *adsiduus* "was often etymologized so as to mean 'rich,'" thus associating it directly with line 1's *divitiae*, in both the cases of the farmer and the soldier.

In addition, *labor* itself is ambiguous. Within the world of Hellenistic poetics, it generally referred to the polished quality of a work that required much toil. As Cairns notes:

> Tibullus doubtless subscribed to this notion, but he goes out of his way to declare his life *iners* in 1.1.5. This self-description is related to his erotic persona, and specifically it reinforces the paradoxical conjunction he makes in 1.1 of his twin roles of lover and farmer. . . . The farmer was traditionally hardworking. Tibullus in 1.1 quite deliberately attributes *labor adsiduus* not to himself but to his antithesis, the soldier. (1979a: 3)

Through his repetition of the adjective *adsiduus*, Tibullus marks his conscious recognition that *labor* has been transferred from the farmer to the soldier to create his pastoral ideal. At the same time, his refusal of the attribute of being *laboriosus* (cf. Catullus 1) within the context of his own Hellenistic poetics can only be read as ironic, and hence as a qualified acceptance of the term as the necessary ground on which his pastoral fantasy of the rejection of *labor* can be erected. Thus, the opposition between farmers and soldiers in terms of *labor* is dependent on a preexisting poetic *labor* that creates the dream world in which this initial thematic antithesis can take place. That poetic *labor*, in turn, must be attributed to the poet whose persona is assuming the role of the *otiosus* farmer.

One might choose to argue that the verbal identity created between these two contrasting formulations of the greedy soldier and the contented farmer through the repetition of *adsiduus* serves merely as a rhetorical means to emphasize their substantive differences (Murgatroyd 1991: 52), or, following Postgate, as a measure of the poverty of Tibullan language (Postgate 1910: xxviii, 67), rather than as a means of denoting some more substantial identity.[18] Nevertheless, there are important reasons to reject such readings, for the contrast between the life of the soldier and that of the farmer is not as clear as it might seem. Tibullus is setting up the contrast and then subtly undermining it (Wimmel 1976: 8). Indeed, the opening couplet applies much better to the situation of a landed squire than to the average soldier. It is the picture of a well-off equestrian farmer, like Tibullus, who possesses "multa iugera." If we slow down the reading process in the manner of Stanley Fish's (1980: 164–84) examination of Milton's "When I consider how my light is spent," then "quem labor adsiduus" is most naturally taken as referring to the labor of farming, a confusion that is not obviated until we reach the word *terreat* in the second hemstitch. And while Tibullus downplays the amount of actual manual *labor*[19] he would have to perform as a farmer, he still imagines himself (*ipse*) planting vines (7), wielding a hoe (29), driving cattle (30), and carrying lost lambs back to their mothers (31–32), menial tasks that his use of the verb *pudet* (29) acknowledges to be unfit for a man of his social status (Lyne 1980: 157). Indeed, as Wimmel (1976: 28) notes, twice within the poem's opening panel's juxtaposing of *rura* and *militia*, the poet paints a picture of ideal pastoral *inertia* in one couplet and then proceeds to undermine it in the next. Thus in lines 5–6 he wishes for a life of inactivity before an unfailing fire, only to picture himself in the next couplet tending his own vines, while in lines 27–28 the poet avoids the heat of the summer sun, lying in the shade on the banks of a murmuring stream, but in the very next couplet pictures himself hoeing his fields and herding cattle.

In this light, whose life is more correctly characterized as one of *adsiduus labor*, the farmer's or the soldier's, is open to question, though from a coldly realistic perspective, in the context of the lives of the equestrian and senatorial landed gentry to which Tibullus and all the other major poets of the first century belonged, the point is moot.[20] When Cicero in the *De Officiis* (1.151) recommends farming as an appropriate career for the *vir bonus*, "he means running one or preferably more large farms, managing an estate on which the work would be done by tenant farmers or hired labourers or slaves" (Lee 1974: 100). Tibullus, the poet, does not intend to pick up the hoe himself. That would be shameful (*pudeat*, 1.1.29) (Veyne 1988: 103). Such labor is characteristic of slaves, not of freemen and certainly not of equestrians, those with the time and leisure to pursue such *artes liberales* as reading or writing poetry (Parkhurst 1995: 47; Ste. Croix 1981: 198–201; Syme 1960: 176). As Littlewood sums up, "The Augustan elegists were sophisticated *literati* who belonged to a still prosperous middle-class which enjoyed both the freedom to remain aloof from governmental and military responsibility and the stimulation of mutual intellectual intercourse" (1983: 2134). They were not manual laborers.

Tibullus in his guise as a farmer portrays himself, not as one who pursues a life appropriate to his actual station (*non pudet*, 1.1.74), but as a *servus* or little better. This is a complex move. First, in so doing he anticipates his own later portrayal as *servus amoris* (slave of love) (1.1.55–58), thereby establishing a continuity of humbleness or humiliation between the amorous and georgic portions of the poem.[21] This observation of a continuity between the scenes in which Tibullus pictures himself performing manual labor and the later scenes of amorous servitude is confirmed by certain stylistic observations made by Wimmel (1976: 40). In response to André's charge that Tibullus's use of the perfect active infinitive in lines 29–30, "nec tamen interdum pudeat *tenuisse* bidentem / aut stimulo tardos *increpuisse* boves" (even so may it not shame me in the meantime *to have held* a hoe / or *to have chided* slow cattle with the goad) was otiose (André 1965: 15), he notes that the use of the perfect active infinitive in place of the present was characteristic of love elegy's diction (cf. Smith 1964: 190–91). Thus, we would expect this passage to have an amorous cast, given its use of one of the genre's signature features. It does not, but the next example of this trope does, lines 45–46, "quam iuvat immites ventos audire cubantem / et dominam tenero *continuisse* sinu" (how happy it makes me lying in my bed to hear the pitiless winds / and *to have held* my mistress to my tender breast). Wimmel argues that these parallel grammatical features indicate a continuity of content between the two passages not otherwise immediately apparent. His case is strengthened by the citation of a similar set of passages from 1.4. There, in lines 47–48, perfect active infinitives are used to describe the kind of servile labors the lover should not be ashamed to undertake if he is to win the favors of his beloved. The description of those labors, however, contains nothing erotic per se. Then, in 1.4.56, the next occurrence of the perfect active infinitive, we see the fulfillment of the desires of the *servus amoris*, repeating the pattern found in 1.1. Wimmel concludes from this parallel that the labors undertaken by the poet in 1.1 are love offerings made to the beloved on the analogy of those in 1.4. I am unwilling to go that far, since no mention is made of Delia in the first half of 1.1, while 1.4 is erotically motivated from the beginning. Moreover, there is every indication that Delia is a thoroughly urban character who does not share Tibullus's agrarian dreams. Consequently, she would not be impressed by an offering of hard manual labor on the farm. Wimmel, however, is correct to see that in both 1.1 and 1.4 Tibullus uses a grammatical form, whose preciosity had become associated with love elegy, to underline the continuity between forms of labor conventionally considered servile and *servitium amoris*.

A second layer of complexity can be seen in the sheer paradox of Tibullus's portraying himself as a farmer whose actions are not characterized

by *adsiduus labor*, but who nonetheless performs manual toil unthinkable
for one of his station. At the same time, he is also described in the poem
as someone who opposes war and wealth, yet somehow also accepts them
as traditional Roman values. This self-portrait creates a subject position
that has no analogue within the available terms of Roman ideology. The
Tibullan speaker is neither farmer nor soldier, freeman nor slave, mer-
chant nor leisured man of *otium*. He is an anomaly that exists only in
poetry, which, in fact, is how Veyne (1988: 101) characterized the elegiac
lover in general. Yet where Veyne (1988: 30) sees the creation of such an
aporetical and oxymoronic figure as signifying that elegy is merely a semi-
otic game, I want to ask: Why this game now? What does the existence
of this game at this particular point in time, the beginning of the princi-
pate, the only time when elegiac discourse as an important literary genre
is possible in Rome, signify? Is not the very incoherence of this subject
position symptomatic of a crisis in Roman ideology, a crisis that we call
the collapse of the republic and the birth of the empire, and whose clear-
est, least mystified witness is the rewriting of what it means to be a free
Roman citizen (Fisher 1983: 1950–51)? The anomaly of the Tibullan per-
sona figures a gap between the Imaginary and the Symbolic through which
History, in the form of the unsignifiable Real, emerges into the text.

Tibullan poetic consciousness, I am arguing, is thus openly split in its
relations to Lacan's two major psychic registers. What this means can be
clarified by examining a passage in Žižek where the difference between
the Imaginary and the Symbolic has been neatly summarized:

> [T]o put it simply, Imaginary identification is identification with the image in
> which we appear likable to ourselves, with the image representing 'what we
> would like to be', and Symbolic identification, identification with the very
> place *from where* we are being observed, *from where* we look at ourselves so
> that we appear to ourselves likable, worthy of love. (Žižek 1989: 105, empha-
> sis in original)

The poet's Imaginary identification with the farmer or the lover is consis-
tently at odds with his Symbolic identification as an equestrian subject in
the Roman social order. Tibullus creates strong Imaginary identifications
with a world of ideal amatory and/or agricultural pleasance throughout
his poetry only to undercut them—as noted by Elder—when they come
into contact with the values and identifications out of which the Symbolic
constitutes our various realities.[22] This same split between Imaginary and
Symbolic can be seen in the earlier example of the theme of wealth. From
the perspective of the poet's Imaginary identifications, the world of ex-
change, which necessarily brings with it the realms of politics and *militia*
as the concomitants of Roman social order, can only be antithetical to his
utopian yearnings. *Divitiae* must, therefore, be morally condemned in an

effort to achieve Imaginary purity. But that condemnation, as the rest of the collection realizes, can only take place from within the Symbolic and its rule-based codes. Consequently, the moral revulsion against wealth, when translated into the exchange values of the Symbolic—as figured from the poet's own equestrian position—becomes the *ressentiment* of those who do not have wealth toward those who do. The two evaluations do not cancel each other out because they address different registers of existence from different positions. Rather they establish oppositions whose logical categories are consistently undermined. In the resulting moment of undecidablity, we encounter the Real in all its unassimilability to the world of sense. Indeed, it is precisely in the fact that the old paradigms are no longer able to make sense out of the raw data from which we construct our Imaginary identifications that the clearest record of a historical shift can be found.[23] The former cohesion, or at least semblance of cohesion, between circumstances, self, and sense has been lost.

The conflict between the Imaginary agrarian ideal and Symbolic "reality" manifests itself on many levels in the poetry of Tibullus. Certainly, the harshness of agricultural labor is made clear in 2.3.9–10, where the poet pictures himself laboring in the fields with sunburned limbs and ruptured blisters on his hands.[24] Moreover, poem 1.9, in a passage that has caused many critical debates, includes the farmer among those motivated by greed. On that score, the farmer, then, is indistinguishable from the soldier, described in the opening couplet, who would pile up tawny gold and hold vast acreages. The opposition between them would seem at least momentarily to have been elided. Indeed, Kennedy (1993: 14–15) suggests that the narrator of 1.1 is best understood *to be* a soldier, thus explaining the frequent use of the optative subjunctive[25] in regard to the activities he proposes to undertake on his ideal agrarian estate. Such a reading also would make better sense of 1.1's relation to 1.3, which opens with Tibullus on Corcyra, left behind after falling ill on a military mission with Messalla, and to 1.2's curse against anyone who would leave Delia behind to go on such a mission (cf. 1.1.65–66; Kennedy 1993: 20), a statement generally read as either an ironic recollection or anticipation of the journey undertaken in 1.3.

In addition, the heaps of fruit and the vats filled with new wine that Tibullus imagines on his farm in 1.1.9–10 recall that very desire for accumulation that he had ostensibly repudiated. Indeed, as Putnam points out, 1.1 has a circular structure, beginning with *divitiae* and ending with *dites* (1973: 50; Ponchont 1967: 8). Of course, the final line of the poem reads "dites despiciam despiciamque famem" (I shall despise wealth and I shall despise hunger), but the mirror structure of this pentameter, which reflects an equivalence of opposites, is predicated on the hexameter's evocation of "ego composito securus acervo" (I without a worry, since my own pile has been amassed), a phrase that reflects both the desire for accumulation stigmatized in the opening couplet and employs the same noun, *acervus*, as that used to designate the heaps of fruit mentioned in lines 9–10. The opposition of *militia* and *rura* that structures the poem's opening panel is, therefore, self-deconstructing, since each term is equally characterized by labor and accumulation: *militia* and *rura* are both opposites and mutually implicated. Consequently, when Lyne writes of poem 1, "Here Tibullus *can* be detected yearning for a primal and idealized (but presumably not totally fictitious) rural simplicity," there is a certain truth to the statement, but it is hardly the whole of the matter (1980: 153, emphasis in original). Riposati (1945: 16) is closer to the mark when he sees 1.1's and 1.10's evocation of rural simplicity as an attempt by the poet to recapture a dreamed-of childhood innocence, before both love and war, before the world of exchange and accumulation. Yet, even this is an oversimplification that fails to do justice to the intricacies of Tibullus's craft.

Indeed, this text manifests a complexity of reference and poetic intention in even the minutest details of its diction. In line 11, after the initial series of optative subjunctives, the poet tells us, in the first use of the indicative in the poem, that he is a man of old fashioned and simple piety who reveres the gods in the traditional rural manner—a statement difficult to square with Kennedy's identification of the speaking subject with the figure of the freebooting soldier:

> nam veneror, seu stipes habet desertus in agris
>   seu vetus in trivio florida serta lapis:
> et quodcumque mihi pomum novus educat annus,
>   libatum agricolae ponitur ante deo.
>   (1.1.11–14)

> For I pay homage, whether a deserted post in the fields
>   or an old stone at a crossroads, it has flowery wreaths:
> and whatever fruit the new year brings to me,
>   is placed as an offering before the god of the farmer.

This evocation of primal rural simplicity, though, is hardly univocal. Indeed, we have to ask: simple compared with what; in what sense is it primal? The sudden use of the indicative is deceptive. We see the speaker in the fields and before his simple altar. But who is he? Just a few lines before (1.1.7–10) when he spoke of his activities as a *rusticus* planting vines with his own hand, the use of the optative subjunctive, *seram*, connoted not an actual state of affairs but a wished for situation (Kennedy 1993: 13–14). Our poet is presumably therefore only a would-be *rusticus*.[26] This is hardly an original pose. As Peter Green notes, pastoral poetry from Theocritus to Vergil, Tibullus, and beyond "is set in the

countryside, its ideals are rural and bucolic, it glorifies summer ripe-
ness—and it is invariably produced by urban intellectuals who have
never themselves handled a spade, much less herded sheep, goats, or
cattle, in their lives" (1990: 233).[27] Thus, the simplicity of which Lyne
and others speak is in fact not simple at all. It is a dream of simplicity
that can only bespeak a sophistication and nostalgia that is everywhere
in this poetry revealed and denied.

How, then, can the simple farmer be contrasted with the greedy, acquisi-
tive soldier if the life of rural piety, on which the contrast is predicated,
is itself internally divided? Moreover, the next use of the indicative, lines
19–22, reveals the poet not as one who shuns the false morality and ac-
quisitiveness of the present in favor of the simple verities of the past.
Instead, he is a member of that vast displaced rural aristocracy whose
fortunes were reduced by the civil war (Murgatroyd 1991: 7; Putnam
1973: 3; Littlewood 1983: 2146),[28] but hardly eliminated:[29]

> vos quoque, felicis quondam, nunc pauperis agri
>   custodes, fertis munera vestra, Lares.
> tunc vitula innumeros lustrabat caesa iuvencos:
>   nunc agna exigui est hostia parva soli.

> You, the Lares, guardians of a now poor estate
>   that once was wealthy, you bring your gifts.
> Then a slaughtered calf cleansed countless bullocks,
>   now a lamb is the small sacrifice of my narrow holding.

Tibullus's nostalgia is in part forced upon him. The simplicity of which
he speaks refers not so much to a primitive time before the fall, or not
only to that, but also to the anxieties of the present.[30] Through its very
doubleness, this presumed simplicity stands as a symptom of the trau-
matic eruption of the senseless world of the Real into the realm of the
Symbolic. It does not offer a reasoned reflection on the social conflicts
that led to the rise of the Augustan regime, or produce a teleological narra-
tive that would aim at containing (though never reflecting) the Real within
the ideological structures of the Symbolic. Instead, the answer of the Real
is seen precisely in the generation of an aporetical text in which the nostal-
gia for a world of ideal agricultural poverty reflects both an inaccessible
utopian dream and the actually existing circumstances of a fallen present
that the dream ostensibly opposes.

Such contradictions concerning the speaker's circumstances, in turn,
recall the earlier paradox of the simultaneous identity and contrast be-
tween rural *paupertas* and martial *divitiae* with which we began. Indeed,
the assertion of unity and difference is a pattern throughout the poem.
The more closely the diction of the poem is inspected, the more overdeter-

mined the relation between its manifest content and its latent multiplicity of meanings is revealed to be. In lines 7–8, the hand that plants the vines and the fruit is called *facilis*. This is a puzzling adjective to characterize the manual labor generally considered beneath the dignity of a man in Tibullus's position (Smith 1964: 187). As Putnam notes, "*facilis* is ordinarily a passive adjective, 'without effort,' a suitable detail in this easy *vita iners*, but perhaps strange for a *rusticus*." He is not the only commentator to note its strangeness. Smith seeks to domesticate this rogue adjective by arguing that *facilis* should be translated as "ready," "skillful," noting that "the shift of adjectives from a usual active to an unusual passive or vice versa is a frequent and characteristic device in poetry" (1964: 187). Yet Smith, by observing that the passive is unusual, in effect concedes that if a Roman reader were to arrive unassisted at the active reading he prefers, it would not be the first interpretation that leapt to his or her mind. Murgatroyd in his commentary goes even farther than Smith, arguing that "such changes in adjectives from passive to active and vice versa are quite common." Perhaps, but that is not the case for this word in Tibullus. In the four other uses of the adjective in the corpus,[31] the active meaning does not appear once. In addition, the main example Murgatroyd cites to bolster his argument, Propertius 2.1.9, is not apposite, since the *faciles manus* with which Cynthia plays the lyre refer to a case in which the root's primary meaning "easiness" or "doability," whether passive or active, is not contradicted by the nature of the activity in question. Playing the lyre, while perhaps not a simple thing to do, is not something that the Romans would normally qualify as *labor*. The planting of vines and of fruit trees is. Cynthia's hand is far more easily pictured as *facilis* than the Tibullan farmer's.[32]

Such attempts to reduce the strangeness of the use of *facilis* in this context are doomed to failure. Not only is the passive meaning usual, as conceded by Smith, but the context that would allow the active meaning to be used without strain is not immediately available. This is not to say that such a meaning would be impossible, but that it would only be accessible after some hermeneutic delay. It is an interpretation arrived at in an attempt to neutralize the strangeness of the more normal sense of *facilis* as "without effort." Accordingly, the secondary meaning, "deft, quick, skillful," is only visible as a palimpsest overwriting a primary meaning, now held under erasure.

Doubleness, however, is the order of the day. This puzzlement on the level of diction is reproduced on that of the passage as a whole, since many critics have felt that the list of manual labors cataloged in lines 7–10 is so out of place in relation to the poet's stated desire for a *vita iners* (life of inactivity) that they have resorted to emending the text, although there is no evidence of corruption.[33] Thus Murgatroyd, who favors the active meaning of *facilis*, also accepts Richter's (1873) proposal to move lines 25–32 of poem 1 immediately after lines 1–6 in order to resolve this seeming contradiction. Yet, there is no conflict between the longed for *vita iners* and the planting of vines or the harvesting of fruit, as Putnam correctly perceives, if the *labor* in question is viewed as easy. Indeed, it could be argued that the active reading of *facilis* all but requires the emendation since such an interpretation does not view the *labor* as "easy" but the hand as "skillful." The opposition between the *vita iners* and manual labor is structurally homologous to that between the passive meaning of *facilis* (easy) and the vigorous activities of planting and pruning described in lines 7–8, and ultimately to that between the *paupertas* of the farmer and the *divitiae* of the soldier. The *vita iners* is opposed to the planting of vines only so long as the labor itself is strenuous; the addition of *facilis* undermines the opposition even as the controversy over its interpretation—based on the fact that the actions themselves are not easy—reinstates it. This simultaneous combination of opposition and concord in turn reminds us of that seen at the beginning of the poem between the *adsiduus labor* of the soldier and the *adsiduus ignis* of the contented farmer's hearth. The result is a complex whole whose multiple layers of meaning vastly outweigh the sum of its parts, while at the same time remaining structurally anchored to the particularities of history understood in their deepest sense. Indeed, not the least irony of the passage is that the man who is *dives*, and therefore would in fact do the least *labor*, is opposed to the one who is *pauper*, and would in reality do the most *labor*, on the clearly fictional basis that the rich man would supposedly endure more *labor* and thus poverty is preferable.

This series of passages, then, can be seen as an example of what Freud in the *Interpretation of Dreams* labels condensation, the production of multiple significations by a single set of terms. Condensation in Tibullus, moreover, is all but invariably generated through the mechanism of displacement, thus reproducing the two basic tropes whereby Freud characterizes the dreamwork. In each case, the fertile contradictions in Tibullus that give rise to this effervescence of meaning are generated by the slippage of an initial term from its primary or initial location in the signifying chain to a secondary or eccentric position. Hence the luster of the first line's riches is transferred to the sixth line's hearth, the constancy of the soldier's labor to the fire that warms the ideal farmer's leisure, the ease of the work of sowing and reaping to the hand that performs the task. Indeed, in lines 7–8, there is a double displacement, a catachresis raised to the second power, because in addition to the problem of the *facilis manus*, the action of planting is described as occurring "maturo tempore," a phrase that more logically governs the act of harvesting:

ipse seram teneras *maturo tempore* vites
rusticus et facili grandia poma manu.

I myself will plant the tender vines at the ripe time,
as a peasant, and the full grown fruits with ease of hand.

One might try to solve the problem by translating *poma* as fruit trees, but the adjective *grandia*, then, makes very little sense, since trees are normally planted when small, not large. Hence, one would assume that the reference is to the fruit itself, which would make better sense of *poma*'s neuter gender, inasmuch as trees are normally feminine and Tibullus uses the neuter to mean fruit in line 13 of this very poem (Postgate 1910: 108; Putnam 1973: 51). The natural assumption, therefore, would be that *maturum tempus* goes with the fruit, since a common definition of *maturus* is "ripe." But why would ripe fruits be planted? Putnam is on the right track when he says that *grandia* "anticipates the productivity of [Tibullus's] seedlings" (1973: 51). In short, the displacement of *maturum tempus* in conjunction with the anticipatory adjective *grandis* creates a series of contradictions on the logical level, but not on the level of the poetic dream text, for through the mechanism of condensation, it allows the presentation of the entire agricultural cycle from planting to the harvest of fruit in a single couplet. Displacement thus leads to condensation, and the meaning of the text is enriched even as the implicit structure of the whole scene as a form of wish fulfillment—since it is based on the anticipation of desired results—is made clear. The notion of the full rural cycle is, in turn, able to be joined directly to the normally opposed concept of the *vita iners* through the displacement of *facilis* from the activity per se to the metonymic hand, allowing the life of leisure and that of rural labor momentarily to seem one.[34]

WHAT'S *AMOR* GOT TO DO WITH IT: MESSALLA AND THE SYMBOLIC

In all the cases examined thus far, we are dealing with the paradoxical assertion of contrasts presented in terms of identity. As such, all these oppositions are structurally homologous with the relation that obtains between *militia* and *rura* presented in the first six lines. As we have seen, the problem of determining precisely the nature of the relationship between *militia* and *rura*, as well as that between their homologues, would appear to be insoluble in its own terms, since each member of these oppositions constantly proclaims both its identity with and its difference from the other. A third term will have to be introduced if so complex an equation is to be solved, or at least fully factored. One such term is *amor*, whose contrast with *militia* occupies the second half of poem 1. There is one important complicating element, though. The section that introduces *amor* also begins with Messalla, whose presence necessarily alters the light in which *militia* is to be viewed.

If we examine lines 53–58, the section that as Gaisser (1983: 59–60) points out introduces the last half of the poem and is organized on the same formal pattern as lines 1–6, we find the soldier's life portrayed in a substantially different way than it was at the beginning of the poem:

> te bellare decet terra, Messalla, marique,
>> ut domus hostiles praeferat exuvias:
> me retinent vinctum formosae vincla puellae,
>> et sedeo duras ianitor ante fores.
> non ego laudari curo, mea Delia: tecum
>> dum modo sim, quaeso segnis inersque vocer.

> It is fitting that you wage war on the land, Messalla, and on the sea,
>> so that your house might display enemy spoils:
> the chains of a beautiful girl hold me bound,
>> and I sit as her doorman before her hard threshold.
> I do not care to be praised, my Delia: so long as I
>> might be with you, I seek to be called lazy and inactive.

Here, the soldier's life is no longer primarily defined by its participation in the ideology of accumulation but is now portrayed as *decus* and the object of *laus* (Murgatroyd 1991: 64). The description of Messalla seems to reverse the earlier condemnation of the soldier's life, but it occurs without explanation. Consequently, the association of military adventure with greed is never retracted, while on the level of diction, though not of theme, it is reasserted: for the use of *exuvias* to end line 54 not only refers to the acquisition of spoils that would be displayed in the *vestibulum* of the house to signal Messalla's achievement and his right to *laus*, but also rhymes with *pluvias* and *vias,* which end lines 50 and 52 respectively, thereby creating a highly unusual series of three rhyming couplets (Murgatroyd 1991: 64; Lee 1974: 105). In this fashion, Messalla's achievement, which seems to be given the poet's stamp of moral approval through his use of the verb *decet*, is inextricably linked both with the *dives* in line 50—able, Tibullus says, to bear storms (*pluvias*) at sea in his pursuit of gain—and with the piles of gold and emeralds that he contends would better perish than for one girl to cry over his own mercantile or mercenary adventures (*vias*) (Fineberg 1991: 135–36).

In 1.3, moreover, *viae* are clearly associated with both the poet's accompanying of Messalla on a military expedition (line 14),[35] and the end of the golden age (lines 35–44), which also marks the beginning of organized agriculture.

quam bene Saturno vivebant rege, priusquam
  tellus in longas est patefacta *vias*!
nondum caeruleas pinus contempserat undas,
  effusum ventis praebueratque sinum,
nec vagus ignotis repetens compendia terris
  presserat externa navita merce ratem
illo non validus subiit iuga tempore taurus,
  non domito frenos ore momordit equus,
non domus ulla fores habuit, non fixus in agris
  qui regeret certis finibus arva lapis.

How well they lived when Saturn was king, before
  the earth was laid open to long roads!
Not yet had the pine held the azure waves in contempt
  and offered the billowing sail to the winds,
Nor had the wandering sailor seeking profits in unknown lands
  weighted down his raft with foreign wares.
At that time the strong bull did not yet submit to the yoke
  the horse did not take the bit with a tamed mouth,
No house had doors, no stone was set in the fields
  that might mark the plowlands with certain bounds.

As we learn from poem 1.7, Messalla is indissolubly linked with the world of *viae*: roads, marches, ways of access to faraway places, and hence the possibility of separation, boundaries, and their necessary crossing (Lee-Stecum 1998: 222; Fineberg 1991: 153).[36] He is also the fly in the ointment with regard to Tibullus's dream of Arcadia, for it is in order to accompany Messalla on campaign that the poet leaves Delia in the first place (Johnson 1990: 103). Moreover, what is *decus* for Messalla in 1.1, the conquest of military glory, is rejected by Tibullus in the same poem in favor of love. Yet, that rejection does not in itself redeem the dream of the pastoral paradise. Just because *rura* and *amor* are both opposed to *viae* does not mean they coincide with each other. Delia is not a creature of the country. The poet only fantasizes her presence there in 1.5, when he imagines her playing hostess to Messalla. She lives in the city, an urban sophisticate whose life represents the opposite of Tibullus's pastoral imaginings, and whose existence is only joined to the country by the roads that Messalla builds, the very presence of which marks the limits of the Tibullan agrarian utopia. Messalla, the city, and Delia, then, all stand in the same essential relation to the Tibullan dream text.[37] They supply the necessary conditions for the dream's content and forms, as well as the leisure and sophistication necessary to create it—yet ultimately prevent its realization (Lyne 1980: 154). They are profoundly related figures.

To begin to explain this conjunction of seemingly different images and characters, we can return to the passage from poem 1 in which we found the poet's initial portrait of Messalla. The paradoxes inherent in his depiction of his powerful patron, and the latter's relation to both Delia (or *amor*) and the city, are given further elaboration when we turn to the way Tibullus portrays himself in these same lines. First, the *rura* that he imagined as his own in the first half of the poem have now vanished and will not reappear for the remainder of 1.1. Second, not only is the poet now pictured before his mistress's door, but also he has adopted the posture of a slave in chains. This of course evokes the standard elegiac trope of *servitium amoris*, but it also puts the greatest possible distance between the *vestibulum* of Messalla's aristocratic abode in which the emblems of his triumph are displayed—thereby validating his claims to the highest ethical and social status accorded by traditional Roman values—and Delia's front door, where Tibullus adopts the position of the lowest of the low, a *ianitor* bound to the house of another and a man subjected to the whims of a woman. This servile posture is standard procedure for Tibullus. In 1.5, he portrays himself as Delia's slave, moving crowds out of the way so she may pass and arranging assignations for her with other lovers (lines 61–66). As we have seen, the homology between servile labor and *servitium amoris* was established in the agricultural portion of 1.1, and repeated in 1.4.

This semiotics of self-abasement reaches its apogee in 2.3 when Tibullus proposes to become a field slave at a neighboring estate so he can catch a glimpse of Nemesis at her *dives amator*'s villa (Cairns 1979a: 154–55).[38] The hard labor of the countryside and the servile qualities of the lover have now shed their romantic sheen (Bright 1978: 193–94). In poem 2.3, *rura* are part of the iron age, not that of gold (Fineberg 1991: 146, 148 n. 64). This in turn clarifies why the golden age is described as a time before agriculture in 1.3 (Whitaker 1983: 84). Agriculture means labor, and the man who must labor, in ancient terms, is no longer truly free. He is subject to external necessity, just as the *servus amoris* portrays himself as subject to the whims of his *domina* (Grimal 1986: 110, 142).[39] Hence, Tibullus's self-portrait as a field slave in 2.3 is in fact the logical development of his earlier juxtaposition of the farmer and the lover in 1.1. There is, then, no real paradox in the transformation of the *rusticus* into the *ianitor* in 1.1; rather, from a class perspective it is a natural progression. Even so, our sense of the necessity governing this sequence is blunted by Tibullus's consistent attempt to portray the impossible subject position of both the farmer whose labors are *facilis* and the *ianitor* whose life is love. This is a romanticization of *amor* and *labor* that book 2 will find harder to sustain, since, as every Roman of Tibullus's station knew, love and labor were both forms of servitude. Indeed, this poetic portrayal of the assumption of servitude by members of the elite, as Veyne points out, constituted much of elegy's humor for its Roman audience (1988: 102–6, 115; Fitzgerald 1995: 9).

Tibullus's assumption of the position of *ianitor* represents the poetic renunciation of his own inherited social and sexual prerogatives,[40] the very things Messalla positively embodies. This rejection of traditional ideology through self-abasement—however comic its intention or effect—is spelled out in lines 57–58, where the poet not only repudiates the desire for praise, but actively signals his desire to be called "segnis inersque," two terms of opprobrium (Lee 1982: 109; Murgatroyd 1991: 65). As Leach notes, the term *iners* "is anathema to the political man but scarcely more appropriate to the Roman farmer or the Augustan poet" (1980b: 60–61). In fact, one of its meanings is "impotent"—hence its use in Catullus 67.26, "iners sterili semine natus erat" (the son was impotent with sterile seed), an unhappy description for either a lover or a farmer.[41]

These terms are hardly chosen at random. *Iners* appears in line 5 of the first passage we examined, referring there to the quiet existence the poet proposes to lead, in opposition to the restless life of accumulation led by the soldier. In the first passage, it seems to imply merely a life of leisure or inactivity, although the verb *traduco* is susceptible of another interpretation than just "to lead": it can also mean "to betray or traduce" (Putnam 1973: 51).[42] Hence, one possible reading would be that Tibullus's rejection of the life of a mercenary is, in fact, a betrayal of his better self, a willful impotence, a form of post-Oedipal castration in which the masculine subject assumes a feminine position outside the phallic order of the Symbolic.[43] Castration is a fate that Priapus wishes on the poet's greedy enemies in 1.4 when he declares:

> at qui non audit Musas, qui vendit amorem,
>   Idaeae currus ille sequatur Opis,
> et tercentenas erroribus expleat urbes
>   et secet ad Phrygios vilia membra modos.
>   (1.4.67–70)

> But he who does not listen to the Muses, who sells love,
>   may that one run after the chariots of Idan Ops,
> and fill three hundred cities with his wanderings
>   and slice off his useless appendages to Phrygian rhythms.

The punishment is appropriate because precisely these sellers of love (and those who pay them), with their total absorption in the realm of phallic accumulation and exchange, have left the poet impotent in his amorous pursuits. The poet, therefore, wishes them to become castrated followers of Cybele (Idan Ops) so that he might be empowered. He is looking at trading places, for the poet through his own desired *inertia*, his rejection of the life of *divitiae* and *militia*, has been severed from phallic power. As Callimachus says in *Iambus* 3—a possible model for both this poem and Catullus 63—in the present world, where money is honored more than virtue, it would be better to be a eunuch devotee of Cybele than a poet (frag. 193 and *Diegesis*; Trypanis 1978; Murgatroyd 1991: 131; André 1965: 53; Luck 1960: 89–90). The irony of Priapus himself uttering these threats in Tibullus 1.4 would have been lost on no one. Tibullus invokes the personification of the phallic to voice a sentiment that aims at depriving those who currently wield phallic power of their attachment to it and transplanting that power to poets like himself. This gesture of appropriation is itself, of course, an implicitly phallic one that presumes the poet already to be participating in the realm of Symbolic exchange, personified at its best by Messalla. Nonetheless, the poet defines the life he chooses to lead, in opposition to that of his honored patron. His life is to be without glory, a life actively disparaged by traditional Roman values. As noted already, the term he uses for this life in the second passage, *iners*, is the same as that which he employed earlier in what had initially seemed a laudatory contrast between the calm life of the farmer and the hectic existence of the acquisitive soldier. To see more precisely how both of these things can be true at once requires that we now examine Tibullus's depiction of Messalla's relation to the golden age.

W. R. Johnson (1990: 96–97) has shrewdly noted that Messalla in Tibullus's poetry plays the role of a father figure, with all the ambivalent feelings that that persona implies. And while Johnson goes out of his way to avoid invoking a crude psychoanalytic reading of this point, in fact, his *praeteritio* serves only to bring this facet of his interpretation into sharper focus: "I refrain of course from calling him a superego or something of the sort" (1990: 104). Johnson lays the groundwork for a Lacanian interpretation of not only Messalla but also the tropes of the golden and iron ages when he observes, "Adults live in the age of iron; the age of gold is the time when children wander freely in the pleasance, which, for them, is at once ideal and real" (Johnson 1990: 102). The father in Lacanian psychoanalysis is the figure who, in the post facto narrative of the subject's "creation," signifies the intrusion of the realm of the Symbolic into the child's world of the Imaginary through the threat of castration. The Symbolic as noted earlier is the world of language and of norms (and hence a more complex entity than the classical notion of the superego, which Johnson rightly avoids). It is the social world that exists between subjects and thus makes subjectivity possible. In the realm of the Imaginary, there are no subjects because there is no Other,[44] only doubles of the same (Julien 1990: 75). The world, as concretized by the mother and her body, exists only for the infant. It is an extension of the self and reflects the image of the infant to itself in the fullest possible plenitude, hence this moment's name in Lacan's early formulation,[45] "the mirror stage." The child is the mother's exclusive possessor. This is similar to the way Tibullus portrays the golden age in poems such as 1.3.[46] Here the world exists only to offer its plenty to its ideal inhabitant. It is a world without war, without labor, without possessions, without otherness or alienation, indeed without doors. The golden age, then, is an evocation of the realm of the Imaginary.[47]

The father, in the subject's retrospective reconstruction of his or her own creation,[48] puts an end to this idyll of infancy by asserting his own claim to the mother and instituting the classic Oedipal conflict that lies at the heart of all psychoanalytic thought. This conflict is resolved through the threat of castration, which hardly need be interpreted in the literal sense (Žižek 1991: 165), but merely implies the paternal function's capacity to remove the source of pleasure and plenitude. In fact, Lacan argues that what is really at stake in castration is the child's entrance *as a speaking subject* into language or the Symbolic—the infant has in reality bathed passively in the Symbolic's norms and expectations since conception. Castration names that primal wound whereby we are separated from ourselves so as to enter language as subjects (Julien 1990: 190, 231; Eagleton 1983: 168; Kristeva 1979: 11). "The speaking subject that says 'I am' is in fact saying 'I am he (she) who has lost something'—and the loss suffered is the loss of the Imaginary identity with the mother and with the world" (Moi 1985: 99). When our Imaginary self-identification most seems to coincide with our subject position in the Symbolic, then the suture that closes this wound is all but invisible. But in times when the Symbolic is in crisis, when it is clearly no longer adequate to the relations our Imaginary selves maintain to the Real, then the wound becomes visible, and the split it marks at the subject's heart is foregrounded (Schneiderman 1983: 113). The concept of castration figures a limit to desire and the necessity of recognizing the existence of others and thus also of the self. Castration, therefore, represents the birth of society and of the subject. Lacan punningly labels this resolution of the primal Oedipal conflict as the introduction of the *nom du père*, which in French means either the *name* or the *no* (*non*) of the father. For with the father's no—with the institution of the world of the Symbolic—the realm of regulated social exchange, whether in the form of language, money, property, or systems of kinship, is instituted (Lacan 1973: 169; Kristeva 1982: 61; Goux 1990: 17, 20–21, 24, 49, 52–53, 55–56; Parkhurst 1995: 51).

This is Messalla's world: the world of politics and military accomplishment, the world that recognizes the value of the enemy spoils he displays in his vestibule amid the death masks of his glorious ancestors. Indeed, in 1.7 Messalla is assimilated to the figure of Osiris, the culture hero who makes civilization possible. In the same poem, Messalla is also portrayed as the patron of farmers in his role as highway repairman. Yet, this is a paradox. As many critics have noted, the world of the farmer in Tibullus is also associated with the golden age, a mythical, carefree world before cities that comes to an end with the overthrow of Saturn by Jupiter, itself a repetition of the initial killing of the divine father, the castration of Uranus by Saturn or Kronos (Kristeva 1982: 61).[49] The present, then, as Tibullus's mythological paradigm defines it, is the product of intracommunal, in fact intrafamilial, violence. This theme would have had a strong resonance for Tibullus's Roman audience. Indeed, the whole series of divine deaths can be read as an allegory of the civil wars through which Rome had just lived (Bright 1978: 74–75; Putnam 1973: 183; Smith 1964: 447; Postgate 1910: 125).[50] In addition, it is from the castration of Uranus, which starts the intergenerational strife that leads to the destruction of the golden age, that Venus (as Tibullus acknowledges in 1.2) is born. Here in that part of the poem that most clearly recalls the classic paraclausithyron, the poet declares that if anyone should see his trysts and gossip about them, "is sanguine natam, / is Venerem e rapido sentiet esse mari" (He will know that Venus was born from blood. / He will know her born from the foam of the sea; 1.2.39–40), a punishment that equates speech and perception with the rebirth of Venus.

In a paradoxical sense, the entry of illicit love into the realm of discourse, the intersubjective world of the Symbolic, will be punished by the rebirth of *amor* and its goddess. Love is a symptom of the fallen age of iron. It is the scar of castration, the visible sign of our desire for a "lost" plenitude, a loss that the entrance into the Symbolic both institutes and seeks to cover over (Lacan 1975: 65, 74–79). In the golden age, under the rule of Saturn, however, there are no love affairs (and how could there be since there are no subjects and no possessions?), and hence no *amor* exists that can be contrasted with *militia* or associated with *rura*. Tibullus's poetry must assume that the golden age has passed, and with it his pastoral ideal (*haec mihi fingebam*). In this light, the inclusion of the farmer at the beginning of poem 1.9's list of those motivated by greed makes better sense. It is not a case of the poet using a "topos without assimilating it," as Bright claims (1978: 251), or a clever means of highlighting the unusual extent of Marathus's greed, as Fineberg argues (1991: 84–87). Rather, it is of a piece with the poet's statement in 1.3 that agriculture is a product of the end of the golden age, every bit as much as commerce and trade. The farmer and the soldier are both symptoms of the same pathological state.

Indeed, love as it is represented in elegy depends on property, not just in the sense that one must have money in order to attract the beloved—itself a sign of the fallen nature of the age—but also in the deeper sense of the ability to possess. Delia can only be Tibullus's in a world that recognizes boundaries, that has doors (and hence paraclausithyra). Yet, this segmentation of the world into discrete, bounded entities or places is the very negation of the golden age (Fineberg 1991: 136–37). The golden age has no love. By the same token, it has no agriculture, because agriculture too needs boundaries, as primitive Roman religion recognized in its worship of the *termini* or boundary markers between fields, portrayed by Tibullus at 1.1.11–12 (Murgatroyd 1991: 56; Putnam 1973: 52; André 1965: 13; cf. 1.3.42–44). To the extent that passion existed in the golden age, it was exercised freely and in the open, a practice Tibullus explicitly associates with the mythic period when men fed on acorns and lived on the earth's spontaneous, if unrefined, bounty (Whitaker 1983: 84; Bright 1978: 204). In 2.3, when he ostensibly despairs over Nemesis's having gone to the country villa of his wealthy rival, the speaker cries, in yet another moment of amorous *ressentiment*, that if he may not enjoy the fruits of the present then let us return to a time before the pleasures of domesticated crops and possessive love, before doors that could be closed:

> o valeant fruges, ne sint modo rure puellae:
> glans alat et prisco more bibantur aquae.
> glans aluit veteres, et passim semper amarunt:
> quid nocuit sulcos non habuisse satos?
> tunc, quibus aspirabat Amor, praebebat aperte
> mitis in umbrosa gaudia valle Venus.
> nullus erat custos, nulla exclusura dolentes
> ianua: si fas est, mos precor ille redi.
> . . . .
> horrida villosa corpora veste tegant.
> nunc si clausa mea est, si copia rara videndi,
> heu miserum, laxam quid iuvat esse togam?
> (2.3.67–78)

Farewell to crops, provided that no girls go to the country:
the acorn will nourish us and water be drunk as when time began.
The acorn nourished the men of old and they made love anytime, anywhere:
what did it hurt them not to have sown fields?
Then, to those whom Love inspired, ripe Venus
openly offered her joys in a shady glen.
There was no guardian, no door to lock out those in pain:
if it is proper, I pray, may that way of life come back.
. . . .
may they cover their shivering bodies with shaggy garments.
Now if my girl is locked away, if my chances of seeing her are rare,
wretched me, what good is my loose fitting toga?

Thus there is a homology, a structural echo, between agriculture and the practice of possessive love, a fact further reflected in the tension between Tibullus's use of the possessive adjective *meus* in the passage's final couplet and his desire to return to a time before possession of any kind. But this wish is an expression of bad faith on the part of the poet's persona.[51] He does not wish to renounce his possession of Nemesis, to share her openly, but rather he desires her to be possessed by no one but him. He is not so much against doors per se as against those that close on him (Whitaker 1983: 85–86; Copley 1956: 73).

We have already seen this homology between agriculture and modern love reflected in the parallel thematics of the servile labors of the farmer and the lover, all of which helps to account for the unusual pairing of these motifs in 1.1. Of course, with boundaries and the determination of "yours" versus "mine," exchange becomes both possible and necessary (Ragland-Sullivan 1986: 42). We enter the realm of the Symbolic: of money and of roads linking places to one another (Fineberg 1991: 137–38), now that places (i.e., others' places) as opposed to simply place (i.e., my place) exist. This is the realm of Messalla, the realm of the father. This realm, which Tibullus both needs and tries to escape, explains why Messalla occupies the mythic place he does in the Tibullan corpus, being both the incarnation of traditional Roman values and in 1.7 associated with Osiris and Bacchus, the founders of agriculture (Johnson 1990: 105; Moore 1989: 424, 428; Bright 1978: 53–54): Messalla figures both the basis of Tibullus's agrarian dream and the mark of the fall from the golden age (Van Nortwick 1990: 118; Moore 1989: 427, 429; Bright 1978: 59). As a figure of mythic proportions, Messalla both provides the space Tibullus needs and stands above that space (Bright 1978: 64–65; Koenen 1976: 157–58). He functions as the unbounded boundary and hence is out of play. He makes possible the dream of the contradictory existence for which Tibullus longs: to experience the boundlessness of the Imaginary dyad, the fantasized fusion with the other, within the bounded space of the possession of his love, his property, his farm, and his gods.[52] Possession and place then become the two key elements of the Symbolic necessary for the dream to exist, but they also represent that which undermines it, because with them comes exchange, travel, and military service. The quasideification of Messalla is an attempt to forestall the violent resolution of this conflict, to move the point of contradiction outside the field of ideological and semiotic play.

This recognition in turn explains why, in 1.5, Tibullus cannot be present in his dream of Messalla's coming to the country, for if Messalla is on the farm then he is no longer above the conflicts that structure the Tibullan dream text. In this scene, Tibullus imagines Delia's serving Messalla the fruits of the harvest (Bright 1978: 46–47). Here the most disparate elements of his imaginings come together: Delia, the country, and the figure who incarnates the opposition to both *amor* and *rura*, Messalla.

> illa regat cunctos, illi sint omnia curae:
>> at iuvet in tota me nihil esse domo.
> huc veniet Messalla meus, cui dulcia poma
>> Delia selectis detrahat arboribus:
> et, tantum venerata virum, hunc sedula curet,
>> huic paret atque epulas ipsa ministra gerat.
> (1.5.29–34)

> Let her reign over everyone, may she be in charge of everything:
>> But let it be a joy to me to be nothing[53] in all the household.
> My Messalla will come here, to whom Delia will bring
>> sweet fruits from the best trees:
> and, having worshiped so great a man, diligently she will serve him,
>> and, as his attendant, she will herself prepare and bring him feasts.

In this scene, rather than the father figure who sunders the Imaginary dyad, since Tibullus has already vanished, Messalla represents the poet's ideal mirror image. He occupies the position Tibullus longs for but of which he cannot truly even dream. Here, Messalla and Delia reflect each other in a brief Symbolic apotheosis of the Imaginary dyad. Each of them is momentarily deified as they enter Tibullus's dream world (Van Nortwick 1990: 116–17; Bright 1978: 47–48), but this can happen only when that world has itself been raised to such a level that the poet can no longer imagine his own presence in it. Tibullus presents this dream in the form of a mirroring relationship, an impossible unity of the Imaginary and the Symbolic that is explicitly recognized as an unrealizable fantasy: "haec mihi fingebam, quae nunc Eureusque Notusque / iactat odoratos vota per Armenios" (These things I imagined for myself, prayers that now the East and South winds / toss about among the perfumed Armenians; 1.5.35–56). It is a primal scene, much like that Freud outlines as lying behind the Wolf-Man's dream, in which the desire both to possess the mother and be possessed by the father, to be the subject of power and be subjected, are conflated. The poet like the child is reduced to the passive observer who must simultaneously fear and long for the castration that would both split apart the impossible unity he desires while rendering the articulation, and hence provisional satisfaction, of his desire possible.[54]

In truth, the only way Tibullus can be present, can even imagine being present, in this unity of the Imaginary and the Symbolic, of the golden age and the institution of those boundaries that would allow him exclusive possession of Delia, is through death (Bright 1978: 28–29). This point is

made clear in poem 1.3. At its beginning, Tibullus, after having reluc-
tantly agreed to accompany Messalla on a military mission to the East,
falls ill and is left behind on the island of Phaeacia, generally identified
with Corcyra in ancient geography (Murgatroyd 1991: 102; Putnam
1973: 74). The Odyssean allusion is one of many in the poem (Kennedy
1993: 49; Bright 1978: 33–36), but it is especially significant in regard to
the golden age and its relation to death. Phaeacia was generally located
in mythological geography near Elysium (Cairns 1979a: 45, citing the
scholia to the *Odyssey* and the *Hippolytus*; Bright 1978: 23). Tibullus's
road has led to a land near death, and in his fevered state he imagines
being led the one short step to Elysium. This, however, is not the afterlife
of heroes found in epic but one for the followers of Venus (1.3.57–66).
Here the fields yield fruits and fragrant flowers without cultivation (Whi-
taker 1983: 72). This is a golden age for lovers, unlike that described
a few lines above (35–48).[55] In that brief description love was nowhere
mentioned. This, however, is an alternative golden age that exists after
death (Cairns 1979a: 47). The original golden age was a realm without
roads, without boundaries, without possession, and indeed there is no
road (*via*) by which Tibullus and Delia may reach this new place except
through death.[56]

At this point, the conflict between the two parts of poem 1 begins to
become clearer. The farmer's quiet retreat cannot be rigorously distin-
guished from the freebooting soldier's ideology of accumulation because
each depends upon the other. The farmer's retreat is always imagined in
terms that include love. Yet love implies subjects and the birth of Venus,
which means castration and the end of the golden age, and the birth of
the world of money, commerce, and exchange. Hence the second half of
poem 1, the part that concerns love, is introduced by the figure of Mes-
salla, the name of the father who both makes love and the farmer's prop-
erty and prosperity possible, as symbolized in his later portrayal both as
Osiris, avatar of the fertility of the Nile, and as the builder of roads and
consequent object of Italian rustics' praise. The rural retreat, which is
ultimately admitted to be only fantasy in 1.5, therefore depends on the
name of the father and love. Love, however, as the last half of poem 1
indicates, takes place in the city—the negation of the country and the
center of culture and wealth, the regulated realm of rule and exchange
(Lee-Stecum 1998: 297–98).

DREAMS, HISTORY, AND THE REAL

In the end, we see that Tibullus must live a life split between the Imaginary
Arcadia of his pastoral dream and the social Symbolic, for neither term
can ever fully comprehend the other. Consequently his paradoxical por-

trait of the relation between *amor, rura,* and *militia,* as mediated by the figure of Messalla, must point to a *tertium quid* that constitutes the ground on which this conflict between the Imaginary and the Symbolic takes place: the world of inarticulate struggle, of life, death, and the material forces beyond our wills; the same world we try to manage and understand through the Symbolic, even as we seek to maintain and assert our Imaginary identities within its bounds. Lacan labeled this realm the *Real.* In Tibullus's mute gesture to this beyond of signification, to what Foucault labels the stutter of language, his elegies discover their profundity. The image with which they leave us is not the wasteland, but a dreamlike plurality of voices in which the policeman, in the form of Messalla, the Symbolic, and the law of the father, is ever present as that which both makes desire possible and keeps it ever unfulfilled. The result is not a balance between extremes, but a tense unease embodied in the opposition between the collection's final prayer for peace (1.10.66–67) and the farmer's drunken erotic violence that immediately precedes it (1.10.51–60). *Amor* and *rura* do not replace *militia* but threaten to become it (Lee-Stecum 1998: 280; Gaisser 1983: 71). Peace and harmony are not established in the final movement of the book but are valiantly wished for in a series of optative subjunctives that parallel those found in 1.1. The dream remains the moment when the contradictory nature of our desires is represented but not transcended.

Tibullus's poetry, thus, in its very plurivocity, in its insistent, repetitive articulation of a desire for the conjunction of the Imaginary and Symbolic registers of existence, stands as eloquent testimony of the early principate's status as a moment of ideological crisis. These texts' very incoherence, their schizoid quality—like those of Eliot in the years immediately following the implosion of nineteenth-century Europe's self-understanding in the trenches of Verdun and the storming of the Winter Palace—are symptomatic of the changing realm of the Real in post-civil-war Rome. These changes, while not reducible to the thematic content of either set of poems, are nonetheless most eloquently expressed in the inability of the imagining of personal identity, as depicted within these texts, to find Symbolic categories adequate to it. In both cases, the Symbolic is no longer able to process the experiential traumas that the world of History and the Real has inflicted upon the subject. The dream through its ability to maintain contradictory relations, therefore, becomes the sole medium able to achieve a momentary and longed-for coherence, even as its status as wish fulfillment insures that in reality it can only be the most insubstantial, utopian articulation of the desire to escape History's nightmare.

Chapter Five

WHY PROPERTIUS IS A WOMAN

[L]a vraie question n'est pas celle de leur inconduite,
mais celle de leur incohérence.
—Maleuvre 1998: 2

In the genre of Propertian love elegy . . . the
narrating ego is constituted as an effeminate voice.
—Wyke 1995: 120

PROPERTIUS BOOK 2 moves from the initial establishment of the poet's style in the *Monobiblos* to its institutionalization and consequent engagement with the recuperative force of Roman ideological norms, embodied in the Symbolic. It is no accident that this book commences with a *recusatio* or that the figures of Maecenas and Augustus loom large over it. Propertius has begun to move in the imperial circle. This, however, does not mean that his poetry becomes less oppositional. Rather to the extent that poetry referring to, or refusing to refer to, the emperor, Maecenas, and their coterie is more prominent in this collection (Gold 1987: 158), then the recuperative pressures of the Roman Symbolic stand in proportionately sharper opposition to the erotic Imaginary's desire for asocial union (as exemplified in words like *nequitia, inertia,* etc.)[1] that stands at the heart of elegiac discourse.

In this chapter, I shall examine four related areas. First, I shall look at the ways in which Propertius in book 2 fashions an anomalous subject position by identifying himself simultaneously with Augustan and anti-Augustan positions, paying special attention to poems 2.15's and 2.16's depictions of the battle of Actium. Second, I shall argue that the Propertian subject position thus created closely approximates that of Woman as defined by post-Lacanian feminists such as Clément, Cixous, Kristeva, and Irigaray. Third, I shall contend that this identification not only helps explain the frequent deployment of the trope of gender inversion in elegiac discourse, but also that it provides a useful explanatory framework for examining the formal rhetoric of elegy in book 2, as exemplified in two important political poems 2.1 and 2.7, in which the poet displays both a newfound closeness with the imperial regime and a refusal of its embrace.

Finally, I shall examine the ways in which these same essential contradictions are also embodied in Book 3, with special emphasis on poems 3.4 and 3.5, even as the field of their articulation is narrowed and their intensity strengthened.

WHEN OPPOSITES ATTRACT

When I say that the recuperative pressures of the Roman Symbolic stand in sharper opposition to the Imaginary's desire for asocial union, I do not mean that Propertius's poetry reflects an oppositional stance in a naive, thematic sense. It is not a question of the poet's "attitude" toward the regime. What I am addressing is an objective structure of the poetry, and its clearest evidence is the unending debates on whether Propertius should be seen as: Augustus's political critic (Hallett 1973: 109; Stahl 1985: 147); his ally (Alfonsi 1979: 37; Cairns 1979b: 201–02; Newman 1997: 6); or an apolitical Callimachean ironist who just happens to be the beneficiary of imperial patronage (Veyne 1988: 3, 30, 108). None of these options does sufficient justice to the complex and contradictory nature of Propertius's later poetry (Santirocco 1995: 226–28), which is simultaneously more and less political than that in the *Monobiblos*. It is more political because aspects of the imperial regime are envisioned as possible themes, as in 2.15 and 2.16 where the poet treats the *princeps*'s recent victory at Actium. It is less political because those same themes are almost always deferred, as in 2.10, where the composition of an epic celebrating Octavian's conquests is promised but put off to the Greek calends (Stahl 1985: 157–60). The complexity of the gesture embodied in such a *recusatio*, as Cameron (1995: 472–73) and Commager (1974: 56–58) note, is heightened by the fact that its structure is dependent upon accepting the superiority of the very genre of eulogistic epic that it is rejecting. Such a poem thus demands a double reading[2] that can take account of both the possibility of infinite deferral and of what many commentators have seen as a sincere promise to provide Maecenas and Augustus the epic they desired (Lachmann 1973: xxi–xxiii; Lemaire 1832: 192; Paley 1853: 88–90; Butler and Barber 1969: 208; Camps 1967: 108–9).

Similarly, when these Augustan themes are addressed, they are dealt with in an ambiguous and problematic fashion. Thus in 2.15.41–46 the poet claims that if only everyone else pursued a life of drunken carousing, then neither would the Actian sea be churning Roman bones nor Rome be exhausted from triumphing over its own citizens (Commager 1974: 48–49; Sullivan 1976: 58; Stahl 1985: 226–27; Gurval 1995: 181). On the surface, this sounds like opposition to the Augustan regime's program of moral reform and martial virtue. It is not a celebration of the victory at Actium. At the same time, however, it can hardly be thought to outline a serious political program. In fact, Rothstein (1979: 1.313–14) reads the passage as implicit praise for Augustus as opposed to the explicit depiction of a decadence that can only recall Antony's portrayal in Augustan propaganda.[3] Is this, then, political opposition, implicit praise, or self-subverting irony? If opposition, then to what and, more important, from what standpoint? Where would it be located on the map of Roman ideology? If the poem is either implicitly Augustan or merely ironic, then how do we explain the disturbing image of Roman bones denied final rest in the churning waters off Actium (Gurval 1995: 181), or the force of the uncanny feat of poetic alchemy whereby those same bones are transformed into dry leaves floating in a wine bowl at the end of the evening's revels (2.15.51–52)? Decadence and death, it seems, await us no matter the path we choose.

Poem 2.15's evocation of Actium, however, cannot be read in isolation from its companion piece, poem 2.16. There in lines 35–40, the poet compares his own "turpis amor" with that of Antony for Cleopatra, a gesture he will repeat in poem 3.11. This is a position that simultaneously puts him in direct opposition to Augustus (Propertius = Antony) and condemns that opposition (Propertius = *turpis*), while attributing *gloria* and *virtus* to Caesar (Rothstein 1979: 1:314; Stahl 1985: 229). Propertius is thus simultaneously pro- and anti-Augustan. But even this contradictory formulation oversimplifies his position. For, on the one hand, while Propertius grants Augustus *virtus*, he defines it as almost the opposite of what it normally means in Roman ideology, "Caesaris haec virtus et gloria Caesaris haec est: / illa, qua vicit, condidit arma manu" (This is the manly courage of Caesar, this is Caesar's fame: with the very hand by which he conquered, he put away his arms; 2.16.41–42). As Gurval has recently observed, "the poet's concluding compliment to Octavian (lines 41–42) is a most unusual manner in which to praise a Roman victor in battle. The *virtus* and *gloria* come not from his courage in fighting or military success over the enemy but from the pardon that the victor bestowed on the vanquished" (1995: 184–85). For Propertius, Augustus can be said to embody *virtus*, but only so long as it does not mean *virtus*.

On the other hand, it would be a mistake to accept Propertius's identification with Antony at face value, in the manner of Jasper Griffin (1977). Indeed Gurval wants to separate Propertius completely from this implied "self-comparison" on the grounds that the poet condemns Antony's *amor* as *infamis* and labels it a cause for shame while blaming it for the destruction of his fleet (1995: 184), "cerne ducem, modo qui fremitu complevit inani / Actia damnatis aequora militibus" (behold the commander who just now filled the waters of Actium with the empty cry of his doomed soldiers; 2.16.37–38).[4] Clearly, there are limits to how far the identification between the poet and Antony can be taken. Propertius's love for Cynthia cannot be posited as the efficient cause of the debacle at Actium, whereas Antony's for Cleopatra was and is so construed.

Gurval's denial of any relationship at all, however, goes too far.[5] There are at least two objections that can be raised to this position. First, Propertius uses *turpis* and *infamis* elsewhere to characterize his own affair and the poetry that pretends to chronicle it (1.16.7, 2.3.4, 2.24.1–10; Wyke 1995: 119). Indeed, as Stahl (1985: 92–93) notes, Propertius consistently adopts the language of those who would condemn him. If both Antony's and Propertius's love can be considered under the same rubric, at least from the standpoint of the emergent imperial ideology, then how different are they? If Propertius were in the same position as Antony in relation to Cleopatra, would he not have done the same thing? Second, if Antony is presented in 2.16 as responsible for the debacle at Actium, and if Propertius in 2.15 portrays his own "Antonian" life-style as a potential antidote to Rome's recent civil slaughter, then, where is the real opposition between Caesar's virtue and Antony's (or Propertius's) vice? Each in turn can be cast as both the cause of war and the agent of peace. From the perspective of the dead at Actium, the pro- and anti-Augustan (or pro- and anti-Antonian) positions would be essentially interchangeable. As Propertius in 3.5 wryly observes, "victor cum victis pariter miscebitur umbris" (the conqueror and the conquered will be equally mixed in the land of the shades; 3.5.15). Each side may define itself as opposed to the other, but each produces the same effect as the other.

What we have in these poems is a very intricate language game in which the poet, by occupying both sides of the opposition but never being wholly present on either side, inscribes the possibility of a third position that can only be expressed in terms of the simultaneous contradiction between and equivalence of both sides. The poet's contradictory self-positionings within this ideological matrix are, therefore, more an indication of the impossibility of a normative Propertian subject within the terms of the late republican and early imperial Symbolic than of the need to assign priority to one of these positions as "truly Propertian" and denigrate the other as either a misreading or a mystification designed to deceive the uninitiated.

Indeed, the search for the true Propertius is a fool's game that can be played *ad infinitum*, as each side of the argument always seeks to trump the other rather than acknowledge that the text always already includes the Other.[6] What we see in book 2 is neither a rebel in Augustus's camp, nor a collaborator, nor an abstracted aesthete, but the vision of an erotic subject who is placed under more and more tension as he is brought into closer and closer contact with the discourse of the Augustan regime. This tension both makes this subject position possible and, at the same time, threatens to implode it. The task of the critic is not to privilege one reading over the other, or to deconstruct the opposition in the name of irony, but to accept the contradiction itself as the fullest instantiation of the Propertian subject.

In the end, the poetic consciousness of book 2 is not only dialogically constituted out of its own intratextual relations (Miller 1994: chaps. 3–4), as in the example of 2.15 and 2.16, but is also projected onto a space that is both manifestly constructed from the terms of contemporary Roman ideology and not able to be precisely located anywhere within it. It is both inside and outside, adopting and inverting traditional Roman values,[7] while projecting images of utopian beauty that are forever tinged with death:

> ac veluti folia arentis liquere corollas,
>   quae passim calathis strata natare vides,
> sic nobis, qui nunc magnum spiramus amantes,
>   forsitan includet crastina fata dies.
> (2.15.51–54)

> And just as the leaves fallen from withered garlands,
>   which you see swimming here and there,
>   piled one on top of another in the wine bowl
> at the end of evening's revels, so perhaps tomorrow holds the fatal day for us,
>   who now breathe the full inspiration of love.

This passage presents a moving image of sensuality and decay that is the counterpart and pendent of the churning bones of Actium. The layering of dead leaves in the wine bowl and the evocation of the carpe diem motif combine to produce a call for absolute commitment to the present moment and for an erotic transcendence that has no place in traditional Roman categories of manhood or *virtus* (Sharrock 1995: 166). Here, in this moment of poetic *jouissance*, with "its strange yoking of ecstasy, pain, and death [that] menaces the Symbolic as the symptom of what cannot enter into the logic of signification" (Janan 1994: 30), the Propertian subject finds its own irreducible kernel of enjoyment, the hard core of its being that is beyond the pleasure and reality principles and beyond the Symbolic categories that make them possible (Kristeva 1979: 13; Žižek 1989: 135; 1991: 169; 1993: 90; Irigaray 1977b: 95).[8]

"WAS WILL DAS WEIB?"

> Je plaiderai . . . en faveur d'une théorie analytique des
> systèmes et des pratiques signifiantes qui chercheraient
> dans le phénomène signifiant la *crise* où le *procès* du sens

et du sujet plutôt que la cohérence ou l'identité d'*une* ou
d'une *multiplicité* de structures.
—Kristeva 1977: 150

The interstitial space of *jouissance*[9] just described for the Propertian sub-
ject is in fact analogous to what Cathérine Clément (1975: 13–14) identi-
fies as woman's eccentric position in relation to communal Symbolic
norms. Woman, she claims, occupies a position that is both radically criti-
cal and deeply conservative, both inside and outside the system. Julia Kris-
teva (1979: 8, 15; Eagleton 1983: 164–65; Moi 1985: 133–34, 163, 166)
echoes this view. What I want to argue is that this psychoanalytically
based and politically charged definition of the feminine not only has the
potential to shed light on the elegiac practice of assuming traits conven-
tionally assigned by Roman ideology to women or effeminate men—pas-
sivity, *mollitia*, and *servitium* (Edwards 1993: 93; Kennedy 1993: 33–
34)—but can also be used to demonstrate a determined and necessary
link between the practice of gender inversion and the elegists' rhetoric of
ambivalence, oxymoron, and paradox. The rhetoric of undecidability and
the practice of gender inversion are two sides of the same coin, which
together reveal the Propertian text to be symptomatic of a profound disso-
ciation between Symbolic norms and the possibilities of self-representa-
tion that lie at the heart of the elegiac enterprise.

Clément's and Kristeva's definitions of "Woman" are, of course,
founded on the psychoanalytic work of Jacques Lacan. Indeed, French
feminism from the 1970s to the present constitutes itself both in reaction
to and in the tradition of Lacanian psychoanalysis.[10] Exemplary in this
regard is the case of Luce Irigaray. A member of Lacan's Ecole Freudienne
at Paris until her expulsion in 1974 after the publication of *Speculum de
l'autre femme,* Irigaray's work is both grounded in the Lacanian theory of
the subject's sexualization in language and deeply critical of it. Of the
many places in which this ambivalent and all but Oedipal relation between
teacher and student is played out, it is perhaps best seen in her essay "Cosi
fan tutti." In this tour de force, she revisits Lacan's *Séminaire XX, Encore,*
on feminine sexuality, and through a strategy of extensive quotation, com-
mentary, and parody presents the discourse of the master in the guise of a
Mozartian comedy of seduction, only with the genders reversed. By chang-
ing Mozart's title "Cosi fan tutte" to "Cosi fan tutti," Irigaray makes us
see the subject presumed to know travestied by the Other.

Parody, as Bakhtin tells us, is always double-voiced.[11] In parodic texts,
by definition the voice being parodied cannot be absolutely distinguished
from the voice of the parodist, if the effect is not to be lost and the dis-
course degenerate into a monologic attack that seeks to annihilate rather
than subvert the other. Two systems of accentuation are present in parodic
texts, each in its most extreme manifestations clearly distinguishable from

the other, but also each overlapping with and mutually determining the other at precisely those moments of contact that make parody possible. Parodic discourse is, thus, always already internally dialogized. Consequently, it must presume the authoritative status of the speech it seeks to inhabit.[12] Parody, like the *recusatio*, therefore, always begins with a concession to the ground of the other, but continues with a simultaneous refusal to grant that territory absolute status and an imperative that the monologic dreams of the other be relativized and opened to the speech of the interlocutor. Such indeed would seem to be the case in "Cosi fan tutti." For, as Elizabeth Weed has argued, "Virtually every element of the essay . . . comes from the twentieth *Séminaire*" (1994: 90). Consequently, the point where Lacan's discourse leaves off and Irigaray's begins is impossible to determine with absolute precision, yet the result is not the annulling of either Lacan's or Irigaray's discursive claims, but rather the opening of the former to the interrogation of the latter. "Cosi fan tutti," then, is one of the purest manifestations of the dialogic possibilities inherent in Irigaray's concept of a feminist mimetic discourse.[13] It also provides a very precise model for the complex relationship maintained between Propertian erotic poetry and the normative Symbolic of the emergent imperial regime.

This inherently complex relationship between Irigaray's and Lacan's texts is further complicated by several factors. In a real sense, Lacan's discourse is self-parodic. When Lacan says of women, "elles ne savent pas ce qu'elles disent, c'est toute la différence entre elles et moi" (1975: 68), it must be remembered that for Lacan knowledge, *le savoir*, is itself constituted within the phallic order of the Symbolic, that realm of ordered rationality and noncontradiction that psychoanalysis, both in spite of and because of its own scientific pretensions, must always see as a mystified realm of rationalization and one whose protocols Lacan's own discursive practice violates at every turn.[14] Women don't "know" what they are saying because the feminine position within the phallic economy is located outside the Symbolic, but it is only within the Symbolic that "knowledge," defined as information processed in accord with the formal dictates of reason (i.e., the laws of Symbolic substitution recognized by a given community), can occur. Lacan, Irigaray, Clément, Kristeva, and Cixous agree that woman is not representable within the phallic order of the Symbolic.[15] For this reason Lacan argues that "La femme" does not exist, since the article "la" implies a universal and the concept of universality is the logical category constitutes the very heart of the Symbolic order.[16] Woman thus represents a hole in the Symbolic, not because she is lacking (although that is the only way the patriarchal Symbolic can represent her) but because she is exorbitant in relation to its totalizing claims. The shudder of her *jouissance* takes place beyond words and thus beyond the Symbolic's power to categorize, anatomize, and atomize. It partakes of that

Real from which the primary repression of our entry into the Symbolic has forever severed us.[17] She gives the lie to the Symbolic's claim to representing universality, *tout*. She says no to that. She is thus the *pas-toute*.[18] She is, as Irigaray argues, the ground on which the phallic figure of totality and totalitarianism is erected, the space that makes its calculation possible.[19] Thus her excess, which the Symbolic figures as lack, is man's necessity. It is precisely this space of intrinsic eccentricity that Propertius occupies in book 2.

"WHEN DOES NO MEAN NO?"

The elegists, in fact, represent a travesty of Roman conventions of masculinity that both questions those conventions and implicitly accepts them as the ground of their questioning (Hallett 1974: 212). This travesty of the masculine and its Symbolic norms, in turn, accounts for the anomalous position of the elegiac beloved or *domina*, who is simultaneously the cruel mistress of the *servus amoris* and the victim of the poet's, and Roman masculinity in general's, complex games of power and manipulation. Thus Propertius, as has been widely recognized, frequently assumes the feminine discursive position and promotes Cynthia to a pseudomasculinity without ever forfeiting his phallic privileges (Luck 1960: 121–22; Stahl 1985: 263; Gold 1993: 89; Wyke 1995: 118).[20] As Gutzwiller and Michelini note, while the elegists followed the lead of the Hellenistic poets in their reversal of normative gender values, "Roman love poets found ways of reasserting traditional male dominance in matters of sex" (1991: 76; see also Gold 1993: 91; Hallett 1993: 64). The rhetoric of undecidability and inversion is not in itself therefore a tool of liberation, as Hallett (1973) in more optimistic times had asserted. Rather it is symptomatic of a disruption in those social structures that produce the gendered subject (Gold 1993: 83). It is precisely this moment of disruption, as manifested in poems 2.1 and 2.7 as well as 3.4 and 3.5, that I examine in the remainder of this chapter. Each text exhibits, as we shall see, an analogously double-voiced strategy that at once deconstructs the laws of gender and genre.

Poem 2.1 is both the opening programmatic poem of Propertius's second book and another example of the *recusatio*, already seen in 2.10, a form whose ambivalent rhetoric simultaneously refuses a closer engagement with an alien kind of discourse (epic, encomium, etc.) and grants that engagement through this negation. It is a form that must assume the rhetorical plausibility of Maecenas's suggesting to the poet that he produce an epic on Augustus (Rothstein 1979: 1.209; Hubbard 1974: 99–100). And some have read 2.1 as a response to stronger pressures still (Stahl 1985: 164; Gold 1987: 127). It is a poem that at minimum stages the possibility of poetry's engagement with political and social power. Throughout this poem, Propertius founds his project in book 2 on both his refusal of the embrace of normative Augustan discourse and his acceptance of it. As such, the specific difference that constitutes elegiac discourse—exemplified as the poet's inability to perform his traditional encomiastic function, his rhetorical impotence—is problematized in the very gesture that marks that discourse's programmatic institutionalization.

More specifically, in 2.1 the poet begins by offering his reader a *mollis* or "effeminate" *liber* (2.1.2) that is inspired not by Apollo or the Muses but by the poet's *puella* or "girl"(2.1.3–4) (Wyke 1995: 117).[21] There then follows a list of possible topics concerning his beloved upon which the poet proposes to write *longae Iliades* (2.1.14). This allusion to epic, so seemingly out of place in the programmatically *mollis* genre of elegy,[22] is anticipated by a specific reference to amorous violence in the preceding line ("nuda erepto mecum luctatur amictu" [Naked she fought with me, her wrap ripped away; 2.1.13]) that at once naturalizes the identification of elegy with epic and underlines the paradox. The overt inversion of genres in this passage is paralleled by an implicit inversion of genders as the epic *hostis* metamorphoses into the *puella* of the poet's *militia amoris* (Kennedy 1993: 31–32). The conflation of genders and genres becomes complete, and the oxymoronic character of the verse explicit, when later in the same poem the possibility of Propertius producing an encomiastic epic on Augustus is rejected. Such *durus versus* (2.1.41) would be beyond the compass of the soft poet. At the same time, Cynthia, the subject of the poet's own *mollis liber*, is also characterized as *dura* (2.1.78), so that the elegiac beloved is attributed the same traits as epic itself (Wiggers 1977: 341; Kennedy 1993: 32–33; Fredrick 1997: 180).

How then are we to understand the poet's claim that the crown of epic lies beyond his grasp? The production of an annalistic epic on the *res gestae* of Augustus and his trusty companion Maecenas—the very topic Propertius says he would treat had he the ability (2.1.25–38)—seems simple compared with the act of sheer rhetorical prestidigitation the poet claims to accomplish: the creation of a "maxima de nihilo . . . historia" (a great history out of nothing; 2.1.16). This phrase moreover follows immediately upon the formulation of the poet's own amorous adventures as *longae Iliades* and directly precedes his apostrophe to Maecenas on his inability to write heroic verse, "quod mihi si tantum, Maecenas, fata dedissent, / ut possem heroas ducere in arma manus" (2.1.17–18). The effect of this juxtaposition is at once to underline the difference between Propertius's amorous epic and the more traditional tales he professes to be unable to recount and to reduce the distance between these poles to the most negligible possible by casting the one in terms of the other (Gold

1987: 159). The masculine genres of history and epic are here subordinated to and surpassed by elegy.[23]

At the same time, there is in these lines a deliberate confusion of form and content, since what Propertius literally says is, "if only the fates granted me this much, Maecenas, so that I might be able to lead bands of heroes in arms." The normal gloss on the pentameter, "i.e. write an epic describing such events" (Camps 1967: ad loc.), erases the line's polysemic character. The basic sentiment does indeed seem to be the same as that expressed later in lines 43–44, "navita de ventis, de tauris narrat arator, / enumerat miles vulnera, pastor ovis" (the sailor tells about the winds, the plowman about his bulls, / the soldier recounts his wounds, the shepherd his sheep) that is, if I were a general I would write epic. However, the literal reading must be maintained as well, if the line is not to lose much of its point, for Maecenas too was not born to lead men into battle. Indeed, he had made a conscious decision to lead a life of equestrian *otium* (Nicolet 1966: 704; Veyne 1988: 104–5), pursuing a career neither in the military nor in electoral politics, a fact that Propertius deliberately exploits in 3.9 to justify his own life of elegiac *mollitia* (Gold 1982).[24] The point becomes all the sharper when we recall that Maecenas himself, unlike Tibullus's patron Messalla,[25] was accused of effeminacy (Juvenal 1.66; 12.39; Seneca, *Epistles* 114). Hence, the conflation of genres implicit in the poet's proposal to write *longae Iliades* on his beloved is doubled by a conflation of genders shared by the elegist and his patron in their mutual *mollitia*. Indeed, this whole unstable constellation of values is nowhere better exemplified than in the poem's final couplets:

> si te forte meo ducet via proxima busto,
> esseda caelatis siste Britanna iugis,
> taliaque illacrimans mutae iace verba favillae:
> "Huic misero fatum dura puella fuit."
> (2.1.75–78)

> If perchance your way should bring you past my grave,
> stop your British gig with its carved yokes
> and weeping utter such words to my mute ashes:
> "a hard girl was the fate of this wretch."

The oxymoron of the *dura puella* has already been discussed, but it is here paralleled by another inversion of gender traits connoted by Maecenas's use of the British war chariot or *essedum*. This was not a vehicle of machismo. Ovid in *Amores* 2.16.49–50 tells us it is the kind of chariot driven by a woman, a sentiment echoed in Propertius 2.32.5. Cicero treats the *essedum* as a sign of effeminate luxury and notes that it is all the more disgusting when driven by Antony while serving in the traditionally virile office of tribune of the *plebs* (*Epistulae ad Atticum* 6.1.25; *Orationes Phlippicae* 2.24).[26] The transformation from epic battle-car to elegiac chick-chariot, which the *essedum* undergoes as the price of entry into the Roman Symbolic, in many ways sums up the entire thrust of this poem, as elegy and epic change places in a dance that Roman culture can only conceive as feminine.

In fact, there is consistent practice of *contaminatio* throughout the poem, as one generic and gendered frame is invaded by another and what appears to be the outside is revealed to be always already inside. This violation of the law of genre—whereby the *mollis* and the *durus*, the masculine and the feminine, epic, history, and elegy are deliberately confused—is, as Sheri Benstock argues in *Textualizing the Feminine* (1991), one of the most consistent features of discourse traditionally marked feminine, even when produced by male writers.[27] The law of genre is, of course, the textual manifestation of the Oedipal law of the father, whose primary social function is to institute the Symbolic and draw clear and distinct boundaries between recognized bodies and maintain category distinctions. Its most striking manifestation is in the incest taboo, but it is at work wherever the "universal" strives to draw clear and distinct boundaries between discrete classes of persons and things so as to regulate their intercourse (Goux 1990: 222–23, 242; Rabinowitz 1993: 15; Althusser 1996c: 27). It is precisely this phallic concept of the boundaries of discourse that Propertius violates at every turn. The clearest example in the present poem of this confusion of inside and outside, and hence of the problematization of the boundaries, is the old controversy over whether 2.1 is one, two, or even three poems,[28] but it is felt at all levels of diction throughout its troubled text.

Thus, the first three couplets present what is on the one hand a straightforward declaration of poetic intent, and on another a sustained meditation on the relation between form and content, signifier and signified, inside and outside:

> Quaeritis, unde mihi totiens scribantur amores,
>   unde meus veniat mollis in ora liber.
> non haec Calliope, non haec mihi cantat Apollo.
>   ingenium nobis ipsa puella facit.
> sive illam Cois fulgentem incedere †cogis†,[29]
>   hac totum e Coa veste volumen erit.

> You ask, why my loves so frequently become literature,
>   why my soft book should be on the lips.
> Neither Calliope nor Apollo sings these things for me.
>   my own genius the girl herself creates.
> If you would have her go forth shining in Coan silks,
>   a whole book will be made from this Coan dress.

We have already noted that *mollis* in line 2 is generally read as program-matic, referring to the subject matter contained in the *liber* (i.e., elegy), rather than the texture of the book itself. Yet the distinctions become much cloudier when we move on to the question, "To whom is the poet referring in the phrase *in ora*, himself or his readers, and what does this mean?" While the majority of readers including Enk (1962: ad loc.) Camps (1967: ad loc.), Richardson (1977: ad loc.), Giardina (1977 ad loc.), and Butler and Barber (1969: ad loc.) read the phrase as monologi-cally and unproblematically referring to the fame the poet achieves through his verse—he is on the lips of everyone—Goold (1990: ad loc.) interprets it as a question of poetics, "how is it that my book sounds so soft upon the lips?"[30] Yet if we look at the immediately preceding hexame-ter and the following couplet, it becomes clear that what is most at issue is the question of origins: "[W]hence does my soft book come softly on the lips?" This reading does not invalidate either the majority position nor that of Goold, for these readings are not mutually exclusive, from a logical point of view, and all are grammatically possible owing to the extreme concision of the line. Rather it reveals their interdependence. For the question of the origin of the poetry (whence it came), its nature (soft upon the lips), and its ultimate destination (as a topic of conversation for its audience) are all three at issue in this poem. But if we cannot make a firm distinction between subject matter (*res*), style (*verba*), and reception (*res publica*), then the difference between inter-, intra-, and extratextual relations becomes impossible to maintain.[31]

Nor is this an isolated instance of the transgression of fundamental boundaries. The violation of the law of genre or gender is pervasive throughout both this passage and the poem as a whole (Greene 2000: 244). Indeed, there is an ambiguity in the very first line: does *amores* refer to the poet's love affair or the poetry that purports to chronicle it (Giar-dina 1977: ad loc.; Gold 1987: 158–59)? This very confusion, however, forces us to pose the even more fundamental question of whether any such distinction can be made. On one level, the poet seems to tell us that his experience dictates the song he sings, "ingenium nobis ipsa puella facit." Nevertheless, even this seemingly straightforward line is problem-atic when read in context, for the poet has just told us that his poetry is not the product of Apollo and the Muses. The next words beneath the reader's eyes are "ingenium nobis." This poetry is not the product of the gods but of the poet's own genius![32] *Ipsa* does nothing to change our mind, since it could as easily be neuter plural as feminine singular. It is only once we reach *puella* that the process of interpretive revision has to take place. The sequence runs as follows: I need no external source of inspiration; my own innate talents are my girl's creation. But if the *amores* themselves, as Giardina points out, serve as a title for book 2, and hence have no necessary referent beyond the book we hold in our hands, then in what sense can the *puella* herself be extratextual?

This ambivalence should come as no surprise. It is now a truism of Propertian criticism that Cynthia stands for Propertius's poetry as much or more than for a consistent character in a novelistic romance, let alone a person of flesh and blood (Veyne 1988: 3, 7, 89; Wyke 1989: 28, 32–34; Gold 1993: 88; Kennedy 1993: 50–51; see also chapter 3).[33] Thus when the poet tells us that if she should wear Coan silks, a fabric known for its see-through qualities, that he will make an entire book from the fabric, he means not only a volume of erotic titillation, but also a deluxe edition fashioned from the fabric itself, whose style like that of Catullus's "libellum . . . pumice expolitum" (slender volume polished with pumice; 1.1–2), will be as smooth as the material from which it is made (Rothstein 1979: ad loc.). It will be silken inside and out. That would indeed be a "mollis in ora liber"![34] Thus from the very opening of 2.1, what falls within and without the realm of elegy, let alone the book roll itself, is deliberately and intensely problematized. Within such a context, the line to be drawn between *mollis* and *durus*, masculine and feminine, epic and elegy becomes problematic indeed.

It is, of course, part and parcel of the *recusatio* both to grant and to refuse the requested verse form, and Propertius not only delivers on this promise by casting elegy in terms of epic but also by providing an example of the kind of encomiastic verse he claims to be unable to write. Indeed, immediately following the poet's profession of epic incompetence, he provides a brief history of the genre's themes from the gigantomachy through Herodotus's *maxima historia* of the Persian Wars to the deeds of Marius. His account of topics that cannot be treated culminates in a fourteen-line excursus on the feats of Augustus himself. Yet the ambivalence expressed with regard to the poet's ability to write encomiastic epic is paralleled in the subjects he proposes to treat if he were to praise Caesar: the graves at Philippi (line 27) and the desecrated hearths from the Perusine War (line 29) (Wiggers 1977: 336). The slaughter of civilians and prisoners at the end of the siege of Perusia was, of course, a topic with which he had already dealt in poems 1.21 and 1.22 (see chapter 3). It was a page from the history of the civil wars that the *princeps* would have far rather had forgotten than memorialized. In fact, Propertius is the only Augustan poet so tactless as to mention it. Yet he not only includes it in his list of possible topics of epic celebration, he highlights it: for, while all the others appear in strict chronological order, the battle of Perusia (41 B.C.E.) is found between Naulochus (36 B.C.E.) and Augustus's triple triumph (29 B.C.E.). Moreover the list of possible topics itself is the longest of any *recusatio* in Augustan poetry. Propertius clearly does not want either his readers or his patrons to miss the point (Nethercut 1963: 11, 46–48; 1983: 1840).

Poem 2.1 thus presents effeminized elegy in the terms of masculine epic, while simultaneously both confessing the poet's inability to produce epic verse and giving an example of that same form that would make the poet's patron thankful for the latter's declining of his invitation. At the same time, the very existence of 2.1 stands as a testimonial to Maecenas's discretion and Augustus's *clementia* and respect for the traditional virtue of *libertas* (Cairns 1979b: 186, 201–2).

MAKING UP IS HARD TO DO

Poem 2.7, likewise, appears on first reading to be a refusal of the existing order. It is generally read as a celebration of the repeal of one of Augustus's moral reform laws and a declaration of pure opposition to the Augustan regime's efforts to rewrite the Roman Symbolic. Instead of celebrating the return of the *mos maiorum*, the poet's vision of himself in a strictly dyadic relation with Cynthia, one that would exclude all forms of third-party interaction, is promoted to the status of a norm ("tu mihi sola places: placeam tibi, Cynthia, solus: / hic erit et patrio sanguine[35] pluris amor" (You alone please me, may I alone please you, Cynthia, and this love will be worth more than a father's blood; 19–20). Yet this reading of the poem is highly problematic, since, as Badian (1985) has shown, and others have agreed (Konstan 1994: 152; Edwards 1993: 41n.26), none of the laws promoted by Augustus had been passed at this time, let alone repealed. Badian's elegant solution to this historical conundrum is to argue that the poems' actual reference is to the repeal by Augustus of a tax imposed on unmarried men by the second triumvirate in order to raise money for the civil wars. The repeal, then, would represent part of the normalization process undertaken by Augustus, commonly referred to as "the restoration of the republic." Implicit in Badian's reading is the idea that 2.7 rather than being an attack on Augustus's moral reform legislation is actually a celebration of his fiscal restraint.

Yet, while Badian's solution to the problem of the legal reference in 2.7 is compelling, it hardly eliminates the interpretive difficulties that beset the poem. What Propertius and Cynthia celebrate is not their ability "to keep what they earn," but their refusal to enter into a recognized marital relationship and to provide citizens for the imperial armies of Rome ("unde mihi Parthis natos praebere triumphis? / nullus de nostro sanguine miles erit" [why should I offer sons for a Parthian triumph? / There will be no soldier from our blood; 2.7.13–14]), neither of which can be seen as supporting what Galinsky (1996: 8) calls the moral basis of the restoration of the republic. Hence, Propertius's support of Augustus's repeal of the repressive triumviral legislation continues to be a statement of opposition to an Augustan ideology whose articulation had begun well in advance of any actually recorded legislation (Besnier 1979: 202; Wallace-Hadrill 1985: 180–84).

Indeed, it is in order to account for the anomaly of the poet's critical stance vis-à-vis the moral tenor of the Augustan regime, even as he remained the acknowledged recipient of its patronage, that Francis Cairns produced the brilliant, if reductive, expedient of interpreting 2.7 as a covert endorsement of the policy it seems to oppose. Cairns (1979: 187, 190) notes that Propertius's casting of himself as the decadent, effeminate poet in opposition to Augustus's policy of moral regeneration merely underlines the evils the *princeps* sought to combat. The poet's lack of moral credibility in traditional Roman terms provides the best possible endorsement for the proposed reforms. Poem 2.7, thus, offers a double-voiced form of discourse analogous to that of 2.1's *recusatio*. As Cairns observes, "In writing what is ostensibly a rejection of his patrons' proposals, but actually giving a favorable impression of them to the reader, Propertius is doing something paralleled in his own work and that of his contemporaries. The best-known Augustan parallels are *recusationes*" (1979b: 200). Poem 2.7, then, presents precisely the same kind of doubleness as that observed in 2.1.

Yet, even this double-voiced reading of 2.7 is an oversimplification. It merely inverts what Galinsky refers to as the "inane dichotomies" of "'pro-' and 'anti-Augustan'" (1996: 5) but does not posit that which eludes such binary oppositions, and hence what makes them possible: a subject position that is both inside and outside the norms of Symbolic discourse, that situates itself in the interstices of the dominant order, and that consequently assumes that feminine position which Propertius elsewhere more explicitly claimed as his own (Clément 1975: 17–18; Gold 1993: 91; Hallett 1993: 63; Wyke 1995 119–20). Cairns's position then cannot really account for both readings of 2.7, but merely demonstrates the possibility of replacing one with the other. Yet, as we saw in 2.1, Propertius's deployment of the *recusatio* form not only grants what it refuses, but it then also calls into question what it has granted by concentrating on Augustus's actions during the civil war. In particular, we noted the reference to the cruelties of the Perusine War in which Propertius lost a kinsman, as he tells us in 1.22. It would be surprising indeed if at the beginning of the next book all this had been forgotten and Propertius been converted into a subtle but unrepentant apologist for the Augustan regime.[36]

Clearly, a more complex and nuanced interpretation is required if we are to account for all the data. Poem 2.7, as we have seen, is capable of being read as a defense of the *princeps'* policy of fiscal restraint, an implicit attack on his soon to be launched moral reform program, and a covert endorsement of that same policy. All of these readings are not only textually but also historically possible and plausible. They bespeak an unresolvable ambiguity in the poet's relation to the realm of Augustan public discourse, and hence to the Symbolic norms of his time, analogous to that already seen in the case of poems 2.15 and 2.16.

This symptomatic undecidablity is evident even on the level of 2.7's poetic diction. Thus in lines 1–6 the poet writes:

> Gavisa est certe sublatam Cynthia legem,
>   qua quondam edicta flemus uterque diu,
> ni nos divideret: quamvis diducere amantis
>   non queat invitos Iuppiter ipse duos.
> "At magnus Caesar." sed magnus Caesar in armis:
>   devictae gentes nil in amore valent.

> Cynthia certainly rejoiced when the law was revoked,
>   at whose proclamation we both long wept
> lest it should divide us, although Jupiter himself
>   cannot split apart two lovers if they are not willing.
> "But Caesar is great." But Caesar is great in arms:
>   conquered peoples are worth nothing in love.

The reference to Jupiter can be read as a covert allusion to Augustus thematically preparing his explicit mention in the next couplet. As Cairns (1979b: 187–88) notes, the association of Jupiter and Augustus is a common encomiastic strategy in Augustan poetry, allowing the poet implicitly to deify the emperor without risking impiety or a political faux pas.[37] The metonymic identification of Jupiter and Augustus, however, is not always benign. The same trope appears in Ovid's *Tristia*, first as an ironic insinuation of despotism (*Tristia* 2) and then as an explicit recognition of the poet's abjection in the face of imperial power. It is because of the inherent ambiguity of the identification with the father of the gods that what is for Cairns an implicit encomium becomes for Nancy Wiggers (1977: 337) a subtle condemnation of imperial brutality.

The text is more elusive still. It neither quakes before the power of Jupiter, nor indicts his brutality, but proclaims the god's inability to separate lovers against their will. Moreover, the juxtaposition of Jupiter and Caesar underlines not only these figures' metonymic identification, but also their substantive difference. Indeed, Caesar is introduced as a potentially more powerful adversary than Jupiter himself, "*At* magnus Caesar" (Postgate 1884: ad loc.; Richardson 1977: ad loc.). This first adversative construction is not, however, allowed to stand alone, but is answered by a second, "*sed* magnus Caesar in armis." It notes that while Caesar is great in arms, and hence a potentially more formidable opponent than the distant Jupiter, his greatness is circumscribed to a realm that has no relevance to lovers. "Conquered peoples are worth nothing in love." Thus, Caesar like Jupiter is impotent before the power of love. The claim of a complete lack of relation between love and war, however, is belied by the poet's own use of the trope of *militia amoris* in both 2.1 and 2.7 (King 1980a: 73). What this string of adversatives and negations points to then is a position that eludes the sterile dichotomies of pro- and anti-Augustan: for, what Richardson reads as a "defiant defense of liberty," Cairns sees as "open praise of Augustus's military glory" (1979: 187); and what Wallace-Hadrill (1985: 184), reads as an attempt to define and limit "Augustus's proper sphere of action," the battlefield but not the heart, Badian (1985) interprets as the celebration of a return to fiscal normalcy and Postgate (1884: ad loc.) as "gross flattery."[38]

To this extent, then, both 2.7 and 2.1, like 2.15 and 2.16, present Propertius as speaking in the feminine, a discourse that eludes the conventional binary oppositions of official and subversive, pro and con, conscious and unconscious. Propertius is a woman because his subject position cannot be precisely located in any one spot within conventional Roman ideological space (Wyke 1995: 120–21). In this context, his inversion of normative gender roles in assuming the pose of *servus amoris* can be seen as part of a wider ideological and rhetorical strategy in which the norms of gender, discourse, power, and desire are called into question in a more radical fashion than the concept of mere opposition can convey. To that degree, the Propertian text can be read as symptomatic of a more profound dissension at the heart of the Symbolic itself, one that figures the norms of discourse as radically incommensurate with the poet's Imaginary reflections of the self's experience. The gap that is thereby revealed is a truer gauge of this poetry's engagement with History and the Real than any reduction of the text to a state of permanent ontological inferiority, to the status of a mere reflection of a preexisting reality, political or otherwise. Unlike other women, however, Propertius, at least theoretically, retains the option of being a man. His appropriation of the feminine position does not imply a new symmetry in sexual power relations so much as a destabilization of the category of the masculine. In the final analysis, it remains an appropriation that was not equally open to all. And that is real power too.[39]

LOVING YOUR ENEMY

The clue may be supplied by one of the ideal demands,
as we have called them, of civilized society. It runs:
"Thou shalt love thy neighbour as thyself." . . . Why

should we do it? What good will it do us? . . . Indeed,
if this grandiose commandment had run "Love thy
neighbour as thy neighbour loves thee," I should not
take exception to it. And there is a second
commandment, which seems to me even more
incomprehensible and arouses still stronger opposition
in me. It is "Love thine enemies." If I think it over,
however, I see that I am wrong in treating it as a greater
imposition. At bottom it is the same thing.
—Freud 1961a: 56–57

Augustus takes on an increasingly prominent role in the
poetry of Book 3, although few of the references to him
could be construed as complimentary. Poem 3.5, which
directly contradicts 3.4.1 in it first line (cf. *Arma deus
Caesar meditatur* with *Pacis Amor deus est*), again
confuses questions of ethics with poetic style.
—Gold 1987: 163–64

Book 3 exhibits the same confusions and conflations of basic categories
that we have identified in Book 2 (Stahl 1985: 189–90).[40] It does not,
however, merely repeat Book 2's problematic: for in it, the circle that
defines the gap between Imaginary self-definition and Symbolic law has
been reduced. The distinctions between elegy and epic, public and private,
masculine and feminine have been more sharply defined in relation to
one another and the distance between them reduced. Book 3 opens with
reflections on the contradictions between martial themes and the poet's
erotic and Callimachean aims (3.1–3)[41] and closes with the dismissal of
Cynthia and amatory poetry (3.24–25; Gold 1987: 163; Wyke 1987: 154;
1989: 30). It juxtaposes the poet's proposed journey to Athens, as a means
of escaping unhappy love, with an exhortation to Tullus to return to
Rome and enjoy the fruits of the Augustan peace (3.21–22; Stahl 1985:
207–8).[42] It stages the poet's own refusal of epic verse as parallel to Maece-
nas's unwillingness to accede to the ranks of the Senate (3.9; Gold 1987:
166–67; Boucher 1980: 304), and it, like book 2 (2.15–16), justifies the
poet's subjugation to a woman by citing Antony's subjection to Cleopatra
(3.11; Gurval 1995: 206–7).

   Poem 3.11 is particularly symptomatic of the kind of ideological conun-
dra presented by book 3's conflation of even the most basic categories,
including those of friend and foe. It closes by celebrating Augustus's
power as equal, if not superior, to Jupiter's own: "haec di condiderant,
haec di quoque moenia servant: / vix timeat salvo Caesare Roma Iovem"
(the gods founded these walls, the gods still watch over them / Rome
should hardly fear Jupiter while Caesar is safe; 3.11.65–66). The state-

ment is problematic. On one level, it is certainly laudatory of Augustus (Fantham 1996: 124–25). On another, it borders on sacrilege by exalting the *princeps* above the father of the gods, a position that sorts ill with his preferred image as the restorer of traditional piety. Propertius goes well beyond the more nuanced position staked out by Horace:

> Caelo tonantem credidimus Iovem
> regnare; praesens divus habebitur
> 　　Augustus adiectis Britannis
> 　　imperio gravibusque Persis
> (*Odes* 3.5.1–4)

We trust that thundering Jupiter reigns in heaven; Augustus will be considered godlike in the here and now by the conquered Britains and through his power over the dread Persians.

In this closing poem of the Roman Odes, Augustus is a god only to those barbarians at the far edges of the known world who are about to be subjected to Roman *imperium*.[43] In Rome, he is merely the first citizen. His reign may be the earthly instantiation of Jupiter's rule (*Odes* 3.1.5–8), but he is not a god himself, let alone Jupiter's superior. His subsequent deification is alluded to by Horace, but his status in this world is clearly that of a man (White 1993: 169–82).

The extremity of the Propertian position cannot help but raise eyebrows. It is deliberately provocative. Is this a compliment or an insult? The question becomes more difficult to answer the closer we look at the poem itself. Jupiter may be compared with Augustus at the end of 3.11, but earlier in the poem he is portrayed as one who, like Propertius, disgraces himself and his household through submission to a woman (3.11.27–28). Jupiter like Propertius, then, functions as an analogue to Antony in his submission to Cleopatra: no wonder Augustus is portrayed as the god's potential superior! Yet Augustus's own line is not exempt from this taint: for the poem's mention of Pompey's death on the shores of Egypt not only calls to mind the origins of the civil wars but also reminds the reader of the deified Julius's own erotic submission to the *noxia Alexandria* (3.11.33–38; Stahl 1985: 237, 242–47; Gurval 1995: 198). This last association is especially important because the deification of Augustus's uncle and adoptive father is what established the warrant for the *princeps*'s own impending divine status, though only once he has left behind the realm of the here and now (cf. *Odes* 1.2.45).

As we can see then, in poems like 3.11, rather than sticking to safe topics, as Hubbard (1974: 95) alleges, Propertius in book 3 has moved into an even closer engagement with the Augustan regime. Such proximity, however, not only more firmly plants Propertius's star in the imperial firmament, it also necessarily exacerbates the contradictory relations that characterize the rapport of elegy with the imperial Symbolic. The ratcheting up of the tensions inherent in this rapprochement is at the heart of the Propertian project in book 3, and it is nowhere better exemplified than in the relation between poems 3.4 and 3.5, a pair whose opening lines both recall and directly contradict each other: "Arma deus Caesar dites meditatur ad Indos" (Caesar the god is planning to take up arms against India; 3.4.1); "Pacis Amor deus est, pacem veneramur amantes" (Love is the god of peace, we lovers worship peace; 3.5.1) (Boucher 1980: 69; Stahl 1985: 196–97; Camps 1966: ad loc.). The remainder of this chapter is concerned with the complex and multivalent relations between these last two poems of the programmatic sequence that introduces the third book (Camps 1966: ad loc.; Nethercut 1983: 1839). These poems intermingle political, erotic, poetic, and generic frames in such a fashion as both to preserve elegy's irrecuperable remainder and to make its posited externality to the emerging imperial Symbolic ever harder to maintain. Propertius is still a woman, but now more than ever he is woman as the formal expression of a simultaneous excess and lack (Benstock 1991: 119)

Poems 3.4 and 3.5, in the manner of all of Propertius's later work, are not simple texts. The difficulties in interpreting 3.4 begin with the very first line. "Arma deus Caesar" echoes the opening of the *Aeneid*, extracts of which were already circulating at the time Propertius was finishing book 2 circa 25 B.C.E.[44] and are explicitly alluded to in 2.34.61–66. This initial reference to the poem has been the cause of critical debate as to whether it is laudatory (Newman 1997: 220), critical of Vergil's lapsing from the orthodox Callimachean line of eschewing epic (Benediktson 1989: 45), or engaged in a subtle polemic about the proper progression of a poet's career (Stahl 1985: 182–85). Nonetheless, it has been difficult to read the final couplet referring to Vergil's forthcoming epic, "cedite Romani scriptores, cedite Grai! / nescio quid maius nascitur Iliade," as less than ironic since Pound's brilliant mistranslation:

> Make way, ye Roman authors,
> > clear the street, O ye Greeks,
> For a much larger Iliad is in the course of construction
> > (and to Imperial order)
> Clear the streets, O ye Greeks!
> (Sullivan 1964: 169)

Thus when Propertius begins a poem "arma deus Caesar"—immediately after being told by Calliope in 3.3 to eschew epic and arms, "Contentus niveis semper vectabere cycnis, / nec te fortis equi ducet ad arma sonus" (you will always be content to be carried by snowy swans / nor will the sound of a brave horse lead you to arms; 3.3.39–40)—it is hard not to see it as a critical echo of "arma virumque cano." Indeed, the only puzzling thing is that no previous commentary has observed this allusion, even as Ovid's "arma gravi numero" (*Amores* 1.1.1) is universally conceded to be an echo of *Aeneid* 1.1 (Green 1982: 268; McKeown 1987: ad loc.; Mack 1988: 54–55; Buchan 1995: 54n.5).

The Propertian allusion, in fact, is more precise than its Ovidian recollection. The substitution of *deus* for *vir* keeps the basic structure of the opening hemistich of *Aeneid* 1.1, in which the agent wielding the *arma* is the second word of the hexameter. At the same time, Propertius's reformulation also makes explicit that the *vir*, Aeneas, was but a stand-in for the *deus*, Caesar, all along, even as it implicitly recalls that both Aeneas and Augustus were really only *viri*. Thus, the use of *deus* for Augustus here, as in 3.11, can be read as both genuinely encomiastic[45] and a covert slap.[46] Likewise, the echo of the *Aeneid* presents the same essential ambiguity on the poetic level—is it complimentary or critical? In addition, the nature of that intertextual relation is in no way made less problematic by the *Aeneid*'s own notoriously complex relation to the *princeps*. Finally, the alliteration between *cano* and *Caesar* drives the parallels between the two passages home.

Such complexities are not limited to the first line. In fact, the whole of poem 3.4 is compounded from a similarly unstable mixture of contradictory elements. Thus, on the one hand, the poem labels the motives for war and the subsequent celebration of triumphs as greed (cf. 3.4.2 "gemmiferi . . . maris [the gem rich ocean]; and 3.4.3, "magna, viri, merces" [great wages, men!]). On the other, the image of Caesar giving laws to the Tigris and Euphrates and recovering the lost standards of Crassus was almost necessarily genuinely encomiastic. These were themes with such broad appeal that they cannot be immediately discounted as simple kowtowing to the party line or as imperial propaganda, nor can they, in themselves, be reduced to mere pretexts for greed (3.4.4–10; Boucher 1980: 117; White 1993: 159–68; *pace* Stahl 1985: 195). It was certainly possible to loot without establishing a constitutional order or giving laws, and there were far easier targets of potential pillage than the feared Parthians.

By the same token, however, Propertius's claim that he will watch Caesar's triumph while propped on his girlfriend's lap is, as Richardson notes, "a flagrant breech of decorum" (1977: ad loc.). Such statements are hardly designed to rally the troops for a program of imperial expansion. Still, the sting of the barb is substantially reduced by the final couplet, which on its own would demand to be read as a simple restatement of traditional Roman values:

> praeda sit haec illis, quorum meruere labores:
>   me sat erit Sacra plaudere posse Via.
> (3.4.21–22)

Let this booty be for those whose labors have earned it:
It will be enough for me to be able to applaud from the Sacred Way.

The sentiment is, "Let the prizes goes to those who earn them; for the rest of us there is nothing to do but express our admiration." This is a mere affirmation of an ideological truism: those who possess wealth and power are those who deserve it. It does not challenge the traditional social order and the system of rewards reserved for *otium* and *negotium* but reaffirms them (Conte 1994: 256). But why then say it? The one question the normative position cannot answer is why someone would choose not to play the game. Yet, that person is precisely the elegist. The very statement of the norm implies the existence of a position that cannot be articulated within its bounds. This is the position of Propertius, of Woman.

The tensions inherent in such a position cannot be reduced without sacrificing much of the poem's interest. Indeed, it is precisely with regard to this sort of aporia that a symptomatic reading of elegy proves its mettle: for, it is in the symptom itself that the force of History is made manifest. As Boucher eloquently observes, "Les contradictions du développement élégiaque sont l'écho des contradictions du poète . . . l'écho des contradictions d'une époque qui sort durement des guerres civiles et d'une révolution" (1980: 386–87).[47] Such contradictions are not to be resolved by critical fiat into a univalent picture of pro- or anti-Augustan sentiment. Rather they are, like woman herself, a symptom, a trace of the Symbolic's own foundational moment of exclusion, its attempt to wrest a self-consistent, and hence monological, system of signification from language's web of infinite difference (Lacan 1975: 68; 1982: 168; Janan 1994: 31). It is less Propertius's attitude toward Augustan ideology that is on display in such undecidable moments than the elegist as the unassimilable remainder, as that which cannot be processed by the categories of Augustan ideology without either falsifying elegy or itself (Boucher 1980: 136–37).

The symptomatic visibility of that remainder is best seen in 3.4's penultimate couplet where the poet achieves a momentary fusion of the amorous and the imperial, in an image that simultaneously gives elegy's blessing to epic and confirms our earlier reading of 3.4.1 as a parody of *Aeneid* 1.1:

> ipsa tuam serva prolem, Venus: hoc sit in aevum,
>   cernis ab Aenea quod superesse caput.
> (3.4.19–20)

> You yourself keep watch over your child Venus: may he live forever,
>   whom you see to be the descendant of Aeneas.

Venus is the appropriate guardian of Augustus since she is the mother of Aeneas, the founder of the Julian line. She is, of course, also the goddess of love and mother of Amor, Aeneas's brother as Ovid reminds us (*Amores*

1.2.51–52). But whereas in Ovid this reference, coming at the end of Amor's triumph over the poet, is a moment of pure irony containing neither a specifiable political content nor a credible encomiastic purpose (Barsby 1979: ad loc.; Mack 1988: 64; Buchan 1995: 64), in Propertius the reference to an Augustan triumph at end of the long-planned Parthian campaign, and in a context evoking the *Aeneid*, must leave open the possibility of a genuinely eulogistic intent (Stahl 1985: 193–94). It is precisely in the gap between the equally plausible positive and negative readings of this couplet that the Propertian subject is situated. Venus is the suture between the realms of Propertius and Augustus, the point of articulation that allows the effeminate world of elegy to be momentarily joined with the masculine, warlike world of Augustus and epic, without being assimilated to it.

At the same time, Venus is the poetic hinge point that allows the poet to prepare the reader for the opposition between 3.4 and 3.5 announced by "pacis Amor deus est" (Love is the god of peace), in which *pax* is substituted for 3.4.1's *arma* and *Amor* for *Caesar*. Propertius does not, however, strictly refuse battle but rather in the following line modulates directly into the *militia amoris* motif, claiming that his *dura proelia* will be with his mistress rather than the Parthians. In contrast to the battles outlined in 3.4, though, his amorous tussles will not be fought for the acquisition of *praeda*. Indeed, where 3.4.2 looked expectantly to the "freta *gemmiferi* . . . maris" (the straits of the *gem-bearing* seas), 3.5.4 directly denies that "bibit e *gemma* divite nostra sitis" (our thirst drinks from a *bejeweled* cup). Moreover, in 3.5.3–18, greed, imperial expansion, and the sack of Corinth are attributed to a congenital perversity of the human spirit that forces us ever to seek new satisfactions for new desires (Liberman 1995: 319), and hence to establish new boundaries to cross and new enemies to crush, as we become embroiled in a continual dialectic between the search for limits and the necessity of their transgression (Barton 1993: 57–58). Each new set of categorical distinctions is annihilated, each new boundary is erased, as the foundation of our desire in an original lack, a marking of the limits of the self, can only be ultimately expunged in the absolute negation that is death (Bataille 1957: 155). Propertius limns this narrative for us in the first half of 3.5:

nec tamen inviso pectus mihi carpitur auro,
    nec bibit e gemma divite nostra sitis,
nec mihi mille iugis Campania pinguis aratur,
    nec miser aera paro clade, Corinthe, tua.
o prima infelix fingenti terra Prometheo!
    ille parum cauti pectoris egit opus.
corpora disponens mentem non vidit in arte:

recta animi primum debuit esse via.
nunc maris in tantum vento iactamur, et hostem
   quaerimus, atque armis nectimus arma nova.
haud ullas portabis opes Acherontis ad undas:
   nudus ad infernas, stulte, vehere rates.[48]
victor cum victis pariter miscebitur umbris:
   consule cum Mario, capte Iugurtha, sedes.
Lydus Dulchio non distat Croesus ab Iro:
   optima mors Parcae[49] quae venit acta die.
(3.5.3–18)

Neither nonetheless is my heart seized by unseen gold,
   nor does our thirst drink from a bejeweled cup,
nor are a thousand rich acres plowed in Campania for me
   nor do I, like a wretch, procure your bronzes, Corinth, with my sword.
Oh unhappy first earth to yield to Prometheus's craft!
   That one wrought the work of a too little cautious soul.
Putting the bodies in order he did not oversee the mind with skill.
   First the way of the spirit ought to be straight.
Now we are tossed about on the sea by so much wind, and we seek
   an enemy, and we lash new arms to arms.
You will not take any riches to the waves of Acheron:
   Fool, you will be carried naked to the infernal rafts.
The victor will be equally mixed with the conquered shades:
   you, captured Jugurtha, will sit with the consul Marius.
Lydian Croesus does not stand apart from Ithacan Irus:
   Best is the death that comes on the day appointed by Fate.

On one level, this is a stinging indictment of the transgressive desire that
powers the dreams of eastern conquest in 3.4 and sets up a clear opposi-
tion between the lover who worships peace and Caesar who plans war.
There is never enough (Stahl 1985: 195–200). New enemies must always
be found, new boundaries established between us and the other, an other
who must always then be annihilated and incorporated into ourselves,
into the dominant order, until we reach the point at which all boundaries,
all distinctions between self and other collapse (Black 1991: 108).[50] The
logical conclusion of this aggressive desire, which Propertius attributes to
us as original sin owed to the fault of Prometheus, is death, the telos to
which the passage leads (Freud 1961a: 65–66, 69; Freud 1961b: 30–33).
This is the only possible complete fulfillment, the erasure of the distinction
between self and other, of the boundaries that constitute the hierarchies
wherein our identity is founded and our subjectivity positioned: Marius
versus Jugurtha, Croesus versus Irus, victor versus vanquished, Roman
versus barbarian, rich versus poor, inside versus outside, same versus

other.[51] The logic of desire, however, is fundamentally deconstructive. It both requires these kinds of binary oppositions and undoes them, including that between lover and soldier. Thus, on another level, this same logic is what aligns Propertius and Augustus within the dialectic of transgression and desire,[52] so that each becomes the ironic mirror image of the other.

This homology is made apparent on a number of levels, the most obvious of which is the poet's deployment of the motif of *militia amoris* (3.5.2). Yet this trope is sufficiently common that, despite its use immediately after 3.4's vision of future triumphs over eastern foes, it might be thought to be purely conventional. More convincing, however, is a pair of textual anomalies that have never been adequately explained, each of which demonstrates the homology of the Propertian and Augustan positions with respect to desire. The first is found in the last line of the passage just cited, "optima mors Parcae quae venit acta die" (best is the death that comes on the day appointed by fate). This line has caused much vexation. The main problem is the word *Parcae*. Barber's Oxford Classical Text (OCT) prints the reading of the best mss., *parca*, in daggers. Lachmann notes that *parca dies* as first explained by Scaliger—"the fated day"—is nonsense in Latin. *Parcae dies*, however, gives excellent sense, is easily explained, and is paralleled in *Aeneid* 12.149.[53] The issue that has impeded its universal acceptance is one of interpretation rather than grammar, paleography, or usage: for, are not all deaths those that come on the day of fate? But if that is the case, then what is the point of the distinction Propertius seems to be drawing between the life (and death) of the lover and the soldier? We all die on our appointed days. Enk admirably sums up the logic of this counterargument:

> apparet eam correctionem sensum dare huic loco non aptum. Nam si quis ob stultiam in mari aut in acie perit, ea quoque mors acta venit die Parcarum. Sensus, quem flagitat contextus arsque logica, hic est: optimum est mori, cum confectus annis vitam relinquis. Hunc sensum restituit emendatio Baeherensii: *carpta*[54] qua recepta etiam lectio *apta*[55] in textu ponenda est. (1962: ad loc.)

> It appears that this correction gives an inappropriate sense to this passage. For if anyone, on account of foolishness, dies either at sea or in battle, that death also comes on the day appointed by the fates. The sense that the context and logical consistency demands is this: the best death is that which comes when you leave life weighed down with years. The emendation of Baehrens restores this sense: *carpta*, whereby the received reading *apta* is also to be placed in the text.

The problem, of course, is that Enk assumes that Propertius's goal is logical consistency and that the purpose of the passage is to present a straightforward rhetorical distinction between two opposed styles of life, which we can for our purposes refer to as the Augustan and the elegiac.[56] But as numerous commentators have noted, the essence of Propertian style is just the opposite: it does not present the reader with unproblematic rhetorical demonstrations, but sharp juxtapositions, unstated transitions, and ironic reversals (Luck 1960: 114; Elder 1962: 71–72; Boucher 1980: 316–17; 370; Benediktson 1989: 29). Moreover, this tidying up of the rhetorical distinctions between the Augustan and the elegiac modes of life is in direct contradiction with the thrust of the passage itself, which states that all such categories are invalid in the realm of the dead, "victor cum victis pariter miscebitur umbris." The fact that, no matter when or how one dies, one always dies on the day appointed by fate does not render the passage meaningless but rather proves its point. Thus, on the one hand, the poet's message is certainly that the pursuit of wealth is to be shunned since "you can't take it with you." However, on the other, since there are no distinctions in the underworld, then the lover and the soldier, the poor man and the rich man are both counted the same.[57] We all share equally in Prometheus's mistake. From this perspective, the poet's deployment of the *militia amoris* motif at the poem's beginning is more than the invocation of a well-worn topos. It is a statement of ultimate equality.

Thus, the first of our two textual anomalies clearly reveals as much the aporetical nature of the poet's relation with Augustus as it does the corrupt nature of the text. Most proposed emendations of Propertius have been efforts to smooth out these contradictions and produce a monological text (Boucher 1980: 117 n.1), rather than to read such cruxes symptomatically from the perspective of the emergence of the Real. The homology of the Augustan and elegiac subject positions is, in fact, most interesting in its simultaneous assertion of formal difference (the lover versus the soldier) and substantive identity (the originary or Promethean lack that is desire). It is the contradiction between these two opposed asseverations that constitutes the final irrecuperable remainder, the moment of the Real that can only be attributed to that which must be excluded from a self-consistent Symbolic economy, to that which must be abjected: that is to woman as the excluded ground that makes the masculinist synthesis possible (Kristeva 1977: 165; Moi 1985: 166; Butler 1990: 93).[58]

The same homological structure that unites the opposed positions of the Augustan and elegist can be seen in our second anomaly as well. The last twenty-two lines of the poem consist of a list of topics the poet will study when love has ceased to hold him in thrall (Rothstein 1979: 2.33).

This repetitive catalog, which occupies almost half the poem, is by far the longest in the Propertian corpus. It is an aesthetic blemish. Its very length serves to undermine the otherwise symmetrical structures linking 3.4 and 3.5 (Richardson 1977: 333). How do we explain such a gaffe? Was the poet simply carried away? Is he so infatuated with Alexandrian learning that he cannot resist detailing all the possible topics in natural science, philosophy, and metaphysics that his later studies might cover? Or might this list, in its very repetitive insistence, relate to the theme of the poem itself, that is, to the fundamental inability of desire to be satisfied (except by death)?

It is helpful at this juncture to recall that desire, from a rhetorical perspective, is metonymic in structure. It is an endless series of displacements and inadequate substitutions; its verbal embodiment is the list (Lacan 1986: 143, 340; 1991: 201–2; Žižek 1991: 7; Guyomard 1992: 50). Propertius in the last half of 3.5 asks us to envision him as moving from one realm of intellectual conquest to the next in the same way that his soldierly counterpart must move from one enemy to the next in the first half of the poem and in 3.4. There is a structural symmetry to their respective enterprises. Similarly, just as the first half of the poem ends in the underworld, so does the second. Thus, the poet will finish his career by investigating whether:

> sub terris sint iura deum et tormenta gigantum,
>   Tisiphones atro si furit angue caput,
> aut Alcamaeoniae furiae aut ieiunia Phinei,
>   num rota, num scopuli, num sitis inter aquas,
> num tribus infernum custodit faucibus antrum
>   Cerberus, et Tityo iugera pauca novem,
> an ficta in miseras descendit fabulas gentis
>   et timor haud ultra quam rogus esse potest.
> (3.5.39–46)

> If the laws of the gods and the torments of the giants exist beneath the earth
>   if the head of Tisiphone rages with a black snake,
> or the furies of Alcmaeon or the hungers of Phineus,
>   are there wheels, cliffs, and thirsts in the middle of water,
> does Cerberus with three throats guard the mouth of the cave,
>   and are there nine little acres for Tityus,
> or does a fictive story descend among the wretched peoples,
>   and is there able to be no fear beyond the pyre?

The question of whether the underworld exists might be thought to contradict the earlier claim that all social distinctions will be erased in the underworld, but as in our first instance we are dealing with a formal assertion of difference that masks an underlying substantial identity: for, how can there be social distinctions beyond the grave if there is no beyond? In either case—"the best death comes on its appointed day" or "there are no rich men in the underworld unless it doesn't exist"—we are all equal before death and desire. What remains in both cases then is an assertion of difference that can neither articulate its own underlying assumptions nor be reduced to the terms of mere opposition to an ideological norm. The moment of difference that it enunciates is precisely that which cannot be assimilated to either Augustan imperial ideology or its opposite. Instead, that difference articulates itself as a kind of circularity embodied in the final couplet of the poem, which both functions as an envoi and returns us to the beginning of 3.4, "exitus hic vitae superest mihi: vos, quibus arma / grata magis, Crassi signa referte domum (this is what the end of life has in store for me: you to whom arms / give more pleasure, bring the standards of Crassus home; 3.5.47–48).

REMAINDERS

> [T]he feminine separates and sutures, it is an effect of
> "the vigilance and failure of censorship."
> —Benstock 1991: 118

> That which will not be pinned down by truth is,
> in truth *feminine*.
> —Derrida, *Spurs*, cited by Benstock 1991: 119

Peter White has taught us that it is a vast oversimplification to view the relationship of poets to the Augustan regime as either one of simple conformity to the dictates of an all powerful patron or of heroic resistance to the forces of tyranny. Neither did Maecenas act as a kind of minister of propaganda nor did Augustus dictate the specific kinds of poems that should be written. Nonetheless, as White also points out, it would be a mistake to see the various kind of encomiastic verse produced not only by Horace and Vergil but also by Propertius and even Ovid as unprompted and spontaneous outpourings of genuine emotion. There was a culture of patronage existing at all levels of Roman society that located the individual within a vast web of mutual obligations to his or her social superiors and inferiors. These were often of an informal nature but had direct political consequences and could have legal force. Such relations were the foundation of traditional republican politics. They were also the social fabric into which the poetry of the period was woven. With the collapse of the republic and the coming of the principate, there naturally occurred a centralization of patronage relations as the cultural and politi-

cal life of the city increasingly came to revolve around the imperial house-
hold and those closest to it (White 1993: 28, 119–22, 138, 145, 150–52,
163–67, 208).[59] In any such environment, in which the legitimacy of a
given form of discourse is founded upon relations that either no longer
obtain or have been fundamentally altered, the choice for the speaker
between conformity and resistance is a false one, predicated more on a
bourgeois view of the subject as a unified source of meaning than on
the semantic conditions of possibility for a given discursive formation
(Habinek 1998: 8). Thus what we see in this period is not the institution
of, and the resistance to, a planned program of poetic propaganda, but
the gradual restructuring of the field of social, discursive, and power rela-
tions that made poetic discourse possible within imperial society. Elegy is
a symptom of that restructuration.

Whereas earlier in the century, the collapse of the republic and of the
normative ideology of Roman aristocratic *virtus* had opened up new dis-
cursive spaces and created slippages in the semiotic system that consti-
tuted the Roman Symbolic, as exemplified in the poetry of Catullus, Gal-
lus, and to a lesser extent the *Monobiblos*, the subsequent consolidation
of the principate recentered discursive norms in a way that altered the
nature of what it meant to be a speaking subject (Cairns 1979a: 32;
Maltby 1980: 4). Who spoke to whom and for what purposes all under-
went fundamental changes in this period. With the collapse of the tradi-
tionally decentered (or better, multipolar) web of associations that regu-
lated discursive power in republican Rome, the privileged interlocutor
naturally became the *princeps* and his associates. This, as White (1993:
139–40, 207) points out, was not a deviation from the conditions under
which poetry was produced under the republic but its natural outgrowth.
Poets wanted maximum visibility and thus sought the support of the most
prominent and influential patrons. With the rise of the *princeps*, a single
center of discursive gravity naturally formed. Augustus did not so much
change the rules of the game as the grounds on which the game was
played.[60] He became the patron of all patrons so that, rather than interper-
sonal relations between the elite being conceptualized on the model of
mutual aristocratic obligation in the pursuit of *negotium*, the norm be-
came one of dependent clientage in the pursuit of a cultivated and thus,
from a traditional perspective, effeminized *otium* (see chapters 7 and 8).[61]
Therefore not only did the poets become women but so did their former
patrons as well (Joshel 1992: 151; Edwards 1993: 85; Barton 1993:
29n.63; Oliensis 1997: 154).[62]

This change itself, however, took place within the existing set of social
institutions and was consistently presented as a return to the status quo
ante, a restoration of the republic. As such, the change itself could only
be articulated, within the terms available, as a contradiction. This history

becomes most manifest to us precisely in the moments of poetic aporia that result from the speaking subject being placed in an impossible position: one that allows it neither to accede to a traditional web of aristocratic mutual obligations nor to reject the values inherent in that web; one that neither allows traditional republican *libertas* nor denies it; one that no longer allows the practice of *virtus* as traditionally understood and yet launches a deliberate legislative, religious, and artistic program to encourage its restoration (Last 1934: 456, 459; Littlewood 1983: 2138; Wallace-Hadrill 1985: 183; Edwards 1993: 41–42 and 1996: 49–50, 57).

Propertius, then, is a woman because her excess is the only authentic place from which he can speak, because she simultaneously marks the gap between the Imaginary and the Symbolic and sutures them together. Propertius is a woman because he articulates the rules of the game of power from a position that both accepts that game and finds itself outside the Symbolic system that prescribes it. Propertius is a woman because under the empire, in spite of the variability of individual responses, even a senator can no longer be a man, at least, as the republic understood *dignitas*, manhood, and *virtus* (see chapter 6). Propertius is a woman because Propertius too is a symptom.

Chapter Six

DECONSTRUCTING THE *VIR*:
LAW AND THE OTHER IN THE *AMORES*

> Transgression is neither violence in a divided world
> (in an ethical world) nor a victory over limits (in a
> dialectical or revolutionary world); and exactly for this-
> reason its role is to measure the excessive distance that
> opens at the heart of the limit and to trace the flashing
> line that causes the limit to arise. Transgression contains
> nothing negative, but affirms limited being—affirms the
> limitlessness into which it leaps as it opens this zone to
> existence for the first time.
> —Foucault 1977b: 35

> The new or postmodern development, indeed, remains
> progressive to the degree to which it dispels any last
> illusions as to the autonomy of thought, even though the
> dissipation of those illusions may reveal a wholly
> positivist landscape from which the negative has
> evaporated altogether, beneath the steady clarity of what
> has been identified as "cynical reason."
> —Jameson 1991: 323

OVID IS IN MANY WAYS our intellectual contemporary, an ironist at the end of history. While everyone from Perry Anderson (1992) to Jacques Derrida (1993: 104) has raised theoretical objections to Francis Fukuyama's thesis (1992) that history has reached its telos with the collapse of communism as a viable form of opposition to liberal capitalism, nonetheless credible alternatives to the world domination of American consumer society and its commodified politics are woefully thin on the ground. The position of externality on which the stance of critique depends has evaporated beneath our feet. There is no obvious outside to the present system (Hardt and Negri 2000: 45; Rabasa 2001: 12). The contemporary social critic is reduced to the position of an ironist whose jibes are as much self-consuming artifacts as catalysts for social change. This is a fair description of Ovid and his relation to Augustan ideology as well. Ovidian transgression, like that described by Foucault, "incessantly crosses and recrosses a line which closes up behind it in a wave of extremely short duration" (Foucault 1977b: 34).

In chapter 4, we argued that the postmodern age had better positioned us to understand Tibullus's repetitive and dreamlike poetics. There, following Žižek's definitions of modernism and postmodernism, we contended that Tibullus could be seen as a postmodernist in the same sense as Kafka or Philip Glass (in opposition to the more modernist Propertius, so dear to the heart of Pound and his followers). In that same chapter, we observed that postmodernism as an artistic style dilates on the abundance of the absurd and the unintelligible, rather than examining the lack at the heart of signification after the fashion of modernism. From this perspective, Ovid is a postmodernist of a uniquely contemporary stripe, more along the lines of Andy Warhol than Samuel Beckett or Eugene Ionesco. He is an author of works whose resistance to the dominant mode of the Symbolic is to be found in their uncanny re-production of it. Ovid on this view is more a deconstructionist than a Brechtian poet of Revolution.[1]

Born in 43 B.C.E., the year after Julius Caesar's assassination, Ovid was but twelve at the battle of Actium. By the time he had reached his late teens, the Augustan regime was not only well entrenched but was all he had ever known (Luck 1960: 142). Thus while many have tried to read Ovid's ironic stance in relation to the Augustan program of moral and religious restoration as political opposition, this seems to be based more on wishful thinking than hard-nosed analysis: it is impossible to say either on what that opposition would be based or to what end it could lead (Conte 1994: 342). Indeed, over the past thirty years Ovid had been located all over the ideological map, pro-Augustan, anti-Augustan, and abstracted aesthete (Nugent 1990: 241, 245). Some of this confusion can be written off to our profound historical ignorance about even this well-documented period of Roman history, but it also reflects an ambivalence that is deeply rooted in the nature of Ovid's style.

Ovidian wit skates over surfaces that conceal not hidden depths but a weightless dispersal of meaning. His poems are tight rhetorical constructions with frequent epigrammatic twists (Parker 1969).[2] They do not strain the structures of the Symbolic to the breaking point in the way that Propertius's tortured syntax does, nor do they pile image on image to produce a complex associative web in the fashion of Tibullus's lost idyll of Imaginary union. These are poems that operate within the Symbolic and reproduce its rational structures, but they are also poems that in that very act of reproduction create a space of ironic distance, a kind of fold in the discursive construction of reality (Albrecht 1997: 802; Boucher 1980: 34, 373–74; Barsby 1978: 20; Luck 1960: 150). Every pun reveals not a hidden truth but another series of double meanings that reflects back on itself to create a depthless *mise-en-abyme*.

Such a style naturally produces conflicting evaluations. Thus T. R. Glover wrote, "No one wrote with more grace, no one can be read with more ease . . . there are no undertones, no harmonics, about Ovid's work; it is all on the surface" (1934: 53), and Peter Green, "His seemingly simple verse draws us into a subtle labyrinth of ironic allusiveness; his mythical constructs reveal sociopolitical undertones" (1982: 59). Both are correct. Ovidian superficiality is less a cover for hidden depths of truth than a synecdoche for the series of disjunctive planes across which his complex irony unfolds (Kennedy 1993: 63). It is perhaps W. R. Johnson who comes closest to the truth when he writes of the *Fasti*, "[Ovid] can continue to distract himself . . . but when the fresh ironies grow boring he is left to look at what the ironies were supposed to shield him from—the terrible emptiness of the present, the widening failure of confidence in life or society or anything" (1978–79: 11). What lies beneath the surface of Ovidian wit is precisely nothing.

Ovid is thus not so much anti- or even un-Augustan (Barsby 1978: 10–11, 34) as para-Augustan. His poetry is the product of an anomie in which the integrated self of the Roman republican past, with its totalitarian emphasis on public life to the exclusion of private fulfillment (Veyne 1987: 95), no longer plays a real part. The political self, the religious self, the erotic self, and the domestic self have become so many semiautonomous realms in which the old homologies between *domus*, *amicitia*, and *res publica*, which lay at the heart of the Ciceronian vision of the ideal citizen, are no longer recognizable. Rather the political has become precisely the realm that delimits and makes possible a field of sexual pleasure that is not subordinated to public life and the demands of the *domus*, but coterminous and parallel with them (Habinek 1997: 27–28, 34–35).[3] Thus, as we have just seen in the previous chapter, *Amores* 1.2 picks up on a motif already used by Propertius in 3.4, the depiction of Augustus as the nephew of Amor.[4] Yet, as we argued there, while Propertius's irony is still tied to political actuality through its evocation of the oft-contemplated Parthian campaign, Ovid's cynicism is more formal. Thus, whereas in book 3 of Propertius the position of the elegiac speaking subject is substantially circumscribed, as the space between the poet's Imaginary desire and the emerging imperial Symbolic had been reduced to the point that both the poet's praise and his critique of Augustus are revealed to have the same ground, in Ovid's *Amores* the elegist's stance has become one of transgression, not negation.[5] The crossing of boundaries has become a moment of pure performativity all but devoid of constative content or of an even presumptive moment of externality. The movement of History thus becomes discernible not so much through the manifestation of the Real as through its progressive occultation.

This chapter investigates this process by examining poem 1.2 and its complex relation to Propertius, Vergil, and the Augustan regime. The intertextual ties between the poets is shown to be not only firmly implicated in the political but also the vehicle of its evacuation as allusion is transformed into the medium of a purely performative transgression. The nature of Ovid's transgressive poetics will then be more closely investigated through a reading of *Amores* 1.4 and its imbrication in a rhetoric of law, property, gender, and sexual possession that extends throughout the corpus of the *Amores*. It is precisely around this double axis of law and transgression that Ovid's erotic elegies rotate. At every step, Ovid will be shown to reproduce in detail the structures of the dominant Symbolic regime and to violate them in such a way as to require their preservation.

THE TRIUMPH OF (THE) DESIRE (OF THE OTHER)

> The apparently isolated reference to the real Augustus in
> 1.2 opens up the possibility of parallel political
> discourses to the "realist" adventures of the love-poet
> throughout the *Amores*, while simultaneously blurring
> the distinction between them.
> —Buchan 1995: 65

> L'Autre, latent ou pas, est, dès avant, présent dans
> la révélation subjective.
> —Lacan 1973: 146

As just noted, in the previous chapter we observed that Propertius 3.4.19–20 anticipates *Amores* 1.2.51–52. Each passage calls attention to the presumed kinship of Augustus and Amor, for the *gens Julia* claimed descent from Aeneas and therefore had a special devotion to the cult of Venus Genetrix. The irony of taking such claims literally, however, becomes immediately clear in the elegiac context in which the rejection of war and epic in favor of love and erotic verse are programmatic elements acknowledged by all practitioners (Mack 1988: 64). Moreover, Augustus the moral reformer sorts ill with Augustus Cupid's cousin. The legislator against adultery makes an odd bedfellow with the god of seduction. Propertius, as we saw, deployed this trope, which was directly taken from Caesarian propaganda, in the context of both an evocation of the *Aeneid* and of Augustus's projected campaign to recapture Crassus's lost standards. It was a context that allowed the passage to be read both as serious praise of what would have been a popular campaign and as an ironic undercutting of epic *militia* in favor of elegiac *otium*.

Ovid's use of this same trope is both simpler and more complex. It is simpler because the specific political context of the mid-twenties in which the Augustan regime is still establishing its uncontested legitimacy is all but gone. The *pax Augusta* is an accepted reality and both civil wars and wars of conquest are to be a thing of the past (Boucher 1980: 34; Conte 1994: 252). As Syme observed, "the empire gave no scope for the display of civic virtue at home and abroad, for it sought to abolish war and politics" (1960: 508). Thus, for the Ovid of the *Amores*, the topical reference for the triumph motif, which appears in Propertius 3.4, and the potential political complexity it implies were vanishing. The triumph was no longer something to be aspired to by all Roman commanders, the pinnacle of aristocratic success. By 19 B.C.E., it had become the exclusive property of the imperial household (Eck 1984: 138–39).[6] As P. J. Davis (1999: 439) recently observed, Amor can be granted a triumph in 1.2 because, as the final couplet acknowledges, he is Caesar's relation.

Ovid's use of the trope, however, is more complex than Propertius's because it is woven into a much denser web of intertextual allusion. The first and most obvious intertext is Propertius 3.4. The latter, as noted earlier, had begun with a reference to the *Aeneid*'s "arma virumque cano." *Amores* 1.2 echoes its Propertian antecedent by including its own invocation of Vergil's master narrative of Augustan Rome. It could not, however, simply repeat the Propertian gesture, for Ovid had already parodied the beginning of the *Aeneid* in the first hemistich of the *Amores*, "arma gravi numero." The difference between his citation of *Aeneid* 1.1 and Propertius's is revealing. Where the Propertian reference immediately leads the reader into the problematics of greed as a motive for conquest, "magna, viri, merces! parat ultima terra triumphos" (great rewards men! The ends of the earth prepare triumphs), and hence into a sustained meditation on the nature of desire, which unites 3.4 and 3.5, Ovid's gesture is purely self-reflexive. It leads to a joke on Cupid's theft of one foot from every other line of the epic hexameter and on the creation of the pentameter characteristic of the second verse of the elegiac couplet ("par erat inferior versus; risisse Cupido / dicitur atque unum surripuisse pedem" (the second verse was the same as the first; Cupid is said / to have laughed and to have stolen a foot; 1.1.3–4).[7]

In 1.2, then, Ovid must look to a different Vergilian intertext to parallel Propertius's choice in 3.4. The passage he picks is one of the most unambiguously pro-Augustan in all the *Aeneid*, Jupiter's prophecy to Venus of Rome's coming greatness and of Augustus's closing of the gates of war on the temple of Janus in 27 B.C.E.:

> aspera tum positis mitescent saecula bellis;
> cana Fides et Vesta, Remo cum fratre Quirinus,
> iura dabunt. dirae ferro et conpagibus artis

claudentur Belli portae; Furor impius intus
saeva sedens super arma et centum vinctus aënis
post tergum nodis fremet horridus ore cruento.
(1.291–96)

Then the bitter age will mellow with wars put aside;
white-haired Fides and Vesta, Romulus with his brother Remus,
will give laws. The horrible gates of war will be closed
with iron and tight fittings; inside, Furor, which recognizes no sense of duty,
sitting on savage arms and chained by a hundred brass bonds
on its back, will frightfully howl with its bloody mouth.

The Ovidian passage is the exact opposite of Vergil's. In it, Furor is set
free and Mens Bona (Good Sense) and Pudor (Shame)—clear parallels to
Fides and Vesta—are made captive (Philips 1980: 275–77; McKeown
1989: ad loc.; Mack 1988: 63):

ipse ego, praeda recens, factum modo vulnus habebo
    et nova captiva vincula mente feram.
Mens Bona ducetur manibus post terga retortis
    et Pudor et castris quidquid Amoris obest.
omnia te metuent, ad te sua bracchia tendens
    volgus 'io' magna voce 'triumphe' canet.
Blanditiae comites tibi erunt Errorque Furorque,
    adsidue partes turba secuta tuas.
(1.2.29–36)

I myself, your most recent prize, shall now be wounded
    and I shall bear new shackles with a captive mind.
Good Sense will be led with her hands bound behind her back
    and Shame and whatever else is opposed to Cupid's camp.
All things will fear you, stretching their arms out to you
    the crowd will sing out with a great voice, "io triumphe."
Flattery, Error, and Furor will be your companions,
    The mob that has always followed your faction.[8]

Where Vergil is writing a moving paean to the end of civil slaughter, Ovid
is proclaiming the virtue of the *amator*'s subjection to Love's empire. The
triumph motif recalls the Propertian intertext as well, but where that
poem presents a private perspective on the public spectacle of Augustus's
projected conquest of the Parthians, this poem makes a public spectacle
of the poet's subjection to the whims of love. In neither case does the
elegist occupy the position of Augustus's ideal public citizen (Grimal
1986: 142)—although who could actually occupy that space, with its im-
possible combination of republican *virtus* and imperial subjection, is far
from clear.

Nonetheless, it is not that Ovid's appropriation of the triumph motif is not subversive. It is. But its inversion of established values takes place within a vacuum. When he reverses the order of Vergil's passage, binding Mens Bona and releasing Furor, he is not simultaneously inverting Vergil's meaning. Ovid denies neither that the civil wars have ended nor does he call for their resumption. Rather his position is predicated on the assumption that Vergil's prophecy has been accomplished, that the doors of the temple of Janus will remain closed, and that the dominant values of the imperial Symbolic can therefore be inverted, precisely because they are fundamentally sound (Du Quesnay 1973: 42). Ovid's Furor represents not the bloody maw of fratricidal strife that haunts Vergil, but the mundane irrationality of the desire for Imaginary satisfaction now allowed to run riot in the well-demarcated and pacified fields of early imperial ideology. It is a rational irrationality that accepts the terms of the Augustan settlement and re-presents them as the conditions of possibility for its own desire (Labate 1987: 96–97). Moreover, it is perhaps this very camp acceptance of the Augustan Symbolic that caused Ovid alone of the elegists eventually to feel the full force of the emperor's wrath. He in the end appeared to be the most dangerous because he alone accepted the new regime for what it was and therefore reproduced its founding contradictions (Johnson 1978–79: 13; Conte 1994: 256; Stapleton 1996: 10).[9] In Ovid, Augustus saw his own inverted but necessary reflection, as Ovid saw his in Augustus. As such, they each in their profoundly duplicitous relationship with the other, conformed to "the classic Lacanian definition of communication, by which the speaker receives from the other his own message in its true, inverted form. It is in the 'essential by-products' of his activity, in its unintended results, that his message's true, effective meaning is returned to the subject" (Žižek 1991: 78). Each in turn, Ovid and Augustus, was the desire of the Other.

This same pattern of ideological inversion through re-presentation can be seen in the last of 1.2's intertexts under discussion. As already noted, the final couplet of the poem in its evocation of Amor as the *cognatus* of Augustus—"aspice cognati felicia Caesaris arma: / qua vicit, victos protegit ille manu" (behold the blesséd arms of your cousin Caesar: / by means of the hand with which he conquered, that one protected the conquered; 1.2.51–52)—recalls Propertius 3.4's use of the same trope. The distich itself, however, also alludes to a passage from another Propertian poem, which makes reference to an even more incendiary context, 2.16.41–42, "Caesaris haec virtus et gloria Caesaris haec est: / illa, qua vicit, condidit arma manu" (this is the manly courage of Caesar and this is his glory: / with the very hand by means of which he conquered, he put away his arms); (Walter 1999: 92; McKeown 1989: ad loc.). We examined this passage from Propertius at the beginning of the previous chapter.

There we noted that these lines refer to Mark Antony and his shameful conduct at the battle of Actium and that this negative description contrasted with the more positive portrayal of Antonian excess as an antidote to civil slaughter in 2.15.

With this background in mind, Hermann Walter's (1999: 94–96) reading of the intertextual relation between 2.16.41–42 and *Amores* 1.2.51–52 is particularly enlightening. Walter demonstrates that Amor occupies the position of Antony in Ovid's text. Amor, he argues, therefore stands for a dangerous Dionysian excess that is in direct opposition to Augustus's own self-chosen model of Apollonian control. Thus in 1.2 Amor, the *princeps*'s *cognatus*, presents a threatening parody of the traditional Roman triumph. He is not the victorious hero who returns to bask in the acclamation of his fellow citizens and reaffirm the integrity of the existing order, but a tyrant whose passion has turned uncontrollably against the adoring crowd, and who treats his own people as a conquered nation. He represents a loss of self-control, the reign of Furor:

> tunc quoque non paucos, si te bene novimus, ures;
> > tunc quoque praeteriens vulnera multa dabis.
> non possunt, licet ipse velis, cessare sagittae;
> > fervida vicino flamma vapore nocet.
> talis erat domita Bacchus Gangetide terra:
> > tu gravis alitibus, tigribus ille fuit.
> (1.2.43–48)

> Then also you (Amor) will burn many men, if we have known you well;
> > then also you will give many wounds as you pass by.
> The arrows cannot be stopped, even if you wished it;
> > the seething flame harms whoever stands near its heat.
> Such was the behavior of Bacchus in the conquered land of the Ganges:
> > you are fearsome[10] with your wings, as that one was with his tigers.

In this Dionysian guise, Amor is the perfect model for Antony who, according to Velleius Paterculus (2.82.4), in 34 B.C.E. celebrated his triumph over the Armenians in Alexandria with Cleopatra rather than returning to Rome. There he portrayed himself as the New Dionysus. From the perspective of Roman propaganda, this was a major gaffe. It was precisely the kind of "eastern excess" that allowed Augustus to portray himself as the defender of traditional Roman order against the dangers of an orientalizing and effeminate tyranny (cf. Propertius 3.11 and Horace, *Odes* 1.37).

The Propertian intertext allows the connection with Antony to be made and exploited in Ovid's poem. Yet that very intertext is also what insists that the two passages produce very different political significations. In 25 B.C.E. when book 2 of Propertius was published, the memory of the

Antonian opposition, of the battle of Actium (31 B.C.E.), of Octavian's triple triumph (29 B.C.E.), and of his being voted the title Augustus by the senate and closing the doors of the temple of Janus (27 B.C.E.) were all fresh. Moreover, for Propertius the horrors of the civil wars were no mere abstraction, as demonstrated by poems 1.21 and 1.22. By the time the first edition of the *Amores* was being published in the teens, let alone when the revised second edition was published in the last decade of the first century B.C.E. or at the beginning of the common era[11] (and there is no way to know whether 1.2 dates to the original edition), the memory of Antony and Cleopatra belonged to the rapidly receding past. Where the Propertian text refers to the battle of Actium, the Ovidian text refers to Propertius (Arkins 1990: 827–28). Ovid uses the Propertian text to sublimate the unresolvable political contradictions it articulates into a formal ironic undercutting of Augustan seriousness that both exposes the contradictions of that ideology (Augustus = the offspring of Venus; Amor = the offspring of Venus; Amor = Antony; therefore Amor = Augustus's evil twin), and yet leaves everything as he found it. Ovid's rational irrationality is not a call to a truly Antonian excess, let alone a call to arms. It is a reflection of the contradictions already contained in the Augustan Symbolic.

These contradictions ultimately call into question the nature of traditional Roman manhood, which defined itself in terms of self-control and domination of those under its *potestas*. Law, politics, and warfare were the primary Symbolic arenas through which masculinity sought the confirmation of its Imaginary self-projection. The Augustan restoration proclaimed both the return to the virtues of the past and made their exercise impossible. The nature of the new situation was nicely captured by T. F. Higham who in 1934 wrote of *Amores* 1.2, "Augustus is compared in the final couplet with his mythical relative (*cognatus*), the victorious Cupid (*Am.* I.2.51f). Rome's victories mean little to Ovid,—beyond the chance of comforting his puella with a blonde wig . . . (*Am.* I.14)" (1934: 113). The pacification of the empire and the "restoration of the republic" were in effect the end of Roman *virtus* as traditionally defined. The principate was, as Syme said, the end of war and politics, of *dignitas* as Caesar and Pompey understood it. This is Augustus's great accomplishment, and Ovid was his faithful reflection.

The political, to the extent that it exists in the *Amores*, is, in fact, rendered all but coterminous with the amorous and the personal, the Symbolic with the Imaginary, and the referential with the intertextual (Buchan 1995: 64–65). The hierarchical relation that subordinated one term to the other is no longer truly functional. The space of difference between these opposites is reduced to that minimally necessary for reflection, a space that is by definition never self-identical and hence ironic. The gap that opened between the Imaginary and the Symbolic in the late republic is closing, but the new order that is emerging is fundamentally different from that which preceded it. The old subordinations and homologies are no longer in place. It is in the context of this duplicitous reflection that the space of Ovidian manhood defines itself. It is in this space of doubling that the Augustan Symbolic lays down the law of genre and gender that the Ovidian elegiac subject transgresses. This space makes possible the *Amores* as we know them.

IT'S A MAN'S WORLD

Unlike the lover, the client is not cushioned by a residual
masculine superiority; when he humbles himself before
his patron, there is nothing between him and the ground.
—Oliensis 1997: 157

Augustus himself was usually tactful enough to
avoid stressing his own dominance in such a way as
to remind senators publicly of what some of them
regarded as their subjection, their *servitus* (literally,
"slavery"); and those of his successors who were proved
"good emperors" (that is to say, emperors of whom
the senate approved) persevered for some generations
in the same tradition. In the early Principate the senator
might well feel irked by his "servitus," but under a good
emperor he would normally feel bound to suppress
such dangerous emotions.
—Ste. Croix 1981: 369

Poem 1.4 of the *Amores* is understudied. McKeown (1989) lists a single article from 1966 in the bibliography of his recent commentary. A quick perusal of the past fifteen year's of *L'année philologique* reveals only one article, published in 1994, while the most recent book-length study of the *Amores*, Boyd's *Ovid's Literary Loves* (1997), contains not a single reference to the poem. Greene's *Erotics of Domination* (1998) offers close readings of 1.1, 1.2 and 1.5, but passes over 1.4 in silence. This neglect is undeserved for a poem that, I believe, is crucial to our understanding of the collection as a whole. Situated between the opening three avowedly programmatic poems and the famous (or infamous) 1.5 in which Corinna finally receives her name, 1.4 represents the beginning of the sequence's narrative proper (Wille 1984: 397; Buchan 1995: 67, 75–76). In this poem, the drama of the *Amores* moves beyond the hollow, specular play of love without an object and a poet without a subject, portrayed in 1.1

and 1.2 (Kennedy 1993: 65), to pry open the narcissistic game of mutual reflection between lover and beloved captured in the final couplet of 1.3, "nos quoque per totum pariter cantabimur orbem / iunctaque semper erunt nomina nostra tuis" (and we shall be sung together throughout the whole world / my name will be ever joined to yours).[12] In fact, 1.4 exposes the asymmetrical dyad of poet as *amator* and *puella* as *materies* (1.3.19; Greene 1998: 76–77) to the gendered laws and expectations of Roman sociality.

Amores 1.4, in short, introduces Corinna's *vir*. The term itself is ambiguous and much debated (Davis 1999: 445–46). On the one hand, it suggests that he is Corinna's husband and hence that the relationship portrayed in the *Amores* is an adulterous one. This reading sees Ovid deliberately flouting Augustus's moral reform and its reconstruction of *virtus*—"virtue," "courage," but also "manliness"—as embodied in the *mos maiorum*.[13] The most prominent advocate of this reading has been Gordon Williams (1968: 528–29, 539, 542), who argues that all the elegiac *dominae*, with the exception of Gallus's Lycoris, were adulterous *matronae*.[14] The use of the term *vir* and the invocation of a quasi-legal arrangement governing their relationship (*iure coacta*, 1.4.64) supports this reading.

At the same time, the *vir* may refer merely to Corinna's man of the moment and reflect her status as a *meretrix*. Stroh is the most forceful advocate of this position. He argues in response to Williams that terms such as *vir, maritus*, and *uxor* were merely metaphors for stable long-term relationships that never rose to the level of legal marriage. He (1979: 331–34) offers a host of parallel passages to bolster his thesis, although a perusal of the available translations and commentaries quickly shows his to be a minority position.[15]

There is, then, a division of scholarly opinion. What does seem clear, however, is that the ambiguity inherent in the term provides Ovid with plausible deniability, allowing him to appear both subversive and submissive at the same time (Green 1982: 272). Indeed virtually everyone agrees that the language used in the poem is deliberately deceptive and that, through it, Ovid is either suggesting the possibility of violating the *lex Iulia's* ban on adultery or he is stepping as close as he can to the boundary without actually crossing over it.[16] The *vir*, then, marks the space of both the law and its transgression, within the symbolic economy of this poem (Macey 1993: 138). Through him, I contend, poem 1.4 constructs an extraordinarily dense web of ideologically charged signifiers, out of whose various threads the text of the *Amores* is woven, creating an all but impenetrable weave of gender, law, love and violence that both deconstructs the values that characterize the Augustan settlement and demonstrates the impossibility of escaping them.

Whither the *VIR*

The inherent doubleness of Corinna's *vir*—as both lover and husband—
is symptomatic of the unstable nature of the category throughout the
Amores: he is a person whose prerogatives are guaranteed neither by natu-
ral law nor agreed-upon rights, but whose very definition invokes both
categories. Indeed, his only consistent characteristic is his opposition to
the desires of Ovid and Corinna. He is a product and the producer of
difference. He represents more a token in Ovid's game of love than a
person. This reduction of the other to a signifier of pure opposition, al-
most without positive content, is nowhere so clear as in the contradiction
between the poet's stance in *Amores* 2.19 and that in 3.4. In 2.19, the
maritus of Ovid's newest mistress (2.19.19–20) is urged to keep closer
watch over his wife (*uxor*, 2.19.46) lest the poet lose interest.[17] In 3.4, the
vir (3.4.1), again identified as a *maritus* (3.4.27), is now admonished to
call off the guards who, the poet claims, only whet his appetite (Mack
1988: 59).[18] The contradictory demands to which the masculine other is
subjected reveal the *vir* to be less a consistent character in a realistic narra-
tive than a logically necessary third position that by imposing the law
makes possible the delights of transgressing it. At the same time, the *vir*
serves a valuable function within the economy of the affairs depicted in
the *Amores*. As the bringer of opposition and difference, he prevents the
love relationship from collapsing into a game of narcissistic reflection (Bu-
chan 1995: 77). He stands for the social norms that elegy famously seeks
to violate (Sullivan 1972: 23; Hallett 1973: 108; Gaisser 1983: 66; Van
Nortwick 1990: 121). The legitimacy of his claim to Corinna in 1.4, his
vir-ility (or should I say *vir*-iness?), is what makes the elegiac love affair
possible in its very self-definition as the opposite of epic and of social
normality (cf. *Amores* 1.1).[19] The possibility of adultery becomes the sig-
nifier of the law itself, the foundation of *virtus* (Copley 1956: 100). Thus
at the end of 2.19 Ovid's persona becomes a forceful, if ironic, advocate
for the *lex Iulia*'s banning of *lenocinium*, or the practice of husbands
pandering for their wives (Davis 1999: 446–47).[20] The *desultor amoris*
has become the unlikely proponent of Augustan moral reform—of course,
only as a means of insuring the continuing possibility of erotic transgres-
sion (Davis 1989: 49). The opposite position is adopted in 3.4 when the
same logic is used to argue that the law only invites transgression. Here
the *vir* is urged to practice *lenocinium* (3.4.45–48) as a means both to
private enrichment and of insuring his wife's fidelity:[21]

> cui peccare licet, peccat minus: ipsa potestas
>   semina nequitiae languidiora facit.
> desine, crede mihi, vitia inritare vetando;
>   obsequio vinces aptius illa tuo.
> (3.4.9–12)

Who is permitted to sin sins less: that very power
   makes the seeds of wantonness grow slack.
Believe me, stop encouraging vices by forbidding them,
   you will better triumph over them by your submission.

The *vir*, therefore, must assert his rights if transgression is to be possible and must allow transgression if he does not wish to lose his rights.

Even this, however, is an oversimplification, for while the *vir* represents Ovid's other, Ovid nonetheless is a *vir*, and his attempts to establish his differences from Corinna's *vir* are consistently undermined. The adulterous triangle, which cannot help but recall that more fundamental triad of the Freudian family romance—wherein the father's function is to introduce Law and difference (Lacan 1975: 71; 1986: 356–57; Althusser 1996c: 27)—is in constant danger of collapsing, inasmuch as Ovid can only advance his claims on Corinna by assuming the position of the *vir*, that is, by taking on the name of the father and becoming a *vir* as well. Thus in 3.11.17–18, when Ovid faces the humiliation of Corinna's having taken another lover, he cries out "quando ego non fixus lateri patienter adhaesi, / ipse tuus custos, ipse *vir*, ipse comes?" (When have I not patiently stayed fixed to your side / I myself your guardian, your *husband/ man*, your companion?). On the one hand, the *Amores* deconstruct the category of manhood (*virtus*), revealing it to be a ramshackle piece of ideological bricolage, founded on difference and deployed as a tool of domination (Greene 1994; 1999; Walters 1997; Spivak 1976: xviii–xx). On the other, the distinction between the position of the narrator and that of the *vir* is revealed to be just as arbitrary as *virtus* itself, so that rather than offering the opportunity to step outside the ruling ideology, the *Amores* remain its ironic reflection.

Indeed, poem 1.4's companion piece, 2.5, shows Ovid to be in precisely the same position as the *vir* in 1.4; the tables have turned but the game remains the same. In this later poem, Corinna deploys against the *amator* the very tricks Ovid had instructed her to use against the *vir* (cf. 2.5.15– 18 and 1.4.17–20, and 2.5.30 and 1.4.40; Booth 1991: 38–39; Stapleton 1996: 16). The symmetry between the two poems is so complete, and the resultant subject position so schizophrenic, that Maleuvre (1998: 195–96) was reduced to the expedient of claiming that we must assume two separate speakers. This seems too high a price to pay merely to preserve the illusion of a stable Cartesian subject in a text that rejects all calls for characterological consistency and instead stages the collapse of the subject as a useful category of analysis in Roman life (Mack 1988: 58–59; Stapleton 1996: 32). The two poems are clearly meant to be read together in the same manner as 2.19 and 3.4, the other pair devoted to adultery and the *vir* (Williams 1968: 53; Du Quesnay 1973: 5; Davis 1989: 78n.42).

Indeed, the four form a set of two diptychs that open and close the collection (Barsby 1978: 9; Booth 1991: 11–12).[22] The parallelism between the two sets of poems is underlined by a textual echo between 2.19.34, the first poem of the second pair, "ei mihi, ne monitis torquear ipse meis" (alas, may I not be undone by my own precepts), and 1.4.46, the first poem of the first pair, "exemplique metu torqueor ipse mei" (I am undone with fear of my own example). In each case, the *amator*'s imagined torture is based on his perception of the commutablity of his subject position with that of the other, with his status as the other's reflection. In both poems, it is precisely the symmetry of their positions that allows Ovid's actions against the *vir* to redound to his own detriment.

The *vir*, then, is both the necessary sign of difference and a representation of the prerogatives and position that Ovid must appropriate if he is to stake his claim to Corinna. Yet the moment he makes that claim, then he has become the *vir* and is open to the same usurpations and appropriations that once defined his own position as the *amator*. He too becomes vulnerable to the interventions of an uninvited third party. The adulterous-Oedipal triangle is reconstituted with Ovid at its head.[23]

> "Quid facis?" exclamo "quo nunc mea gaudia defers?
>   iniciam dominas in mea iura manus.[24]
> Haec tibi sunt mecum, mihi sunt communia tecum:
>   in bona cur quisquam tertius ista venit?"
> (2.5.29–32)

> "What are you doing?" I shout "On whom are you bestowing my joys?
>   I will lay a master's claim to what is mine by right.
> Your joys are held in common with me, mine are held in common with you:
>   why does some third person partake of these goods?"

The anomalous character of the *vir* reveals the *Amores* to be less a work critical of Augustan culture than one that plays ironically upon the impossibility of escaping the deployment of competitive gendered power in the *urbs aeterna*.[25] No outside can be envisioned here. No alterity is postulated: only an endless repetition of the same moves as *amator* and *vir* change places around the fixed point of the *puella*.

In developing the initial portrayal of this masculine minuet, poem 1.4 consistently mixes images of property and legitimacy, violence and barbarity, lovemaking and rape in ways that purport to establish strict distinctions between the roles of *amator* and *vir* but which, on closer examination, undermine them. Whereas in Tibullus and Propertius the possibility of a utopian space beyond the traditional confines of republican and Augustan ideology is always at least posited—if then placed under erasure—in Ovid the utopian beyond has vanished or become indistinguishable from the dystopia of the present. As he cynically observes in the *Ars Amatoria*, we already live in the golden age, "aurea sunt vere nunc saecula: plurimus auro / venit honos, auro conciliatur amor" (this is the true golden age: the largest part of honor comes from gold, love is won by gold; 2.277–78). The Ovidian universe is a closed system. The outside is unthinkable and will remain so even once he must experience it directly when exiled to Tomis. It is for this reason that J. P. Sullivan identified the *Amores* as symptomatic that "the counter-revolution had already been effected" (1976: 90). In Ovid, the oppositional element of elegy, so commonly, if problematically, identified in Propertius and Tibullus, is subverted in the very act of its assertion. Adultery is ultimately indistinguishable from marriage; *amator* and *vir* are both identical and opposed.[26]

Just between Us Boys

Thus in 1.4, after the introduction of the *vir*, Ovid compares himself to the Centaurs (*ambiguos . . . viros*, 1.4.8) at the banquet of the Lapiths. Far from being an exemplum that, as Whitaker argues, "has little or no illustrative value" (1983: 150), this image of drunken sexual violence, of contested rights of sexual possession, in many ways sums up the poem as a whole. It recalls the bestial rapes by Jupiter of Io, Leda, and Europa described in 1.3.21–24, which already hint at the violence that goes by the name of seduction. Indeed, as more than one commentator has noted, this is an odd series of exempla to use to illustrate the happy lot awaiting the beloved if she follows Ovid's instructions, "te mihi materiem felicem in carmina praebe" (offer yourself to me as the happy subject of my songs) (Lyne 1980: 257; Davis 1989: 71; Stapleton 1996: 10–11; Greene 1998: 74–77). In this same poem, Ovid ironically begins by referring to himself as the *praeda* or booty of the as-yet-unnamed Corinna, a term he had used in 1.2 when describing himself as a captive in Cupid's triumph (Kennedy 1993: 68). Hence, the fundamentally violent and coercive nature of amorous possession, as something that implies the forceful seizure of a prize that belongs to another, and so entails the loss of freedom in the name of proprietary rights won by force, has already been established. The words *praeda* or *praedata* occur seven times in book 1 of the *Amores*, in each case concerning a conflict over who controls the rights of amorous possession and involving implicit or explicit violence.[27] *Praeda* reappears in 2.12's recapitulation of 1.2 and 1.7's triumph motifs (2.12.1–8)[28] and in 2.17's revisiting of the theme of *servitium amoris*,[29] where Ovid appears as his mistress's spear-won slave (2.17.5–6).[30] In all cases, *praeda* points to the asymmetrical power relations that invariably mark Ovidian erotic intrigue[31] and to the accompanying violence that transgresses, defends, and undergirds its concepts of *virtus* and law.

Thus the legitimacy of the claims of the *vir* in 1.4, whose proprietary rights over the *amator*'s beloved are doubly asserted in the repetition of the possessive adjective *tuus* in 1.4's opening couplet, is initially contrasted with the violence and barbarity of the centaurs who in a drunken frenzy assaulted the bride of their host (Olstein 1980: 295). However, this same comparison of *amator* to centaur also explicitly establishes the *amator* as a *vir*, if more violent and less couth than the *vir* described in lines 1–6, and hence more ambiguous. Still, we must ask ambiguous in what sense? The barbarity of the centaur, his semibestial quality, indicates that the *vir* must walk a fine line between an overrefinement that traditional Roman ideology sees as a sign of softness, and hence effeminacy, and an undue harshness or lack of refinement that threatens the nature of *virtus* and virility every bit as much. Moreover, insofar as Ovid's later contention is that the *vir* extracts his kisses from the beloved by force (1.4.63–66), while those received by the *amator* are freely given, the contrast in terms of violence versus legitimacy that underwrites the opposition between *vir* and centaur is difficult to maintain.

oscula iam sumet, iam non tantum oscula sumet
    quod mihi das furtim, iure coacta dabis.
Verum invita dato (potes hoc) similisque coactae:
    blanditiae taceant sitque maligna Venus.

Now he will take kisses, now he will take not only kisses:
    what you give to me secretly, you will give to him forced by law.
Truly, give it to him unwillingly and like someone who is forced (you can do this):
    let all sweet talk be silent and the sex bad.

In this passage, we have an inversion of the normal relations of property to legitimacy in Roman life. The *amator*, who is cast as a thief or *fur*, is making a claim to legitimacy based precisely on the fact that he has no proprietary claims to Corinna's love and thus it is freely given by her. This inversion aligns law, violence, and the *vir* on one side of the equation and places transgression, legitimacy, and the *amator* on the other. Law is depicted as a type of illegitimate primal violence that forces people to act under coercion, in the manner of slaves who do not control their own bodies (Cicero, *De Officiis* 1.150–51).[32] This equation between law and subjection is made apparent in the final poem of book 1 when Ovid writes:

Quid mihi, Livor edax, ignavos obicis annos,
    ingeniique vocas carmen inertis opus,
non me more patrum, dum strenua sustinet aetas,
    praemia militiae pulverulenta sequi

nec me verbosas leges ediscere nec me
ingrato vocem prostituisse foro?
(1.15.1–6)

Acid Envy, why do you charge me with having wasted my years
  and why do you say that poetry is the work of a lazy soul?
Why do you object that, while my age still permits such strenuous pursuits,
I do not in the manner of our ancestors seek the dusty honors of the soldier?
Why do you object that I neither explicate longwinded laws
  nor prostitute[33] my voice to the thankless forum?

Here Ovid, while invoking the standard elegiac defiance of customary Roman morality, by refusing the career paths of the army, jurisconsult, or advocate, specifically equates the practice of law with a form of prostitution (Davis 1993: 68). This had already been suggested in 1.10.41–44's immediate juxtaposition of the lawyer who accepts a fee from his clients with the free woman who prostitutes herself by using her beauty to add to the family fortune, either through her husband's practice of *lenocinium*, as in 2.19 and 3.4, or through a fortunate marriage (Tracy 1978–79: 58–59; McKeown 1989: ad loc.).[34] Thus in 1.10 and 1.15 marriage, the law, and prostitution are, if not directly equated with one another, at least figured as possible metonymic substitutions, occupying structurally analogous positions in the collection's signifying chain.[35] In all three cases, the *matrona*, the *meretrix*, and the advocate take up a position where they must offer themselves (*prostare*) in return for a possible benefit, and thus they come under the compulsion of others (Davis 1989: 74), a subjection whose rights can in turn be codified according to a rule or law (*ius*).[36] The equation produced is something like the following: *matrona* and *meretrix* both yield their favors due to external coercion. Therefore *matrona* = *meretrix*. Lawyers must prostitute themselves. Therefore *orator* = *meretrix*. Hence the logical conclusion would be, although it is never drawn, *orator* = *matrona*, making only the extralegal *amator* a real *vir*.[37] Thus, the *matrona* and *meretrix* occupy both inverted and identical positions in much the same fashion as the *vir* and the *amator*, the self-confessed centaur or "*vir ambiguus*."

Moreover, the monstrous quality of the lover as centaur clashes with the role of *praeceptor amoris* that the poet subsequently assumes as he instructs Corinna in the art of deceiving her *vir*. This latter identity, a traditional pose of the elegiac poet, self-consciously defines itself as soft or *mollis* in opposition to the hard masculinity of normative Roman *virtus*, embodied both in elegy's generic opposite, epic, and in the *vir*'s *rigidum pectus* (1.4.36; Kennedy 1993: 31–34, 62; Edwards 1993: 63–66, 93; Buchan 1995: 74). As Sharrock notes, "The lover must—paradoxically— be weak to be strong, yield to win and even fail as a lover to succeed as a poet, for the classic paradigm of elegy is the locked out lover. Ovid has it both ways: making a sexual and poetic virtue (*vir*-tue) out of his failure" (1995: 157, see also 162–63, 174). The paradox then is that the poet portrays himself as simultaneously more barbarous (i.e., a centaur) and less harsh, *durus*, than the *vir*. Yet this contradiction, in terms of Roman sexual ideology, is more apparent than real. For inasmuch as *mollitia* was defined as a loss of self-control, then the centaurs and the elegiac poet were all equally *mollis* in relation to the *vir*, even as they might appear to be polar opposites. It is as if in their very excess of virility the centaurs have become a group that is to be dominated rather than dominant. They are not fully men and hence they are, in the zero-sum game of Roman sexual politics, necessarily effeminate. Everyone is getting screwed here.

Masculinity, thus, is revealed as a highly fragile construction, prey at any moment to flip over into its opposite. It is defined not as a positive essence but as a moment of pure difference, neither x nor y, always open to loss and appropriation (Kremer-Marietti 1985: 253–56; Kennedy 1993: 39; Edwards 1993: 75, 81). In addition, it is precisely this moment of pure difference—the phallus understood in its psychoanalytic essence[38]—that the *amator* must appropriate in asserting the legitimacy of his claims to the *puella* in contradistinction to those of the *vir*. The difference between these two rivals must be firmly drawn if Ovid is to usurp the *vir*'s position: for if they were identical no subversion would be necessary. Yet usurping the *vir* puts the *amator* in the paradoxical position of having to make a move in which the difference that empowers him is what he must ultimately deny. "The goal is to outwit the rival . . . by, in effect, exchanging roles. The *vir* becomes the intruder into Ovid's private relationship with the girl" (Tracy 1978–79: 59–60).

UNHAND ME

Indeed, the coincidence of the *amator* and *vir*'s virile identities is underlined by the diction in the opening passage. In the last line describing the *vir*, before the invocation of the battle between the Lapiths and the centaurs, the *amator* envisions his rival engaging in amorous play with his beloved. He asks incredulously, "iniciet collo, cum volet, ille manum?" (will that one put his hand on your neck whenever he wishes? 1.4.6). The primary meaning of *inicio* here is generally thought to be "embrace" (McKeown 1989: ad loc.), but I have chosen to stick with a more neutral translation, "put," to highlight Ovid's subsequent wordplay: for, the figure of the *manus* constitutes an important ideological signifier in this poem, marking the nexus where violence and eroticism, law and its violation, *vir* and *amator* meet.[39] Indeed, as we shall see, this same line can also be read as a formula claiming legal ownership whose currency can be traced back to the third of the Twelve Tables (Davis 1993: 65). The complications become apparent almost immediately. Thus in line 10, we find the *amator*, on analogy with the centaur, confessing, "vix a te videor posse tenere manus" (I scarcely seem able to keep my hands off you). Again the erotic sense predominates, but the violent context of attempted rape evoked by the simile alerts us to undertones that are more sinister. As Henri Bornecque notes, "L'expression latine veut dire aussi—et plus souvent—'se retenir de frapper' " (1961: 103).[40] This latter meaning is illustrated in 1.8.109–12 when the poet stands behind the door listening to the *lena*, Dipsas, explain to Corinna how she should be dunning the *amator* for gifts. He exclaims:

> vox erat in cursu, cum me mea prodidit umbra,
> > at nostrae vix se continuere manus
> quin albam raramque comam lacrimosaque vino
> > lumina rugosas distraherentque genas

> She was talking away, when my shadow betrayed me,
> > and my hands were scarcely able to restrain themselves
> from tearing to shreds her thin white hair,
> > her eyes bleary with wine, and her wrinkled cheeks.

This passage, while there is no possibility of an erotic interpretation, necessarily colors its earlier erotic counterpart. The very existence of an exclusively violent reading of the phrase, "vix se continuere manus," means that the earlier erotic passage in 1.4, "vix . . . posse tenere manus," can never be reread outside this context. Law, violence, ownership, rape, and lovemaking momentarily become one in the act of laying hands upon another. The implicit violence of 1.4's simile comparing Ovid with the *viri ambigui*, the centaurs, here becomes explicit. Of course, *praeda*, amorous triumph, and bestial rape were already established in 1.2 and 1.3 as the currency of Ovid's erotic realm. In this passage at the end of 1.8, with its echo of the phrasing of 1.4.10, the playful abstraction of *militia amoris*—which is elaborated into the collection's most memorable conceit in the next poem, 1.9 (Olstein 1980: 291)—is concretized in a chilling moment that deconstructs both the opposition between the figural language of amorous play and literal violence, as well as the gender hierarchies that opposition subtends.[41] Thus, Stapleton notes, the end of 1.8 invites scrutiny precisely because it exposes the *amator* "for what he is" (1996: 20).[42]

Moreover, the conjunction of *manus* with *praeda* but a few lines earlier in 1.8.92, where the *lena* urges Corinna to enlist her mother, sister, and nurse in the effort to shake down the *amator*, cannot help but recall a more sinister collocation of these terms in poem 1.7, where the poet's *manus* are the feared instruments of amorous violence (1.7.1, 1.7.4, 1.7.28, 1.7.62), and he has himself become the *praeda* of blind anger (1.7.44). Indeed the threatened attack on Dipsas's face echoes the "real" attack portrayed in 1.7 and prepares the way for 1.9's ironic apotheosis of amatory violence.

> ante eat effuso tristis captiva capillo,
>   si sinerent laesae, candida tota, genae.
> aptius inpressis fuerat livere labellis
>   et collum blandi dentis habere notam.
> (1.7.39–42)

> Let the sad captive go before, her hair undone,
>   white as marble were it not for her wounded cheeks.
> Her neck would have been more appropriately bruised by our passionate kisses
>   and better borne the mark of an amorous tooth.[43]

This passage recapitulates Amor's triumph over Ovid in 1.2, but, whereas in that poem love remains a rococo fantasy, here we are exposed to the cruel reality of the situation. Ovid has become Amor's *praeda*, and Corinna has become his (Stapleton 1996: 19). At the same time, the wish that the bruises and bites had been caused by passion instead of rage reveals the violence inherent in the *Amores*' games of amorous possession. Indeed, how does one tell the difference between bruises? When is to lay hands upon another an act of violence, and when is it an act of love, and by what standard is that determination made? Questions of rights and law become central in determining the *amator*'s relation to both Corinna and the *vir*.

The threatened attack on the *lena*'s cheeks and hair in 1.8 clearly recalls the actual assault from the previous poem as well as the personification of the *manus* as the agents of that attack (Olstein 1980: 298). It also recalls an earlier passage from the same poem, "certior e multis nec tam invidiosa rapina est: / plena venit canis de grege praeda lupis" (loot taken from many is both more dependable and less resented: / a herd supplies copious booty to the gray wolves; 1.8.55–56). In addition to the recurrence of the booty motif, there is a clear pun here on *lupa* as common slang for a prostitute, as McKeown notes (1989: ad loc.). Thus, the same Corinna who in 1.4 was treated as if she were an *uxor*, and hence potentially a *matrona* (Lyne 1980: 240), is here equated with a prostitute. As we have already noted, Ovid elsewhere makes the equation between *meretrix* and *matrona* based on the fact that each acts under external compulsion and does not control her own person. Ovid's relation to Corinna in her role as mercenary *meretrix* is thus structurally no different from the *vir*'s relation to her as his *uxor*.

In poem 1.4, the *manus* of the *vir* and those of the centaur are opposed in terms of legitimacy and barbarism, and yet they each also bear inverted significations that testify to an actual unity underlying their superficial identity. Thus, while the lover-centaur's inability to keep his hands off the *puella* is in the first instance read as bearing primarily an erotic signification, as we have seen, it also threatens rape or worse. Indeed, the poet can't keep his paws off her.[44] Those same hands and fingers, which the poet turns into instruments of long-distance lovemaking through the elaborate set of signs and signals he teaches the *puella* (1.4.24 *manus*, 26 *digitis*, 27 *manu*), become instruments of probing and penetration in 1.4.37, "nec sinus admittat digitos." Here while *sinus* permits two possible translations, cloak and vagina, the phrase *admittere digitos* is most often used according to McKeown (1989: ad loc.) for probing wounds, examining corpses, or tasting pies, all three involve images of penetration, probing, and either morbidity or what Bakhtin terms the lower bodily stratum in which images of food, sexuality, and the grotesque become one (Bakhtin 1968: esp. 23). In this context, where love ends and violence begins is impossible to determine.[45] Heavy petting and the probing of morbid flesh have become one. This duality of signification is in turn homologous with that seen earlier in the simile of the lover and the centaurs.

Laying Down the Law

Finally, the phrase used to describe the *vir*'s own embrace of the beloved's neck, *iniciet manum* is, as mentioned earlier, first attested as a legal formula for claiming ownership, the coercive nature of which is underlined by the adverbial clause *cum volet* (Olstein 1980: 295). He lays his hands upon her when he wishes, not when she does. Likewise, it will be recalled that the *amator* defines the difference between the *oscula* the *vir* compels by law and those he receives by stealth as that between those extracted by force and those freely given, so that lawful love is depicted as if it were rape and adultery as the only legitimate love. The point is made clear in 1.10.21–24 when, as we have seen, the same vocabulary of force versus free will is used to contrast the prostitute with the true beloved.[46] There is a very subtle game going on here in which the wife defined as *iure coacta* in 1.4.64, and thus as acting under external compulsion, is aligned with the *meretrix* who *corpore iusso . . . coacta facit* (1.10.22–24), and so acts under another's control. Freedom, then, is defined as that which exists outside of any structure of power or coercion and so, according to Ovid, can only occur in a relationship that is without legal sanction. Legitimacy equals that which the law labels illegitimate, in which case the opposition between it and violence or barbarism collapses since each can only be defined as its own opposite.

This *coinicidentia oppositorum* can be seen most vividly in 1.4.39–40, when Ovid warns Corinna against kissing her *vir* in his presence. He here invokes the same terms used of the *vir* in 1.4.6:

> oscula praecipve nulla dedisse velis.
> oscula si dederis, fiam manifestus amator
> et dicam "mea sunt" *iniciamque manum.*
> (1.4.38–40)

> And especially you had best not wish to have given him kisses.
> if you will have given kisses, I shall become a confessed lover
> and I shall say "those are mine" and seize them.

In this latter passage, the primary sense is not erotic but juridical: for, as noted earlier, the phrase "inicere manus" is also a legal term for asserting ownership (McKeown 1989: ad loc.). More precisely, Ovid here invokes the formula of the *vindicatio* through which one claims property or slaves stolen from their rightful owner (Gaius, *Institutes* 4.16; Daube 1966: 227; Kenney 1969: 254–58). The irony of the *servus amoris* undertaking this procedure against his *domina* for giving her kisses to the *vir* who had a legitimate claim on them would not have been lost on Ovid's audience. A legalistic reading of this passage is supported by the technical vocabulary found in the surrounding context (*nulla dedisse velis*, 1.4.38; *manifestus*, 1.4.39; see McKeown 1989: ad loc.).[47] Of particular interest in this regard is Ovid's parody of the legal formula *ne quis fecisse velit* in his use of the combination of the subjunctive *velis* with the perfect infinitive *dedisse* and the negation *nulla* in 1.4.38. Daube has shown how this "rather rare . . . form . . . originates in ordinances by magistrates to ensure public order and decency" (Daube 1966: 222; see also Ollfors 1967: 36–42). Again, the irony of Ovid's deployment of language designed to police morals in order to assert the legitimacy of his illegitimate demand is part of the fun. Ovid asserts a legal claim to Corinna appropriate only to a *vir* and not an *amator*.[48] This reading is confirmed by the passage cited earlier from 1.4's companion poem 2.5, where the *amator* asserts, "iniciam dominas in mea iura manus" (I shall lay a master's claim to what is mine by right, 2.5.30). The conjunction of the *manus iniectio* with the invocation of *iura* and the pun on *domina* makes what is at stake in 1.4 painfully clear (McKeown 1998: ad loc.).

Recollecting the earlier uses of *manus* in poem 1.4, as well as its meaning in the vocabulary of marriage, in which the possessor of *manus* is he who has power over the bride—the person under whose thumb she must ultimately live (Lilja 1965: 33–34)—brings the point home: Ovid seeks both to usurp the *vir* and to separate himself from him. This double game has clear ramifications. On the one hand, the distinction that Ovid draws between the *vir* and himself undermines his quasi-legal claim to possess Corinna. On the other, his very invocation of that claim denies him access to a status different from the *vir*, even as their vocabulary is identical. He is, as he explicitly acknowledges, hoist on his own petard:

> multa miser timeo, quia feci multa proterve,
>   exemplique metu torqueor ipse mei:
> saepe mihi dominaeque meae properata voluptas
>   veste sub iniecta dulce peregit opus.
> (1.4.45–50)

> A wretch, I have much to fear because boldly I have done much,
>   I myself am tortured with the fear of my own example:
> often my mistress and I have had a quickie,
>   finishing off our sweet work with her cloak tossed over us.

The irony of Ovid's use of the participle *iniectus* here should not be lost. On a purely semantic level, it appears to be redundant and is all but untranslatable.[49] Its clear purpose, however, is to remind us of the omnipresent formula, *inicere manus*, while assimilating it to a quasi-public act of mutual masturbation. When Ovid administers this injection, he is both asserting a claim of sexual possession and depicting a transgression of the very law that makes that claim possible. In this light, Ovid's claim that Corinna's kisses are given to him freely, whereas those given the *vir* are forced by law, rings hollow (1.4.63–64). In the end, he requests that Corinna deceive him as he had taught her to deceive the *vir*. The circle is complete and Ovid's difference from the other is both invoked and denied. He, like the centaur and the other, is a *vir ambiguus*.

REFLECTION AND SELF-CONSCIOUSNESS

> If we observe the interdiction, if we have submitted to it, we are no longer conscious of it. But we experience, at the moment of transgression, the anguish without which there would be no interdiction: it is the experience of sin. This experience leads to achieved transgression, to the successful transgression, which maintains the interdiction, maintains it *in order to enjoy it*. *The inner experience of eroticism demands of he who seeks it no less a sensitivity to the anguish founding the interdiction than a desire leading to its infraction*. (Bataille 1957: 43, emphasis in original)

What Bataille admirably captures in this passage, and what Ovid in his own less apocalyptic tone clearly understood, is the predication of erotic transgression on the maintenance of the law that forbids it. This is the essence of not only poems like 2.19 and 3.4, but also of the very definitions of *virtus* and law that undergird 1.4. Transgression, as Ovid knew, is the seat of the erotic, a fundamental crossing of borders both bodily and Symbolic. It is also the site of that very consciousness that gives the law forbidding transgression its reality. Without transgression there is no law, because there is no consciousness of it and hence no desire, only behavior. The transgressor is thus always necessarily the reflection of that which poses as his opposite. Thus the *amator* and the *vir*, Amor and Augustus, law and its infraction, are revealed by the *Amores* to be two sides of the same coin.

Ovid in a typically deconstructive move constantly inverts these oppositions and shows their hierarchies to be arbitrary, while simultaneously demonstrating the impossibility of escaping them. As fundamental oppositions, they remain dependent on a formal assertion of difference, which in turn is the foundation of language, meaning, and individual consciousness per se. The Law, as an arbitrary assertion of power, as the demarcation of fundamental limits that grounds the Symbolic order, is what makes individual experience possible (Janan 2001: 31). Consciousness is thus always ironic precisely to the extent that it recognizes itself in the world as a moment of difference and reflection (Julien 1990: 176; Moxey 1991: 990; Frow 1986: 65).

This is the unhappy consciousness of Ovidian irony, but it is also the foundation of its sheer enjoyment of transgression. The Ovidian *amator* is a reflection of the Augustan order it seeks to transgress, and the act of transgression requires that order's maintenance. Yet the fact of reflection also presumes a difference, a moment of nonidentity that is also the moment of re-presentation. It is precisely the self-consciousness of Ovidian reflection, its recognition of nonidentity, that makes it so dangerous. It presents Augustan culture to itself and thus reveals the fundamentally arbitrary nature of its founding Symbolic distinctions of law, gender, and genre while simultaneously accepting them as the ground of its desire. It is in this moment of the Symbolic order's attempted closure, within the circle of reflection, that the Real, as the necessity of an unaccountable difference, continues to exert its pressure even in the moment of its occlusion.

Chapter Seven

DISPLACING THE SUBJECT,
SAVING THE TEXT

A recent critic tells us "there is a peculiar emotional
incoherence" in the Tarpeia poem. It would be better
to admit—with many scholars—that our texts are bad
and our understanding of them partial.
—Wellesley 1969: 93

The elegy [4.6] leaves its reader with the impression
that the New Propertius knows no other loyalty than
to his Emperor and his country. There is no longer any
visible split between façade and core, because all his
speech is homogeneously patriotic.
—Stahl 1985: 254

THESE TWO STATEMENTS sum up the problems surrounding Propertius
book 4. These poems present both a widely perceived incoherence and a
sense of ideological closure. One result of this perceived psychological
incoherence has been a flood of emendations that propose to smooth out
the inconsistencies and, in the words of Margaret Hubbard, make Pro-
pertius read "more like . . . Ovid" (1974: 5). My contention is that these
two seemingly contradictory movements—toward a disintegration of the
speaking subject's "emotional coherence" and toward a form of ideologi-
cal totalization—are intimately related. The numerous textual and inter-
pretive difficulties found in the book are less signs that our texts are bad,
though in a few cases they manifestly are, than symptoms of a displace-
ment of the speaking subject.

In many cases, the cruxes revolve around polar errors, that is, textual
problems where the proposed solutions are not merely different but di-
rectly opposed to the reading of the vulgate.[1] Subject and object, Venus
and Vesta, text and context, elegy and epic are conflated. The proposed
emendations, however, are not so much wrong—the problems they re-
spond to are very real—as they are misconceived.[2] They attempt to impose
on these poems a stable order of clearly delineated subjects, objects, and
fields of reference in which both can be located, when it is the existence
of those very entities that is called into question (Janan 2001: 82–83).

On the one hand, the poems in book 4 certainly present an at least superficial incoherence. In 4.7, Cynthia is dead, in 4.8 alive again. In 4.5, Propertius curses Cynthia's dead bawd, Acanthis, but she returns from the grave to indict the poet for his faithlessness and turns his own poems against him (Janan 2001: 85–99; Wyke 1987: 166). In 4.3, Arethusa in her letter to Lycotas illustrates the plight of Roman soldiers' wives, left home during long and dimly understood campaigns. At the same time, she eroticizes warfare from a feminine point of view, thus providing a neat reversal of the traditional *militia amoris* motif and the gender roles it encodes (Janan 2001: 53–69; Wyke 1987: 158, 160; Hallett 1973: 117). In 4.6, on the one hand, Apollo must admonish Augustus not to be frightened by the hollow painted prows of Antony's ships (4.6.49–50). On the other, *divus Iulius* takes the ensuing victory as evidence that he is indeed a god (4.6.69–70), implying his adoptive son's military prowess. In 4.4, Tarpeia is a Vestal Virgin, yet driven wild with passion (4.4.69–70). She longs to trade places with Tatius's horse (4.4.37–38; Rothstein 1979: ad loc.), offers to let him avenge the rape of the Sabines on her own person (4.4.57–58), and claims that her *torus* (couch) will soften his *arma* (arms) (4.4.62), a common euphemism for penis (see chapter 3).[3]

Frames of reference dissolve as soon as they arise in this strange world. The one constant is the displacement of the poet and his persona from pride of place as both speaking subject and object of the narrative. Book 4 represents a turn away from recounting what books 1–3 portrayed as the poet's amorous experiences and toward a narrative of Roman history and institutions (Wyke 1987: 153–54; Boucher 1980: 154; Alfonsi 1979: 71). The statue of Vertumnus, the fusion of the Romans and Sabines through Tarpeia's *felix culpa*, the temples of Palatine and Actian Apollo, the cult of the Bona Dea, and the commemoration of the death of Augustus's stepdaughter, Cornelia, are all recounted.[4] In poem 1, Propertius announces "sacra diesque canam et cognomina prisca locorum: / has meus ad metas sudet oportet equus" (I shall sing of rites, dates, and places' ancient names: / toward these posts my courser ought to strive; 4.1.69–70). Yet in the next couplet, an astrologer of dubious credentials named Horos, who purports to speak for Apollo himself, challenges this statement:

> "Quo ruis imprudens, vage, dicere fata, Properti?
> non sunt a dextro condita fila colo.
> accersis lacrimas cantans. aversus Apollo:
> poscis ab invita verba pigenda lyra."
> (4.1.71–74)

Why do you rush off foolishly to pronounce the fates of things, oh lost Propertius? These threads are not drawn from a propitious distaff. Singing you summon tears. Apollo is opposed. You demand words that will cause regret from an unwilling lyre.

The poet has announced his intention to produce a neo-Callimachean *Aitia* on patriotic topics only to be told that such topics are beyond his and elegy's grasp: "tum tibi pauca suo de carmine dictat Apollo / et vetat insano verba tonare Foro, / at tu finge elegos, fallax opus" (Apollo then grants to you only a small portion from his song and forbids you to thunder in the insane Forum; you rather make elegies, that two-faced work; 4.1.133–35).[5]

The shift in speakers and poetic programs has made many critics argue that the manuscript tradition is corrupt (Gunther 1997: 130–31; Goold 1990; Stahl 1985: 266–74; Camps 1965; Butler 1926). They divide 4.1 into two poems, A and B, at the point where Horos's speech begins. The division is given added credibility by the fact that in many poems in book 4 the poet either does not speak or is only a marginal presence in the poem. Hence, 4.1B could easily stand as a poem in its own right. Yet, there is no textual evidence that these two movements in 4.1 originally constituted separate poems. The wish to make them appear so is a desire to establish two self-consistent and freestanding speaking subjects. Yet, it is precisely this view of the subject that book 4 consistently undermines in the name of creating Propertius's new "two-faced work," *fallax opus*. Poem 4.1, in its double movement, deconstructs the oppositions between epic and elegy, between the Roman and the Callimachean, and between the poet's Imaginary self-projection as an elegist and his interpolation by the Symbolic structures and institutions of the Augustan state (Edwards 1996: 6, 42, 55–56; Albrecht 1983: 59–61; Anna 1983: 57). This is book 4's poetic program.

One paradoxical result of this displacement of the speaking subject is the production of a set of poems that to many appear to have been assimilated to the dominant order (Fantham 1996: 110–11; Boucher 1980: 158–59; Ross 1975: 129; Grimal 1952: 325; Alfonsi 1979: 72). In part at least, this is because a clearly delineated elegiac subject, such as that found in books 1–3, is no longer visible (Cairns 1984: 148). The point of elegiac resistance both to the emerging Augustan Symbolic and to traditional republican ideology is no longer in evidence; gone is the contradictory and aporetical subject position that like Janus faced in opposite directions, unassimilable to both old and new and hence marking an opening to the process of history.[6] The irony that was constitutive of the elegiac subject position now floats free of any single Imaginary projection of self, allowing every statement to turn into its opposite. In book 4, Propertius carries to its logical extreme the Ovidian erasure of stable constative content observed in the *Amores* (chapter 6). The movement of History now becomes discernible not so much through the manifestation of an intractable Real at the heart of the subjective construction of experience, as through the progressive veiling of that experience itself.

The poems in book 4 ultimately represent a crisis in naming. The degree of stylistic elaboration and linguistic estrangement in this book is well documented (Arkins 1989: 246–51). A simple line such as 4.4.94, "o vigil, iniustae praemia sortis habes" (o night watch, you have the rewards of an unjust lot) produces endless scholarly debate as readers try to determine who is the *vigil* (Jupiter, Tarpeia, or her father, Tarpeius)[7] and what are the rewards of an unjust lot (are the rewards unjust, or is Tarpeia's lot, and if one or the other, how so?).[8] Grammatically simple sentences lead to referential labyrinths and textual conundra. The deconstruction of the opposition of the individual Imaginary self-projection to dominant Symbolic values, the opposition on which the elegiac subject position was predicated, has been all but completed, and the object world that was that subject's intentional focus has come unmoored.[9]

In the *Monobiblos*, the speaking subject sought through the figure of the *puella*—as object of both competition and exchange—a lost wholeness, a stable Imaginary community of masculinist self-reflection conjured in the figure of Cynthia/Hylas (chapter 3). In books 2 and 3, that same subject in its increasing engagement with the emerging Augustan regime had come to occupy the eccentric Symbolic position of woman herself, being simultaneously inside and outside the dominant semiotic regime (chapter 5). In book 4, the elegiac subject has become definitively displaced, no longer speaking as if it were the poet (Wyke 1989: 30), nor having been consolidated into the anonymous narrative voice of epic (Wyke 1987: 155). Instead, we have a figure that sometimes represents Propertius (4.1A, the narrator of 4.4), but who has no discernible location and seems oddly separate from the first-person speaker of books 1–3. At others, we have a vatic speaker (4.6) who assumes, however ill fitting it may be, the mantle of impersonal authority, of the officiating priest. This *ego* is analogous, as Cairns (1983b: 106–7; 1984: 139–40) notes, to that of the "I" found in choral lyric and hymns.

Lastly, while Propertius may no longer be a woman in book 4, woman here speaks as never before (Wyke 1995: 121). Thus Grimal (1952: 438) notes that all five poems in book 4 with substantial amorous content (3, 5, 7, 8, 11) have female speakers, to which we should add Tarpeia's speech on her love for Tatius in 4.4. Indeed, in this latter poem, Tarpeia replaces the elegist and speaks the words of the love struck *exclusus amator*, leading more than one commentator to argue that Propertius here speaks in the guise of Tarpeia (Wyke 1995: 122; Stahl 1985: 279–80, 283; La Penna 1977: 87).[10] Hence, even when Propertius is not the speaker, he is, yet not as himself (Stahl 1985: 298–99). The subject in book 4 is always displaced, always speaking from elsewhere. The move in book 4 is not so much toward "objectivity" as toward a studied Callimachean indirection (Wyke 1987: 154; 1989: 30; Boucher 1980: 197;[11] Pillinger 1969: 175–76).

Thus, Wellesley is correct. To speak of Tarpeia's "emotional incoherence" is wrongheaded. The problem is not fundamentally that of Tarpeia or of emotion. It is that the position from which the subject speaks has vanished, making it impossible to specify the place from which a statement is made, the object toward which it is intended, and its consequent ideological inflection. As Michael Holquist observes:

> Each of us makes an entrance into a matrix of highly distinctive economic, political, and historical forces—a unique and unrepeatable combination of ideologies, each speaking its own language, the heteroglot conglomerate of which will constitute the world in which we act. It is only in that highly specific, indeed, unique placement that the world may address us: in a very real sense it is our "address" in existence, an address expressed not in numbers, but by our proper name. It is only from that site that we can speak. (1990: 167)

In book 4, the elegiac subject has become homeless. This very dispersal of the subject, and the consequent dissolution of its fundamental opposition to the Other, allows Stahl to claim that the gap between "façade and core" has disappeared under the guise of a new homogeneity of patriotic speech. Yet, as Stahl (1985: 265) also argues, what we see in Propertius Book 4 is not the beginning of his career as imperial panegyrist, but the end of elegy. Likewise, Wellesley and others may rightly reject "emotional incoherence" as explaining the poem's shape, but they continue to detect incongruities that, given their assumption of a unified speaking subject, they can only address through textual emendation.

Here Lacanian psychoanalysis's rejection of the subject of ego-psychology, the unified Cartesian ghost in the machine, proves its mettle (Ragland-Sullivan 1986: 158; Lacan 1973: 143; Julien 1990: 14–15). For where psychology can see in book 4 only aesthetic failure or textual corruption, psychoanalysis allows us to read the symptomatic text, charting the progressive shrouding of that moment of the Real that is the subject's hard kernel of irrational desire (Ragland-Sullivan 1986: 218). As the possibility of an independently imagined self-projection becomes more and more problematic with Augustus's consolidation of the principate (Stahl 1985: 259; Boucher 1980: 34; Alfonsi 1979: 34), the speaking self assimilates to a new set of Symbolic norms, and the ironic moment of its original constitution, its founding moment of nonsense (Ragland-Sullivan 1986: 43; Lacan 1973: 236), diffuses across a complex semiotic whole that can no longer be located within the confines of single subject position no matter how internally complex or contradictory.[12] We are, thus, left with the task of saving the text, not through emending it but through preserving both it and the displacement of the subject that is its constitutive moment.

The remainder of this chapter examines two cases. I begin with a lengthy reading of Propertius 4.4, paying special attention to textual problems and the history of the proposed emendations. Following the path first suggested in an article I wrote with Charles Platter (1999), I examine these cruces as a symptomatic text that in itself reveals more about the structure of the poem and its ideological and social substructure than about the state of our manuscripts. The textual problems in 4.4, I argue, are a symptom of the displacement of the speaking subject resulting from the more general reconfiguration of the speaking subject's relation to the community[13] under the later Augustan principate. I then turn my attention to 4.6, the Actium poem that has been termed "a thoroughly bad poem" (e.g., Williams 1968: 51), a masterpiece of parodic wit (e.g., Johnson 1973), and a sincere Callimachean hymn to the virtues of Augustus (e.g., Cairns 1984). My argument is that the same forces, which on the micro-level give rise to the textual controversies of 4.4, on the macro level, produce the interpretive cruces of 4.6.

A City Betrayed, a Desire Redeemed

[T]he madness of love is stronger than the identity
of the individual possessed by it. Tarpeia feels this
as Propertius himself once did.
—Stahl 1985: 287

[E]legy 4.4 interrogates the very binary logic
implied in framing its loyalties as either
"pro-Augustan" or "anti-Augustan."
—Janan 2001: 71

Poem 4.4 is an etiological poem in the manner of Callimachus that tells the story of how the *Mons Tarpeius*, later renamed the Capitoline, and the Tarpeian rock upon it, received their names (Varro, *De Lingua Latina* 5.41; Plutarch, *Romulus* 18; Alfonsi 1979: 72–73). Tarpeia was the daughter of Septimius Tarpeius, commander of the Roman garrison when the Sabine Tatius attacked the city. In the story told by Livy (1.11.6–9), she betrayed the city because she coveted the gold bracelets the Sabines wore on their left arms. Her reward was to be buried beneath the Sabines' shields, when she asked for what their left arms bore. Livy's story is the shortest and the most straightforward of those that survive. Even in his laconic account of Roman origins, however, there is a hint of ambiguity: he notes the presence of an alternative tradition according to which Tarpeia deliberately sought to disarm the Sabines in order to foil their assault on Rome. Dionysius of Halicarnassus (*Antiquitates Romanorum* 2.38–

40) cites the *Annals* of L. Calpurnius Piso Frugi as the source of this story and uses it to explain the otherwise curious fact that Tarpeia's tomb received sacrifice each year from the Vestal Virgins during the *Parentalia*. In many ways, this sounds like a later rationalizing account of an otherwise mysterious ritual practice. Yet, as Gansiniec (1949: 20–24) points out in her survey of the source material on this myth and its reception, Piso's second century account is one of the oldest sources we have for this story, and the sole source to mention the annual sacrifice at the tomb. It cannot therefore be simply ignored in favor of Livy's later, more streamlined retelling (see Staples 1998: 143–44; Butler and Barber 1969: 343). Moreover, as Varro (*De Lingua Latina* 5.41) and Propertius both agree, Tarpeia herself was a Vestal.

Tarpeia, as she comes down to us, is an inherently ambiguous figure. A Vestal Virgin who betrayed her vow and, with it, the city whose hearth fire—its very heart and what made it the *urbs aeterna*—she was charged with keeping (Livy 5.52.6–7; Horace, *Odes* 3.5.5–12; Dumézil 1996: 311), she nonetheless received yearly sacrifice. Vestals convicted of breaking their vows and thus of extinguishing the hearth fire of the city were buried alive, but they too remained sacrosanct and received sacrifice at their tombs (Plutarch, *Quaestiones Romanae*, 96; Staples 1998: 34, 151). It has been argued that Tarpeia's death beneath the Sabines' shields served as an *aition* for the subsequent practice of ritual burial (Rykwert 1976: 152). This practice itself was the embodiment of an ambiguity at the heart of the Vestal cult. The convicted virgin was led "voluntarily" to a chamber dug in the city wall, where small amounts of food and water were placed. She was then sealed up (Plutarch, *Numa* 10). What happened after that was the gods' affair. Her death was, from a ritual perspective, another form of life, a new liminal existence. Her spot of burial in the walls placed her neither inside nor outside the city. The maiden whose ritual denial of her own fertility insured the continuing vitality of the city, became an offering when she had violated her vow, yet one that did not formally involve a sacrificial loss of life (Miller and Platter 1999: 449–51; Miller 1995: 226–27). Her fault receives formal cultic honors even as the site of her new abode mediates between the city's inside and outside, between same and other. The Vestal is the site of contradiction. Even her treachery is ultimately a safeguard for the city (Rykwert 1976: 160–61).[14]

In the same way, Tarpeia, in her act of betrayal, makes possible the acceptance of the rape of the Sabine women as a recognized form of marriage and the reconciliation of Tatius and Romulus.[15] If it were not for her, the Sabines would not have mounted the Capitoline hill, and the final confrontation between them and Romulus's Romans would have never occurred, nor the intervention of the Sabine women between them, begging the two armies not to make them widows and orphans (Livy 1.13). Tarpeia thus effects the second foundation of the city. Hers is the *felix culpa* on which subsequent Roman history depends (Janan 2001: 75; Grimal 1951: 209–10). Tarpeia is the other whose very existence is constitutive of the norm. She is the un-Roman, the un-manly, the un-chaste virgin who made Roman *virtus* and *pudor* possible. She stands for the contradictions that lie at the heart of Roman identity (Janan 2001: 78).

In this, she is an echo of Rhea Sylvia, the first Vestal to betray her vow and the mother of Romulus and Remus after her rape by Mars. As Rykwert notes, Rhea's "is the earliest name of a Vestal to appear in legend, Tarpeia's the second. And both are Vestals of Alba Longa not of Rome, and both are faithless, though in different ways" (1976: 153). Moreover, just as Livy's recounting of the Tarpeia legend strives for a univalent interpretation, but leaves the door open to an ambivalent one more hospitable to elegy's *fallax opus*, so his recounting of the birth of Romulus and Remus opens the door to a more negative view of the twins' relation to sexual transgression when he records the story that the *lupa* who saved the boys from the river was not a she-wolf but a prostitute (1.4). In either version of Rome's founding, sexual transgression drives history (Staples 1998: 135). It is the violation of purity, the crossing of liminal boundaries, that allows those boundaries to be maintained and expanded, even as purity itself is reasserted (Macey 1993: 138; Jameson 1981: 68; Derrida 1978: 274–75; Bataille 1957: 43, 75).

This cycle of transgression is a recurrent pattern throughout Rome's mythic history. Servius Tullius, the founder of the city's orders, the builder of its walls, and thus the guarantor of its boundaries both internal and external, was born of a virgin mother, Ocrisia, who while tending the hearth fire, *vesta*, was impregnated by a fiery phallus.[16] The Vestals themselves were not only the keepers of the hearth fire but also of the phallic god Fascinus charged with the protection of children and triumphing generals, and thus with the city's political and generational continuity (Pliny, *Historia Naturalis* 28.7; Miller 1989: 76; 1995: 226; Rykwert 1976: 159).[17] A cognate legend is found at Praeneste where there is the tale of an inseparable pair of divine brothers who found the city and are sired by a phallus from the hearth. Plutarch records the same story as a variant legend for the birth of Romulus and Remus. In this version, it is only through the intervention of Vesta that the twins themselves are saved from wrath of the girl's father, a certain Tarchetius whose name is suspiciously close to Tarpeius (Plutarch, *Romulus* 2; Dumézil 1996: 55–56). Finally, at Praeneste there is also the story of Caeculus, the aboriginal founder of the city, "who was conceived by a slave girl of a spark from a hearth," and who was saved from exposure by virgins seeking water (Servius, *ad Aeneid* 7.678; Dumézil 1996: 252–53; Rykwert 1976: 154–59). In all cases, these stories include fires, phalluses, virgins, and miraculous foundations.

The Vestals, like other analogous figures in Indo-European myth and religion, embodied both fertility and sexual abstinence.[18] They were associated with fire and water through the hearth and the spring they daily visited to clean the shrine. These same elements (fire, water, virginity, and fertility) recur in the foundation myths of Praeneste and Rome, as well as in these stories' Vedic analogues (Plutarch, *Numa* 9, 13; Staples 1998: 150; Dumézil 1996: 56, 252–55, 313–19). The connection of fire and water to passion and fertility is, in turn recognized throughout Roman culture. Romulus solemnized the marriage of the Sabine women to their husbands with the sharing of fire and water. This story served as an *aition* for the later Roman marriage ceremony (Dionysus of Halicarnassus, *Antiquitates Romanorum* 2.30; Miles 1992: 162). Together these two opposed elements were said to represent life itself (Staples 1998: 149–50). Thus, exile was signified by a ban on sharing fire and water, and for this reason was equated with death (Claassen 1999: 11; Staples 1998: 16). The Vestals in their profound connection with the foundation and essence of Rome were figures of inherent transgression embodying the meeting point of opposite forces (fire and water, sexuality and abstinence, male and female, inside and outside). They marked the liminal space through which the community constituted itself, and out of which life arose.

Propertius's Tarpeia poem recounts the story of how the Roman community came to constitute and reproduce itself through the violation of its own purity. Tarpeia's treason and her betrayal of her Vestal vow become the transgression through which the Law founding the Roman Symbolic community is established (Butler 1990: 76). Propertius is unique in joining the theme of Tarpeia's love for Tatius[19] with a foregrounding of her status as a Vestal Virgin (Beltrami 1989: 268; Veyne 1988: 26). In the process, he joins a common Hellenistic motif—the betrayal of a father's city (Tarpeius) by a daughter who falls in love with the enemy—with a reflection on some of the most archaic practices and lore of the Roman community (Hubbard 1974: 119–20; Rothstein 1979, 2.243–44).

Propertius, in fact, takes the already inherently contradictory figure of the Vestal Tarpeia and, without violating the internal logic of the myth, raises it to the second power. The two most common images characterizing Tarpeia in Propertius 4.4 are those of fire and water (Rutledge 1964: 70–71), frequently in close juxtaposition as in 4.4.15–18:

> Hinc Tarpeia deae *fontem* libavit: at illi
> urgebat medium fictilis urna caput.
> et satis una malae potuit mors esse puellae,
> quae volvit *flammas* fallere, Vesta, tuas.

From here, Tarpeia made an offering of the *spring* to the goddess; but the clay urn pressed down on the center of her head. And one death was not enough for a girl who wanted to fool your *flames*, Vesta.

and 4.4.45–46:

"Pallados exstinctos si quis mirabitur *ignis,*
ignoscat: *lacrimis* spargitur ara meis."

"If anyone will be shocked that the *fires* of Pallas[20] have gone dead, let him be forgiving. The altar is sprinkled with my *tears*."

Her very nature is as the *coincidentia oppositorum.* Propertius's Tarpeia is the Vestal whose death means life, whose act of treachery is a self-sacrifice, whose virginity is a form of sexuality, and whose status as a foundational figure of Roman mythic identity is portrayed in terms that are recognizably Greek.

The Augustan Symbolic quintessentially operated to recuperate the alien, through a complex movement of dialectical synthesis. By the mid-teens, when these poems were being written, Rome was both a republic and monarchy. It was ostensibly returning to the *mos maiorum,* even as it laid the groundwork for the most extensive revision of the Roman constitution since the expulsion of the Tarquins (Ste. Croix 1981: 375; Elia 1981: 70–71; Thibault 1964: 34). The poetic program of the two most orthodox Augustans, Horace and Vergil, was centered on the simultaneous adherence to tradition (the "Roman Odes," the *Aeneid*) and its thorough renovation to make it conform to Greek and Hellenistic norms (White 1993: 167; Cairns 1979a: 13–14).

In many ways, Tarpeia and the Vestal cult were the perfect signifiers for the subtle ideological minuet that was the Augustan settlement. On some level, Augustus and his supporters must have recognized this because they minted denarii that featured the *princeps*'s image on one side and Tarpeia's beneath the Sabine shields on the other (Gansiniec 1949: 24–26; Butler and Barber 1969: 344). The Basilica Aemilia also featured a frieze (14 B.C.E.) depicting Tarpeia's death in which she is dressed as an Amazon, one breast bared (Warden 1978: 180–81).[21] Augustus from the perspective of these works is portrayed as both the scourge of treason, who recuperates and incorporates the transgressive, and the direct beneficiary of Tarpeia's act. Indeed, as Pierre Grimal brilliantly deduced, Propertius 4.4 can be read as recapturing Tarpeia's offense for Augustus's glory. The *princeps* not only descends from Titus Tatius, through the latter's supposed genealogical ties to Julius Caesar's grandmother, Marcia (Suetonius, *Divus Iulius* 6), but the equestrian statue of *divus Iulius* in the *forum Iulii* was on the very spot where Propertius imagined Tarpeia seeing Titus on his war-horse, the moment she fell in love with him (Grimal 1951: 208, 212–14; 1952: 317; 1986: 15–16; see also Alfonsi 1979: 78). These are not the sole ties between Augustus and Tarpeia. In 42 B.C.E., the young Octavian chose the Parilia to announce the divinity of his fallen uncle, the same day on which Propertius portrays Tarpeia's betrayal (4.4.73–77) and the anniversary of Romulus's foundation of the city.[22] The Parilia was a day of purification, in which farmers used a special powder prepared by the Vestals (*suffimen*) to insure their family and their livestock's continuing fertility. The holiday featured milk offerings to the goddess Pales and the ritual leaping over of burning piles of straw by drunken peasants. Thus, the Parilia, Tarpeia's treason, the foundation of Rome, and the deification of Julius Caesar are all tied together in a complex ideological and imagistic network linking the Vestals with fertility, purification with betrayal, and fire with water or milk, both liquids associated with women (Staples 1998: 47, 155; Dumézil 1996: 39–44). That these ties were fortuitous strains credulity. That Propertius was unaware of them is equally unlikely.

Nonetheless, while on the one hand the Augustan move to domesticate and incorporate its opposition was sophisticated, on the other, Tarpeia and elegy are possessed of an irreducible ambivalence. Thus, while Tarpeia was the perfect symbol for the principate's own double business, she carried with her a fundamental alterity that Propertius did not soften but heighten. Far from the ideal *virgo* of the *carmen saeculare*, or even the greedy girl of Livy's narrative, Propertius's Tarpeia is transgressive and calls forth the poet's seeming condemnation even as her sacrilegious passion is a double for that of elegy (Beltrami 1989: 267, 271–72; Wyke 1987: 162; Sullivan 1976: 136–37). In Propertius 4.4, although a Vestal, Tarpeia betrays the city for love, not greed. She is the ideal elegiac beloved. When the poet asks, "Satis una malae potuit mors esse puellae?" the question can be read as a form of self-condemnation. However, if 4.4 were truly meant to be a simple indictment of Tarpeia and of elegy's past, why make her plight so peculiarly affecting (La Penna 1977: 87; Alfonsi 1979: 87)? It is all but impossible not to empathize with her even as we are invited to condemn her passion, just as we empathize with and condemn Dido's in the *Aeneid*, a text Propertius echoes at several turns (Platter 1995: 222–24; Warden 1978: 184).

At all events, Propertius has managed the difficult feat of combining a variety of genres to create a new hybrid unlike anything seen in elegy's past. First, the poem is an amatory elegy, even if the protagonist is not the poet speaking in the first person. Second, the poem is a Callimachean *aition*. Third, it is patriotic poetry in the traditional heroic Roman mold (King 1990: 235–36), telling the great stories of the past, ostensibly to inspire virtue and discourage vice. Fourth, it is a poem that begins in the bucolic mode, recalling a world of pastoral serenity that is lost in the very moment of the telling. A vision of a Rome in the golden age is evoked, a city without walls, haunted by the rustic god Silvanus, nymphs, and other markers of the *locus amoenus* (2–6, 13–14, 25). Yet, the violence of the hostile Sabine camp (11–12) and the mention of Tarpeia's tomb already stain that pastoral paradise. Thus, at the opening of the poem, the possibility of a Rome without violence is simultaneously envisioned and denied, its purity already compromised.[23] Propertius would not have been insensitive to the ironies such hybrid constructions breed. They are in fact the formal corollary to those produced by and reflected in the displacement of the elegiac subject onto the profoundly ambivalent figure of the Vestal Tarpeia and her complex ideological rapport with the principate.

"Loco" *AMOENUS*: 4.4.1–18

Tarpeium nemus et Tarpeiae turpe sepulcrum
    fabor et antiqui limina capta Iovis.
lucus erat felix hederoso conditus antro,
    multaque nativis obstrepit arbor aquis,
Silvani ramosa domus, quo dulcis ab aestu
    fistula poturas ire iubebat ovis.
hunc Tatius fontem vallo praecingit acerno,
    fidaque suggesta castra coronat humo.
quid tum Roma fuit, tubicen vicina Curetis
    cum quateret lento murmure saxa Iovis?
atque ubi nunc terris dicuntur iura subactis,
    stabant Romano pila Sabina Foro.
murus erant montes. ubi nunc est Curia saepta,
    bellicus ex illo fonte bibebat equus.
hinc Tarpeia deae fontem libavit: at illi
    urgebat medium fictilis urna caput.
et satis una malae potuit mors esse puellae,
    quae volvit flammas fallere, Vesta, tuas?

I will sing of the Tarpeian wood and the foul tomb of Tarpeia, and the captured thresholds of Jupiter. There was a lush grove hidden in an ivy covered grotto, and many a tree rustles in reply to the waters that sprang up there naturally, there was the branching home of Silvanus, where the sweet pipe ordered the sheep go and drink to escape the summer heat. This spring Tatius rings round with a maple palisade, and he crowns his trusted camp with piled up earth. What was Rome then when the Sabine trumpeter shook the neighboring rock of Jupiter with his low roar? Sabine javelins stood in the Roman Forum, where now laws are dictated to conquered lands. Hills were the city wall. Where now the Curia stands enclosed, a war-horse was drinking from that spring. From here, Tarpeia made an offering of the spring to the goddess; but the clay urn pressed down on the center of her head. And was one death able to be enough for a girl who wanted to fool your flames, Vesta?

The opening of 4.4 is much vexed. Butler and Barber (1969) write of these lines, "an extremely difficult passage, admitting of no certain explanation. As it stands *nemus* (1) must be identical with *lucus* (3), while *aquis* (4) must be the *fons* of 7, 14, and 15. But (i) If Tatius palisaded the spring, how did Tarpeia find access to it?" Likewise, Janan in the most recent treatment of this poem observes that the opening passage is a mass of incongruities:

> Take, for example, the fatal body of water that initially brings together Tarpeia and Tatius. The paths of Sabine king and Vestal Virgin cross at a shepherd's spring that Tatius palisades for his military camp; Tarpeia sees him when she draws water from the spring, and falls passionately in love. But how she *can* draw water despite Tatius's barricade has baffled commentators. Emendations and line transpositions have been freely offered to try to bring these puzzling verses into sensible coordination. Some scholars make two springs from one, or banish one of the irreconcilable allusions to it; others poke holes in the barrier; still others try a combination of approaches. Yet each suggested change to the text garners trenchant objections and small assent. (2001: 71, emphasis in original)

If little has changed in the scholarly consensus on the state of our text between the time Butler and Barber first published their assessment in 1933 and Janan's recent evaluation, it is time to try another approach. The essential problem noted by all critics is the illogicality of the geography as presented, the porous boundaries that allow one object to bleed into another. At the same time, this topographical confusion is compounded on the thematic and generic level by the image of a golden age *locus amoenus* transgressed.

Janan begins the process of offering an alternative to the dead end of positivist textual criticism when faced with problems of intelligibility that transcend grammar, meter, and variants within the tradition of transmission. She proposes a symptomatic reading of 4.4 in terms of the connection between the already noted predominance of images of water and liquidity in the poem and Propertius's dramatization of feminine desire.[24] Starting from Luce Irigaray's (1977f) concept of "fluid mechanics," Janan (2001: 70–81) argues that the slippage between such categories as subject and object, inside and outside, Augustan and anti-Augustan that critics have noted throughout the poem is not the product of textual corruption but of a feminine undermining of the masculinist categories of binary logic. This is an important contribution to our understanding of the poem. It allows us to accept complexity on its own terms rather than as something that must be contained within the confines of a linear and univalent logic. Nonetheless, Janan's reading is not the final word on the subject. It does not account for two elements. First, it does not historicize 4.4 relative to Propertius's oeuvre as a whole. Consequently, it does not recognize the full importance of the displacement of Propertius as the speaking subject in this text. As we argued in chapter 5, Propertius already in books 2 and 3 had occupied the Symbolic position of woman, interrogating the binary logic of masculinist Roman ideology and undermining its strict separation of categories. What is new here is that the woman has now superseded Propertius himself.

Second, while water as Janan and Irigaray note may undermine all oppositions, the poem is also predicated on an opposite, more aggressive phallic undermining of boundaries associated with fire. Tarpeia, as a Vestal, represents the contradictory unity of these two opposed elements and their associated gender valences. Thus, as was noted earlier, the Roman marriage ceremony was solemnized by the sharing of fire and water. Within this binary logic, woman was associated with water and man with fire (Staples 1998: 15–17, 149–50, citing a vast array of ancient sources). Yet, as I have shown elsewhere, *furor* and feminine passion in the *Aeneid* are also associated with fire in scenes such as Dido's madness and the burning of the ships. Fire too, like water, threatens to elude containment and undermine boundaries (Miller 1989, with bibliography; 1995). The sacred flame is the sign of Vesta, the patron goddess of the Vestal Virgins who are to be shielded from phallic invasion and yet tend Fascinus as well. I am not arguing, then, that water is inherently feminine and fire masculine, or that one element represents the undermining of stable boundaries and the other containment, but rather that these images represent two modes of potential transgression that we can refer to as labile and phallic respectively. Each of them occupies a particular position relative to the Symbolic, and though they may be notionally gendered, those positions can be assumed by members of either sex without collapsing into an undifferentiated unity (Ragland-Sullivan 1986: 55, 283; Irigaray 1977f: 105, 110; Lacan 1975: 74). Tarpeia in 4.4 functions as an instantiation of this impossible unity that exceeds any single subject position, even a subversive one.

To contextualize these abstract speculations more firmly within the poem in order to use them as a ground for reading its problematic opening, let us look at lines 69–78, evoking first Tarpeia's erotic furor, followed immediately by a description of the Parilia:

> Vesta, Iliacae felix tutela *favillae*,
> culpam alit et plures condit in ossa *faces*.
> illa ruit, qualis celerem prope *Thermodonta*
> *Strymonis* abscisso pectus aperta sinu.
> urbi festus erat (dixere Parilia patres)
> hic primus coepit moenibus esse dies,
> annua pastorum convivia, lusus in urbe

cum pagana *madent* fercula divitiis,
cumque super raros faeni *flammantis* acervos
traicit immundos ebria turba pedes.

Vesta, blessed guardian of the Ilian *ember*, feeds her blame and plunges many a *torch* into her bones. She is swept away, like a woman from the *river Strymon* near the swift *Thermodon*, her breast bare with her cloak torn apart. There was a holiday in the city (the ancestors named it the Parilia), this was the first day inside the battlements, the annual shepherds feast, playtime in the˙city, when rustic trays of food *drip* with abundance, and when the drunken crowd leaps over piles of *burning* hay with its dirty feet.

The first two couplets describe the fire of Tarpeia's passion and picture her as both a Bacchant from Thrace and an Amazon running along the banks of the river Thermodon, a geographically and imagistically impossible collocation that signifies a more general strategy of paired oppositions throughout the poem (Janan 2001: 76–78; Warden 1978: 182–86; Rutledge 1964: 71–72). This initial pairing of fire and water is echoed in the image of the *fercula* dripping with abundance and drunken peasants leaping over the flames. We have, then, fire and water, Vesta and sexual passion, virginity and fertility immediately conjoined. The fire of the Parilia was envisioned as simultaneously purgative and generative. Tibullus pictures a shepherd praying for the fertility of his wife and livestock during its rites (1.1.35–36, 2.5.87–94). The holiday concerns female sexuality, but only from the male perspective of providing legitimate issue and economic utility (Staples 1998: 46–47; Dumézil 1969: 274–75).[25]

How more precisely does water relate to fire in the poetic and ritual complex defined by Propertius 4.4? As noted, both elements are similar in their refusal to accept containment and in their relation to sexuality, and yet they are opposites with one leading to the annihilation of the other (see 4.4.45–46). Both are also used in rites of lustration. In a traditional ritual context, their opposition would have been mediated by the communal norms; ritual would have deployed these gendered elements in a way that reinforced the forms of conduct and sexual power established by the institutions of marriage, family, cult, and state. The milk of Pales and the fiery phallus were harnessed to the ideology of masculinist reproduction. Fire and water were to be held in the balance defined by the Vestal cult in its intimate relation to the origins of the family and the state. In the late republic, however, there was a widely perceived collapse of these traditional subordinations. It was this crisis that Augustus sought to redress in his moral reform program and in his appropriation of traditional ritual iconography and cult—including the Vestals, the Parilia, and Tarpeia herself—as symbols of the legitimacy of his own power.[26]

Poem 4.4, however, is a poem of transgression in which the proper subordinations do not obtain: Tarpeia seeks a forbidden marriage, without paternal consent, that would be a violation of her Vestal vow, and a betrayal of the nascent Roman state (Rothwell 1996: 841–42; Beltrami 1989: 267, 271–72). In their unmediated conjunction in this poem, the opposed elements of fire and water reveal a Symbolic that can no longer make sense of its own terms, a universe of binary oppositions that lacks an anchor in Law and in an Imaginary projection of the subject's relation to the Law. Tarpeia's tears for Tatius threaten to drown the fires of Vesta in lines 45–46, yet in lines 69–70 those same flames become the fires of passion burning her very marrow "Vesta, Iliacae felix tutela favillae, / culpam alit et plures condit in ossa faces" (Vesta, blessed guardian of the Ilian ember, feeds her blame and plunges many a torch into her bones). Vesta is both the cause of Tarpeia's tears and that which they threaten to extinguish. The goddess is agent and victim, subject and object,[27] the opposite of Tarpeia's passion and its source. This fact has seemed so bizarre that more than one commentator has proposed emending Vesta to Venus in this passage (Goold 1990: ad loc.; Richardson 1977: ad loc.; Kraffert 1883: 147), noting that Vergil uses almost the exact same image to describe Dido's passion (*Aeneid* 4.300–303). Yet, there is no textual evidence for such an alteration, only a desire to arrest the endless play of oppositions.

To summarize, fire represents sexual passion from a masculinist point of view (recall the phalluses that conceive Servius, Caeculus, the divine twins of Praeneste, and Romulus and Remus). Such a conception of sexual pleasure is what Lacan referred to as the *jouissance de l'organe* or *jouissance phallique* (1975: 13, 75; 1982: 168; see also Julien 1990: 210). Water, on the other hand, and associated fluids, as Irigaray (1977f: 112) notes, gesture toward a *jouissance féminine*. Masculinist ardor is given a focal point in fire. Fire cannot simply be masculine, of course: it informs female passion—but only female passion as it is conceived from a masculine perspective, as in the Parilia or the *Aeneid*. Fire represents desire as conceived within the object world of the Symbolic, whereas *jouissance féminine* is an ecstasy of the Real. That which lies beyond the oppositions of the Symbolic, that which is opposed to those oppositions per se, is associated with water's protean nature (Lacan 1975: 69–71; see also Janan 1994: 30; Kristeva 1979: 13; Irigaray 1977c: 95). The opposition of fire and water thus points to the Real as a moment of pure negation, a moment in which the Symbolic becomes an anchorless set of oppositions without a masculinist subjective projection. Tarpeia's watery passion is both the unspeakable beyond of this projection and its unspoken ground. She is a locus of pure contradiction that both represents a radical interrogation of the ground of the speaking subject, as well as its consequent displacement, and threatens the integrity of the text itself.

Lines 1–18 enact this combination of subjective displacement and tex-tual disruption on a variety of levels. The first textual problem is the word *nemus*. A Tarpeian wood or grove is mentioned nowhere else in ancient literature and, though Propertius says in epic tones (*fabor*) that this will be the first object of his song (Rothstein 1979: ad loc.), it does not recur in 4.4. Kraffert (1883: 147), therefore, proposed emending *nemus* to *scelus*. Enk (1978: ad loc.) accepts the emendation, as do Camps (1965) and Goold (1990), and it is listed as "tempting" by Shackleton Bailey (1967: ad loc.). Many of the same critics attempt further to remedy the situation by transposing lines 9–14 immediately after 1–2 (Goold 1990; Shackleton Bailey 1967: ad loc.; Butler 1912). This makes the referent of the opening couplet more clearly the heart of present-day Rome and grounds the poem in an intelligible topography. It also avoids the repeti-tion of *fons* in lines 14 and 15.[28] The aim is to create a rational narrative, with a beginning, middle, and end, that reflects a coherent perspective on, and position in, the world. In no case, however, is there any textual, grammatical, or metrical warrant for these conjectures.

Richardson (1977: ad loc.), who accepts *nemus*, takes it to refer to the grove that initially topped the Capitoline hill where Tarpeia was buried, noting that Livy (1.8.5) tells us that the space between the hill's twin peaks was referred to as "inter duos lucos" (between two groves).[29] In that case, however, the *nemus*, the *sepulcrum*, and the *limina capta Iovis* become functionally synonymous, since Plutarch (*Romulus* 18.1) says Tarquin de-stroyed Tarpeia's grave when he built the temple of Iuppiter Capitolinus. This reading makes the passage otiose and forces us to distinguish be-tween the *lucus* of line 3 and the *nemus* of 1, since the *lucus* is the site of the spring from which Tarpeia draws water, the same spring that, as Janan pointed out, Tatius has supposedly walled off (Perrone 1989: 51–52; Rothstein 1979: ad loc.). Moreover, why would Propertius put two virtu-ally synonymous terms in close proximity to one another (*lucus* and *nemus*), and then force us to distinguish between them analytically, while at the same time treating three heterogeneous terms (the grove, the tomb, and the temple) as marking the same space?

What we see, then, in the first four lines is an apparent incoherence. Closer inspection, however, reveals there is nothing random. The lines of undecidability, of ironic undercutting, are precisely drawn and follow a clear pattern throughout the poem. Identity and difference are consis-tently asserted as opposed and yet interchangeable terms. This ironic undercutting, rather than being located within the perspective of a partic-ular speaker, becomes generic to the site of Rome itself. The *nemus* logi-cally must be both identical with and separate from the *lucus* (Janan 2001:

73–74). The *fons* whose water the *lucus* hides (*conditus*), therefore must be both part of the *nemus* (Butler and Barber 1969: ad loc.)—hence available to Tarpeia, but separate from her, and encloseable by Titus (*hunc Tatius fontem . . . praecingit*) (Marr 1970: 167–68).[30] Alternatively, multiple groves and multiple springs are alleged (Marr 1970: 168; Rothstein 1979, 2: 246–47), in which case *nemus* becomes synonymous with the *sepulcrum*—marking the grave of a traitor as a sacred grove—and with the temple of Jupiter, which is both captured (*capta*) and yet not in fact built till the time of the Tarquins.

This same assertion of polar opposites is found on the level of diction as well. The phrase *Tarpeiae turpe sepulcrum* features the play of identity and opposition on a number of levels. *Turpe* is a paronomasia on Tarpeia, suggesting the shamefulness of her deed (Wellesley 1969: 94). This wordplay, as Boyd (1984b) observes, is echoed in the popular etymology of *sepulcrum* as *sine pulchritudine*, hence *turpe*. Yet Tarpeia as an erotically available *virgo* and elegiac *puella* would have conventionally been *pulchra*, as moreover would have been the *nemus* that marks her *sepulcrum*. The contradiction was sufficiently strong that several of the later manuscripts actually "correct" *turpe* to *pulchre*.

The logic by which the beautiful turns into the ugly and vice versa, even as the *nemus* becomes the *turpe sepulcrum*—which necessarily recalls the *pulchrum* or "the beautiful"—and then metamorphoses into the lush *lucus felix* of the *locus amoenus* is the same as that which characterizes the poem as a whole. It is identical to the simultaneous assertion of golden age purity and its transgression in the opening ecphrasis, the contrasting imagery of fire and water, and the inherently contradictory nature of Vesta, whose fires are both opposed to and identical with those of Venus. The same pattern gives us a spring that is encircled by a maple palisade and open to both Tatius's horse and Tarpeia's urn. This is also the logic of the *felix culpa* as Tarpeia's treason becomes the ground of Rome's future glory. Finally, it is the same pattern of opposition and inversion that characterizes the poem as a whole in its status as an elegy that tells the origins of Augustan Rome and the emergent imperial house. Thus, elegy becomes epic even as Tarpeia herself speaks in the manner of an elegiac lover.

Is elegy thereby condemned or redeemed in its new relation to epic and the Augustan Symbolic? The problem is summed up in the final couplet of this passage: "et satis una malae potuit mors esse puellae, / quae volvit flammas fallere, Vesta, tuas?" (And was one death able to be enough for a girl who wanted to fool your flames, Vesta?). The passage can be read as both a serious and an ironic condemnation of Tarpeia's passion. This potential duality of meaning, however, is raised to the second power when we realize that each of those positions can be read as both pro- and anti-

Augustan. Thus, there is the initial tone of righteous indignation, but it is easily undermined by both the reader's recollection of Propertius's past poetry, which endorsed erotic transgression, and the question of what would it mean to fool Vesta's flames, given that they are said to cause Tarpeia's passion (Miller and Platter 1999: 447–51). Would the desire to deceive Vesta's fires mean to consummate Tarpeia's love or abstain from it? Moreover, as Grimal pointed out and as was noted earlier, it is only because of Tarpeia's sin that the son-in-law and later the grandson of Tatius, Numa Pompilius and Numa Marcius respectively, officially established Vesta's cult in Rome. The latter was the eponymous ancestor of Julius Caesar's grandmother, Marcia, and one of the founders of Augustus's line (Grimal 1951: 211; 1952: 316). Hence, the violation of Tarpeia's Vestal vow, her "fooling" of the sacred flames, is the condition of possibility of both the cult itself and the principate. From the perspective of this *felix culpa*, all condemnations must be simultaneous celebrations. Nonetheless, others see in this couplet a true condemnation of Tarpeia and hence a repudiation of the poet's elegiac past as well as a sign of his reconciliation with Augustus. These critics read the same pro-Augustan message into the couplet as Grimal, but for opposite reasons (see Janan 2001: 70).

The passage, it seems, anticipates all possible interpretations and converts each to its opposite value. Coming immediately after the opening tableau, this couplet has been judged so difficult that many editors have sought to transpose it to another position in the poem that might neutralize its ambiguity. None of the proposed solutions, however, has won wide assent. The enigmatic quality of the couplet is less a factor of its position in the poem than of the double logic to which it alludes.[31] As we have seen earlier in this chapter, Vesta's flames do not so much mark out a univalent position within Roman ideology as point to a threshold occupied equally by eros and virginity. The Vestal vow links chastity and conception in an unstable bond that must be continually violated in order to remain intact. Moreover, the violence, signaled by the camp of Tatius, whose presence marks the end of the golden age finds an echo in the flames of Vesta through the fires of the Sabine camps, the "ignes castrorum" (31), that are the first words of Tarpeia's speech. Thus, the threshold of sexuality and the threshold of violence are imagistically linked in the poem, at the same time as each is characterized by an identical logic of articulation and transgression.

At the center of this swirling mass of articulated contradictions is a lacuna. Not only is the poet here both Augustan and anti-Augustan, but he is no longer "Propertius." The projected Imaginary coincidence between poet, persona, and speaking subject that was at the heart of elegiac discourse no longer obtains. Indeed, as discussed earlier, elegy itself is no longer elegy but an unstable mix of generic conventions (epic, bucolic, patriotic etiology) framing a long first-person speech by a lovestruck *puella* reminiscent of the form's erotic realizations in Propertius's earlier books. Each term in this unstable mix is conjoined with its opposite in such a way that it points to an absent center, a vanishing mediator: "Propertius" and his relationship to Augustus. "Propertius," however, is not there. The only person left to occupy the position of the subject is Augustus himself. Yet, the *princeps* does not appear in the poem, and if he did, he would have to occupy the position of Propertius, the absent center of meaning that gives the poetic speech act an anchor and location—in Holquist's terms, an address. The price of stable meaning has become the loss of the elegiac subject, its displacement onto the emerging imperial Symbolic. In 4.4, Propertius cannot yet pay that cost. He can only articulate its semiotic necessity.

"Sum Deus"

> This contains a splendid eulogy on Augustus for
> his victory over Antony and Cleopatra at Actium.
> —Paley 1853: 295

> [I]t must be admitted, even by those who insist on
> an espousal of a public ideology, that Propertius
> conspicuously fails to glorify the victory or exalt
> the achievement, except for the manifest intervention of
> the god. The implications of the elegist's outcry in line
> 65–66 are unmistakable. The defeat of one woman . . .
> does not merit a triumph; the *mulier* is no Jugurtha.
> —Gurval 1995: 271

If Propertius and Augustus are both absent in different ways from 4.4, they are both present in 4.6. The narrative voice of the poet is strong in 4.6, and Augustus's victory at Actium, his subsequent dedication of the temple of Actian Apollo, and his inauguration of the temple of Apollo on the Palatine are its subject matter. Yet, this is all a bit too glib. In what sense is "Propertius" present? Cairns (1983b: 107–11; 1984: 137, 142, 150–51) has demonstrated that the speaker of these poems is not the individual "ego" of books 1–3 but the choric "ego" familiar from the Greek hymnic tradition.[32] The invocation of the *vates* figure in line 1, "sacra facit vates" (the prophet performs a sacrifice) recalls the speaker of Horace's "Roman Odes," which, as I have argued before (1994: chap. 8), attempts to incorporate a new collective dimension into the private sphere of the Catullan lyric self. At the same time, the numerous reminiscences of Calli-

machus's "Hymn to Apollo" and "Hymn to Delos," explicitly thematized
in the evocation of the *Cyreneas . . . aquas* (4.6.4), bring to mind the
image of the consummate imperial ironist.[33] Few would dream of deduc-
ing a personal statement from Callimachus's witty panegyrics (Miller
1994: chap. 7; Sweet 1972: 169). Questions of sincerity are out of order
when addressed to such poems as the "Lock of Berenice" or the descrip-
tion of Delos's wandering (Veyne 1988: 19–23; Whitaker 1983: 57; Lyne
1980: 61; Ross 1975: 17).

More important, though, Propertius directly announces the rejection
of the subject position adopted in books 1–3 and explicitly refers to his
own previous work to underline the new form of lyric subjectivity he
assumes in 4.6. At lines 11–12 he writes, "Musa, Palatini referemus Apol-
linis aedem: / res est, Calliope, digna favore tuo" (Muse, we shall tell of
the shrine of Apollo on the Palatine: the affair is worthy of your favor,
Calliope). The juxtaposition of Apollo and Calliope here directly recalls
2.1.3–4: "non haec Calliope, non haec mihi cantat Apollo. / ingenium
nobis ipsa puella facit" (Neither Calliope nor Apollo sings these things
for me. My own genius the girl herself creates). That poem, it will be
recalled, was a *recusatio* (see chapter 5) in which one of the topics the
poet says he would cover, if he could, would be Augustus's triple triumph
after Actium (2.1.31–34). But alas, he informs us, he does not have the
strength (2.1.41–42). All he can do is narrate his own "experience":

> Navita de ventis, de tauris narrat arator,
>   enumerat miles vulnera, pastor ovis;
> nos contra angusto versantes proelia lecto:
>   qua pote quisque, in ea conterat arte diem. (2.1.43–46)

The sailors tells of the winds, the plowman of his oxen, the soldier recounts
his wounds, the shepherd his sheep; in contrast we turn out erotic epics on
our narrow bed: each man wears away the day in his own way.

Thus in 2.1 Propertius says, Apollo and Calliope do not dictate my song.
I can only sing what I know. Hence, I shall sing of my girl. Yet in 4.6
Apollo's temple will be the poet's subject and Calliope his muse. The
battle of Actium, which the poet said in 2.1 he was not able to treat, is
now the centerpiece, and Cynthia is nowhere to be found. If the poetry
of 2.1 is predicated on the claims of personal experience or its Imaginary
projection, 4.6 deliberately renounces all such claims.[34]

The poetic voice of 4.6 is not "Propertius," then, but the negation of
that voice. It is the ironic counterimage of the poet's past. Does that make
this poem a pro-Augustan recantation, and hence a resignation to—if not
a direct celebration of—the fact that Augustus alone occupies the position
of subject in the world of the principate?[35] Or, does such irony and self-

subversion necessarily satirize and covertly attack this same reality?[36] This question, which has preoccupied scholarship on this poem for the past fifty years, is poorly formulated. Irony cuts both ways.[37] What irony cannot subvert are the terms of its own existence. The inversion of expected meaning, the foregrounding of difference and undecidability, only takes place within the terms of a determinate problematic. The task of the critic is not to nail down some elusive notion of poetic intent, however understood, but to define the parameters of the problematic that make this particular poetic statement possible. Thus, Cairns's (1983b: 107–08) observation of a collective speaker in 4.6 does not guarantee the seriousness of Propertius's praise, but only the absence of an accountable first-person subject. Likewise, Sullivan's observation of hyperbole and abrupt transitions does not prove parody but merely confirms his own desire to be "rid of some embarrassing personal and poetic aspects of this elegy" (1976: 146–47). What both readings testify to, however, is the inability to confine the meanings generated by this poem to a space recognizable as that occupied by the "Propertius" we thought we knew. Previously, the central contradictions of Propertius's signifying practice were localizable within a certain subject position and its troubled relation to the communal norms embodied by a residual republican and emerging Augustan Symbolic. Now the Imaginary space of that subject is no longer visible. The central problem of 4.6 is the disappearance of that space and the attempt to define what has taken its place—that is, the new locus of contradiction and difference in signifying practices. "Augustus" occupies that new locus, but that proper name does not mark a place from which the poetic subject can authentically speak.

In fact, the temporality envisioned in 4.6 expressly eliminates the possibility of effective agency. This can be seen in three passages. The first is 4.6.43–44. Here Apollo admonishes Octavian to release from fear the *patria*, "quam nisi defendes, murorum Romulus augur / ire Palatinas non bene vidit avis" (which if you do not defend, Romulus as augur of the walls did not see the Palatine birds to give good omen). This couplet is an allusion to the time when Romulus and Remus were deciding where to found the city of Rome. They took auspices or bird signs. Remus saw six vultures over the Aventine hill, but Romulus saw twelve over the Palatine, so the initial wall was built there. Propertius's point is that if Augustus does not defend the city, then Romulus's augury was mistaken.[38] What is most interesting here is the way temporality is portrayed. Either the victory at Actium is predestined, in which case Apollo need not admonish Octavian, or time itself is reversible and later acts can undo earlier ones. In both cases, the power of the subject, or at least the subject's illusion of power, is undone. In the first, predestination renders all human action a dumb show of delusion. Scipio, Propertius, Maecenas, or any other self-conscious agent may have thought his acts were meaningful, but in fact they were all leading to a predetermined end that none could resist: the principate. Alternatively, time itself is reversible by Augustus's action, and a single act seven hundred years after Romulus's initial augury could undo the flow of history, depriving of efficacy all the acts between the first and the last in the sequence. Under either construction of the passage, there is only one real subject: Augustus. Only his acts are meaningful and all history leads up to his act.

The same temporal structure can be found in Apollo's address to Augustus in 4.6.37–38, "o Longa mundi servator ab Alba, / Auguste, Hectoreis cognite maior avis" (O savior of the world from Alba Longa, Augustus, proven greater than your Hectorean forefathers). There are two indicators of anachronism and of a nonconsequential depiction of time in this passage. By nonconsequential, I mean a view of time wherein later events do not flow from earlier developments as a consequence of discrete actions (see Bakhtin 1981b). The most obvious anachronism is the term *Augustus*. The dramatic date of Apollo's address is 31 B.C.E., the eve of the battle of Actium, but Octavian was not voted the title by the senate until 27. The discrepancy may well seem innocent flattery, but it fits a larger temporal pattern. The second instance is subtler. One common meaning of *maior* was "elder," and in Rome's conservative ideology "elder" necessarily meant "greater," hence the deference to the *mos maiorum*, and hence Augustus's strategic use of that phrase when he contended that he was restoring the republic, not elaborating a new constitution. The notion that a descendant could be a *maior* therefore was a non sequitur, unless he were predestined and could claim a necessity to exist that preceded the birth of his ancestors. This, of course, is precisely the paradox Vergil invites us to contemplate in the *Aeneid* (8.675–81) when he shows Augustus winning the battle of Actium on the shield of Aeneas, a text to which Propertius alludes throughout this poem (Gurval 1995: 278; Johnson 1973: 160; Sweet 1972: 171). The wordplay implicit in *maior* is further underlined by ending the line in *avis* (grandfathers), which is a homonym of *avis* (birds) the final word of our first example. The poet invites us to examine the couplets together, drawing our attention to the emerging portrait of a temporal universe in which individual purposive action is meaningless, except as a reflection of the absolute subject, Augustus, who can negate augury and trump his own ancestors.

If that is so, the question, then, becomes the following: to the extent that the subject has been robbed of agency, and to the extent that the only significant actions are those of Augustus, how could "Propertius" be present? The only meaningful Imaginary projection of the self once you accept the Symbolic construction of history and communal life on offer in 4.6 is as a reflection of the *princeps*, which is to say as a negation of the self. The subject position of the poet has become inherently ironic. From this perspective, the antinomies of interpretation that have characterized this text are not a product of misunderstanding, ignorance, or political bias but of the structure of the poem itself. The question is not whether 4.6 represents a sincere or an ironic acceptance of the historical necessity of Augustan rule. There can be no difference between them. The only difference is in our reactions.[39]

The clearest example of this temporal pattern, its ideological implications, and the variety of critical responses to it can be seen in what may be the most problematic couplet in the poem, lines 59–60. Immediately after Apollo finishes his speech (4.6.54), the poet gives a highly compressed narrative of the battle of Actium. At its end, one finds the following couplet, "at pater Idalio miratur Caesar ab astro: / 'Sum deus; est nostri sanguinis ista fides' " (But father Caesar expressed wonder from his Idalian star: 'I am a god; that is the proof of blood'). It is impossible to read this couplet without a chuckle. The irony of Julius Caesar being confirmed in his godhood by the actions of his nephew is impossible to miss. Moreover, the contention that Octavian's actions are proof of both the nature of Caesar's blood and proof that Caesar's blood flows in Octavian's veins is doubly hyperbolic since the latter had only become Caesar's heir by adoption.

For those bent on a univocal reading, the only recourse has been emendation. Enk (1978: ad loc.) notes that the text became a target of "correction" from the time of the earliest Italian humanists. Following Baehrens, he proposes *tu meus* in place of *sum deus*. Lachmann (1973: ad loc.) in his commentary is particularly scathing, "Deum autem sese esse inepte nimis hic affirmabat Caesar, cum illud esset potius agendum, Augustum esse veram et dignam patre Caesare prolem" (Here Caesar excessively clumsily affirms that he is a god, when what should happen is that he affirm Augustus to be his true heir and worthy of his father, Caesar). Lachmann therefore proposes, "Tum deus: En nostri . . ." Lastly, Fedeli (1994: ad loc.) accepts Richter's proposed "Tu deus," making Augustus the true god, not Caesar.

For those who accept the text as transmitted, there are a number of solutions proposed to the problem of interpretation. Individually no one is satisfying, but collectively they point to a profound aporia, the impossibility of a satisfying Imaginary projection for the elegiac subject when the *princeps* has become the locus of both meaning and contradiction. Cairns (1984: 167) offers a reading of the passage that aims to reduce its complexity and claims for it an unproblematic laudatory intent. He notes that the Romans believed that "a man could retrospectively confer glory on his ancestors." Yet, such a notion is not unique to the Romans. The idea that even those who have passed on gain in glory by the deeds performed by their descendants is common. This is fundamentally different from saying that your father's recognition that he has become a god, a fundamental change in his ontological status, is dependent on your actions or that those actions confirmed your blood tie to him when you were merely adopted. Nor do any of the examples Cairns cites say more than the commonplace. Cairns, however, is too perceptive a reader to think that matters are quite so simple. He recognizes the problematic nature of the couple by reserving a separate appendix for it and by noting the resemblance between it and 4.6.43–44, as well as 4.6.37–38, the two passages where we first observed Propertius's deployment of a nonconsequential temporality.

Rothstein (1979: ad loc.) makes no brief for Propertius's sincerity but merely argues that "sum deus" represents the kind of flattery characteristic of court poetry. Similarly, Boucher (1980: 140), qualifies the passage as "*normal*," that is to say "expected" or "typical." In short, they see 4.6 less as a moment of political conversion, than as a product of the sophisticated court society in which it was produced and consumed. Richardson (1977: ad loc.) concedes that the passage was not meant to be taken seriously, but argues that a sophisticated Roman audience viewed deification with wry detachment and would have admired the cleverness of the conceit. Lastly, Johnson sees the couplet as a hilarious send up, "What we are seeing in this couplet is how Propertius emphasizes the facts of anxiety and skepticism. Julius reveals his own (and our own) doubts about his divinity by affirming it with gleeful amazement" (1973: 168). The fact is that these interpretations are not mutually exclusive. Skepticism and anxiety in no way preclude the belief that the actions of later generations can confer glory on earlier ones. Sophisticated court flattery in no way implies the abolition of irony.

What is perhaps most important to appreciate in this controversy, however, is the very impossibility of nailing down the poet's response to the consolidation of the Augustan regime and the beginning of the empire. Book 4 stages the displacement of Propertius as the subject of his own experience. In 4.4, the poet as speaker is replaced by Tarpeia, nor is his attitude toward her easy to specify, for she is explicitly condemned within the text of the poem, but her position is also revealed to be the direct analogue of the elegist's. Similarly, in this poem, Augustus is explicitly praised, but the praise is so extreme that it is hard to take seriously. Yet, hyperbole is not the same as attack. It does not take up a position hostile to the Augustan regime, but one whose place is ironic, that is to say, not self-identical.

To ask what is the poet's real attitude is the wrong question; rather we should say that Propertius in book 4 speaks from a position that no longer really exists, from nowhere. He creates a poetic hall of mirrors in which any given passage reflects its opposite. In such poetry, there can be no sincerity, only duplicity and wit. This is typical of certain styles of court poetry that would be common in the West up through the Enlightenment. It also signals the end of elegy, for elegy defined itself in contradistinction to certain ideological norms that it both mocked and accepted. If the position from which that opposition sprang no longer exists, then the genre has lost its reason for being. In book 4, the elegiac speaking subject has been reduced to a figure of pure difference disseminated across the whole of the emerging Augustan Symbolic.

Chapter Eight

BETWEEN THE TWO DEATHS: TECHNOLOGIES OF THE SELF IN OVID'S EXILIC POETRY

Between classicism and mannerism his minimalism
is the metaphor of severance: between life and death,
meaning and nonmeaning.
—Kristeva 1989: 136–37

The proud and preeminently powerful Romans of
the last century of the Republic and the first century
of the Empire, were in a kind of collective state of shock.
They were enthralled by deformity, disgrace, and
dishonor (the *dehonestamentum*), particularly their
own; tirelessly rehearsing their own debasement
and degeneration. The Romans were enthralled because
they were thralls. They were enthralled in order
to set themselves free.
—Barton 1993: 106

IN BOOK 4 of Propertius, the first-person speaking subject of amatory elegy has all but vanished. The "I" of the *Monobiblos*, whose search for a lost ideal of homosocial bonding had been travestied in books 2 and 3, is all but elided. As our reading of poems 4.4 and 4.6 demonstrated, amatory elegy's public dramatization of a private sphere that both engages socially constituted norms of individual conduct and insistently calls them into question can no longer find a place from which it can be directly spoken. Instead, we see the inversion of elegiac norms in the figure of Tarpeia, whose conflation of the positions of the *amator* and the *puella* eliminate that of the traditional elegiac speaker, even as her clear recollection of that speaker's generic traits makes it impossible to take the narrator's condemnation of her at face value. Likewise in poem 4.6, the tensions constituting the unique nature of the elegiac subject position, as outlined in 2.1's brief for amatory elegy as opposed to eulogistic epic, have been sublimated into the figure of the communal *vates* whose praises of Augustus's victory at Actium are all but indistinguishable from an ironic condemnation.

Nonetheless, the tensions constitutive of the elegiac subject position are not so much resolved or elided as displaced in the last decades of the first century B.C.E. The overtly contradictory position of a Tibullus, who accepts a life of traditional martial virtue for his patron Messalla but rejects it for himself (1.1), of a Propertius, who casts his love for Cynthia in terms recalling Antony's for Cleopatra while praising Caesar's victory at Actium (2.15, 2.16), of an Ovid, who invokes the power of *ius* while proposing stratagems of adultery (*Amores* 1.4), no longer seems possible. The ideological space required for this type of openly split subject is no longer available except as an ironic gap (Boucher 1980: 34–35). Instead, we see a new model emerge in which the subject is always already absent from view, always already speaking from nowhere, from a place beyond the contingencies of the here and now (Newman 1989: 1501).

In the case of Ovid, after the initial composition of the *Amores*, elegy is transformed into a voice of pure complaint in the *Heroides*. Here the writing subject is abstracted from the concrete verities of contemporary Roman life and exists instead as a series of stylized poses. In the *Ars Amatoria*, the elegiac subject becomes systematized as a series of ironic precepts whose very rule-based nature serves as a reflection of the hardening of the Augustan Symbolic into a set of increasingly rigid norms (O'Gorman 1997: 109; Labate 1987: 111). In this brave new world of system and irony, there is no longer a place for the anarchic excesses of the Catullan ego or the self-subverting meditations of a Tibullan "I."

It is with audible relief then that many critics turn from this artificial world to the exilic poetry. Yes, it is repetitive, and even whining, but here readers since Pushkin claim to hear the accents of authenticity. Here poet and persona coincide as never before. Here we have a truly personal poetry (Delpeyroux 1993: 181; Little 1990: 27; Dickinson 1973: 158). To the extent that this is true, we might very well question the inclusion of the exilic poetry in a study of Latin love elegy at all. Might it not more profitably be compared with Horace's and even Cicero's letters, to which it makes clear allusions?[1] Perhaps, but it would be a mistake to see the exilic poems as belonging to a separate genre from that of their amatory cousins.[2] The exilic works not only recall erotic elegy through their metrical identity, their arrangement of short poems into structured books, and their explicit defense and/or renunciation of the poet's past erotic career. They also do so through numerous well-documented and specific thematic,[3] lexical,[4] and rhetorical[5] recollections of the *Amores*, the *Heroides*, and the *Ars Amatoria*. The exilic poetry does not abandon the subject position of amatory elegy but recasts it.

As Plutarch (*Cicero* 32.5) said of Cicero during his exile, Ovid in exile is longing for Rome. He is an unhappy lover, an *exclusus amator* singing his paraclausithyron before the locked door that stands between him and the object of his desire. Now, however, what the poet seeks is not the charms of a *docta puella* or the thrill of transgression, but the *urbs aeterna*, Augustus, and, ultimately, death itself (Claassen 1999: 89; Edwards 1996: 118; Bonjour 1985: 14, 16–17). At *Ex Ponto* 2.7.38, he stands before the *laetitiae ianua clausa meae* of Rome, while in *Ex Ponto* 1.7.35–38 he fears that the *domus* of Messalinus has become *clausa* to him through a "misplaced" fear of Caesar's wrath. Finally, at *Tristia* 3.2.21–24, we find the distraught poet tormented by his *desiderium* of *Roma* and of his *domus*, while locked out before the door of death that would provide the ultimate respite from his pain. Thus paradoxically, through the figure of *exclusus amator*, death, Rome, and Caesar all come to function as metonymic substitutions and their substitutability is recognizable precisely because of the poet's use of the themes, rhetorical schemata, vocabulary, and meter of amatory elegy. What we have in these poems then is not a naive coincidence of poet and persona, but an aesthetic shaping of the self that is at once the product of a complex intertextual weave and an immediately convincing portrait of personal authenticity under conditions of emerging political absolutism. The two moments, however, cannot be dissociated. The recontextualization of Ovid's every statement of contrition or despair at his current lot within the framework of amatory elegy is both that which necessarily ironizes it and what guarantees its authenticity by underwriting the contrast between the artificiality of the world of the *amator* and the all too real world of the *exul* (Cutolo 1995: 26–27, 29; Green 1994: xxxii).

This, of course, is not to say that Ovid gives us an accurate depiction of his life in Tomis. It is, in fact, a conscious fiction. We know that many of the tribes Ovid describes as his neighbors lived hundreds of miles away (Videau-Delibes 1991: 164). Tomis was not an isolated barbaric colony but a Greek settlement that archaeological evidence shows enjoyed a high level of provincial culture (Claassen 1999: 196; Habinek 1998: 158; Williams 1994: 7; Green 1994: xxiv–xxvi). The description of the local population as bearded barbarians wearing pants and carrying poisoned arrows is a pastiche of well-worn commonplaces, not ethnography (Claassen 1990b: 72–73). The conditions of unceasing winter, complete with frozen wine served in slices (*Tristia* 3.10.23–24), which the poet ascribes to the region, are borrowed from Vergil's description of Scythia in *Georgics* 3 and from Strabo or his sources. Tomis itself sits at the same latitude as Boulogne and enjoys a climate not much different from that of northern Italy.[6] The Getae may have driven horses over the frozen Danube on rare occasions but it could hardly have been a regular means of attack as Ovid alleges (Claassen 1999: 195; Williams 1994: 10).[7] Finally, Ovid's description of his voyage up the coast of the Black Sea and of the cities he passes recapitulates precisely Strabo's order of exposition, only in reverse (Green 1994: xxiv; Videau-Delibes 1991: 56, 68; Claassen 1990b: 68–69).

The striking realism of the exilic poetry is a literary effect, produced through the systematic contrast of the conditions of the poet in exile with those of his earlier, more familiar elegiac environs (Claassen 1999: 122, 190; Videau-Delibes 1991: 116; Chomarat 1988: 19; Viarre 1988: 152–53). This is not to say the poet never spent a cold night in Tomis, never was lonely or felt endangered by the proximity of hostile tribes,[8] but rather that the exilic poetry creates the effect of sincerity intertextually. The Real emerges, not through self-expression, but in the fleeting recognition that the very Symbolic resources that produce the accents of authenticity—through this contrast in elegiac modes of self-presentation—are those that insure their own ironic undercutting. The recognition of generic conventions as such—which is necessary if the contrast between the poet's current exilic plight and his amatory past is to be acknowledged—reveals a gap between Symbolic construction and Imaginary self-recognition that only becomes visible in the assertion of their identity. It is precisely in the self-conscious moment of fictive elaboration, of the fabrication of an immediately convincing reality that will be recognized as such, that the aporetical nature of this subject position becomes apparent.

Thus on one level the naive reading is correct. The poet who portrays himself as standing unheeded before the door of death (*Tristia* 3.2.21–24) *is* the persona of the *exclusus amator*. Yet, this coincidence of poet and persona is not a sign of unmediated sincerity. It is the traumatic trace of a death in one realm, the civic community of Rome, that awaits its answer in another, the Real (Claassen 1999: 239–40; Videau-Delibes 1988: 31–32, 35; Chomarat 1988: 18). The subject of erotic elegy has been removed to a world beyond that recognized by the speaking subject in Rome. He exists in limbo. Indeed, as the poet tells us, he has been relegated both to the realm of the dead (*Tristia* 3.11.25–26), and to the world of those who cannot die (*Ex Ponto* 1.2.37–38).[9] His existence is spectral and thus neither of, nor beyond, this world. In Tomis, he lives in a realm of absolute subjection to external contingency and imperial power, yet through his poetry, he says, he finds a means of transcending time and space (*Tristia* 4.1.41–44). His exclusion from Rome and the publicly recognized system of honors and rewards is the necessary condition for his elaboration of this radically separate, transcendental world. That this elaboration is never complete, and never could be, goes without saying. Nonetheless, it is the tension between the poet's Symbolic construction of this other world, complete with his Imaginary investment in it, and his desire to regain the world of the living, with its endless and fleeting satisfactions, that makes the exilic poetry so fascinating.

Indeed, the poet's death, as he acknowledges, opens up a realm of art and self-fashioning that is beyond the world of the *princeps* and the emerging imperial court, yet inconceivable without it. The phenomenal world of the exilic poetry is one in which Augustus is both the sole means of restoring the poet to wholeness and the first cause of division and rupture. The *princeps* represents simultaneously the traumatic emergence of the Real as that which sundered Ovid from a lost realm of Imaginary plenitude—envisioned in terms of *domus, amici,* and *patria*[10]—and the center of the new Symbolic universe that recognizes Augustus as the apex of a pyramid of interlocking social ties in which individuals are recognized as subjects only to the extent that they are subordinated to his authority. As Anne Videau-Delibes observes:

> Il importe de retenir comment les *Tristes* composent une image peu cohérente de l'empereur, tantôt positive, tantôt négative. Il n'est pas question ici de tenter d'y déceler les intentions politiques d'Ovide ni de deviner comment s'y reflètent les réactions complexes de l'exilé réel qu'était l'auteur mais de chercher comment cette image d'Auguste s'inscrit dans le cadre de la poétique des *Tristes* et comment elle en est une clé de voûte.[11] (1991: 234–35)

Augustus in the exilic poetry is the *pater patriae* (*Tristia* 2.39, 2.181, 2.574, 4.4.13), and in the role of phallic (and thus implicitly castrating) father he leaves no place for his heirs except that of subjection and Imaginary identification with the Symbolic community of which he is the image (Videau-Delibes 1991: 250; Lacan 1986: 355–57). Ovid and his peers can never aspire to assuming the name of the father and a position of independent communal Symbolic recognition that is not simultaneously one of recognized submission to the center of authority. Augustus has become the phallus, that which names "the impossible desire to be recognized as Absolute Subject" (Janan 1994: 21).

The Augustan imperial Symbolic, as portrayed in the exilic poetry, with its multiple layers of embedded authority leading to a single center, had abolished the multipolar world of late republican factional politics, with its competing loyalties, complex alliances, and space for individual maneuver[12] (Ste. Croix 1981: 370; Thibault 1964: 9). Thus in *Ex Ponto* 1.7.21–22, addressed to the son of the poet's former patron Messalla Corvinus, M. Valerius Messalla Messalinus, Ovid asks: "Quis se Caesaribus notus non *fingit* amicum? / Da veniam fasso: tu mihi Caesar eras" (What person of any note does not *fashion* himself to be a friend to the Caesars? Have pity on one who is weary. You were my Caesar). This seemingly innocuous bit of flattery to a potential patron is revealing. The emphasis on self-fashioning, "fingis," implies an alteration or tailoring of the self that is necessary if one is to be ranked among Caesar's friends. This is not a natural process, or one in which transparent sincerity is presumed. Rather, the elaboration of a certain subject position by members of the elite is the sign by which Caesar's power is recognized. The fictive nature of the process is manifest. Far from undercutting its political efficacy, it renders it all the more powerful. Whereas the ideology of aristocratic *amicitia* in the republican period was founded on a sense of reciprocity that served both to mask status differences and to reinforce the sense of obligation they implied (Bowditch 2001: introduction), there could be no real reciprocity in a situation wherein an *amicus* must of necessity be *fictus*. Moreover, who could maintain a relationship of reciprocity with Caesar? Messalinus fashions himself into Caesar's friend, a relation that implies a process of subjection even within the image of friendship, and Ovid has done the same in relation to Messalinus.

The same image of embedded layers of personal subordination leading to a single center is found in *Ex Ponto* 1.9 addressed to Cotta Maximus, Messalinus's brother. This poem on the death and funeral of the sometimes poet, Albinovanus Celsus, asks Cotta to show the same concern for Ovid, who can be numbered among the dead ("et nos extinctis adnumerare potest"), as he has for those who are actually dead (1.9.55–56). The crucial image, however, comes earlier in the poem (1.9.35–36). Here, in the context of recalling how Celsus cultivated Cotta's patronage, he refers to Cotta's home as a temple wherein Celsus observed certain rites, the same rites Cotta observes in the houses of those gods that rule the world, that is, the imperial household. The image, even if tinged with ironic wit, not only alludes to the emerging cult of emperor worship, it also casts the role of Celsus and Ovid in relation to Cotta as analogous to that between Cotta and Augustus. Moreover, the term used to refer to the house of Caesar, "terrarum dominos . . . deos" (the lords of the earth that are gods) implicitly casts those who worship them as *servi*. The ideological corollary of the *dominus* was the *servus*, just as that of the *domina* was the *servus amoris*, an echo of amatory rhetoric that was unlikely to be fortuitous.[13] By the same token, the postponement of *deos* to the end of the line insures that the deification of the imperial family is highlighted for maximum effect.[14] Thus where once Ovid played at being the slave of a woman to pursue the object of his desire, he now must submit to Cotta as *dominus* in the same way as Cotta submits to the "terrarum dominos." In this context, the only freedom that is left is one that implies a withdrawal from social relations and the establishment of an Imaginary self-identification that is itself a form of internal exile or Symbolic death.

Finally, in *Ex Ponto* 2.2.121–24, Ovid makes his most explicit portrait of this emerging model of embedded imperial subjectivity. In another address to Messalinus, he portrays the young aristocrat, whom he hopes will be his patron, as a priest who can transmit the poet's prayers to the imperial deity. The implication of this model of patronage as divine intercession is made clear in the next poem's address to Cotta as the *princeps* of the poet's friends (*Ex Ponto* 2.3.31–32). Ovid's relation to the sons of Messalla is analogous to their relationship to Caesar, and as he is a god to them so Ovid can only approach the gods through them:

> Qui quoniam partria toto sumus orbe remoti,
>   nec licet ante ipsos procubuisse deos,
> quos colis, ad superos haec fer mandata sacerdos,
>   adde sed et proprias ad mea verba preces.
> (*Ex Ponto* 2.2.121–24)

Since we are removed a world away from the fatherland, we are not allowed to prostrate ourselves before the gods themselves, whom you worship. As a priest bear these requests to the immortals, but add also your own prayers to my words.

Ovid is two steps removed from the source of Symbolic legitimation. The poet is thus doubly subjected.

At the center of a vast interlocking web of social and personal relations that stretches from the edges of the civilized world to Rome is the figure of the emperor who is treated as a living god (cf. *Tristia* 3.8.13–14; *Ex Ponto* 3.6.23–24; and Claassen 1999: 227). It was through the figure of the *princeps* alone, first Augustus and then Tiberius, that Symbolic integration could be achieved and desire satisfied. The *princeps* is presented as that union of opposites in which inside and outside, individuality and integration, poet and persona, Imaginary and Symbolic are reconciled (Videau-Delibes 1991: 267, 315; Labate 1987: 110). Yet wholeness and satisfaction are ultimately indistinguishable from the extinction of desire in death, from the assumption of the self into a totalizing system in which desire is no longer recognized. As the emperor is officially indistinguishable from his role, so are his subjects (Janan 2001: 49). On this reading, then, we have all become dead, or have at least ceded to that death—that moment of absolute externality—that is implicit in our having become objects or made things (*ficta*).[15] Thus Ovid says in *Ex Ponto* 4.1.27–36 that he has become a work of art fashioned by his new, hoped for patron, Sextus Pompeius.

What the exilic poetry reveals Augustus to have made impossible is not desire but the continuing series of metonymic displacements and erotic substitutions that kept the space of the desiring subject open, that made the unstable and self-contradictory world of the elegiac subject possible. Within the phenomenology of the subject presented in the *Tristia* and the *Ex Ponto* that space no longer exists, and the subject of exile can only speak from a realm that defines itself as beyond its confines. Like Cornelia in Propertius 4.11, Ovid in the poems of exile speaks from the realm of the dead.

There, of course, may be no small irony in Ovid's presentation of the imperial family as the gods or masters of the earth. The implicit accusation that Augustus has turned the rest of Rome, including the noble sons of Messalla, into slaves cannot be discounted (Williams 1994: 158; Videau-Delibes 1991: 233–34). Nonetheless, that irony is often indistinguishable from flattering acceptance. In addition, the scope of ironic play becomes progressively narrowed as we move from the first books of the exilic corpus to later works such as the passages from the *Ex Ponto* just cited (Habinek 1998: 153; Fantham 1996: 122; Evans 1983: 24, 31, 48, 72). Thus at *Ex Ponto* 2.1.17–18, the poet writes in a poem on Tiberius's celebration of his triumph over the Dalmatians in 12 C.E., "gaudia Caesareae mentis pro parte virili / sunt mea: privati nil habet domus" (the joys of Caesar's mind are my own to the utmost of my ability: that house has nothing private).[16]

The manifest eulogistic content of the couplet is not in question. What is far more interesting are its subtler implications. On the one hand, if Caesar's household has nothing private, then all its dirty laundry—which in the case of Tiberius and his marriage to Julia was considerable—would need to be aired in public. On the other, two further readings have an equal claim on our attention. First Caesar's house has become the public face of Rome. It has nothing private. It is the image of the Roman Symbolic, and the *pater patriae* is the foundation of our identity. Second, if Caesar's house has nothing private, if it is totally public and the totality of what is defined as public, then the rest of the population has nothing but the private. As the poet says in *Tristia* 4.4.15, "res est publica Caesar" which can be translated in three different mutually reinforcing fashions.[17] First, "Caesar is public property," and therefore we all have an equal right to praise and address him. Second, "Caesar is the republic." He is the state. Third, Caesar is the public sphere. To the extent that public life continues to have meaning in Rome, it does so only through Caesar. Caesar has nothing private because the *res publica* is Caesar.

What we see in these passages, even as the possibility of ironic undertones persists, is that the unified subjectivity that was the founding myth of traditional Roman ideology has been definitively rent asunder. The seamless integration of public and private life that Cicero celebrates in *De Officiis*, and whose schism the elegists exploited, has now been split into two incommensurate halves. The cultivation of the one no longer has any necessary relation to the other. All men have become exiles in their own homes and must cultivate a purely internal freedom. Thus, at *Ex Ponto* 2.8.19–20, a poem in which Ovid professes joy at receiving from

Cotta Maximus two images of the imperial family, probably coins (Claassen 1999: 285n.99), that he sets up as icons to be worshiped, we find, "hunc ego cum spectem, videor cernere Romam; / nam patriae faciem sustinet ille suae" (when I look at this man [i.e., Augustus], I seem to make out Rome, for he maintains the appearance of his fatherland).

Augustus here again is equated with the image of the *res publica*. The pun on *facies* in reference to a portrait of Augustus stamped on a coin is of course rich with ironic possibilities,[18] but at the same time, as Peter Green notes, the equation of Caesar with Rome echoes one of the standard tenets of imperial Roman Stoicism, "which virtually equated the Roman Empire (symbolized in the person of the Princeps) with the eternal divine cosmos controlling the world" (1994: 326). The later imperial Stoics may have resisted individual emperors, but their equation of the state with its government and the cosmic order, and their cultivation of a realm of internal freedom separate from the contingencies of the communal Symbolic system, also made them the model for a new split subjectivity whose elaboration can be first glimpsed in the exilic poetry (Francis 1995: 1–11). Thus, Ovid may hint that the new face of Rome is founded on a crass materialism (i.e., the coins) and allude to the absurdity of worshiping such idols, but he also maintains that this *is* the face of Rome and these *are* the deities we must worship. Not only is no alternative model proposed, none even seems conceivable. The assertion of Julio-Claudian supremacy is taken at face value (Green 1994: 325; Evans 1983: 25–26).

In what follows, four interrelated topics are examined. First, we look briefly at recent work on imperial philosophy and its arguments that the philosophical discourse of the period functioned as a set of technologies of the self that purported to establish a realm of inner freedom (*apatheia*, *ataraxia*, or *autonomia*) through a deliberate process of intertextual and aesthetic self-construction. Second, we examine how this same aesthetics and ethics of self-fashioning, or at least its precursors, can be found in Ovid's exilic poetry. Particular attention will paid here to the strange confluence of images of the poetic subject's death and his ability to transcend space and time in the *Tristia* and *Ex Ponto*. Third, we discuss how this aesthetics of self-fashioning functions simultaneously as a means of resistance to the new imperial Symbolic and a model of subjection. Finally, we examine how this ambivalence in the textual and intertextual construction of the self as a realm of Imaginary freedom plays itself out in Ovid's *Tristia* II and the later exilic poetry. In the process, we discover the specter of the *tenerorum lusor amorum* (the playboy of tender love poems, *Tristia* 3.3.73) to have been displaced into a limbo between Symbolic death and final annihilation.

The Writing of the Imperial Self

> It was Caesar Augustus (so Tacitus affirms)[19] who
> first made words as well as actions liable to indictment:
> Cassius Severus furnished the occasion, through his
> "famosi libelli" harrying men and women of high rank,
> he was condemned after a trial by the Senate and
> banished to the island of Crete. . . . prosecutions could
> now be extended to take in personal attacks on the
> ruler or criticism of the government; and praise of the
> Republican past was held to reflect ominously on
> the present dispensation.
> —Syme 1978: 213–14

> The *conversio ad se* is also a trajectory; a trajectory
> thanks to which, by escaping all dependencies and
> enslavements, one ends up by returning to oneself,
> as to a harbor offering shelter from storms or to a citadel
> offering the protection of its ramparts.[20]
> —Foucault 1984: 82

In the last years of his life, Michel Foucault turned to the problem of self-fashioning as it was explored by the philosophers of the empire. In these writers, he discovers a new interest in what he terms "technologies of the self," methods of constructing a subject in much the same way as one might create a poem or other aesthetic object. This is a very different vision of what it means to be a subject from that of the classical Platonic model in which the self is a transcendent presence whose primary task in the labor of self-realization is the recollection of what it already is. In fact, Foucault argues, it is less the experience of dialectic that produces the ideal self of the philosophers of the empire than what we might term intertextuality. Thus Plutarch, he notes, recommends learning the discourses of others as a drug that guards the soul against illness. Subjectivity itself, following this model, becomes a function of citation. Where Plato in the *Phaedrus* rejects writing, as mere *hupomnēsis* instead of *mnēmē*, the philosophers of the empire, Foucault observes, directly advocated the keeping of *hupomnēmata*,[21] or notebooks, not as a substitute for memory—conceived of by Plato as vital and interior to the soul—but as a form of practice, a technology of the self (Foucault 1994d: 417–19; 1994e: 360–61; 1994f: 793–96). Foucault observes that in the Stoics, and indeed all the philosophers of the imperial period, the exclusion of writing is completely discarded (Foucault 1994e: 361). Philosophical pedagogy had changed, he notes, so that the truth became something one received from a master or professor. "The Platonic culture of the dialogue cede[d] its place to a culture of silence and the art of listening" (Foucault 1994f: 796).

Writing, rather than undermining the presence of the *logos* to itself or representing a form of discourse whose author is never present to defend the integrity of his intentions, actually renders the absent party present, according to Seneca (*Letters* 4.40.1; Foucault 1994d: 425). Writing is not the foreign element that threatens the interiority of the soul but rather the technology that makes the construction of subjectivity possible. The philosopher strives to construct his own world of *apatheia* through the aesthetic elaboration of a self formed through a rigorous process of study, note taking (*hupomnēmata*), and meditation. Such a subject is no longer fully present either in the Platonic sense of ideal immediacy or in the Ciceronian sense of the subject of effective public action (Foucault 1994c: 627; 1994d: 426–27; 1994e: 361; 1994i: 700). Foucault states:

> The *hupomnēmata* ought to be resituated in the context of a very palpable tension during this period: inside this culture that was so affected by tradition, by the recognized value of the quotation, by the recurrence of discourse, by the practice of "citation" under the seal of age and authority, an ethics was in the process of developing that was very openly oriented by the care of the self toward some very precise objects: the retreat into oneself; the interior life; independence; the taste for oneself. Such is the objective of the *hupomnēmata*: to make the memory of a fragmentary logos transmitted by teaching, listening or reading, a means of establishing a relation with oneself as Adequate and perfect as possible. (1994c: 625–26

What Foucault sees in the philosophers of the empire is a kind of scripting or writing of the self, that in its very fictive nature, became a practice of freedom under conditions of empire (Miller 1993: 340; Foucault 1994g: 711; Newman 1989: 1501).

In particular, Foucault sees in the work of such philosophers as the Stoics Seneca and Epictetus, and the neo-Platonist Plutarch, a turn to the self that, through various practices of examination and study, seeks to fashion a beautiful existence in which the subject attains perfect mastery over itself (Foucault 1994e: 356):[22]

> In the philosophical tradition inaugurated by Stoicism, *askesis*, far from denoting self-abnegation, implies the progressive consideration of the self, the mastery of the self—a mastery one attains not by renouncing reality, but by acquiring and assimilating the truth. The ultimate goal of the *askesis* is not to prepare the individual for another reality, but to permit him to accede to the reality of this world. In Greek, the word that describes this attitude is *paraskeuazō* ("to prepare oneself"). The *askesis* is a set of practices by means of which the individual is able to acquire, to assimilate the truth, and to

transform it into a permanent principle of action. *Alétheia* becomes *ēthos*. It is a process of intensifying subjectivity. (Foucault 1994f: 800

Stoic *askesis* is not designed to root out hidden desires, nor to decipher the reality of who we are beneath appearances, but as a device to mold behavior. This self-surveillance is less disciplinary, in the sense of being designed to make the individual conform to a single preestablished end, than shaping. It is a technology of the self that allows the subject to attain mastery over its thoughts, feelings and reactions to external events (Foucault 1994c: 610, 615, 626–27; 1994e: 359, 364–65; Miller 1998a: 184–88). Self-mastery, on this view, is an end in itself. Stoic *askesis*, as such, conforms to Foucault's definition of ethics as the "mindful practice of freedom" (1994h: 711–12). It is less a purely cognitive activity than a practice, or in the words of Pierre Hadot, a "spiritual exercise" (1987: 15–16; 1995: 82–83).[23]

The goal then is the establishment of inner freedom through the internalization of certain precepts, the meditation upon them, and the consequent shaping of a self that is able to exist as a detached object, separate from the sphere of public life and yet continuing to function within it. Writing was the means of creating this interiority, and meditation upon one's own writings and those of others was the method by which individuals kept to hand the wherewithal necessary to meet the challenges of daily life with the desired degree of indifference (Foucault 1994d: 417, 420–21; 1994e: 360–62; Newman 1989: 1478–80, 1489, 1498). As Carlin Barton observes: "In the indifference of fascination Stoic and Sceptic *ataraxia* meet. The apathy of the wise man was a kind of autointoxication or autofascination, which according to Plutarch (*Quaestiones conviviales* 7.8 *Moralia* 711b) rendered him proof against enchantment ('akeletos'). The Stoic was immunized by insensibility against the malice of another" (1993: 100–101). What the practice of the philosophical writing of the self aimed to achieve was the production of a realm of internal freedom: the Imaginary investment of a self-contained realm that was separate from the communal Symbolic. It did not withdraw per se from the public sphere of law, politics, and military achievement, but set up an internal division wherein public life and the aesthetic fashioning of the self were neither isomorphic, as in the republican ideal, nor contradictory, as in much elegiac poetry, but separate parallel universes (Henderson 1993: 129–30).

One of the prime examples Foucault offers of the kind of subject produced by this ethic is Pliny the Younger. Without being the adherent of any dogma he devotes great care to both his married life and his individual self, yet this in no way implies a withdrawal from the duties and obligations of public and political life (Foucault 1984: 63, 97–98, 188–89).[24] Pliny experiences an increased disjunction between internal and external power relations compared with that of the republican era, but no opposition between those realms. He does not posit himself in an antagonistic relation to the social world of political power and honors but essays to preserve his tranquillity (1984: 105). Thus we picture Pliny easily moving between the realms of light poetic composition, the pondering of his own ethical obligations, professing passionate love for his wife, and fulfilling his duties as a provincial governor by writing to the emperor for advice on handling those troublesome Christians. The worlds in which he lives are not mirror images of one another, but neither are they antagonistic.

For Ovid, exile marks the moment of fissure in which the subject's Imaginary identification with the state, and the Symbolic community thus constituted, is definitively cut off. Tomis, as he argues in *Tristia* 3.9.27–28, derives its name from the Greek *temnō* and refers to the spot where Medea butchered her brother to slow her father's pursuit. Tomis therefore is the place of dismemberment where reunion with the father (*pater patriae*, Rome, etc.) is once and for all made impossible (Videau-Delibes 1988: 29). Where imperial philosophy accepts and ultimately valorizes this splitting, Ovid is on its cusp. The exilic poetry as the last authentic moment of the elegiac subject is the point where we see its transformation into the subject of empire.

None of this is to say that Ovid had become a philosopher.[25] In fact, the exilic poetry deliberately shuns the whole tradition of consolatory literature on exile. There was a vast genre of philosophical writing that had sought to show victims of political exile that theirs was a time for study, reflection, and the exhibition of personal fortitude. Ovid will have none of it, just as Cicero in his letters from exile found no consolation in the philosophical platitudes he so liberally dispensed (Claassen 1999: 21, 165–67, 184; Green 1994: xlvi–vii; Chomarat 1988: 19). My argument, then, is not that Ovid was influenced by certain philosophical doctrines, just as Foucault's thesis is not that a specific philosophical school produced a given set of concepts that was then widely adopted. Rather, like Foucault, my concern is with the subject's relation to itself (Davidson 1994: 118). Thus my contention is that in Ovid's exilic poetry we see the beginnings of the elaboration of a model of subjectivity that will become characteristic of a certain mode of aristocratic self-formation in the imperial period.

Indicative of this is the fact that, although Ovid may not have been extensively influenced by Stoic or other philosophical writings on exile, he was himself influential on the philosopher Seneca (Green 1994: xlvii). The epigrams attributed to Seneca concerning his Corsican exile reveal imitations of the exilic poems as well as other Ovidian works (Claassen 1999: 242, Prato 1964: 9–16). Likewise, the *ad Polybium* shows clear borrowings from a variety of exilic poems, with special emphasis on *Tris-*

tia 3.14. Moreover, Seneca, like Ovid, has been criticized for what seems like servile adoration of Caesar and his freedman, Polybius. Others have chosen to see the same passages as ironic. Nonetheless, as observed earlier in the context of *Ex Ponto* 2.8 and as is explored in the last section of this chapter, the distinction between these two subject positions, that of the ironist and the flatterer, can be difficult to discern and their effects are all but identical (Claassen 1999: 92, 96, 263n.79; Degl' Innocenti Pierini 1990: 112–17, 143–45). Lastly, it should be noted that Seneca in his *consolatio Ad Helviam*, written to his mother, seeks to console her for the loss of her infant grandson as well of her son, Seneca himself, since as an exile he speaks from the dead. This last trope, of course, is familiar from Ovid's exilic poetry.[26] One particular novelty on Seneca's part is that it is the voice from the dead who seeks to console the living, for it is the dead who are able to exhibit Stoic *apatheia* (Claassen 1999: 90–93). Thus, exile and death become implicitly equated with that very distance from the communal Symbolic that is the aim of Stoic *meditatio* and imperial philosophical practice.

Ovid, of course, was not completely innocent of philosophy. At *Tristia* 3.4.4–6 he urges his anonymous addressee to live in obscurity. Here he not only adopts a theme of Epicurean philosophy already articulated by Horace at *Epistles* 1.17.10–12, but he also, as just observed, describes a form of life that by its very invisibility is all but indistinguishable from death.[27]

> vive tibi et longe nomina magna fuge.
> vive tibi, quantumque potes praelustria vita,
> saevum praelustri fulmen ab arce venit.

Live for yourself and flee far from the famous. Live for yourself and, as much as you are able, avoid magnificent things, fierce lightning comes from the magnificent citadel.

The pun on *vita* is particularly adept. In the final position, it is impossible definitively to determine on metrical or phonetic criteria alone whether it is the noun, "life," or the imperative of the verb, "to avoid," although the possible parallelism with "nomina magna fuge" shows the verb to be a clear possibility. Nonetheless, the anaphora of *vive* also makes the noun a natural expectation and the adjacent adjective *praelustria* could be a modifier, it is only when we read the pentameter that we realize that *vita* must be the verb and *praelustria* a neuter plural substantive. The potential confusion is reinforced by the fact that *praelustria* is a hapax legomenon. What seems initially an admonition to live a pure life in isolation changes into one to avoid the magnificent. If, however, we derive *praelustria* from *lustrum* "bog or morass" and by extension "debauchery," rather than *lustrum* "purification" and hence "that which has been made bright," then the pure life is transformed into its opposite by contact with the illustrious.[28] Thus the maintenance of purity is defined precisely as the avoidance of the compromises of public life, which leads only to Jupiter's thunderbolt, a common metaphor for Augustus's anger throughout the exilic poetry (Williams 1994: 190; Luck 1977: ad loc.). The pure life in turn is defined later in the poem as a kind of invisibility that in the eyes of the Symbolic, the place from which we are recognized as subjects by the Other, equals death (Žižek 1989: 101; 1991: 44, 74; Moxey 1991: 990; Lacan 1973: 222): "bene qui latuit bene vixit" (He who has hid well has lived well; *Tristia* 3.4.25).[29] Thus, exile, death, the philosophical *conversio ad se*, and life under the conditions of empire—that is to say, under the threat of Jupiter's thunderbolt—become if not completely equated then at least recognized metonymic substitutions.

"I'M NOT DEAD YET"

> The work of art that insures the rebirth of its author and its reader or viewer is one that succeeds in integrating the artificial language it puts forward (new style, new composition, surprising imagination) and the unnamed agitations of an omnipotent self that ordinary linguistic usage always leaves somewhat orphaned or plunged into mourning. Hence such a fiction, if it isn't an antidepressant, is at least a survival, a resurrection.
> —Kristeva 1989: 51

> Conditions in Rome have now reached the stage where the excessive rhetoric of adulation has become unconvincing by its own totality but has throttled all possiblities of expressing deviation.
> —Stahl 1985: 253

This philosophical vision of the self as the telos of a process of construction that is separate from experience, that is textual and intertextual rather than natural, consolidates and valorizes a rift that had opened between the subject and the actual political, historical, and existential circumstances of its life. It offers the vision of a self whose very presence is a kind of absence. This is a self whose life is envisioned as a series of discontinuous synchronous moments outside the flow of a collective history. Freedom is defined as a moment of absolute self-presence beyond the necessary complicities and disappointments embodied in the Other and in problematic emotions like hope (Citti 2000: 31, 127).[30] As such, this self is an ideal model for the subject of empire, a subject who is always already in exile, and one who is most resistant to power when absent, unreachable, elsewhere, who is dead to the world in which power reigns. This is also the model that most accurately describes Ovid's self-construction throughout the exilic poetry, but one that has special relevance to *Tristia* II, the *Apology to Augustus*.

In this poem, perhaps more than any other, Ovid chooses to speak the truth to power (Williams 1994: 161–62). While ostensibly offering a humble defense of his life and art, the poet launches into what at times reads more like a satire than a petition for imperial clemency (Nugent 1990: 244; Kenney 1983: 150). On one level, the poetic persona appears not to be attacking but praising the emperor, yet, as Claassen notes, "excessive adulation and lip-service to the emperor's ideal of national poetry, and also many examples of *praeteritio* create an atmosphere of criticism" (Claassen 1989: 265). Still, Ovid never calls into question the legitimacy of Augustan power (Evans 1983: 16–17), but rather presents "dependency and subjection . . . as the necessary condition for enjoyment of the benefits of the imperial system" (Habinek 1998: 151). Moreover, Ovid's *apologia* is constructed through a series of complex intertextual appropriations that allude not only to his own earlier offending works, particularly the *Ars*, but also to Horace and the neo-Callimachean tradition of the *recusatio*.[31] Ovid in this poem is thus most himself precisely when he means the opposite of what he says, while saying what he means. He is most authentic when he appropriates the words of others. His creation of this ironic textual subject allows him to be most fully present where he is absent. Like Plutarch, whose valorization of writing Foucault admires, Ovid fashions his text less out of his experience than as a palimpsest of previous texts, or what in contemporary Plutarch studies have been termed clusters (Van der Stockt 1999a; 1999b).[32] The Ovid constructed by and through the exilic poetry thus becomes the perfect metaphor for both exile and the subjections of empire, whose simultaneous self-constitution and nonexistence render him an ideal citizen of this brave new republic. As Mario Labate (1987: 114) argues, the exilic poetry marks the point where the ideological and ethical concerns of the late republic are translated into a de facto imperial code of conduct.

Indeed, as the poet himself notes throughout these poems, he is in a real sense dead (Williams 1994: 12–13; Claassen 1988: 168),[33] or rather, in Lacanian terms, he is caught between the two deaths, the Symbolic and the Real. Thus, as we have already seen, the poet in *Tristia* 3.2.23–24 presents himself as the *exclusus amator* before the door of death, paradoxically seeking to die as a release from the death of exile (Green 1994: 325; Evans 1983: 66). In 3.3, when Ovid fantasizes about his own death while ill in Tomis,[34] we find the image of his wife gathering his bones to be taken back to Rome. The poem then modulates into the story of Antigone doing the same for her brother (3.3.65–68). In the next poem, 3.4, which we examined for its use of the Epicurean theme of avoiding the great and its equation of "living well" with Symbolic death, Ovid is depicted as occupying "the borderline between the human and the nonhuman" (Williams 1994: 133).[35] In this same interstitial realm Lacan, in his seminar on the ethics of psychoanalysis, locates Antigone in her confrontation with Creon. Moreover, it is her relegation to this limbo that makes possible her *autonomia*, her rejection of the good as understood by the dominant mode of the Symbolic embodied in Creon's decrees (Lacan 1986: 291, 315–29; 1991: 120; Žižek 1989: 117, 135):

> Antigone presents herself as *autonomos*, the pure and simple relationship of a human being to that which it miraculously finds itself carrying, that is the rupture of signification, that which grants a person the insuperable power of being—in spite of and against everything—what he [*sic*] is. . . . Antigone all but fulfills what can be called pure desire, the pure and simple desire of death as such.[36] She incarnates this desire. (1986: 328–29)

Antigone's choice, her desire, is pure precisely to the degree that it rejects all claims of otherness and encloses itself in what Patrick Guyomard, in his response to Lacan's reading, sees as an incestuous narcissism. For this latter day French psychoanalyst, it is precisely Creon's bitter ability to learn from his mistakes, rather than Antigone's suicidal purity, that presents the real ethical model (1992: 45, 52, 62–64, 75). But for Lacan (1991: 13), it is the beauty of Antigone's choice of a Good beyond all recognized goods, beyond the pleasure principle, that gives her character its monumental status and makes her an ethical model. Beauty for Lacan represents the perfect moment between life and death, a moment both articulated by and beyond time and desire, a moment whose true achievement can only be imagined as the incarnation of a pure desire beyond any recognizable object (1986: 291, 344; 1991: 15, 154; Julien 1990: 114–15; Žižek 1989: 135). For Lacan, then, as is the case for Foucault (Foucault 1994d: 415; 1994c: 617) in his turn to antiquity, the search for an ethics leads to an aesthetics of existence, to the search for the beautiful life.

This same *autonomia*, or "self-law," Ovid invokes in his repeated claims that the emperor may physically remove him from Rome, the land of the living, but cannot control his mind (Claassen 1999: 198; Edwards 1996: 122–24; Williams 1994: 197; Barsby 1978: 43). Thus at *Tristia* 3.7.43–48, in a poem addressed to Ovid's stepdaughter and fellow poet Perilla, he asserts the immortality of the gifts of genius and of the heart while noting that Caesar's law can have no power in this realm.[37] Poetry thus offers access to a realm of freedom and autonomy. The poet gains this freedom through being transformed into a work of art, that is through a textual self-fashioning that is immune to the vicissitudes of experience (Delpeyroux 1993: 186–87). By the same token, poetry in *Tristia* 4.1.41–48 is portrayed as a *spiritus*[38] that raises one above merely human evils and shields one from pain. It intoxicates and numbs its devotee as the mysteries of Bacchus do the Bacchant:

> utque suum Bacche non sentit saucia vulnus
> dum stupet Idaeis exululata modis,
> sic ubi mota calent viridi mea pectora thyrso,
> altior humano spiritus ille malo est.
> ille nec exilium, Scythici nec litora ponti,
> ille nec iratos sentit habere deos.
> utque soporiferae biberem si pocula Lethes,
> temporis adversi sic mihi sensus abest.

> As the injured Bacchant does not feel her wound so long as she is benumbed, having shrieked in Idaean rhythms, so when my heart warms and has been moved by the green thyrsus, that spirit [of poetic *furor*] is more exalted than mere human ill. It does not sense exile, the shores of the Scythian sea, nor that the gods are enraged. As if I were to drink cups of sleep-bearing Lethe, all sense of my difficult situation is gone.

Poetry here transcends the limitation of human time and space (i.e., exile and the Scythian sea),[39] and for this reason it is like a draught of the river Lethe. The realm of the *autonomos*, of poetic and aesthetic freedom beyond the demands of the Other, is effectively the realm of death. The aesthetics of self-fashioning is inseparable in the exilic poetry from the poet's depiction as dead and yet desiring death, as caught between Antigone's two deaths. Likewise, in *Ex Ponto* 1.2.27–28 the poet says his only surcease from pain comes when a deathlike stupor overtakes him "et similis morti pectora torpor habet" (and a numbness like death holds my heart). This numbness in its description is indistinguishable from both the insensibility to pain ascribed to the Bacchant in *Tristia* 4.1.41–42 and the immortal oblivion of poetry's river Lethe in lines 47–48.

It is likewise this same *autonomia*, this same combination of autonomy and self-nullification, that is cultivated by the Foucauldian sage in the construction of its intertextual self.[40] In this regard, an anecdote about Zeno of Citium, the founder of Stoicism, is particularly interesting: it is told that when he went to the oracle at Delphi to ask how he should lead his life, the response came back "that he should mate with the dead. He understood this to mean that he should *read* the *ancients*."[41] In this story we see three interrelated terms: self-fashioning (how one should live one's life); communion with the dead; and intertextuality. These are the same terms that form the core of Ovid's exilic poetics. Yet where Antigone embraces her death and willingly locates her desire beyond the pleasure principle (Žižek 1989: 166–67, 132; 1991: 25), and where the philosophers of the empire, Zeno's heirs, seek the freedom that results from *apatheia* and total self-regulation (Foucault 1984: 82; Henderson 1993: 128–30; Newman 1989: 1478, 1498–1502), Ovid still pursues his dreams of resurrection and the possibilities of a fully embodied enjoyment. It is this pursuit of return, however deluded, that denies Ovid's plight the tragic status of Antigone's (Lacan 1991: 154; Videau-Delibes 1991: 119, 127) and leaves him instead in what many see as the pathetic and contradictory position of ironist and flatterer.[42]

Yet, what has not been fully appreciated in the previous criticism is the extent to which these two positions are not contradictory but homologous: for each necessitates the thematizing of a moment of performative self-consciousness that exceeds the pure constative or observational content of even the truest of factual statements.[43] The ironic statement only exists to the extent that it calls attention to the way it exceeds its own denotative content and thereby forever loses its ability to recover a purely constative status as a transparent proposition about the world.[44] Flattery only functions to the extent that it calls attention to its own excessive, hyperbolic nature. It is the sly rhetorical wink that says, "this is a compliment," that says "I am exalting you and recognizing the power differential between us." The court poet is thus always already both flatterer and ironist (Videau-Delibes 1988: 17). He cannot praise without recognizing the subordination that makes that praise possible and necessary and, in so doing, calling into question the nature of that praise. Yet the very recognition of the poet's self-conscious subordination to the new system of embedded vertical power relations described in the opening of this chapter—a recognition that seems to the modern reader to be an ironic undercutting of those relations—is also simultaneously a recognition of their absolute hegemony (Bartsch 1994: 177; Labate 1987: 99, 104–5, 110–13; Evans 1983: 29). As Ovid says approvingly when he instructs his wife on approaching Livia to seek mitigation of his fate, "sentiet illa / te maiestatem pertimuisse suam" (she will feel that you have feared her greatness; *Ex Ponto* 3.1.155–56)—and may well be disposed to grant your suit.

Likewise in *Ex Ponto* 3.6, the poet starts by telling us that we can see how merciful Caesar is from the example of his own lot, for he merited much worse (3.6.7–10). The fact that the poet consistently proclaims his misery may undercut the assertion of Caesar's *clementia*, but it also makes clear the unquestionable nature of Caesar's power. Moreover Ovid's basic assertion in these lines is also a simple factual statement. Augustus did show mercy. He could have easily had the poet killed (Thibault 1964: 60). Our discomfort with that fact does not change it. Thus, as Paolo Cutolo

has observed, *Tristia* 2.122–38, where the poet thanks Augustus for spar-
ing his life and not forcing him to submit to a public trial in the Senate,
is not so much a covert allegation of despotism and denial of due process
(Claassen 1999: 149), as it is a frank recognition that the Senate would
have felt obliged to deal with the poet even more severely. The very fact
of a public trial on charges brought by Augustus would have required
all who wished for the *princeps*'s favor to demonstrate their loyalty by
demanding the harshest possible penalty (Cutolo 1995: 40–41). Is the
poet's thanks ironic here or sincere? How would we know the difference:
for it is the very denial of the due process of law owed a Roman citizen
that constitutes the emperor's mercy. Indeed, as Ovid observes in *Ex
Ponto* 1.2.37–38, he is kept alive "in order" (or "with the result") that
his suffering may not end. He thus becomes a living object lesson. In fact,
as he notes in *Ex Ponto* 3.1.49–50, his exile has if anything made him
better known.

Caught between the two deaths, like the later philosophers,[45] he culti-
vates in his poetry, under the image of what may be read as resistance,
that which the empire most needs: a new model of Roman subjectivity
(Habinek 1998: 151–53). Ovid is allowed to publish from exile because
it serves Caesar's interest.[46] The *princeps* is shown to be clement and lib-
eral while providing a vivid example to all those who would think of
offending him in a similar manner (the very mystery of Ovid's *error* may
be part of the point [*Tristia* 2.207]). Thus in *Ex Ponto* 3.6 we modulate
from the ambivalent proclamation of Caesar's mercy to a direct assertion
of his godhead (3.6.23–24) followed by the claim that many of the victims
of Jupiter's thunderbolt did not deserve their fate (3.6.27–28). Jupiter and
Augustus, as noted earlier, are associated with one another throughout
the exilic poetry. In these two couplets, the very arbitrariness of Caesarian
power becomes the sign of its absolute status. He is merciful in the same
way as the Calvinist god is merciful even as he assigns sinners to their
arbitrarily predestined hell.[47] Yet Ovid assures his addressee, who fears to
be named, that the latter's timidity defames Caesar since "there is no need
to fear sharp rocks in calm seas" (3.6.43–44). The image nicely captures
the duality of Ovid's discourse: Caesar is merciful, but he is also the jagged
rocks that can shipwreck a poet's life should a storm arise.

The question of sincerity in these poems is not only beside the point, it
is not even posable.[48] Under these conditions, the poet here can only mean
what he says on one level if on another level he does not.[49] The split nature
of his existence[50] can only be authentically expressed through a manifest
bad faith (O'Gorman 1997: 115). His position is ironic, but that irony is
not subversive per se—it is rather a recognition of the inherent power
differentials in play. It is *sincerely ironic*.[51] More precisely, while the poet
may reserve a realm of internal freedom through poetic transcendence

and a writing of the self—which as we have seen is portrayed in terms identical with death, torpor, and *apatheia*—to serve as a locus of resistance, the very severance of that realm of freedom from the communal Symbolic, and its very ironic structure, renders it indistinguishable from complicity.

One of the most salient examples, for our purposes, is *Tristia* 2.287. Here the poet argues that the *Ars Amatoria* is no more to blame for vice than other Roman institutions that are equally susceptible of misuse. This includes temples, and he says with a wink "quis locus est templis augustior?" (What place is more august than temples?). The passage is susceptible to three logically—but not rhetorically—mutually exclusive readings. The first, which I label the constative, reads the statement as being essentially tautological, "What place is holier than temples?" (Luck 1977: ad loc.) This, as Cicero, and Ennius, attest (Cicero, *Actio in Verrem* 6.186; *De Deorum Natura* 1.19; Ennius, *Annales* 502), would have been the only interpretation of *augustior* prior to the *princeps* receiving his cognomen in 27. The second reading, which I term the ironic, sees a pun on Augustus's name and notes the wit of associating the *princeps* with places of possible seduction, particularly in a poem that seeks to defend its author against charges of corrupting the morals of young women. According to this interpretation, Ovid is no more to blame for the misuse of the *Ars* than Augustus is for the seductions that occur in holy/august temples. This reading gains in complexity when we realize that the temples the poet names were all built or reconstructed by the *princeps* and listed in the *Res Gestae* as among his proudest accomplishments (*Tristia* 2.277–302; *Res Gestae* 19.1–21.1; Williams 1994: 201–2).[52] Thus, what could be more like Augustus, *augustior*, than these temples that he himself built or refurbished? And it is precisely this very play on words that also allows the line to be read as a form of flattery that need in no way question the legitimacy of the emperor but rather acknowledges precisely those attributes he claimed for himself. Ovid, according to this third flattering reading, merely defends the *Ars* in its own terms and says even the holiest of places, those most associated with the *princeps*, are subject to misuse and misinterpretation (Evans 1983: 16–17).

The key thing to recognize is not that we must choose between these last two readings, as the vast majority of criticism of the exilic poetry has done (Evans 1983: 10–11), nor even that the choice is undecidable and hence founded on a deconstructible binary opposition, but that on the most basic level they are the same. They both depend on the same verbal forms, and they both function precisely to the extent that they simultaneously presume and exceed the constative reading by calling attention to their performative natures in the same way. The point can be pushed further. The ironic reading gains in cogency when the reader recognizes that the temples and porticoes mentioned in the passage are precisely those listed in the *Ars Amatoria* as ideal places to pick up girls (*Ars Amatoria* 1.67–262; Williams 1994: 202–3).[53] In the *Ars*, the entire Augustan building plan is appropriated for erotic purposes (Edwards 1996: 24). For this reason, critics have in the past interpreted this passage in the *Tristia* as an attack on "Augustus's well-known sensuality" (Holleman 1969: 54; see also Wiedemann 1975: 270). Nonetheless, the whole point of *Tristia* 2's defense of the *Ars* is that works "rarely succeed in having only the consequences their creators intended. . . . The readings of a poem . . . cannot be controlled by the author; the interpretations of a monument cannot be controlled by the builder" (Edwards 1996: 25). The same kind of "misreading" that sees the *Ars* as a source of vice would also claim that the temples themselves cause the seductions that take place within their precincts. To "misread" Ovid's recollection of the *Ars* in *Tristia* 2's catalog of temples as anti-Augustan is to perform the same "misreading" as those who would accuse Augustus of promoting seduction by building the temples in which it occurs. Poems don't pervert *matronae*, *matronae* do. The ironic reading thus folds back into the flattering reading precisely at the point where the admission of the ironic reading as a separate possibility would convict the reader of the same perversion as the *matronae* who allow themselves to be seduced in temples (Williams 1994: 158, 168; Dickinson 1973: 172). *Quis locus est . . . augustior?*

Ovid is even so generous as to provide exemplary misreadings of the temples by a posited perverse *matrona*. Thus in *Tristia* 2.295–96 we find "venerit in magni templum, tua munera, Martis, / stat Venus Ultori iuncta, vir ante fores" (she will have come into the temple of great Mars, Venus stands joined to the avenger, her husband before the door). The temple of Mars Ultor, dedicated in 2 B.C.E., was vowed by Augustus in return for his victory over the assassins of Julius Caesar (Luck 1977: ad loc.). It featured a statue of Venus, the patron deity of the *gens Iulia*, joined with that of Mars in an allegorical representation of the alliance of the power of war to the imperial clan. This would be the constative reading and its flattering gloss. *Iuncta*, however, can have clear sexual connotations. The ironic reading, thus, has Venus and Mars engaged in an act of sexual congress (Traill 1992: 505–6). *Vir*, moreover, refers to Vulcan, a representation of whom was placed outside.[54] Venus's husband is reduced to the figure of the elegiac *exclusus amator*, in a neat reversal of roles similar to that envisioned in *Amores* 1.4. Nonetheless, what we have here is also an accurate description of a perfectly pious temple, erected for the glory of the *princeps* and his clan. The ironic, erotic interpretation of these statues could only be construed by the same sort of fevered imagination that would be corrupted by reading the *Ars* (Traill 1992: 506–7).

The interpretive choice in *Tristia* 2.287, then, is not as Williams (1994: 49) argues between a naive and a sophisticated reading, for both the flattering and the ironic reading present the same level of self-conscious excess in relation to the naive constative understanding of *augustior*. Indeed, as Habinek and others have recently argued, Ovid valorizes the power his irony ostensibly resists. "Far from repudiating Augustus or those around him, Ovid's *Tristia* and *Epistulae ex Ponto* acknowledge the legitimacy of their dominance" (Habinek 1998: 164–66; see also O'Gorman 1997: 104–5). But this is not to say there is no irony. Nor is it to deny the possibility of change as the collection progresses. In fact, what we see is a constricting of the scope of ironic interpretation as we move from *Tristia* 1 and 2 to the later books of the exilic poetry. We finish this section by examining two passages that admit of the same basic structure of reading as that just examined. In the process, however, we shall observe the gradual effacement of the last remnants of the contradictory space that defined the elegiac subject.

Let us start with *Tristia* 4.4.13–16, part of which we have already examined:

> ipse pater patriae (quid enim est civilius illo?)
> sustinet in nostro carmine saepe legi,
> nec prohibere potest, quia res est publica Caesar,
> et de communi pars quoque nostra bono est.

> The father of our country himself (for what is more public/civil/ like a citizen than that?) allows himself often to be read in our poetry, nor is he able to prohibit it, because Caesar is public property and part of our common wealth.

The pun on *civilius* in the context of the initial rhetorical question possesses the exact same structure as that on *augustior*, but here the range of meanings is more constricted. The constative reading would again be essentially tautological: what could be more characteristic of the Roman *civitas* and civic identity than the *pater patriae*? The ironic reading would be the acknowledgment of the tautology and the recognition that the city is now being defined as much in terms of Augustus as vice versa. The flattering reading would then attribute the virtues of civility and civilization to the *princeps* who is the *pater patriae* and therefore both the reflection of the city and the source of that reflection's meaning. The ironic and the flattering reading thus fold into one another so that each only makes sense in terms of the other. Yet, where in the case of *augustior* the arc described by the analogous folding of the ironic into the flattering reading passed through the accusation that Augustus's temples promoted adultery, there is no reading here that even momentarily undermines the position of Caesar: for while the ironic reading flirts with the accusation of despotism, it also acknowledges Augustus as the phallic father, the *fons et origo* from which the meaning of the *civitas* derives. This same reading is confirmed in the next couplet, where the clause "res est publica Caesar," as we observed at the beginning of this chapter, can be translated in three different fashions: the constative sense, "Caesar is public property"; the ironic sense, "Caesar is the republic"; and the flattering sense, "Caesar is the public sphere." Here again, there is no sense that Augustus would not wish to be disseminated. The couplet may well give the lie to the notion of restoration of the republic, but in 12 C.E. when Roman political life was dominated by the intrigues surrounding Tiberius's succession, only the most naive reader could have been shocked by that insinuation.

More daring is Ovid's treatment of Tiberius's relation to Augustus in *Ex Ponto* 2.8. In the course of an address to Augustus's image, the poet prays to the *princeps* "perque tibi similem virtutis imagine natum, / moribus adgnosci qui tuus esse potest" (by the son similar to you in the image of his virtue / who can be recognized to be yours by his character) (31–32).[55] On the constative level, the poet here asserts a similarity between the character of Tiberius and his adoptive father, Augustus. On the ironic level, Ovid clearly invites us to think of the more common way a father is recognized in his son: physical appearance, hence his use of the words *similis*, *imago*, and *adgnosco*. This impression is redoubled if we recall that Ovid here is contemplating the faces of Augustus, Tiberius, and Livia as they appear on coins sent to him by Cotta Maximus. A locus classicus for this trope of recognizing the father in the son is Catullus's marriage hymn to Manlius Torquatus where the recognition is proof of the bride's chastity:

> sit suo similis patri
> Manlio et facile insciens
> noscitetur ab obviis,
> et pudicitiam suae
>   matris indicet ore.
> (61.214–18)

May he resemble his father Manlius, and unawares may he be easily recognized by all he meets, and may he prove his mother's honor by his appearance.

The possibilities for irony are rich once the intertext is seen. Not only was Tiberius not Augustus's biological son but Livia was pregnant with him when Octavian caused her to divorce T. Claudius Nero. He was hardly, therefore, a testimony to his mother's exclusive devotion to Augustus. Moreover, it should be remembered that Augustus's daughter, Julia, the wife of Tiberius through an arranged marriage, had been exiled for adultery at the same time the *Ars Amatoria* was published and that her daughter, also named Julia, had been exiled on the same charge when Ovid received his relegation. Many scholars posit a connection between these two events (White 1993: 153; Thibault 1964: 57–58). Finally, it must be recalled that Octavian himself had been adopted by Julius Caesar. His legitimacy in the early years of his reign was based on the acceptance of his claim to being Caesar's true heir. This was also the foundation on which his claim to being *filius divi*, "son of the divinized," rested.

On the one hand, to a modern sensibility this reads like the most hilarious irony. And, on a certain objective level, it is. But, on the other, none of this was news. All of Rome knew these facts. If Ovid thought this would expose the emperor or his family, tear the veil off their pretensions to an undeserved legitimacy, he must not only have been unbelievably naive, he must have been suicidal. We tend to assume that sincerity was both valued and possible in such a situation. Rather, the greatest flattery, the most abject subjection to the powers of the emperor, would come precisely in accepting imperial claims at face value in spite of all indications to the contrary. This is the logic of absolutism. As Žižek observes, "An ideology really succeeds when even the facts which at first sight contradict it start to function as arguments in its favor" (1989: 49). The more flattery signals its acceptance of the power differentials between the parties involved, and as a consequence the more the performative moment becomes visibly separate from the constative in the act of enunciation, the more ironic subversion and flattering acceptance become, both structurally and functionally, indistinguishable. At this point, as the contradictory space of the elegiac subject becomes elided, it has no more place from which to speak. It has become a voice from the dead.

Thus, as noted at the beginning of this chapter when discussing lines 19–20 of this same poem, when Ovid looks at Caesar's image, he seems to see Rome, "hunc ego cum spectem, videor mihi cernere Romam." The emperor has become the source of all civic meaning ("quid enim est civilius illo?"). He is the central point from which the individual can found his difference only by falling away from this self-reflecting and suffocating plenitude, only through a loss of Symbolic substance or death. That loss is found precisely in an excess of signification that highlights the gap between the subject internal to the speech act, the "I" of the sentence, and the subject of the speech act, the maker of the sentence. There is more meaning than a seamless identification of the subject of the sentence and the subject of the speech act can process. This ironic excess locates the subject in a position exterior to the content of the actual speech act, beyond a virtual river Styx, in a realm of pure performativity. To the extent that this separate realm becomes an autonomous cultivated sphere of scripted reflection, then the subject who is imaginatively invested in that realm must die to the world of declarative public meaning and recognized "facts." The construction of this separate world, one beyond the contingencies of the Other, is the task of imperial philosophy and its technologies of the self. This new form of subjectivation seeks to create a self that exists at a remove from the immediate, and which is constructed around the valorization of the infinite deferral of meaning, a self first glimpsed in the exilic poetry.

News From Pontus

In the same letter . . . Kafka . . . relates a dream:

> Very late, dearest, and yet I shall go to bed without deserving it. Well, I won't sleep anyway, only dream. As I did yesterday, for example, when in my dream I ran toward a bridge or some balustrading, seized two telephone receivers that happened to be lying on the parapet, put them to my ears, and kept asking for nothing but news from "Pontus"; but nothing whatever came out of the telephone except a sad, mighty, wordless song and the roar of the sea. Although well aware that it was impossible for voices to penetrate these sounds, I didn't give in, and didn't go away.

> News from "Pontus"—as Gerhard Neumann has
> shown, in pretechnical days was news from Ovid's Black
> Sea exile, the quintessential model for literature as a love
> letter. Letters of this kind, necessarily received or written
> in their entirety by women,[56] were replaced by the
> telephone and its noise, which precedes all discourse and
> subsequently all whole individuals.
> —Kittler 1999: 56

> Ovide, si classique souvent d'un point de vue purement
> formel, pratique l'excès avec un talent très rare chez les
> Latins, surtout avant l'âge néronien. Son esthétique
> s'avère souvent baroquisante, on le sait, par la
> place qu'elle fait aux ruptures, aux mouvements
> démésurés, etc.[57]
> —Viarre 1988: 155

The final question is how does this elegiac irony of the emerging imperial subject, of the subject of exile, relate to that displayed earlier in the genre's history? The answer, as we have already noted, is that in the exilic poetry the moment of performative self-consciousness is located in the realm of the dead, or more precisely of the undead. It is the ghostly consciousness of a poet trapped in a limbo between the two deaths. Whereas Tibullus's wry juxtaposition of *arma*, *rura*, and *amor*, momentarily posits a golden age of pre-Symbolic self-identity (1.1), Propertius in his embrace of *nequitia* imagines a utopia in which Cynthia alone would constitute his *domus* and *parentes* (1.11.23). In Ovid's *Amores*, we find less a utopia than a heterotopia, an otherness lodged in the very heart of Augustus's Rome. Poems such as 1.9 do not posit an alternative universe from which the subject's performative discourse can emerge, a space outside of the constative, but revel in the aporiae of the Augustan Symbolic, its self-generated moments of nonidentity. The performative self-consciousness of the *Tristia*, however, can only posit an atopia of nonexistence.[58] Thus where Propertius, Tibullus, and the Ovid of the *Amores* all produce ironic discourses that are structurally homologous with, and therefore often interpreted as, discourses of flattery, they do so from a position of radical otherness that resists being folded back into the dominant Symbolic order. It is precisely this moment of radical otherness, what Lacan terms the Real, that has become attenuated in Ovid's exilic poetry.

The difference between Ovid and Foucault's philosophers of the imperial age is that Ovid does not yet know, or at least does not yet accept the fact, that he is dead. He still hopes for resurrection and reprieve. He is not beyond the pleasure principle. Thus where the philosophers of the empire seek to construct a self at once beautiful and beyond the reach of contingency, Ovid constructs an intertextual self whose very absence bespeaks its desire for the delights of presence. Where Antigone in the face of the uncomprehending Creon pursues a good that is beyond those recognized by communal Symbolic norms, it is precisely the absence of those norms that steals Ovid's pleasure. Indeed, it is the ghostly wraith of Ovidian enjoyment that constitutes the lingering elegiac difference of the poems from exile. It is this haunting that marks them as the final sigh of the genre of Catullus, Gallus, Propertius, Tibullus, and the *tenerorum lusor amorum*.

Yet Ovid in exile remains dead. The news from Pontus, like Kafka's nightmarish roar, presents not an act,[59] but an acceptance of the current horizon of expectations. His resistance to empire comes only and precisely in his proclamation of an "autonomia" that is also a confirmation of the empire's powers of subjection. Ovid can not envision the grand world-historical gesture of Vergilian epic or even its ironic reflection in the *Metamorphoses*. In the world of empire it is no longer possible to revision the world as a collective endeavor or project. All that is left is the micropolitics of self-fashioning and ironic resistance, functionally indistinguishable from flattering acceptance: a condition not that different from our own.

NOTES

CHAPTER ONE
TOWARD A NEW HISTORY OF GENRE: ELEGY AND THE REAL

1. "Catullus and Ovid . . . represent a recognizable beginning and end of the elegiac tradition" (Benediktson 1989: 21).

2. Roughly 300 years, from the beginning of the second century B.C.E. to the end of the first C.E.

3. Roughly three hundred ninety years, from circa 160 B.C.E. to circa 130 B.C.E.

4. Roughly 600 years, from the first half of the fourteenth century to the end of the nineteenth.

5. Roughly 400 years, from the beginning of the seventeenth century to the present.

6. For dates, see 7 B.C.E. (McKeown 1987: 1.84), 2 B.C.E. (Barsby 1979: 6), and 1 C.E. (Conte 1994: 340; Lyne 1980: 239).

7. Pliny tells us that elegy was a kind of cottage industry in the household of the Propertii and that Passenus Paulus Propertius later changed to Horatian lyric. The one citation we have "Prisce iubes," as Courtney notes (1993: 371), appears to be the opening of an epigram. It is impossible to judge the content of these verses, let alone the subject position they imply. The best guess is that they represent a rehashing of the work of a famous ancestor and were "plane in Properti domo scriptum." They thus did not make any new contribution to the genre and were regarded as a kind of family curiosity.

8. If we assume that the epithalamium Statius wrote for Stella represents his work as an elegist—an admittedly risky assumption, but it is the only evidence we have—then it testifies very clearly to the collapse of the tensions that I argue constitute the elegiac subject position. Lucius Arruntius Stella was a member of a consular family from Patavium who assumed political office himself and became suffect consul in 101 or 102 (*Silvae* 1.2.66–73; Groag and Stein 1933; Hardie 1983: 68). His elegies were written to court Violentilla who became his wife, whereupon he ceased practicing the genre (*Silvae* 1.2.24–40). His manner would appear to have been that of Catullus in the *passer* poems according to Martial (1.7; 7.14). Elegy, then, far from testifying to tensions in the constitution of the subject of desire as it did in Propertius, Tibullus, and Ovid, has now become a tool of legitimate seduction leading to marriage and a respectable government career, whereupon it is promptly put aside and the poet assumes the more respectable role of patron (*Silvae* 1.2.194–200; Martial 12.3; Hardie 1983: 111–13). The elegist, far from posing as the irregular who rejects marriage and a profitable career in government and the military for *otium*, *inertia*, and *nequitia* is now "Ausoniis multum gener ille petitus / matribus" (the son-in-law much sought after by Italian mothers; *Silvae* 1.2.76–77). All translations are my own unless otherwise noted.

On the case of Sulpicia, see Miller (2002: 2, 3, 17, 23–24, 159–65).

9. On Persius's satires as a reproduction of absolutism, see Henderson (1993: 127).

10. See Winthrop-Young and Wutz in Kittler (1999: xxii): "[D]iscourse analysis does not deny interpretation; it merely concentrates on something more interesting. First of all, it focuses on the fact that certain texts were produced—rather than not, and rather than others."

11. See also Albrecht (1997: 814–16).

12. Cairns (1979a: 225) notes that Varro of Atax's *Leucadia* may have represented another such precursor, but no fragments survive and we have only Ovid's (*Tristia* 2.439) and Propertius's testimony (2.34.85). See Courtney (1993: 236–37).

13. See, however, Gutzwiller and Michelini's (1991: 73–75) very important observation that the "excessive objectivity" and lack of sincerity often attributed to Callimachus are in part a function of his frequent adoption of a feminine persona. This inversion of gender values becomes a very important feature of Latin love elegy, see especially chapter 5.

14. See Riposati (1945: 195); Lilja (1965: 79–81); Quinn (1969: 50); Hubbard (1974: 10); Ross (1975: 17); Cairns (1979a: 221–24); Lyne (1980: 61); Whitaker (1983: 23, 54–55); Veyne (1988: 19–23); Gold (1993: 84–85); Cameron (1995: 305, 315); Fantham (1996: 105–6); Albrecht (1997: 743).

15. Other important sources for elegy include Roman comedy and the uniquely personal perspective offered by Lucilius's satires (Konstan 1994: 158–59; Newman 1997: 35), as well as the writers of erotic epigram cited by Aulis Gellius in 19.9, Aedituus, Porcius Licinus, and Quintus Catulus.

16. See Copjec (1994: 47) on Bergson's critique of Aristotelian teleology on the ground that it destroyed time. Foucault's attempt to produce a discontinuous history is designed precisely to avoid the traps of evolutionary teleology and restore real historical difference to the study of the past (Kremer-Marietti 1985: 9–10, 22–28, 102–3, 110; Morris 1988: 22; Flynn 1994: 43). In the process, however, as I have argued elsewhere, he effectively renders historical explanation impossible (Miller 1998a).

17. See Albrecht (1997: 746); Grimal (1986: 138); Kenney (1983: 124); Syme (1978: 204–5); Sullivan (1976: 74); Luck (1960: 172).

18. The elaboration of a theory of "emergence" that could explain how new modes of personal or social organization could arise out of preexisting forms, without being seen as already contained by those forms, and so effectively subsuming the emergence of the new within a vision of the given, was seen by Althusser as one of the central problems of both Marxism and psychoanalysis if they were to overcome their idealist roots. In this struggle, he saw Lacan as one of his principle allies (1996b: 59–60).

19. For contrary positions, see James (2003); Konstan (1994: 151–58); Wyke (1989: 40); Veyne (1988: 3, 7, 89); Cairns (1979a: 189); Hallett (1973: 105).

20. There will undoubtedly be those who will object to the use of Marxist categories on the grounds that the fall of the repressive governments of Eastern Europe has demonstrated their inadequacy. As Derrida (1993: 90) notes, however, the manic jubilation with which the death of Marxism is repeatedly trumpeted merely demonstrates how much it continues to haunt the capitalist mind.

21. See, most notoriously, Derrida's chapters from *Of Grammatology*, "The Outside and the Inside" and "The Outside is the Inside" (1976: 30–65).

22. See Eagleton (1976: 69); Todorov (1984: 17–18); Bakhtin /Medvedev (1985: 14, 17); Voloshinov (1986: 10); Frow (1986: 64); Moxey (1991: 987–89).

23. "An ideology really succeeds when even the facts which at first sight contradict it start to function as arguments in its favour" (Žižek 1989: 49).

24. On the Freudian basis for the distinction between reality and the Real, see Lacan (1966: 83).

25. At the limit, separation from the Symbolic order is the Lacanian definition of psychosis (Žižek 1991: 40).

26. As Lacan puts it, an act always participates in a structure, which gives it meaning, and concerns the Real. The example he gives is the Japanese practice of *seppuku* (1975: 60).

27. See also Levine (1993b: 4–6); Hayles (1993: 39–40); Jordanova (1993: 275–76).

28. The New Physics has, of course, shown the limitations of Newton's "universal" laws.

29. See Frow's (1986: 24) excellent, if difficult, formulation of Althusser's concept of knowledge, which is based on principles similar to those outlined earlier: "To say that the production of knowledge occurs wholly 'within thought' does not mean that thought is 'a faculty of a transcendental subject or absolute consciousness confronted by the real world as *matter*,' nor that it is 'a faculty of a psychological subject'; rather it is 'the historically constituted system of an *apparatus of thought*, founded on and articulated to natural and social reality. It is defined by the system of real conditions which make it . . . a determinate *mode of production* of knowledges.' . . . Its determinate conditions include the state of the raw material it works, and this is always 'an ever-already complex raw material, a structure of "intuition" or "representation" which combines together in a peculiar "*Verbindung*" sensuous, technical and ideological elements' . . . . Knowledge therefore never confronts a 'pure' (real) object; it is neither a reflection nor a representation of the real but a structure of discourse which *constructs* its object through an ordered transformation of pretheoretical values" (emphasis in original). See also Lacan (1975: 45, 188); Ragland-Sullivan (1986: 188); Žižek (1991: 120); Parkhurst (1995: 52).

30. To the extent that Kant's "Ding" is considered as existing in a shadow world of the noumenal that duplicates the phenomenal in a fashion analogous to Plato's Forms, then it remains vulnerable to Hegel's criticism that it is a limit internal to the experience of knowledge itself. This is a criticism that both Lacan and Jameson would accept (Žižek 1989: 172, 177, 204–5, 214; Copjec 1994: 35).

31. See Lacan (1973: 103); Jameson (1981: 102); Schneiderman (1983: 132); Ragland-Sullivan (1986: 189); Parkhurst (1995: 45).

32. Lacan developed a theory of "knots" to explain the mutual interdependence and inseparability of his three primary categories, the Imaginary, the Symbolic, and the Real. See Mitchell and Rose's explanation (Lacan 1982: 171n.6).

33. See Lacan (1975: 32–33) on Marx's insight that history is the possibility of completely subverting the function of discourse; hence, history is that which demonstrates the contingency of a given Symbolic system and its consequent inad-

equacy vis-à-vis the Real. On Althusser's concept of history being based on Lacan, see Jameson (1981: 34–35).

34. See Žižek (1993: 23, 109); Jameson (1991: 5–6, 1981: 91, 95, 97–98, 1972: 193–94) Adorno (1983: 53, 140–43).

35. Foucault's later concept of the *dispositif*, while replacing that of the *épistémè*, differs from the original concept "primarily because it encompasses the non-discursive practices as well as the discursive" (Dreyfus and Rabinow 1982: 121; Macey 1993: 355).

36. Foucault argues that the question of genesis can only be posed when the descriptive task of archaeology is complete, in effect postponing it till the second coming while providing no theoretical guidance on how this topic might be broached (Foucault 1966: 64–65). See also Rouse (1994: 94) and Macey (1993: 94).

37. For a good accounting of Veyne's virtues, see Fitzgerald (1995: 7–9).

38. Copjec admirably sums up the differences between the two approaches in the following: "These two powerful discourses—psychoanalysis and historicism, represented here by Lacan and Foucault, respectively—have in common the conviction that it is dangerous to assume that the surface is the level of the superficial. Whenever we delve below this level, we are sure to come up empty. Yet the lessons each discourse draws from this conviction are strikingly divergent. Psychoanalysis, via Lacan, maintains that the exclusivity of the surface or of appearance must be interpreted to mean that appearance always supplants or routs being, that appearance and being never coincide. It is this syncopated relation that is the condition of desire. Historicism, on the other hand, wants to ground being in appearance and wants to have nothing to do with desire" (1994: 13–14). Many thanks to Micaela Janan for drawing this passage to my attention.

39. The text is Shackleton Bailey's (1999).

40. "The lack of a representation is a clue not only to such a crisis in a negative sense but also to a potentiality in an ontological sense. That is to say, the lack of a homogenizing representation is a fundamental condition of the multiplication of representations" (Villalobos-Ruminott 2001: 33).

41. This is what in Hegelian and Marxist terms is known as the "negation of the negation." It "does not entail any kind of return to positive identity," but the recognition of negation as the condition necessary for any identity's positive existence (Žižek 1993: 176; see also 177).

42. See Lacan (1986: 118–19); Ragland-Sullivan (1986: 299–300, 305); Jameson (1981: 153); Žižek in Hanlon (2001: 12).

43. See Duncan Kennedy's brilliant dismantling of the assumptions underlying Jasper Griffin's "rhetoric of realism" (Kennedy 1993: 2–4; citing Griffin 1985).

44. "But when Lucius Domitius as a candidate for consul openly threatened to do what he had not been able to do as praetor and take his army, Caesar brought Pompey and Crassus out to the city of Luca in his province, so that they might seek another consulship for the sake of throwing out Domtius, and Caesar brought it about through the two of them that his command was prolonged for five years. With this encouragement, he added to the legions that he had received from the republic, others at his own expense. One was even recruited from the Transalpine region. It was also called by a Gallic word—for it was named Alauda.

When he had instructed it in Roman discipline and dressed it in Roman arms, he then gave the whole legion citizenship."

45. See Livy 105, 107; Dio Cassius 39.34–37, 40–41; Plutarch, *Pompey* 52, 54, *Cato* 41–43, *Caesar* 28–30, *Cicero* 35; Cicero, *Pro Milone*. Gruen (1995: 147, 152, 311, 314, 356, 397, 433, 443), of course, is well aware of these facts and has complete command of the sources.

46. See Tacitus, *Annales* 1.2; Syme (1960: 313–18); Scullard (1963: 219–20); Littlewood (1983: 2138); Edwards (1996: 49–50, 57).

47. See Galinsky (1996: 8), who argues that at the core of the ideas and values inspired by the Augustan regime "was the revitalization of the mores of the *res publica*; a program of moral legislation, to give but one example, had been urged by Cicero on Caesar (*Marc.* 23–24). These guiding ideas, which do not amount to an ideology in the modern sense, received further elaboration from all sides and therefore their expression was anything but uniform." This statement is good as far as it goes, but the use of the term "ideology" here is anything but contemporary, inasmuch as it refers to a closed and rigid system of ideas of the sort that is only referred to in the pejorative sense, as in "they are blinded by ideology, but we can see the truth." This is not the sense of the word being used in this book.

48. See Syme (1960: 514–15); Brunt (1971a: 74–111); Ste. Croix (1981: 359–60); Nippel (1995: 33–34); Wallace-Hadrill (1997: 22).

49. See Nippel (1995: 90–91) on the changes in the powers of the magistrates that had already occurred well before the principate. The Roman constitution was in a state of flux that made any sort of return to a pure republican *libertas* more an exercise in wish fulfillment than Realpolitik.

50. See Syme (1960: 441–42); Scullard (1963: 23); Brunt (1971a: 11–15, 19); Ste. Croix (1981: 358); Miller (1989: 63–64); Nippel (1995: 30–31).

51. See Ste. Croix (1981: 352–53); Nippel (1995: 72); Brunt (1971a: 127–28); Gruen (1995: 228–29, 445).

52. "As great as was the confusion during these years; so difficult was it, at the moment when one reevaluated 'humanity,' to determine the place that madness should occupy; so difficult was it to situate it in a social space that was in the process of being restructured."

53. On the later republic's "confusion of moral systems," see Gowers (1993: 10–11).

54. On how these themes are manifest in the *Aeneid* and its relation to the elegists, see Miller (1989; 1995).

55. See Eleanor Leach's (1999) wonderful argument on the way Caesar himself constitutes precisely such a monster of the Real in Cicero's letters of the forties, revealing a crisis in the orator's self-constitution as a desiring subject in the wake of the republic's collapse.

56. One of the most intriguing suggestions has recently come from Trevor Fear (2000) who argues that elegy deliberately seeks to conflate the roles and expectations of *matronae* and *meretrices* at the same time as the *princeps* in his reform laws was trying to reestablish the polarity between them. See also Williams (1968: 542); Boucher (1980: 447–50); Green (1981: 22–25); Veyne (1988: 3, 7, 89); White (1993: 90); Konstan (1994: 151–52, 158); James (2003).

57. Religion had long provided a source of ideological prestige and power for the Roman *nobiles*. This power in turn was often associated with the regulation of sexual behavior. See the case of the repression of the Bacchic cults in the early second century B.C.E. (Edwards 1993: 44; Nippel 1995: 29–32).

58. On the Augustan age's ambiguous relation to the past, see Cairns (1979a: 13–14).

59. Plutarch dates this crisis in the Roman Symbolic, in the system of coded values that described what it meant to be a Roman, to the time of Cato the Elder in the second century B.C.E. See Gowers (1993: 10).

60. For a good summary of the inconsistencies and contradictions that structure the elegiac ego's world, see Veyne (1988: 2–3, 7, 50–51, 89).

61. It is the moment of "interpellation" where the subject's Imaginary identity becomes invested in its Symbolic position that in Althusser's terms gives rise to the subject and is the consequent basis of his theory of ideology. See Althusser (1971b); Eagleton (1983: 186–87); Dowling (1984: 82–83, 91); Žižek (1989: 43–44, 101); Copjec (1994: 21).

62. Tränkle (1983: 154–55) argues that elegy presupposes the instability of the late republic and early principate, and that the successful passage of the moral reform laws effectively spelled the end of the genre.

63. For a parallel example of the political and personal redefinition of what he labels the "language of self-performance" during this same period, see Krostenko (2001: esp. 26, 83–84).

64. A close friend might well be referred to with the more intimate term *sodalis* rather than the formal *amicus*, as at *Tristia* 1.3.65–66. See Helzle (1989: 22–23).

65. See Krostenko (2001: 52), "*Bene facere*, indeed, is something of a technical term for social services rendered (cf. *benefactum*)," as well as Lee-Stecum (1998: 20) and Saller (1982: 26).

66. Hellgouarc'h (1963: 17–25) defines *fides* as the moral-contractual relation binding patron to client or as the relationship binding those who seek the same political ends. *Fides* was also the force that bound sworn oaths (Cicero, *De Officiis* 3.104). *Fides* and *beneficia* were commonly used to refer to monetary loans between *amici* (Edwards 1993: 183). *Fides* at root referred to "a scrupulous regard for all aspects of procedure" (Krostenko 2001: 166).

67. Cicero, *Pro Murena* 70–73. See Krostenko (2001: 171); Helzle (1989: 46, 50); Wiseman (1982: 30); and Syme (1960: 343).

68. This was not per se an original observation on my part. Here, I was clearly building on the work already done by numerous scholars including Syme (1960: 12–13); Pucci (1961: 254–56); Ross (1969: 81–88; 1975: 10–14); Nethercut (1976); Lyne (1980: 24–25); Saller (1982: 11–15); and Veyne (1987: 95). Although there have been disputes about the range of particular terms, and the extent of the Catullan and neoteric innovations, there is a broad and general consensus that has held up over the past forty years among scholars from a variety of traditions and perspectives. See most recently, Krostenko (2001: 239–46) and Nappa (2001: 96). On the cross-fertilization of the terms *amor* and *amicitia* in the later elegiac tradition, and their necessary invocation of asymmetrical power relations and the Roman institution of patronage, see Oliensis (1997).

69. On the contradictions of *dignitas* in the late republic, see Barton (1993: 27–28).

70. Compare Ragland-Sullivan (1986: 157); Eagleton (1983: 186–87). For more on *dignitas* and the aristocracy's self-conception, see Ste. Croix (1981: 363–64).

71. See Kaster's (1997: esp. 7, 11–12, 17) very useful meditations on the nature of *pudor* and its relation to *dignitas*, and Tatum (1997: 483).

72. See Lyne (1980: 68–69); Fisher (1983: 1950–51); Gaisser (1983: 65–66); Grimal (1986: 142); Van Nortwick (1990: 121).

73. As Ragland-Sullivan notes "Any ultimate pursuit of the moments of join between Imaginary and Symbolic leads back . . . to a point of fading and primal repression where identifications (fusions) initially merged with the Real" (1986: 150).

CHAPTER TWO
THE CATULLAN SUBLIME, ELEGY, AND THE EMERGENCE OF THE REAL

1. "I am the dark one—the widower—the unconsoled, the prince of Aquitaine in the destroyed tower."

2. "And we always search how to fool ourselves, we try to accede to the perspective of continuity, which presupposes the surpassing of a limit, without leaving behind the limits that define this discontinuous life. We wish to reach the beyond without taking the step, prudently remaining within the bounds of this world. We cannot conceive of anything, imagine anything, accept within the limit of our life, beyond which it seems to us that everything disappears."

3. Luck (1960: 48); Lilja (1965: 31); Putnam (1973: 9–10); Sarkissian (1983: 1); Williams (1980: 45); Lyne (1980: 65); Skinner (1981: 106); Grimal (1987: 256); Gold (1993: 84–85); Conte (1994: 150, 324); Albrecht (1997: 744).

4. Sarkissian sees poem 68 as anticipating the work of the later elegists in the separation it makes between poet and persona.

5. Whitaker (1983: 62) elaborates on this notion arguing that the Laudamia and Protesilaus simile in 68 is more complex than anything found in later elegy.

6. As noted earlier, this rigid separation of Catullus from the elegists is a minority position. On the importance of Veyne's reading of elegy as well as his inconsistency with regard to the question of sincerity when dealing with Tibullus's Marathus poems, see Konstan (1995: 162n.50). For a reading of the elegists that embraces Veyne's critique of the conventional assumption of elegiac sincerity without necessarily accepting the exclusion of Catullus, see Kennedy (1993). Finally, Fitzgerald (1995: 7–9) has recently applied Veyne's theoretical assumptions to Catullus himself, producing a very important and stimulating reading.

7. Wray (2001: 41–42) notes that the possible echo of an epigram by Philodemus undercuts a straightforward reading of poem 85 as lyric outcry. The existence of a formal intertextual irony overlaying and relativizing the mimetic agony of 85.2's *excrucior* (I am torn apart) confirms my basic thesis of a subject that is not only bifurcated, but fundamentally not whole. For a line-by-line analysis of this poem, see Miller (2002: 119).

8. All translations of Bataille are my own.

9. For a related reading of this same passage, using the vocabulary of film theory, see Fitzgerald (1995: 146–49).

10. For another example of the use of Bataille to examine the limits of the self and their transgression in Roman ideology in the late republic and early empire, see Barton (1993: 57–58).

11. For Lacan deriving his concept of the Real from Bataille's notion of the "heterological," see Roudinesco (1997: 135–36, 216–17). The heterological in medical terminology refers to unassimilable pathological tissue. Hence Kristeva refers to the symptom as "a language that gives up, a structure within the body, a nonassimilable alien, a monster, a tumor, a cancer that the listening devices of the unconscious do not hear, for its strayed subject is huddled outside the path of desire" (1982: 11).

12. This notion of erotic lack and completion is, of course, ultimately Platonic. For Lacan's reading of Plato, see Miller (1999). For the importance of Plato to understanding Catullus, see Janan (1994: 10–33).

13. See Michael von Albrecht's penetrating comment in regard to poem 63's drama of religious fanaticism and self-castration: "In a period of great revolutions such as that of Catullus, such experiences of 'alienation' begin to be made by human beings in the most different spheres. Intoxication and enthusiasm drive them towards radical destruction" (1997: 349).

14. On the necessity of a third outside standard for the comparison between entities to be valuable in society, and hence for all exchanges—monetary, linguistic, or exogamic—to be possible, see Goux (1990); and Irigaray (1977a), both of whom rely on Marx's account of commodity fetishism at the beginning of *Capital*, vol. 1.

15. See Lefèvre (1991: 312); King (1988: 388); Hubbard (1984: 48n.44); Bright (1976: 109n.81); Salvatore (1965: 103). For Lachmann's (1873: ad loc.) reading of *Manius* as *praenomen* and *Allius* as *nomen gentile* for the same person, see Kroll (1980: ad loc.); Williams (1980: 46n.13); and Garrison (1995: ad loc.). For *Mallius* as *mi Alli*, see Williams (1980: 46n.13); Bright, (1976: 88–90). For *Allius* as paranomasia for *Mallius*, see Hubbard (1984: 33, 45n.13). Quinn (1973: ad loc.) refrains from pronouncing on the textual question but assumes that the same person must be referred to in 68a and b. Merrill (1893: ad loc.) argues strongly for two different persons with two different names, as does (Thomson 1997: ad loc.), Courtney (1985: 95); and Fordyce (1978: ad loc.).

16. Cairns (1979a: 163–64) notes that *Eclogue 6* has the same dual structure. He uses this as an argument for the unity of the two sections. Williams (1980: 50) sees similarities with *Eclogue* 10 and Propertius 4.1 as well as Catullus 64, so does Janan (1994: 112–13). Both see this as evidence of the poem's unity. Bright (1976: 90, 108–11) sees 68 as the model for Propertius 2.28 as well as the *Ciris* and sees the poem as consisting of three parts (68a, b, c) forming a unified trilogy.

17. On 66 repeating elements from 65 in the same way that 68b repeats elements from 68a, see Fitzgerald (1995: 200).

18. On 67's relation to 68 being essentially the same as 69's to 70, see Wiseman (1985: 164).

19. On 65–68 as a coherent sequence anticipating the themes treated in the epigrams, see King (1988: 390).

20. This recognition of parallel but noncoincident registers of meaning in the poem is also seen in Hubbard's contention that 68a and 68b represent opposed rhetorical strategies that deconstruct each other but are "always already implicated in" one another (1984: 43); and Williams's observation that myth in 68 "functions paradigmatically in relation to the contextual ideas, but structurally it functions as a type of synechdoche" (1980: 52).

21. In general, I use Mynors's OCT text (1958), but I depart from it here in favoring the manuscript reading in G, R, and M as opposed to the later Pal. which emends *hic* to *ac*. Fordyce prints Mynors's text but offers compelling arguments against it. Eisenhut, Thomson, Merrill, and Quinn follow the better attested manuscript tradition. Quinn argues that the emendation is in fact the symptom of a deeper structural confusion as to whether 57–62 and 63–65 both refer forward to Allius's *auxilium* in line 66 or they represent two different similes, the first referring back to Catullus's tears and the second forward to Allius's aid. The ability to make such distinctions in this poem is precisely what is at issue in this chapter. In any case, the emendation rests on an interpretive position that it then seeks to justify. This reasoning is circular and offers no compelling argument for abandoning the manuscript tradition.

22. All translations of Catullus are my own.

23. The relation between these two sets of interlocking similes goes even deeper; as Feeney (1992: 37–38) points out, the hot springs at Thermopylae (l. 54) were created by Athena for Hercules' bathing.

24. *Mulier* is susceptible of either translation and both are contextually appropriate.

25. On the Homeric (*Iliad* 9.14–15) precedent for a simile comparing tears to a stream, see Sarkissian (1983: 49n.36) and Merrill (1893: ad loc.).

26. This, of course, does not imply that the various critics agree on the details of the arrangement. And this lack of agreement, as I argue shortly, signals the presence of that very metonymic subversion of clearly ordered rhetorical partitions that forms the Imaginary counterpoint to the poem's Symbolic construction. See inter alia, Quinn (1973: ad loc.); Whitaker (1983: 61); Hubbard (1984: 38); Janan (1994: 177–78); Lefèvre (1991: 320); Courtney (1985: 96); Edwards (1991: 78–79); Bright (1976: 112); Ferguson (1985: ad loc.); and Shipton (1987: 55–59).

27. I owe this citation to Sharon Diane Nell.

28. It will have been noted that metonymy is most often associated with Lacan's concept of the Imaginary in this chapter rather than with the Symbolic as is normally the case (Fineberg 1991: 10). This alteration has been necessary because metonymy is used within the poem to create a series of metaphorical identifications, metaphor being the privileged trope of the Imaginary. This interdependence of two tropes is in fact characteristic of rhetorical practice according to Barthes; each figure ultimately depends on the existence of the other. Without the syntactic dispersion characteristic of metonymy there would be no metaphor, and without metaphor's paradigms of substitution there would be no possibility of defining one signifier in terms of another, and hence no signification (Barthes 1967: 60, 88). At the same time, Lacan argues for the interdependence of these tropes' associated psychic registers: the Imaginary, the Symbolic, and the Real. This relationship is most famously expressed in Lacan's hermetic doctrine of the Borromean knots

(Julien 1990: 213–14, 221; Lacan 1982: 171n.6; Ragland-Sullivan 1989: 4, 131). It should also be noted that Lacan also argues that metonymy is characteristic of the Imaginary in the "mirror stage" (1966b: 84–85). The momentary instability of the relations between the Imaginary and Symbolic, and the way their schism leads to the emergence of the Real in the form of a series of interpretive cruxes, is, of course, the subject of this chapter.

29. On the functional identity of Lesbia and the poet's brother, both within 68 and throughout the corpus, see Janan (1994: 123); Sarkissian (1983: 31); and Edwards (1991: 77).

30. Catullus's allusion to this incident is elliptical in the extreme. The sources vary as to their depiction of the circumstances of Laudamia's suicide (Sarkissian 1983: 17–18) and, unless one is willing to accept Sarkissian's speculative emendations of the text, are not crucial to our understanding of 68 (Sarkissian 1983: 28–30; Shipton 1987: 64n.9). One of the poet's sources was almost certainly Laevius's *Protesilaodamia*, but unfortunately our fragments (see Courtney 1993: 130–34, frags. 13–19) are so small as to be of little value in elucidating Catullus's poem (Sarkissian 1983: 42; Grimal 1987: 254; Dollar 1997: 51–53), although Hinds (1998: 77–79) notes some parallels in diction and word placement. Another important source for the poem's structure, as noted by both Grimal (1987: 254) and Dollar (1997: 18–19, 30–34) was epinician, which is likewise presented as a gift and structured around a central mythic comparison.

31. Compare Wray (2001: 197) on poem 65.

32. On Protesilaus corresponding to Iphigeneia, thus revealing yet another level of gender inversion, see Shipton (1985: 65). If Catullus corresponds to Aegisthus, the adulterer, then, as M. J. Edwards (1991: 76) points out, the most apposite myth in 68 for illustrating Catullus and Lesbia's relationship is not that of Laudamia and Protesilaus but rather Helen and Paris, the exemplum that directly frames the poet's apostrophe to his dead brother. Thus the poet metonymically associates his brother's death, and that of his entire household (line 94), with his adulterous affair with Lesbia. On verbal and thematic parallels between Catullus's depiction of Paris and Helen, Laudamia and Protesilaus, and Catullus and Lesbia, see Janan (1994: 131).

33. For a summary of the scholarship on this poem, see Miller (1998a: 186–92).

34. Compare Janan's remarks, "The tense conflict in the elegiac treatments of [the dichotomies characterizing Catullus' love] is not evident by the end of the poem [68]. Reconciliation no longer matters: both levels of perception float one on top of the other, while the mind (and the poetry) moves in between. This is *Aufhebung* of the object—abolition of it as concrete fact, while retaining its principles not for stasis but for a push forward into the next spiral of the dialectic of desire."

35. As my colleague David Larmour observed to me, their saltiness anticipates that of the sea.

36. For an analogous critique of persona theory as generally practiced, see Wray (2001: 163–65). Nappa (2001) uses persona to mean a fiction without a unified author behind it. This is clearly preferable, but one then questions why

the term is needed at all other than to exorcise the lingering ghost of biographical criticism.

37. Gunderson more recently employs Derrida and Lacan in a similarly ahistorical fashion "to examine . . . a passion felt by all men of letters" (1997: 207).

38. Hubbard (1984: 36) notes that this sequence is paralleled by a similar progression in the use of the word *amor* corresponding in line 69 to Catullus's lovemaking with Lesbia, in lines 73, 83, 107, and 117 to the married love of Laudamia and Protesilaus, and his familial love for his brother in line 96.

39. The whirlpool image itself, in turn, introduces the Hercules simile, which Bright (1976: 98–103, 112) notes is the first of the three featuring birds and which corresponds to the three we have examined in detail at the beginning of the poem. For a great example of how the correspondences between various elements of the poem create a series of identifications so complex that they ultimately undermine any attempt to discern a unitary structure, see Courtney's (1985: 95–97) tortured explanation of why stylistic correspondences must be rigorously distinguished form structural ones.

40. See Hallett (1973: 112–13); Edwards (1991: 72–73); Garrison (1995: ad loc.); Quinn (1973: ad loc.); Mynors (1958: ad loc.); Helm (1963: ad loc.); Merrill (1893: ad loc.); Kroll (1980: ad loc.).

41. See Thompson (1997: ad loc.); Shipton (1983: 870–71); Eisenhut (1983: ad loc.); Pöschl (1983: ad loc.); Sarkissian (1983: 16), who also has a good review of the previous scholarship; Fordyce (1978: ad loc.), who prints *dominae* but argues for *dominam*; and Cornish (1962: ad loc.).

42. Mynors (1958) following Marcilius posits a lacuna here. I follow Quinn (1973) and Pöschl (1983).

43. On the centrality of the *domus* to the Catullan moral universe, see Nappa (2001: 31).

44. "The basic implication of the word *barathrum* is that it is not merely a chasm but a type of chasm from which escape is impossible" (Shipton 1987: 56).

45. On Catullus's invocation of traditional Roman values, see Wiseman (1985: 113, 209).

46. For a more detailed reading of the present poem and its relation to the Catullan corpus, see Miller (1994: 59–61, 138–39; 1998a: 188–92).

47. On the need for Catullus to invent a new vocabulary of emotional commitment by borrowing terms current in other realms, see Lyne (1980: 24–25) and Fitzgerald (1995: 118), as well as the final section of chapter 1 of the present work.

48. The primal law is of course that of the incest taboo, the demand for exogamic relations, which as a form of repression also creates the desire for its transgression (Bataille 1957: 75; Butler 1990: 76, 79; Goux 1990: 79).

Chapter Three
Cynthia as Symptom: Propertius, Gallus, and the Boys

1. "That which signifies but the possibility of our sociality, of our culture, can it be attributed to a hommo-sexual monopoly? The law that orders our society is the exclusive valorization of the needs/desires of men, and the exchanges between

them. What the anthropologist designates as the passage from nature to culture can therefore be attributed to the installation of the empire of hom(m)osexuality. Not as an 'immediate' practice, but through its 'social' mediation. . . . Omnipresent in its reign, but forbidden in its use, hom(m)osexuality is played out across the bodies of women, its matter or sign, and heterosexuality is up to the present only an alibi for the proper functioning of the relations of man to himself, of the relations between men."

2. The identification of Lesbia with Clodia Metelli rests on three major pieces of evidence and several ancillary elements: Apuleius's identification of Lesbia as a certain Clodia (*Apology* 10); poem 79's implication that Lesbia prefers the company of her brother Lesbius to that of Catullus (Clodia Metelli was very close to her brother Clodius Pulcher; indeed, Cicero in the *Pro Caelio* repeatedly insinuates an incestuous relationship as Catullus does in 79); and the strong resemblance between the kind of slander of Clodia Metelli's sexual excesses found in the *Pro Caelio* and Catullus's picture of Lesbia in poems such as 11 and 58. Such an identification is given added credence by the presence of Caelius in Catullus's own poetry, and by his acknowledgment that Lesbia was married at the time the affair began. It also nicely accounts for the ambivalent tone of poem 49's praises of Cicero, if we assume it to be a response to the *Pro Caelio*. The identification of Lesbia with Clodia Metelli is thus all but universally accepted by Catullan scholars. Wiseman (1969: 50–60), however, on the basis of chronology, believes Lesbia might be her sister.

3. For a fuller discussion of these translation issues, see chapter 6.

4. Cicero's assertions in the *Pro Caelio* must be taken with a grain of rhetorical salt. His aim in the oration was to blacken Clodia's character and deflect blame from the young Caelius who was charged with plotting her murder. To that end, Cicero portrays Clodia as if she were a *matrona* turned common prostitute. No doubt, Clodia was unfaithful to her husband and even promiscuous, but that she was open to all comers is belied by her class and political status. For a good critique of the way Cicero's perspective on Clodia has been unproblematically adopted by modern Catullan studies, see Fitzgerald (1995: 21–24). Of course, as Judith Hallett points out to me, the real difference between Lesbia and Cynthia is that Cynthia is portrayed as interested in money (and hence potentially a *meretrix*) and Lesbia is not.

5. See Courtney (1993: 262), Anna (1983: 46), Nisbet (Anderson et al. 1979: 151), and Alfonsi (1945: 14–15) for the majority position and Ross (1975: 109–10) for a highly original revisionist reading that reverses the chronology.

6. Compare Propertius 2.10.25–26, a clear reference to this passage.

7. Hesiod.

8. Tränkle (1960: 24) argues for another direct imitation of Gallus at 1.18.8.

9. Or "love poems."

10. *Amica* is also a common term for girlfriend. See Catullus 72.3.

11. See also Nisbet (Anderson et al. 1979: 150).

12. In fact, the difficulties of Propertius's style are well known and account in part for his appeal to modernist poets like Ezra Pound. Thus Propertius's syntax is notoriously convoluted and the transitions in his poems notoriously abrupt (Fineberg 1991: ii; Benediktson 1989: 29; Boucher 1980: 370; Hubbard 1974: 1;

Elder 1962: 71–72; Luck 1960: 114). In this regard, he is the antithesis of Tibullus. For more on this comparison of the two styles, see chapter 4.

13. See Fantham (1996: 58–59); Stahl (1985: 122); Nethercut (1963: 30; 1983: 1824–25); Ross (1975: 74–75); Hubbard (1974: 98–99); Davis (1971: 210–11). Nicholson (1999: 149) argues that Gallus and Propertius's relative may not be the same person, but that the poet clearly encourages the identification.

14. Indeed, Cairns (1983a: 90) argues that the interlacing and symmetrical arrangement of the Gallus and Tullus poems is so tight that it can only be accounted for by concluding that both men were Propertius's patrons. There is no external evidence to support this view, but Cairns's expedient offers vivid testimony to the centrality of these poems as well as the importance of Propertius's relations to both men for understanding the *Monobiblos*.

15. Cynthia thus is the paradigmatic illustration of Irigaray's dictum that in patriarchal society women (borrowing Marx's terminology) have no inherent "use value," only "exchange value": "La valeur d'une femme échappe toujours: continent noir, trou dans le symbolique, faille dans le discours. . . . Ce n'est que dans l'opération de l'échange entre femmes que quelque chose—d'énigmatique, certes—peut s'en pressentir. La femme n'a donc de valeur que de pouvoir s'échanger" (1977a: 172).

16. Irigaray argues that heterosexuality itself is founded on relations between men (1977b: 189–90).

17. This term was first coined by Lacan (1975: 79) to designate the hegemony of a masculinist model of desire even over women.

18. See Greene (forthcoming); Fredrick (1997: 172–73); Oliensis (1997: 154–57); Konstan (1997: 148); Boucher (1980: 92, 100); Irigaray (1977a: 172–73, 176).

19. On the Gallus poems as a structuring principle for the *Monobiblos*, see Rothstein (1979: 1.89).

20. Maleuvre (1998: 89) has recently claimed that the Gallus of 1.21 is also Gallus the poet, a most unlikely scenario but illustrative of the extremes to which readers are driven to solve the conundra with which Propertius has presented them.

21. See, for example, Hubbard (1974: 25), who argues for a third Gallus who was a member of the Etruscan gentry. Fedeli (1983: 1878) makes a similar argument. For an overview of the various positions, see King (1980b: 212n.2).

22. Lacan (1976: 4) defines the symptom as the "Tout, mais pas ça," a formulation linked to his dictum of woman as the *pas toute*, or that which is excluded from the masculinist universal. Thus if woman functions in the masculinist Symbolic economy as a symptom, she functions as that which allows the economy of exchange to function by masking the exclusion on which it is founded: "Tout," everything, "mais pas ça," but not that. *Ça*, it should be noted, is the conventional French translation of the German *es*, which in English translations of Freud is rendered *id*. Thus, the phrase could just as easily be translated, "anything but the id." For a fuller discussion of woman as the *pas toute*, see chapter 5. Obviously, in this context, to label Cynthia a symptom is to speak of her figurative function in Propertian discourse, not to cast aspersions on her character.

23. On the poetics of collective trauma and its symptomatic manifestations, see Steele (2000: 41–55).

24. Davis (1971: 211) also sees 1.21–22 as a double poem similar to 8a and 8b as well as 11 and 12 earlier in the corpus. This reading is aided by the fact that the oldest manuscript, N, reads 1.21 and 1.22 as a single poem. Many manuscripts (A¹FP) also do not separate 1.21 from 1.20, presumably owing to the confusion arising from having two poems in succession featuring the name Gallus.

25. Heiden (1995: 166) conjures up the equally desperate expedient of viewing 1.21 as a speech given by Gallus to his brother before committing suicide, thus allowing the brother to escape rather than be slowed by the necessity of caring for his gravely wounded sibling. The scenario, however intriguing, has no textual support. It does nicely demonstrate that these poems elude comprehension within the narrative framework provided by the *Monobiblos* (Nicholson 1999: 146; Traill 1994).

26. Even Tränkle (1983: 150) notes the startling difference between Propertius's explicit treatment of the death of a relative at Perusia with Horace and Vergil's poems from the same period. See Stahl's (1985: 102–21, 165) subtle and convincing argument that while 1.22 by itself may be read as politically neutral, the combination of it and 1.21 reveals a far greater alienation from the Augustan regime.

27. Putnam (1976: 96–97) notes that *semper* can be seen either as modifying *quaeret*, with which it fits grammatically, or *amicitia*, which word order indicates. Both meanings are relevant. If their *amicitia* is truly eternal, then why must Tullus always be asking these questions?

28. For this reason Leo (1960: 169–73) assumed that 1.22 was a fragment of a larger poem in which Tullus's questions would have been answered in full.

29. On parallels between Hylas and Cynthia, see King (1980b: 228).

30. "Cornelius Gallus is the last poet of prominence to end up a prefect; the others pass from a youthful experiment with political or military participation to an exclusive commitment to poetry; Propertius, Ovid and so many others dedicated themselves directly and only to poetry."

31. See also Alfonsi (1979: 16, emphasis in original) for the contrast between the "contenuto gnomico o guerriero" of Catullus and the later "*dolorosa* vita dell'amore" of Propertius.

32. For a complete collation of the sources on Gallus's life, see Courtney (1993: 259–61).

33. Ovid, thus, in *Tristia* 4.10.33–54 elaborates a parallel concept of poetic aristocracy with its own genealogy and which rejects the political values of the forum.

34. The *Aeneid*'s elaboration of a model of self-abnegation to Rome's historical calling is as much a paean to the lost possibilities of individual fulfillment as it is a celebration of the new Augustan definition of the *civis Romanus*. Scipio, Marius, Sulla, Caesar, and Cicero would not have recognized themselves in the image of Aeneas, even if they would have granted the merit of his *pietas*.

35. Another parallel passage noted by Parsons and Nisbet (Anderson et al. 1979: 141) is that between line 3's "maxima Romanae pars eris historiae" and Propertius 1.21.4's "pars ego sum vestrae proxima militiae."

36. Thomas (1979: 203–4) observes that the nonliterary reading of the poet as voyeur in isolation from the literary reading is "ridiculous." See Lyne (1980: 112–13) for an example of such a straight mimetic reading.

37. Ovid in *Tristia* 4.10.47–48 identifies both Bassus and Ponticus. See Suits (1976: 86).

38. Sharrock (1990: 570–71) observes "this may well be right" but adds the additional thesis that *alternis vocibus* means "elegiac verse" and refers to the alternating hexameters and pentameters of the elegiac couplet. These two readings are not mutually exclusive, but reinforce one another. For, if the reference is first to elegiac verse, then that seals the literary reading, and since the dramatic situation of 1.10 indicates that Gallus and his *puella* are conversing, then, they would therefore be trading elegiac couplets.

39. This thesis had already been advanced by Anna Benjamin (1965) before the discovery of the Gallan papyrus.

40. On the themes of mirroring and the confusion of subject-object relation in the poem, as well as the relation between Hylas and Narcissus, see Hodge and Buttimore (1977: 202–4, 208); Rothstein (1979: 1.198); and Butler and Barber (1969: 185–86).

41. See Fedeli (1983: 1878); Lyne (1980: 110); Syme (1978: 99–100); Hodge and Buttimore (1977: 105); Hubbard (1974: 25); Camps (1961: 57); Enk (1946: 55); Butler and Barber (1969: 161); Rothstein (1979: 1.9–10).

42. Those supporting the identification are Janan (2001: 36–37); Sharrock (2000: 268n.13; 1990); Nicholson (1999: 159n.48); Oliensis (1997: 159); O'Hara (1989); Cairns (1983a: 83–84, 95, revising his more skeptical position from 1979a: 228); Kennedy (1982: 380); King (1980b: 225); Thomas (1979: 204n.84); Sullivan (1976: 33n.17); Ross (1975: 82–83); Benjamin (1965); Alfonsi (1943: 54–56; 1945: 9); Skutsch (1906: 144–46). Crowther (1983: 1637–38) and Fantham (1996: 58–59) identify the Gallus addressed in 1.20 as the poet but do not explicitly pronounce on the other poems.

43. But, as Crowther points out (1983: 1638), even if one accepts the biographical reading, there is no prima facie reason to reject the possibility of a close personal friendship.

44. See inter alia, Larmour et al. (1998: 22–33) for a complete overview of the question. See also Carnes (1998: 119–20); Parker (1997); Halperin (1995); Edwards (1993: 66); Konstan (1994: 119–22); Wiseman (1985: 10); Foucault (1976; 1984; 1994c; 1994h).

45. See Konstan (1994: 119–20) and Grimal (1986: 106, 121).

46. He says only "pueri tangar amore minus" (I'm less touched by the love of a boy).

47. Maleuvre (1998: 88), typically, acknowledges the validity of the problem and then proposes an absurd solution by claiming that the Gallus of 1.20 is Vergil.

48. See, however, Syme (1978: 99–100).

49. "Muiskos, when he had shot his arrow with his eyes at me, who until that time was unwounded in my breast by Desires, shouted the following: 'I caught the presumptuous one; behold! I trample with my feet on that insolence in the eyebrows of royal philosophy.' And having only caught so much breath, I said

this to him: 'Dear youth, why do you marvel? Eros brought Zeus himself down from Olympus."

50. On the sinister implications of this epithet for Poseidon and how it ties him to the Hercules simile that follows, see Commager (1974: 14–15).

51. Green (1982: ad loc.) notes the same pun in *Amores* 3.3.19 as does Claassen (1999: 265n.122) at *Epistulae ex Ponto* 4.9.49.

52. See Janan (2001: 35); Fedeli (1983: 1894); King (1980b: 214); and Richardson (1977: 181).

53. Enk (1946: ad loc.) sees this as evidence that Propertius was driven to seek solace in the arms of a prostitute.

54. Stahl (1985: 38) argues for excluding evidence from later poems, but such a reading would only be convincing the first time. And if our reading has established anything, and Stahl's as well, it is that these are subtle and complex texts not meant for a single reading.

55. See Janan (2001: 38–39); Sharrock (2000: 268–69); Albrecht (1997: 745); Gold (1987: 146); Fedeli (1983: 1867); King (1980b: 221–22); Fedeli (1980: ad loc.); Ross (1975: 31, 63, 85, 90–91). Ross also argue that lines 25–29 contain further allusions to Gallus.

56. As Camps (1961: ad loc.), Rothstein (1979: ad loc.), and Suits (1976: 88) note.

57. Catullus's Gallus is unidentifiable. Chronology excludes Cornelius Gallus.

58. Although the arguments of King (1988), Skinner (1988), Minyard (1988), and others make it quite likely that Catullus arranged the epigrams in the order we have them today, even if one accepts the thesis of a posthumous editor, there is every reason to believe the edition of Catullus we possess today was in circulation by the time Propertius was writing the *Monobiblos*, twenty years after Catullus's death.

CHAPTER FOUR
"HE DO THE POLICE IN DIFFERENT VOICES": THE TIBULLAN DREAM TEXT

1. "Agrarian life is till now only one aspect of his existence, it represents the element of a split. It is not fully 'integrated' into his lifeworld."

2. "The principle motif of the song announces itself from the beginning in a general form, like the opening of a symphony; then it gets lost in the undulation of thoughts and sentiments, of images and new visions."

3. As when Veyne declares elegy a semiotic game that has "no other referent than itself" (Veyne 1988: 11–12, 30, 112; Kennedy 1993: 95–96, 99).

4. See, for example, Mugatroyd's (1991), and Postgate's (1915) acceptance of Richter's (1873) proposal to move lines 25–32 of poem 1 immediately after lines 1–6 to remedy what they see as a contradiction between the opening lines' *vita iners* and the emphasis on manual labor that comes after. Lee (1982), Smith (1964), and Putnam (1973) reject this suggestion. The locus classicus for the twentieth century's negative view of Tibullus is Jacoby (1909 and 1910).

5. For direct evidence of Pound's effect on the poem, see the facsimile edition of the *Wasteland* (V. Eliot 1971).

6. Lyne in this passage is echoing Elder's earlier evaluation that, while "the individual sections" of a Tibullan poem "may seem, superficially, to have little or no connexion with one another . . . . 'behind the scene' of every section is present the same figure, Tibullus being tortured in love" (1962: 103).

7. For an excellent discussion of the difficult topic of *urbanitas* and its relation to neoteric poetry, see Fitzgerald (1995: 87–113). On Tibullus as the continuator of the neoteric tradition both in terms of increasing stylistic refinement and the "conquest" of a new sense of interiority, see Riposati (1945: 24–25) and Lyne (1980: 188).

8. On 1.4 as the first poem in the collection to link wealth with *munera*, see Wimmel (1976: 4) and Leach (1978: 89).

9. Littlewood (1970: 661–69); Leach (1980a: 81); Dettmer (1980: 70–71; 1983: 1964); Ball (1979: 6). Marathus is, of course, mentioned in 1.4 but only at the end. The poem as a whole is not dedicated to him per se, but see Powell (1974: 107–12).

10. Elder (1962: 91) sees 1.4 as "a reflective pause between 1.3 and 1.5."

11. On this recursive pattern of reading as the hallmark of the lyric collection, see Miller (1994: 1–8, 52–77).

12. Murgatroyd (1991: 71); Leach (1980a: 87); Cairns (1979a: 166–67); Putnam (1973: 10); André (1965: 21); Smith (1964: 208); Copley (1956: 107).

13. Tibullus partly achieves this smoothness of transition in poems that are longer and more heterogeneous in theme than the other elegists' (Bright 1978: 10), through the repetition of key words and through internal and end rhyme, in addition to his well-known use of anaphora. In 1.1, Wimmel (1976: 11, 16, 29) points to the repetition of *ante* in two different senses in lines 12 and 14, the use of *agna* in lines 22, 23, and 31, and the employment of an elaborate rhyme scheme in lines 8 and 10, in which the three words in "grandia poma manu" each rhyme with their counterparts in "pinguia musta lacu." Cairns (1979a: 94–95, 104) notes the etymological play on the root *fac* in 39–40 and between *spes* and *spicea* in lines 9–16, pointing out that Varro had derived both words from the same root (Varro, *De Lingua Latina* 5.37; *De Re Rustica* 1.48.2), while also examining how 41–42 pick up themes from 19 and 9, and 43 echoes 25. Ponchont notes, "la pièce se trouve ainsi fortement encadrée et liée, malgré la nonchalante aisance avec laquelle se poursuivent les dévelopements et l'abandon qui se marque jusque dans les négligences de la forme, les répétitions de mots ou les libres apostrophes" (1967: 8). Repetitions of other terms in 1.1 are examined later in this chapter.

14. Fineberg (1991: 57–58); Veyne (1988: 33); Putnam (1973: 11–12); Luck (1960: 74); Elder (1962: 103); Riposati (1945: 11–12, 168).

15. Bright (1978: 261–62) does claim that Tibullus is a linear poet, but he means by that not that the poet follows a logical point by point progression, but rather that he proceeds in a metonymic or associative style, as opposed to the circular style of ring composition. Cairns, in contrast, sees ring composition as typical of Tibullus, but, as he and Dettmer concede, the poems are susceptible to more than one kind of analysis (Cairns 1979a: 208–9; Dettmer 1983: 1963).

16. Ovid, however, often undercuts the value of his logic at the poems' end. See Parker (1969).

17. See Lee-Stecum, "Power in Tibullus Book One . . . manifested in a series of relationships which can be conceived as relationships of exchange" (1998: 23, as well as 27–28).

18. *Adsiduus* in line 6 is emended to *exiguus* by Heyne without comment in his 1817 edition in order to avoid the repetition.

19. As David Wray points out in an excellent forthcoming article that engages an earlier version of this chapter, *labor*, from a military point of view may actually exclude agriculture (Caesar, *Bellum Gallicum* 6.21–22), although in other contexts it certainly means agricultural labor in the way we understand it (Wray cites Tibullus 1.7.39). The passage from Caesar is less decisive than Wray contends. If quoted in full, it reads:

> Vita omnis in venationibus atque in studiis rei militaris consistit: ab parvulis labori ac duritiae student. Qui diutissime impuberes permanserunt, maximam inter suos ferunt laudem: hoc alii staturam, alii vires nervosque confirmari putant. Intra annum vero vicesimum feminae notitiam habuisse in turpissimis habent rebus; cuius rei nulla est occultatio, quod et promiscue in fluminibus perluuntur et pellibus aut parvis renonum tegimentis utuntur magna coporis parte nuda.

> Agri culturae non student, maiorque pars eorum victus in lacte, caseo, carne, consistit. Neque quisquam agri modum certum aut finis habet proprios; sed magistratus ac principes in annos singulos gentibus cognationibusque hominum, qui una coierunt, quantum et quo loco visum est agri attribuunt atque anno post alio transire cogunt. Eius rei multas adferunt causas: ne assidua consuetudine capti studium belli gerendi agri cultura commutent.

> [Their life consists in hunting and military pursuit; from the time they are small they seek *labor* and toughness. Those who have remained unmarried the longest receive the greatest praise among them. Some think their stature to be established in this, others their strength and vigor. Indeed, they hold that to have had the knowledge of a women in one's twentieth year to be among the most shameful of things; in this regard there is no concealment, because they bathe openly in rivers end they use skins or small coverings of fur leaving a great part of their bodies nude.

> They do not pursue agriculture, and the great part of their food consists in milk, cheese, and meat. Nor does anyone have a certain border or boundary of a field as their own; but the magistrates and headmen allocate to the tribes and families who are present how much and what sort of land they see fit, and force them to change after a year. They allege many reasons for this affair: lest having been captivated by constant habit they change from the pursuit of waging war to farming.

Wray's claim that *belli gerendi* here is contrasted with *agri cultura*, while not impossible, is in no way necessary. Caesar tells us that *labor* and *duritia* are the center of the Germans' existence. He then outlines in what that *labor* consists. Next he tells us that farming is not an important part of their existence and is thought to distract from the pursuits of the arts of war. This need not mean Caesar, or the Latin language, assumes that *agri cultura* cannot be conceived as a form of *labor,* but merely that it is one fundamentally to be distinguished, at least by the Germans, from *studium belli gerendi.*

20. Miller (1994: 125–26); Ste. Croix (1981: 41–42); Taylor (1925: 161–70; 1968: 469–86); Nicolet (1966: 441–56).

21. Compare Lee-Stecum (1998: 90).

22. "C'è in Tibullo un antitesi fra la realtà e il sogno; di qui le note discordanti del contrasto, della nostalgia e del rimpianto, di quei subitanei turbamenti dell'animo, e di quel perenne oscillar di fanciullo fra opposti sentimenti" (Riposati 1945: 93–94).

23. This can be compared with Kuhn's (1962: esp. 43–76) notion of the increase in anomalies as indicating an impending paradigm shift in "normal science."

24. Indeed, the prospect of labor is less idealized in book 2 (Lyne 1980: 165; Bright 1978: 192, 194). *Labor* is also frequently used in military contexts. For a good bibliography, see Boyd (1984a: 273–74n.2).

25. On the use of the subjunctive throughout 1.1, see Riposati (1945: 99), Wimmel (1976: 17, 21–22, 28n.55), and Bright (1978: 130).

26. Wimmel terms the use of the indicative in an analogous passage, 1.35.36, an "Art Überkonjunktive" or "a kind of hypersubjective," since it imagines the realization of the desired state.

27. On the relation between elegy and pastoral, see Veyne (1988: 101).

28. Riposati (1945: 16–17) does note that land distributions were made in 41 B.C.E. to the veterans of Phillipi in the region of Pedum, thought to be Tibullus's native land.

29. On the pose of *paupertas* and external evidence for Tibullus's *divitiae,* see Putnam (1973: 3–4) and Riposati (1945: 18).

30. As Lee (1974: 99) notes, the proposition that one should live content with little as a way of avoiding anxiety was a philosophical truism of the time.

31. As presented in Postgate's Oxford Classical Text (OCT) edition (1915) and Luck's Teubner edition (1988).

32. All parallel passages listed in the *Thesaurus Linguae Latinae* date from a period after Tibullus and are liable to the same sort of objections. None refers to a labor in any way comparable with the farmer's: *Ars* 1.160, smoothing a pillow; *Fasti* 3.536, keeping time to music; Seneca's *Octavia* 483, Fortune's ease in handing the reigns of government to Nero; *Epistulae Morales* 121.5, the art of painting. Only Apuleius, *Metamorphoses* 8.5, comes close when referring to the act of running through a boar, though this passage is much later and not listed as parallel by the *Oxford Latin Dictionary.*

33. For a complete discussion of the controversies surrounding this passage, see Ball (1983: 23).

34. Wimmel (1976: 10) is surely right when he refers to the "exquisite arrangement" of 1.1.8, and indeed one could say this of the whole couplet.

35. "cuncta dabant reditus: tamen est deterrita numquam / quin fleret nostras respiceretque *vias* (All things foretold return: but she is never deterred / from weeping or viewing our *departure* with alarm")."

36. See Ball on the tension between Messalla and Tibullus at the beginning of the collection. For 1.7 as a poem in which the complementary but opposed worlds of Tibullus and Maecenas find a momentary balance, see Moore (1989: 423–30).

37. For a further homology between Delia and Messalla, see Lee-Stecum: "the girl is in the same position as Messalla . . . just as he has the spoils of war outside his home, the *formosa puella* has the spoils of her conquest" (1998: 48; f. also 225).

38. Nemesis, as Bright (1978: 186) remarks, is the negative side of Delia.

39. Wimmel (1976: 39) notes that by introducing the word *domina* in 1.1.46, at the end of the agricultural section of poem 1, he is returning the word to its "altrömisher" significance as the mistress of a rural household who would supervise the work of the house slaves. See also Grimal (1986: 160–61).

40. See more explicitly 2.4, where Tibullus proposes to sell his ancestral lands in order to be able to buy trinkets for Nemesis. This would be the ultimate rejection of his own position as an equestrian within the Roman Symbolic (Bright 1978: 214).

41. See also Lyne (1980: 155) and Boyd (1984a: 277).

42. The passage calls attention to itself through its unusual syntax. One expects *vitam* to be the accusative object of the verb; instead, by putting *vita* in the ablative, the poet in effect treats his inactive life as the medium through which *paupertas* leads or betrays him (Wimmel 1976: 7).

43. On men being able to assume the feminine position in discourse and women being able to assume the phallic position, see Weed (1994: 81, 89); Janan (1994: 30); Moi (1985: 136–37); Kristeva (1983: 223–47); Irigaray (1974: 165; 1977a: 183; 1977b: 189); Lacan (1975: 34, 39, 67–75).

44. See Lacan (1975: 71), "Comme ça se produit grâce à l'être de la signifiance, et que cet être n'a d'autre lieu que le lieu de l'Autre que je désigne du grand A, on voit la biglerie de ce qui se passe. Et comme c'est là aussi que s'inscrit la fonction du père en tant que c'est à elle que se rapporte la castration."

45. The succession of "periods" in which these events are staged, as Lacan makes clear subsequently, is logical rather than strictly temporal. See Janan (1994: 20) and Lacan (1975: 53).

46. In Ovid's *Fasti* (1.193–94), however, the rule of Saturn is already characterized as a time of greed (Edwards 1996: 58). On there being two different golden age traditions in the ancient world, one similar to the ideal described by Tibullus and Vergil and another characterized by hard work and greed, see Fitzgerald (1995: 275n.15). Vergil's vision in *Eclogue* 4 is perhaps the most idealized and least troubled of the lot (Boyd 1984a: 275).

47. "Que l'imaginaire se supporte du reflet du semblable au semblable, c'est ce qui est certain" (Lacan 1975: 77).

48. In point of fact, as Julien (1990: 67) makes clear, both the Imaginary and the Symbolic are assumed to be present from the beginning in Lacan's teaching after 1953.

49. On Jupiter's overthrow of Saturn as a form of castration, see Lacan (1973: 276).

50. Cairns (1979a: 82–83) points out that 2.5, where Apollo is pictured as singing Jupiter's victory ode after Saturn's defeat (lines 9–10), also recalls the

prodigia seen after the death of Julius Caesar (67–82). For a contrary view, see Murgatroyd (1994: 174).

51. See Bright (1978: 194), "the premises of 2.3 are sheer pretense," and Cairns (1979a: 154–55).

52. According to Žižek (1991: 167), "the respective domains of fantasy and symbolic law are radically incommensurable. That is to say, it is in the very nature of fantasy to resist universalization: fantasy is the absolutely particular way every one of us structures his/ her 'impossible' relation to the traumatic Thing. It is the way every one of us, by means of an imaginary scenario, dissolves and/or conceals the fundamental impasse of the inconsistent big Other, the symbolic order."

53. I have chosen to translate *nihil* literally as "nothing," even though it is somewhat awkward in English. The Latin contains within it not only the more obvious sense of "without significance, unimportant" but also suggests complete nonexistence.

54. I owe this last observation to David Oberhelman. See Freud's (1955: 29–47) analysis of the Wolf Man's dream.

55. Obviously, I do not completely accept Cairns's position (1979a: 54) that the description of the golden age (lines 35–48) and that of Elysium are to be equated, though clearly they are very similar. There are two key differences: in the golden age, love is not mentioned; in Elysium, everyone is dead. My argument rests on the contention that such differences are not insignificant. See also Lee-Stecum (1998: 120).

56. On the golden age as the negation of Tibullus's situation as described at the poem's beginning, see Whitaker (1983: 67–68).

CHAPTER FIVE
WHY PROPERTIUS IS A WOMAN

1. See, for example, Propertius 1.6.25–26; Tibullus 1.1.57–58; Gaisser 1983: 65; Wimmel 1976: 37–38; Veyne 1988: 106; Copley 1956: 100; Sullivan 1976: 62; and Tracy 1979: 343, "*Nequitia* in the Roman elegists has been defined as the freeing of self from community consciousness, the retreating into one's own 'I.' "

2. See Enk (1962: 2.151) citing Fleischmann, "Nihil certi promittere voluit Propertius hoc carmine Augusto; 'itaque fit, ut quae altero versu elatiore quodam animo et singulari quadam alacritate se aggressurum promittat ea iam altero versu refringat et quodam modo retrahat.' "

3. Butler and Barber (1969: 217) agree but assert "there is no real inappropriateness." Giardina (1977: 157) is similarly ambivalent, "Minime ad Antonium refertur sermo eiusque amores." Tränkle (1983: 157) argues that 2.16's condemnation of Antony shows that 2.15 should be read in a negative light as well.

4. All translations are my own. All texts are cited from Barber's 1953 OCT unless otherwise noted.

5. As Walter (1999: 94) shrewdly observes, Propertius is less concerned with his personal likeness with Antony than with the opposition between Antony and Augustus and the homologous one between the excessive Dionysian lover and the restrained Apollonian image of Augustus.

6. This is precisely the problem with Stahl's brilliant and provocative reading of the poet. He posits a double structure to later Propertian poetry, but feels consistently compelled to demonstrate that such duplicity can be resolved back into a monological whole once the "truth" is recognized. "The discrepancy cannot be denied: there is no bridge leading over the abyss between the poet's true feelings and the public statements he has felt obliged to make" (1985: 209). The question of what gives him the epistemological and ontological privilege to distinguish the true from the false, especially if as he says they share no point of contact, is never answered. What is at stake, as Duncan Kennedy observes, is a desperate effort to save the unified liberal, male subject of the Western "ideology of the individual" (1993: 35–38). The search for the one true meaning lurking behind the necessarily deceptive appearances ultimately produces a paranoid style of reading in which all ambiguities and ambivalences must be ruthlessly shorn away. The best, recent example of this paranoid style is Maleuvre, whose recent book on elegy acutely diagnoses the incoherence of the elegiac subject position and then proceeds magisterially to resolve it by demonstrating how the entire elegiac canon can be shown to be an elaborately encoded allegory of Augustus's seduction of Maecenas's wife Terentia (1998).

7. On Propertius as both inside and outside traditional Roman ideology, see Platter (1995). On elegy performing "the ambiguities of equestrian status," see Fitzgerald (1995: 9).

8. Žižek admirably sums up the psychoanalytic theory behind this reading when he writes, "what lies beyond [the pleasure principle] is not the symbolic order but a real kernel, a traumatic core. To designate it, Lacan uses the Freudian term: *das Ding*, the Thing as an incarnation of the impossible *jouissance*" (1989: 132).

9. On *jouissance* as essentially feminine, see Lacan (1975: 13, 76–77).

10. See inter alia, Moi (1985: 99), "Cixous, Irigaray, and Kristeva are all heavily indebted to Lacan's (post-) structuralist reading of Freud"; and Weed (1994: 87).

11. Bakhtin (1984: 127): "[P]arody was inseparably linked to a carnival sense of the world. Parodying is the creation of a decrowning double; it is that same 'world turned inside out.' For this reason parody is ambivalent." On the distinction between negative, monological satire and the ambivalence of carnival laughter, see Miller (1998b).

12. Bakhtin (1981a: 68–69, 75–76); Morson (1989: 63, 65, 73).

13. Irigaray (1977a: 183), "elles sont 'objets' pour et entre hommes et ne peuvent, par ailleurs, que mimer un 'langage' qu'elles n'ont pas produit"; Irigaray (1977a: 176–77); Herndl (1991: 11); Schwab (1991: 57–59); Weed (1994: 82).

14. Weed (1994: 89), "Lacan . . . sees the knowledge (*savoir*) involved in symbolic processes as indissociable from the knowledge (*connaissance*) produced in the early imaginary demarcations of 'psyche' and 'body,' a *connaissance* that is, in turn, activated differently in the symbolic depending on whether the subject is sexed through language as male or female. If anything, Lacan sees women as knowing they don't know what they're saying—by virtue of their position in the symbolic order—while men are dupes of Truth." On the Symbolic as realm of ordered rationality, see Janan (1994: 35, 79); Butler (1990: 82–83).

15. Janan (1994: 28): "[F]or Lacan, Woman is a position outside clear meaning and grammatical language—she is *hors-sens*, 'outside meaning/sense.' As such, Woman signifies the antithesis of masculine certitude, based on identification with rules, order, Law. Thus the feminine is for Lacan an attitude toward knowledge and procedure, rather than a category defined strictly by gender"; and Goux (1990: 223). On woman as unrepresentable within the symbolic, see Lacan (1975: 74); Herndl (1991: 16); Moi (1985: 117, 133–34, 163, 166); Irigaray (1977a: 184): "Les femmes . . . vont assurer la possibilité de l'usage et de circulation du symbolique sans y être pour autant partie prenante. C'est le non-accès, pour elles, qui établit l'ordre social"; Irigaray (1977e: 25); Butler (1990: 9–10, 27–28, 154n.27); Goux (1990: 147); Weed (1994: 81, 88–90).

16. Lacan (1975: 53, 54, 57, 64, and 68): "Il n'y a pas *La* femme, article défini pour désigner l'universel." See Kristeva (1979: 15) for her reading of this passage.

17. Lacan (1975: 13, 57, 69, 76–77); Janan (1994: 30); Julien (1990: 173, 176, 208); Irigaray (1977c: 87–88, 95; 1977f: 109); Butler (1990: 56); Eagleton (1983: 168).

18. Lacan (1975: 69): "Ce n'est pas parce qu'elle est pas toute dans la fonction phallique qu'elle y est pas du tout. Elle y est *pas* pas du tout. Elle y est à plein. Mais il y a quelque chose en plus." See also 13 and 75.

19. Irigaray (1977c: 106–7), "Donc le 'tout'—de x, mais aussi du système— aura déjà prescrit le 'pas-toute' de chaque mise en relation particulière, et ce 'tout' ne l'est que par une définition de l'extension qui ne peut se passer de projection sur un espace-plan 'donné,' dont l'entre, les entre(s), seront évalués grâce à des repères de type ponctuel."

20. For a brief synopsis of passages in which Propertius plays the woman, see Wyke (1995: 116).

21. Bramble (1974: 44): "Sexual overtones load the vocabulary of the critics: *tener, mollis, fractus, effeminatus enervis*, and their opposite epithets like *fortis* or *virilis*. This patently moralistic terminology often acted as substitute for rational criticism, as at Quint. 12. 10.12, where we hear that in his own day, Cicero was taxed with being "in compositione fractum, exultantem, ac paene, quod procul absit, viro molliorem."

22. Lemaire (1832: 145); Rothstein (1979: 1.210); Enk (1962: 13–14); Giardina (1977: 90); Richardson (1977: 211).

23. As Wiggers (1977: 339) points, out the later comparison of Cynthia's fidelity to Helen's adultery (2.1.49–50) implicitly, if perversely, argues for elegy's superiority to epic on the grounds of moral seriousness.

24. On the pursuit of *otium* as linked to *mollitia* or effeminacy, see Edwards (1993: 85).

25. Here, the contrast with M. Messalla Valerius Corvinus, the patron of Tibullus, the young Ovid, and his niece Sulpicia is striking. Messalla was heavily involved in both the political and military struggles in the period between the assasination of Julius Caesar and Octavian's consolidation of power in the aftermath of Actium. As a youth, Messalla won military glory fighting with Brutus and Cassius at Philippi, before defecting to the side of Octavian and Antony when the battle was lost (Plutarch, *Brutus* 40–42, 45, 53; Velleius Paterculus 2.71). He was a member of Antony's faction until 36 or 33 B.C.E. when he defected to the side

of Octavian, possibly in the wake of Antony's 34 B.C.E. Alexandrian triumph where Cleopatra was honored by the legions as queen. He subsequently wrote anti-Antonian pamphlets and replaced Antony as consul (Valvo 1983: 1670–72; Cassius Dio 47.11, 49.16, 38, 50.10). In 26 or 25 B.C.E., after celebrating a triumph over the Aquitani in 27 (Tibullus 1.7), he was named prefect of the city, but stepped down after only a few days, alleging according to one account that he lacked administrative ability (Tacitus, *Annales* 6.11), a fact belied by his previous military and political experience. According to another version, he claimed that the recently created office had more power than was proper for a citizen to hold (*incivilem potestatem*, Saint Jerome, *Chronica* 164H). This is sometimes seen as a subtle critique of the increasing concentration of power in the hands of the *princeps*.

There need be no conflict between these competing versions. The first may well represent the official version accepted by Augustus. The second, however, would represent the view Messalla shared with his friends (Valvo 1983: 1673–74). That there was no open rift with Augustus is shown by Messalla's being chosen to propose that the Senate offer the *princeps* the title Pater Patriae (Suetonius, *Divus Augustus* 48). Nonetheless, with his resignation of the post of *praefectus urbi* Messalla essentially withdrew from an active political career.

Messalla at first seems to be a very different figure from Maecenas. A senator who took an active part in military affairs but who nonethless supported an important poetic circle while being a writer of no small accomplishment (Valvo 1983: 1674–80), he appears to represent the image of lost wholeness attributed to Gallus by Propertius in the *Monobiblos* (see chapter 3). As he is celebrated by the anonymous writer of the *Panegyricus Messallae*, "quis te maior gerit castrisve forove?" (Who has greater military or forensic accomplishment than you?) (39; see Schoonhoven 1983: 1682–84). Unlike, the historical Gallus, however, Messalla understood the implications of Octavian's supremacy. And though he might have had his reservations about the principate, and certainly does not ever seem to have suggested that the members of his poetic circle should produce Augustan propaganda, in the end he recognized that the only role for senatorial ambition under the new regime would be that of the patronage of and the participation in equestrian *otium*.

26. See Lemaire (1832: ad loc.); Rothstein (1979: ad loc.); Enk (1962 ad loc.); Hubbard (1974: 102n.1); Giardina (1977: ad loc.).

27. Benstock looks not only at H. D., Stein, and Woolf, but also at Joyce and Derrida.

28. For a good review of the early literature on this point, see Enk (1962: 8–9). The contemporary consensus is for the unity of the text; see Boucher (1980: 381).

29. Either the manuscript tradition is corrupt and *cogis* needs to be emended (Lachmann 1973, Lemaire 1832, Paley 1853, and Butler and Barber 1969 propose *coccis*; Enk 1962, Camps 1967, and Goold 1990 follow the *codices deteriores* with *vidi*) or *cogis* here has the attenuated sense of *adducere*, which is all but unexampled (Rothstein 1979; Butler 1926; Shackleton Bailey 1967: 61). Many simply mark the text with daggers in despair (Barber 1953—though he proposes *iuvit* in the *apparatus criticus*; Giardina 1977; Richardson 1977; Fedeli 1994). I

have chosen to translate the consensus reading of the best manuscripts in what seems a reasonable fashion, following Butler (1926), while leaving the OCT's daggers to denote the perilous nature of any such reading.

30. Butler (1926) prints the reading of the Neapolitanus, *in ore*, and translates in the same way. Rothstein (1979) reads *in ora*, but takes it to mean not "in the mouth" but before the eyes.

31. On Propertius's deliberate undermining of the classical distinction between *res* and *verba*, see Benediktson (1989: 30–31).

32. Thus Rothstein (1979: ad loc.) notes that these lines far from reflecting modesty actually equate the poet's *ingenium* with divine inspiration, if they do not claim its outright superiority.

33. See 2.24.1–2, "Tu loqueris, cum sis iam noto fabula libro / et tua sit toto Cynthia lecta foro?" ("Do you speak, when you are now a story in a well-known book / and your Cynthia is read in all the forum?"). These lines in addition to treating the name Cynthia as the title of the poet's book also play on the joke that characters in books cannot speak.

34. On this whole passage, see Fredrick (1997: 180), with whom I am in substantial agreement.

35. There is no good reason not to follow the manuscripts here and read *sanguine* instead of Postgate's *nomine*.

36. On 2.1's deliberate echoes of 1.22, see Gold (1987: 158).

37. See inter alia, *Odes* 3.1.

38. Tränkle argues for interpreting the poem simultaneously as an "elegy of praise full of respect and distance" (1983: 155, my translation).

39. The fact that racial, gendered, class, and sexual subject positions may be in large part social constructions does not mean that they are all equally available to everybody. See Steele (1997: 202).

40. On 3.1 continuing the themes and style of 2.1 and 2.34, see Stahl (1985: 190).

41. On 3.1–5 as a response to Horace's "Roman Odes," see Sullivan (1976: 14); Cremona (1987). On the apparently Callimachean pose adopted by the poet actually being profoundly imbued with Roman models, see Cameron (1995: 473–74).

42. Gold (1987: 155–56) notes that 3.21 and 3.22 represent a rejection of the position taken by the poet in 1.6, where the poet stays home and Tullus goes abroad.

. 43. Of course, the Horatian subtext is made clearest in elegy 3.11's relation to *Odes* 1.37. See Sullivan (1976: 23–24).

44. The exact dating of Propertius's books is open to question, depending on whether one accepts Lachmann's thesis that book 2 was originally two separate books. There is strong evidence of manuscript corruption in book 2, as evidenced by the widespread disagreement over how many poems the volume contains, ranging from thirty-four to forty-six depending on the editor (Hubbard 1974: 44–45), and many have found the notion of dividing the second book attractive, especially in light of 2.13.25–26's reference to there being three books, that is, the *Monobiblos* plus two others (Lachmann 1973: xxi–xxii; Paley 1853: ad loc.; Hubbard 1974: 41–42; Sullivan 1976: 6–7; Lyne 1980: 120; King 1980a; Günther 1997:

6–10). This notion has not won universal assent, but the alternative explanations that "three" either represents an indefinite number (Richardson 1976: ad loc.; Camps 1967: ad loc.) or a selection of representative books from Propertius's library (Rothstein 1979: ad loc.) are not convincing. King's (1980a: 66, 70, 80) argument that poems 2.1 to 2.12 form a coherent unity in terms of both thematic and numerical correspondences has much to recommend it, while Fredrick (1997: 182) observes the dominance of the Iliadic theme in poems 2.1 to 2.15. If one accepts Lachmann's thesis then Hubbard's and Sullivan's datings of the books seem reasonable: *Monobiblos* 29–28, book 2a 28–27, book 2b 26–25, book 3 22–21, book 4 after 16 (Hubbard 1974: 44; Sullivan 1976: 3, 7–8). In any case, 2.34's reference to the *Aeneid* only makes sense if the poem's basic outline was already known; it is therefore not unreasonable to assume that by 22 B.C.E. the circle of poets gathered around Maecenas had heard some version of the poem's opening lines.

45. Richardson (1977: ad loc.); Camps (1966: ad loc.); Butler and Barber (1969: ad loc.); Newman (1997: 250).

46. Rothstein (1979: ad loc., citing Philo *leg. ad Gaium* 23); Hubbard (1974: 104); Stahl (1985: 194).

47. "The contradictions of the development of elegy are the contradictions of the poet . . . the echo of the contradictions of an epoch that with difficulty has just come through the civil wars and a revolution."

48. This line is much disputed. I have chosen to follow Lachmann (1873), Lemaire (1832), Paley (1853), Rothstein (1979), Butler (1926), Paganelli (1964), Richardson (1976), and the reading of the better codices rather than that offered by Barber's (1953) OCT or pick one of the numerous other emendations that have been advocated by Enk (1978), Butler and Barber (1969), Shackleton Bailey (1967), Camps (1966), Goold (1990), and Fedeli (1994), and have yielded no better sense nor garnered much assent.

49. I have adopted the reading of Lachmann et al.

50. See Butler (1999: 6): "[D]esire according to Hegel, is the incessant human effort to overcome external differences, a project to become a self-sufficient subject for whom all things apparently different emerge as immanent features of the subject itself."

51. Bataille (1957: 26–27); Lacan (1986: 341); Black (1991: 110, 205); Guyomard (1992: 53–54); Butler (1999: 9).

52. On the fundamental structure of eroticism as the violation of boundaries and the dissolution of the closed structure of being, see Bataille (1957: 22).

53. Thus Lemaire (1832: ad loc.); Rothstein (1979: ad loc.); Camps (1966: ad loc.); Shackleton Bailey (1967: 145–46); Fedeli (1994: ad loc.).

54. Butler (1912) and Goold (1990) also follow Baehrens.

55. The oldest of the manuscripts, N, has the reading *acta*, this is accepted by Lachmann (1973) and those who agree with him. It is also the reading of Butler (1912), Barber's OCT (1953), and Richardson (1977). Some of the later manuscripts read *apta*, as do Paley (1853), and Butler and Barber (1969).

56. See also Rothstein's (1979) comments on line 3.

57. Paley (1853: ad loc.) and Richardson (1976: ad loc.) each defend the original reading of the manuscripts, taking *parca* as an adjective meaning "poor" or "mean." Neither offers any parallel passages for the phrase *parca dies* meaning

"day of poverty." Both interpret the passage to mean that the best death comes when one is poor. The reasoning here is unclear, nor does it address the passage's fundamental point that death treats rich and poor alike. Paganelli (1964) too accepts *parca*, but treats it as a proper name without explanation. This is a position that cannot be defended. The most important thing, however, is not which reading of the text to accept, but rather to see the confusion itself as symptomatic of the instability of the fundamental Symbolic categories out of which, and in opposition to which, Propertius constructs the elegist's subject position (see Miller and Platter 1999). It thus becomes increasingly difficult to define a position outside of Augustan norms, as the very gestures of opposition themselves become assimilated to the structures of the emerging imperial ideology.

58. The abject is precisely that which links us most firmly with the Real, the reminder/remainder of our pre-Symbolic origins. It is literally non-sense. On the ideological equivalence of cadavers, feces, mentstrual blood, and sexual fluids, see Bataille (1957: 64).

59. See also the valuable discussions of Gold (1987); Cairns (1979b: 202); Boucher (1980: 37); Santirocco (1986: 154); Ste. Croix (1981: 342); Wyke (1989: 30); and Conte (1994: 251).

60. As Habinek (1998: 121) makes clear, the normative function of Roman literature was to contribute "to the amalgamation of Roman identity to subject status and help reconstitute the potentially free reader of the widely circulated literary text as a subject of an imperial regime."

61. On the case of Messalla, see note 24.

62. On the collapse of the republic and the collapse of the traditional discourse of aristocratic manhood or *virtus*, see Edwards (1993: 57); Fredrick (1997: 179).

Chapter Six
Deconstructing the *Vir*: Law and the Other in the *Amores*

1. See Nugent (1990: 240), "If Augustus dreams of a morally reconstructed Rome, Ovidian cynicism implicitly deconstructs that dream and the imperial propaganda promoting it."

2. On Ovid's use of traditional rhetorical and legal forms of exposition, see Martyn (1981: 2446).

3. See our discussion of these issues in the final section of chapter 2, as well as Du Quesnay (1973: 41); and Otis (1966: 43).

4. This, of course, places Augustus in the same blood relationship to Amor as he was to his adoptive father Julius Caesar.

5. For the distinction between transgression and negation, see Miller (1998a).

6. While Ovid may have begun reciting his poetry in public as early as 25 B.C.E. (*Tristia* 4.10.57–60), *Amores* 1.2 must be later. The first edition of the *Amores* is generally thought to have been published in separate books over the course of the teens. This poem, as one of the three opening programmatic poems in the second edition (Davis 1989: 69; Wille 1984: 397), is likely to have been written for publication, and hence would not be part of the juvenilia aimed at the more immediate audience attending Ovid's early recitations at Messalla's home. For more on the dating of the two editions of the *Amores*, see my subsequent discussion.

7. For a fuller reading of this passage, see Buchan (1995: 54); Cameron (1995: 456–57); Kennedy (1993: 59–61).

8. All translations are my own. The text is from Kenney (1961).

9. See Derrida (1978: 274): "[T]ransgression of discourse (and consequently of law in general, for discourse establishes itself only by establishing normativity or the value of meaning, that is to say, the element of legality in general) must, in some fashion, and like every transgression, conserve or confirm that which it exceeds." See also Boyne (1990: 82) on Foucault's concept of transgression as a "non-positive affirmation" or "a pure movement across a limit, a movement which neither repudiates the place from whence it came nor welcomes the place to which it is bound."

For an excellent account of the basic contradictions of Augustan ideology, see Janan's (2001: 12–14) reading of the iconography of the Forum Augustum.

10. There is a pun in *gravis* that is impossible to translate. *Gravitas* is the traditional quality of a serious Roman. Its opposite is *levitas* or "frivolity." Literally, *gravis* means "weighty" or "heavy," and so "gravis alitibus" is an oxymoron that nicely translates the paradox of Amor leading the weightiest of all Roman processions, the triumph. This paradox in turn distills to its essence the founding tension that underlines the standard elegiac motif of *militia amoris*.

11. The composition of the original five-volume edition dates predominantly to the teens (McKeown 1987: 75–84; Conte 1994: 340). The revised three-book edition is dated variously to 9 B.C.E. (Green 1982: 267), 7 B.C.E. (McKeown 1987: 1.84), 2 B.C.E. (Barsby 1978: 6), and 1 C.E. (Conte 1994: 340; Lyne 1980: 239).

12. The irony is, of course, that at this point Corinna has not even been named so that all we see in this hall of mirrors is Ovid's own reflection (Kennedy 1993: 69).

13. See Commager (1974: 42): "Lucilius in the course of a rambling definition of *virtus*, proclaimed the orthodox hierarchy: 'commoda praeterea patriai prima putare, / deinde parentum, tertia postremaque nostra.' 1337–38 (Marx)."

14. See also Mack (1988: 56–57); Bornecque (1961: 15); Du Quesnay (1973: 2, 40–41); Tracy (1978–79: 59–60); Lyne (1980: 240); Showerman (1977: 328); Barsby (1979: 56–57), while admitting the possibility of ambiguity; and Melville (1990: 7), with qualifications by Kenney (1990: 177).

15. See Munari (1970: 116n.3); and McKeown (1989: 76–77), with reservations.

16. Williams (1968: 540, 542); Stroh (1979: 337); Wallace-Hadrill (1985: 181–84); Davis (1989: 45–46; 1993: 67); Konstan (1994: 157n.39); McKeown (1998: 407).

17. Corinna is even offered as a positive example of a mistress who knew how to keep the *amator*'s attention (2.19.9–10). This line invites us to imagine that the relationship between Corinna and her *vir* is analogous to that between Ovid's new love and her *vir-maritus*. As Davis (1999: 446) notes, the use of the terminology of maritus and uxor makes the identification of the couple as man and wife probable if not absolutely necessary.

18. On 2.19 and 3.4 as a pair, see Du Quesnay (1973: 5), Davis (1989: 77–78), Stapleton (1996: 27).

19. On the figure of the *vir* in the opening lines of the *Aeneid* as a means to distinguish a masculinized epic from a feminized elegy, see Buchan (1995: 56).

20. On the legal definition of *lenocinium* and its being perceived as a real and continuing problem in later imperial society, see Davis (1989: 47–48, 54–55).

21. Stroh (1979: 338–39); Lyne (1980: 275, 280); Davis (1989: 51); Booth (1991: 91–92); Greene (1998: 102–3).

22. These sorts of complex relationships reveal the problem with overly rigid studies of arrangement, such as Wille's, that cannot take account of clear pairings that transcend the division into books. See his schematic chart (1984: 422).

23. It is precisely the demonstration of this kind of movement that is the burden of Lacan's seminar on "The Purloined Letter" (1966c).

24. The phrase *inicere manus* plays a crucial role in our reading of 1.4.

25. Thus Kennedy (1993: 56) argues that *servitium amoris*, while ostensibly an inversion of traditional gender roles, is in fact a method of domination; Gold (1993: 91), following Gutzwiller and Michelini (1991), argues that the elegists' inversion of traditional roles was in fact designed to reassert "traditional male dominance." Hallett (1993: 64) acknowledges the strength of this reading as a supplement to her 1973 characterization of elegiac counterculture.

26. See Tracy (1979: 343), Mack (1988: 56, 59), and Benediktson (1989: 20–21) on the well-documented tendency of poems in the *Amores* to undercut their own premises and to deconstruct the representational unity of poet and persona found in the other elegists. On Ovid's "opposition" being so constructed as actually to support Augustus's "position of domination," see O'Gorman (1997: 104–5).

27. 1.2.19, 1.2.29 (Ovid as booty in Cupid's triumph), 1.3.1 (Ovid won by the girl), 1.7.44 (Corinna as booty in Ovid's triumph), 1.8.56, 1.8.92 (*praeda* as gifts extracted from lover), and 1.10.48 (gifts extracted from lovers that lead to the girl's destruction).

28. Booth (1991: 64–65) here notes a reminiscence of Propertius 2.15, the companion piece to 2.16 alluded to in *Amores* 1.2.

29. As Davis (1989: 68) observes, the themes of the triumph and its relation to *servitium amoris* are already present in 1.2's invocation of the *praeda* motif.

30. The irony is, of course, that this is a poem in which Corinna is portrayed as the one who lays down the law (Tracy 1979: 345–46). 2.17.23–24 is followed by 2.19 in which Corinna is said to give the example to Ovid's new mistress of how his interest is to be piqued by coming up with a thousand little obstacles. Thus Ovid's profession of faithful *servitium* is immediately followed by evidence of his faithlessness. Therefore, while 2.17 may appear to reverse the power relations depicted in 2.12, the shift is merely tactical as Ovid claims the power, through his poetry, to make or unmake Corinna's reputation, and even to replace her with another who already claims to be her (2.17.29–30).

31. On asymmetrical power relations as characteristic of Roman sexuality in general, see Parker (1997).

32. See Lee-Stecum (1998: 19): "Writing recently of the relationship between slave and master in the Roman world, K. R. Bradley defended his decision to examine slavery as an institution partly by pointing to the pervasiveness of such a power structure in Roman culture: 'The relationship was just one, as it happens,

of a sequence of asymmetrical relationships in Roman society that tied individuals together.' Roman elegy is a genre which in its most characteristic elements exploits the ideology of such power structures, not least of course the master-slave relationship itself." See also Ste. Croix (1989: 198); Joshel (1992: 64–68, 152); Edwards (1993: 195); Konstan (1997: 140).

33. See the analogous uses in 1.10.17, 42.

34. See McKeown (1989: ad loc.) on Augustus's revival in 17 B.C.E. of the *lex Cincia* against advocates accepting remuneration for their services. This would be but one year after the passage of the *lex Julia* forbidding *lenocinium*.

35. For more on this view of metonymy, see Fineberg (1991: 10, 158), Janan (1994: 117), and Miller (1995).

36. See Wallace-Hadrill (1985: 182), "Indeed, there is a small handful of passages where Ovid makes fun of marriage. Wives are under compulsion to make love to their husbands (*Ars* II 685); they cannot therefore love them (ib. III 585). Quarreling is typical of marriage, but not of true love: *dos est uxoria lites* (ib. II 155). Only lovers can enjoy true love since they know no legal compulsion: 'non legis iussu lectum venistis in unum/ fungitur in vobis munere legis Amor' (ib. II 157–58). Here the reference to Augustus's law is unmistakeable."

37. On Ovid's use of logic to reach perverse conclusions by ostensibly reasonable means, see Lyne (1980: 276) and Connor (1974: 26, 38).

38. The phallus, in Lacanian psychoanalysis, represents the moment of difference that splits the Imaginary unity of mother and child, and so is identified with the function of the father, the institution of Law, and the possibility of regulated Symbolic exchanges (Moi 1985: 99; Ragland-Sullivan 1986: 55, 281–82). It is the marker of difference and so is always absent, but claimed as present by those who seek legitimacy in the wielding of social power, in this case the *vir* but, as we shall see, Ovid as well.

39. O'Gorman (1997: 113) has observed the personfication of the *manus* and its associations with fratricide in *Heroides* 7 (Dido) and 14 (Hypermnestra). In *Amores* 1.7.1–4, the hands are personified as the agents that beat Corinna and consequently should be thrown in chains. See Olstein (1980: 298).

40. Munari (1970: 116n.6) echoes Bornecque almost word for word.

41. On the necessary interimplication of figural and literal language in general, see De Man (1979: 3–19). On the ideological underpinnings implicit in the attempt to distinguish between the literal and figurative use of the vocabulary of warfare and aggression in love elegy, see Kennedy (1993: 54–55) and Lee-Stecum (1998: 15).

42. On Dipsas as the double of the *amator*, see Davis (1999: 449).

43. See McKeown's (1989) very astute commentary on this whole passage.

44. See Frécaut (1972: 55–56) on the predominance of images of touching, handling, and manipulation in this poem.

45. On the homology between beating and sexual penetration in Roman ideology, see Walters (1997: 37–40) and Veyne (1988: 32): "[T]he Roman assimilated the gestures of making love to a fight."

46. Who, of course, in fact is to be completely subjected to the *amator*'s will (Tracy 1979: 348).

47. For more on the use of legal language in this text, see Stroh (1979: 334–35), Lyne (1980: 264–65), and Davis (1989: 46–47; 1993: 65–66, 69). On Ovid's use of legal terminology generally, see Kenney's table (1969: 253).

48. Compare Tracy (1978–79: 58): "In *Amores* 3.4 Ovid affirms the right to interfere in a marital or quasi-marital relationship. Pleasure lies as much in cheating the *vir* as in winning the girls. The seducer becomes the rightful owner and the husband must forfeit his rights (*iura* 44) over his wife. It is characteristic of Ovid ironically to employ legal language (33, 44) while seeking to undermine the legitimate claims of the *maritus*."

49. Showerman (1977), Green (1982), and Melville (1990) all choose to solve the problem by not translating the word.

CHAPTER SEVEN
DISPLACING THE SUBJECT, SAVING THE TEXT

1. Briggs (1983) has a nice survey of this type of textual crux, with some apposite remarks on Freud's speculations regarding the unconscious origins of such errors.

2. See Boucher's apposite warning, "le principe même de la correction qui vise à rendre facile l'exemplum de Properce, est contraire aux principes de la critique puisqu'on cède à ce qui est le défaut de la tradition, la banalisation croissante qui substitue à la 'lectio difficilior,' au texte abrupt une variante commune et aisée" (1980: 316–17).

3. Rothstein (1979: ad loc.) is the first to note the erotic color of this line.

4. Poem 4.11 is interpreted both as the restoration of traditional values, with elegy reclaimed for the dominant ideology (Wyke 1987: 171–73), and as a critique of the Augustan regime (Hallett 1973: 119–20). This kind of polarity of interpretation, while not uncommon in Propertius's earlier work, is particularly evident in book 4, where it is exacerbated by the reader's inability to localize the contradiction within the frame of reference provided by a single speaking subject.

5. In fact, as Boucher notes (1980: 184–85), the image of the thunder not only recalls the recusatio in 2.1.39–40, but is itself directly taken from the *Aitia* lines 19–20.

6. Thus, Alfonsi notes (1979: 68), quite correctly, that in spite of book 4's ostensibly patriotic etiological program and poems such as 4.6 on Actium, book 3 is more politically engaged than book 4, where actuality is displaced by ritual and myth.

7. Jupiter: Richardson (1977: ad loc.); Goold (1990: ad loc.). Tarpeia: Rothstein (1979: ad loc.); Shackleton Bailey (1967: ad loc.); Butler (1926: ad loc.); Marr (1970: 173); Wellesley (1969: 103), with emendation; Camps (1965: ad loc.); Rutledge (1964: 73). Tarpeius: Paganelli (1964: ad loc.); Paley (1853: ad loc.); Lachmann (1973: ad loc.). Butler and Barber (1969: ad loc.) search in vain for a univalent reading, while Janan (2001: 84) sensibly concludes that the ambiguities are irreducible and an inherent part of 4.4's poetic structure.

8. See the discussions in the authorities cited in the preceding note.

9. The psychoanalytic concept of the gaze is crucial here, because unlike its Foucauldian and phenomenological counterparts, it situates the subject in relation

to its object as much as the object in relation to the subject (Lacan 1973: 109–10). The object of our gaze, in fact, frames us as the vanishing point in a reverse tableau of our own desires and social situation (Lacan 1973: 103, 204). It is the breakdown in the dialectical co-constitution of elegiac subject and named object that we observe in book 4 and that produces the consequent textual instability on which all students of it have remarked.

10. For a discussion of both sides of this question and more bibliography, see Janan (2001: 70–71) and the accompanying notes.

11. Boucher (1980: 141–43), however, argues that the thematic differences between books 2–3 and book 4 have been exaggerated. Books 2–3 have substantial political content, and book 4 is hardly devoid of interest in love. I would agree, but note that the major difference between book 4 and the preceding books is not in terms of theme, but in terms of the constitution of the speaking subject and the status of its relation to the object world.

12. Lacan (1966c: 54), "Le programme qui se trace pour nous est dès lors de savoir comment un langage formel détermine le sujet."

13. The one can never be separated from the other. See Voloshinov (1986: 12, emphasis in original), "Signs can arise only on *interindividual territory*. It is territory that cannot be called 'natural' in the direct sense of the word: signs do not arise between any two members of the species *Homo sapiens*. It is essential that the two individuals be *organized socially*, that they compose a group (a social unit); only then can the medium of signs take shape between them. The individual consciousness not only cannot be used to explain anything, but, on the contrary, is itself in need of explanation from the vantage point of the social, ideological medium."

14. On the liminal status of the Vestal's sexuality, see Beard (1980).

15. See Dumézil (1996: 68).

16. Livy 1.39, 42; Ovid, *Fasti* 627–30; Pliny, *Historia Naturalis* 36.204; Nagy (1990: 125n. 47); Rykwert (1976: 154).

17. On the rural worship of Fascinus and his connection with Liber Pater as well as general agricultural fertility, see Grimal (1986: 29–30). On the worship of the ithyphallic Mutunus Tutunus by *matronae*, and the relation between the Vestal's worship of Fascinus and suggestions of divine marriage, see Grimal (1986: 27–28) and Rykwert (1976: 159).

18. Miller and Platter (1999: 450–51); Puhvel (1987: 265–67); Calame (1977: 287); Nagy, (1974: 265–69). See the snake cult at Lanuvium, discussed in Propertius 4.8, where the town's fertility is dependent on the virginity of the young girls offering cakes to snakes in a sacred cave at a festival for Juno Sospita (Aelian, *De Natura Animalium* XI).

19. Plutarch (*Romulus* 17) records a version of the story by the otherwise unknown Greek poet Simylus that also portrays Tarpeia's primary motivation for betraying the city as love (Brenk 1979: 166). Simylus, however, has her betray the city to the Gaul Brennus. We cannot say whether Simylus wrote before or after Propertius. Hubbard points (1974: 120–21) out that the story about the Sabines' golden bracelets, found in Livy, makes more sense in the case of the Gauls than primitive Sabines. She notes that a Gallic chief named Brennus invaded Greece in the third century.

20. A reference to the Palladium kept by the Vestals.

21. Vergil uses Tarpeia as the name of one of the Amazons accompanying Camilla (*Aeneid* 11.655; Warden 1978: 189).

22. In 12 B.C.E., the city of Praeneste began a series of annual sacrifices to Vesta in honor of Augustus's accession to the post of Pontifex Maximus (Grimal 1952: 196).

23. See Janan (2001: 74); Miller and Platter (1999: 451); Rothwell (1996: 839–41); O'Neill (1995: 57); King (1990: 228); La Penna (1977: 86); Burch (1966: 420–21). It is surely no accident that the opening of 4.4 resembles that of Tibullus 2.5, which also concludes with a celebration of the Parilia (Rothwell 1996: 830).

24. Brenk (1979: 174) first noted the poem's explicit dramatization of the connection between "water and feminine passion." Yet, already in 1964 Rutledge had established the relation between water and "women who suffered in their erotic desire" (70) in the poem's mythological exempla.

25. As Newman (1997: 366) notes there is an implicit pun between the Parilia and Tarpeia's own wish to give birth to Tatius's royal issue (*pariam*, line 55). The critics that seek to emend the text here on the grounds that a Vestal Virgin would never envision herself giving birth miss the point. See, however, Goold (1990), Hanslik (1979), Richardson (1977), Shackleton Bailey (1967), Paganelli (1964), Barber (1953), and Enk (1978). Perrone (1991b: 288) objects to *pariam* on the ground that an elegiac puella never envisions maternity. While he is right to read overtones from Propertius's earlier work into this later poem and to bring up the mixed signals sent by Propertius's strange mélange of genres, such reasoning is hardly definitive. Rothstein (1979: ad loc.) sensibly notes that *pariam* is the corollary of the envisaged royal marriage.

26. For the material discussed in this paragraph, see Edwards (1996: 49–50); Wyke (1989: 39–40); Wallace-Hadrill (1985: 183); Littlewood (1983: 2138); Lefkowitz (1981: 18); Hallett (1973: 104–5); Riposati (1945: 30).

27. For another example of the conflation of subject and object, see lines 33–34, "o utinam ad vestros sedeam captiva Penatis, / dum captiva mei conspicer ora Tati!" The problem lies with the repetition of the word *captiva*. In line 31, it must agree grammatically with the subject of "sedeam," but in line 32 it may agree either with the subject of "conspicer," Tarpeia, or with *ora*, so that we may translate it either "would that I, a captive, might see the face of my Tatius," or "would that I might see the captive face of my Tatius," this latter possibility envisioning a reciprocal love match in which each would be the captive of the other. In the first possibility, the anaphora is peculiarly unproductive, and thus the grammatical tension that attracts *captiva* to *ora* is not obviated. In the second possibility, the repetition of the adjective exhibiting the same morphology, but agreeing with two different nouns is extraordinarily harsh, since the reader's natural tendency is to interpret the same word in the same way.

The second *ora* is a conjecture by Gronovius for the otiose *esse* of the manuscripts but is widely adopted (Günther 1997: 106; Perrone 1991a; Goold 1990; Barber 1953; Butler and Barber 1969; Butler 1912; Enk 1978: ad loc.; Paley 1853; Lachmann 1973). Otherwise *conspicer* must be taken as a rare true passive rather than a deponent (Richardson 1977: ad loc.; Fedeli 1994: ad loc.; Camps 1965: ad loc.; Rothstein 1979: ad loc.), an unprecedented usage in poetry and one of which there are only two disputed examples in prose before Apuleius (Günther 1997: 106; Enk 1978: ad loc.). Likewise, *esse* itself adds nothing to the passage and if there is one agreed upon characteristic of Propertian style, it is its concentration (Perrone 1991a; Marr 1970: 171; Butler and Barber 1969: ad loc.).

28. Enk (1978) moves 3–6 after 12. Perrone (1989: 56) notes that the repetition has ample precedent in Propertius.

29. See also Wellesley (1969: 96); Rothstein (1979: ad loc.).

30. Perrone (1989: 52–54) tries to solve the problem by having Tatius enclose the spring only from two sides, leaving both ends open. This would allow Tatius's horse to drink from one end (line 13) and Tarpeia to dip from the other (line 15). But what purpose such an open palisade would serve is anyone's guess, since, as he notes, the goal of such a fortification would be to deny the enemy access. The answer that only Tarpeia knew the path is neither textually founded nor particularly convincing. Rothstein (1979: 2:245) makes a similar argument.

31. Kraffert (1883: 147) moves the couplet after 92. Enk (1978) and Goold (1990) concur. Hanslik (1979) following Wellesley (1969: 96–97) moves it to after 2. Shackleton Bailey (1967), Paganelli (1964), Camps (1965), Fedeli (1994), and Butler and Barber (1969) leave it in place, while Richardson (1977) prints it in brackets, questions its authenticity, and proposes moving it to after 44. Lachmann (1973) notes that the problem is the couplet itself and not the placement. He proposes emending *una* to *urna* and *mors* to *sors*.

Rothstein (1979: ad loc.) and Beltrami (1989: 269–70) note that only here do we learn that Tarpeia is a Vestal. The image of the urn pressing down on her head in line 16, a reference to the ritual cleansing of the shrine, is a bad omen that both foretells her fall and juxtaposes water and fire. They argue that all the proposed transpositions or emendations would destroy this coherent pattern.

32. On the collective ego of archaic lyric, see Miller (1994: chap. 5).

33. Cameron (1995: 478–79); Cairns (1983b: 115); Boucher (1980: 198–99, 204); Sweet (1972: 171); Pillinger (1969: 193–94, 196–98); Rothstein (1979, 2.280–81).

34. The irony that Callimachus is claimed as the inspiration of both poems should not be missed. Callimachus's appropriation for Roman elegy is tactical. Different aspects of this complex poet are appropriated for different ideological and poetic purposes.

35. Anna (1986: 69); Stahl (1985: 252–53, 259); Connor (1978: 1–2); La Penna (1977: 89); Grimal (1952: 192–93, 446).

36. Gurval (1995: 250, 267–68, 272–74); Sullivan (1984: 31); Nethercut (1983: 1841); Connor (1978: 9); Sullivan (1976: 65); Johnson (1973).

37. Alfonsi's (1979: 79) claim that this is one of the poet's most solemn poems is hard to understand, since it does not even allow for Callimachean wit. See also Boucher (1980: 158–59).

38. The dispute between Romulus and Remus was the first example of that fratricidal strife, the culmination of which was Actium. It was this strife over the wall that led to Romulus slaying Remus (Livy 1.6–7).

39. To his credit, Ralph Johnson had recognized the need for a larger structural understanding that could encompass both the pro- and anti-Augustan positions in 1973. He said that he could not yet articulate such a structure and that for

reasons of aesthetic and political preference, he thus chose the interpretation that gave the poem the greatest artistic integrity and put Propertius on the side of the angels (174–77).

CHAPTER EIGHT
BETWEEN THE TWO DEATHS: TECHNOLOGIES OF THE SELF IN OVID'S EXILIC POETRY

1. On Horace's *Epistles*, see Habinek (1998: 156–57); Evans (1983: 14); Nagle (1980: 39); Barsby (1978: 44). On Cicero's letters from exile, see Claassen (1999: 107); Edwards (1996: 112); Green (1994: xlvii); Chomarat (1988: 18).

2. On the distinction between genres, subgenres, and forms, Miller (1994: chap. 3).

3. Claassen (1999: 13, 71, 110–11); Edwards (1996: 118, 121–22); Stapleton (1996: 5–6); Williams (1994: 30–31, 69–70, 124); Videau-Delibes (1991: 265, 320–21); Colakis (1987: 210); Labate (1987: 93–94, 129); Bonjour (1985); Barsby (1978: 44–45).

4. O'Gorman (1997: 121–22); Labate (1987: 93–94).

5. Claassen (1990a: 105; 1999: 130, 214); Habinek (1998: 135); Labate (1987: 93–94).

6. Claassen (1999: 191, 194–96); Edwards (1996: 117); Green (1994: 236) Williams (1994: 10–11); Videau-Delibes (1991: 112–13, 166–67); Bews (1984: 56); Barsby (1978: 45). Ross (1975: 93–94) notes that Vergil in the *Georgics* uses unending cold as a metaphor for poetic sterility. Such sterility is also a topos of the exilic poems (cf. *Tristia* 5.12 and *Ex Ponto* 4.2; Williams 1994: 57, 74), in spite of the fact that Ovid's produced on average a book a year during his time there (Claassen 1989: 254).

7. Although a Romanian friend, Christian Moraru, who did his military service in Dobrudja, assures me that his grandparents could remember winters when sleighs were driven on the ice, it never happened during his lifetime.

8. This is the extreme position adopted by Fitton Brown (1985) who argues that Ovid's exile was a poetic fiction. He never gives a motive for why such a charade would be maintained or tolerated for nine years. He is convincingly refuted by Little (1990).

9. For more examples of this kind of paradoxical juxtaposition, see Viarre (1988: 154–53).

10. "Dans l'imaginaire des Tristes, Rome représente le lieu de l'unité perdue et passionément souhaitée que célèbre l'élégie 4,2" (Videau-Delibes 1988: 29). See also, "Les Tristes ne contiennent pas seulement le souvenir d'une union idyllique du héros avec ses proches, ni le constat d'une fêlure irrémédiable révélant l'altérité mais une tension vers la restauration de l'unité passée" (Videau-Delibes 1991: 201).

11. "It is important to remember that the *Tristia* do not compose a very coherent image of the emperor, one moment positive, the next negative. It is not a question of trying to uncover Ovid's political intentions, or of divining how the poetry reflects the intentions of the actual exile who was their author, but of searching to understand how this image of Augustus was inscribed within the

framework of the poetics of the *Tristia* and how it functioned there as a key stone."

12. As illustrated in the careers of both Cicero and his archnemesis, Clodius.

13. See also *Tristia* 4.1.3–14 where the poet compares his fate as an *exul* to that of a variety of servile occupations. The point there is that all turn to song as a source of relief from their pain.

14. See Tacitus, *Annales* 1.2, on Augustus's conversion of the nobility to a form of *servitium* through patronage and honors, as well as Fear (2000: 236); Joshel (1992: 151); and Ste. Croix (1981: 36).

15. "Le signifiant, vous commencez peut-être à l'entendre, matérialise l'instance de mort. Mais si c'est d'abord sur la matérialité du signifiant que nous avons insisté, cette matérialité est *singulière* en bien des points dont le premier est de ne point supporter la partition" (Lacan 1966c: 33). See also Guyomard (1992: 53–54).

16. As Judith Hallett points out to me, there is also a sexual pun in *pro parte virili. Gaudia*, moreover, is a euphemism for orgasm.

17. On the relation between these two passages, see Luck (1977: ad loc.).

18. For the case that this is a directly comic poem, see Claassen (1999: 237).

19. *Annales* 1.72.3.

20. Citing Seneca, *Letters to Lucilius* 82.5. All translations of Foucault in this section are my own.

21. The importance of the *hupomnēmata* as a genre of philosophic writing that was designed to serve as a spiritual exercise, and hence a technology of the self, was first discussed by Pierre Hadot in reference to Marcus Aurelius's *Meditations* (1992: 40–49; Davidson 1995: 10–11).

22. On the convergence of the various philosophical schools of the imperial period in their focus on philosophy as an *askesis*, or technology of the self, see Davidson (1995: 30–31) and Hadot (1987: 206; 1995: 59). Hadot 1995 is ostensibly a revised English translation of Hadot 1987. The revisions, however, are in some cases quite extensive and the reader is advised to consult both texts.

23. On Hadot's criticism of Foucault's reading of the Stoics as too narrowly focused, see Davidson (1995: 24–25) and Hadot (1995: 206–13; 1987: 229–33).

24. Citing *Letters*, 1.9, 1.10, 4.9, and 7.5.

25. The paradox of Ovid's relationship or nonrelationship to philosophy is nicely captured in his excusing the poverty of his poetic production in exile by alleging that Socrates himself would have written nothing if he had to endure the same conditions (*Tristia* 5.12.11–16). Of course, Socrates did write nothing, and Ovid in exile was very productive.

26. For the generality of this trope in ancient philosophy, see Claassen (1999: 20); Labate (1987: 94); Luck (1977: 1–2).

27. See Green (1994: 239); Videau-Delibes (1991: 406); Degl' Innocenti Pierini (1990: 150); Labate (1987: 120–21); Luck (1977: 18).

28. Inasmuch as *praelustria* is a hapax (*TLL*), each Roman reader would have been thrown back upon his own devices to construe its derivation.

29. Compare also *Tristia* 5.12.41–42, "non adeo est bene nunc ut sit mihi gloria curae: / si liceat, nulli cognitus esse velim" (Now is not the time for glory to

be a concern for me, if it were allowed, I would wish to be known by no one): a wish realizable only in social death.

30. Thus in *Ex Ponto* 2.7.79–80 Ovid claims to hang on to hope because that alone keeps alive the will to live, but in 3.7.21–24 the poet accepts the Stoic renunciation of the delusions of hope, "spem iuvat amplecti, quae non iuvat inrita semper: / et, fieri cupias siqua, futura putes. / proximus huic gradus est bene desperare salutem, / seque semel vera scire perisse fide" (it is useful to embrace hope, what is not useful is always to embrace its disappointments: and if you desire something to happen you will think that it will. The very next step is to despair of salvation and to know oneself to have perished from one's own true faith). This juxtaposition of two poems occupying analogous points in respective books is clearly intentional. As a number of scholars have shown, *Epistulae ex Ponto* 1–3 constitute a carefully arranged collection of three books, in spite of Ovid's assertions to the contrary, designed to serve as a replacement and make amends for the *Ars Amatoria* (Claassen 1999: 120; Labate 1987: 93; Evans 1983: 146–47).

31. Claassen (1999: 215; 1989: 258–59); Habinek (1998: 156–57); Edwards (1996: 24–25); Williams (1994: 54); Evans (1983: 14); Nagle (1980: 36, 39, 125–26, 128n.25); Helzle (1988: 74); Avery (1958: 247).

32. Thanks to my colleague Jan Opsomer for alerting me to this concept and the associated bibliography.

33. For a complete list of the numerous passages in which this notion is found, see Claassen (1999: 309n.37).

34. Green (1994: 236) notes the intertext of Tibullus 1.3. For the same poem's echoes of the *Georgics* and the *Aeneid*, see Bews (1984: 55). It is a veritable tapestry of allusions.

35. Cf. 3.4.51–52, "ulterius nihil est nisi non habitabile frigus. / heu quam vicina est ultima terra mihi!" (Beyond this frozen waste there nothing but the uninhabitable/ o how close is my land to the end of the world!).

36. See Moi (1985: 101): "If we accept that the end of desire is the logical consequence of satisfaction (if we are satisfied, we are in a position where we desire no more), we can see why Freud in *Beyond the Pleasure Principle,* posits death as the ultimate object of desire—as Nirvana or the recapturing of the lost unity, the final healing of the split subject."

37. "Caesar in hoc potuit iuris habere nihil" (*Tristia* 3.7.48). Luck (1977: ad loc.) notes the Epicurean character of this whole passage.

38. On the independence of the *animus* from contingent circumstances and its ability to restore the body's strength, see *Ex Ponto* 2.7.75–76.

39. On this same theme, see also *Tristia* 4.2.57–64, *Ex Ponto* 3.5.48–56, Claassen (1990a: 109) and Bonjour (1985: 21).

40. On the close relations between Lacan's ethics as embodied in his reading of the *Antigone* and Foucault's, founded on his understanding of imperial philosophies of self-construction, see Miller (1999).

41. Nietzsche citing Diogenes Laertius, *Vitae Philosophorum* 7.2, quoted by Kittler 1999: 8 (emphasis in original).

42. On Ovid as Augustus's ironic critic, see Claassen (1989: 265; 1999: 150, 180); Williams (1994: 161–62, 204–5); Nugent (1990: 247–49); Barsby (1978: 43); Holleman (1969: 42–54). On Ovid as flatterer, see Habinek (1998: 166);

Evans (1983: 10–12); Barsby (1978: 42–43). On the inherently contradictory position he occupied that produces both effects, see Cutolo (1995: 23); Videau-Delibes (1989: 21; 1991: 425–29, 509).

43. Stahl's statement relative to the conditions that gave rise to Propertius book 4, quoted as an epigraph to this section, shows an inkling of the convergence of these ostensibly opposing positions. What he fails to recognize is that the "rhetoric of adulation" can never be anything but "excessive." Likewise, Williams (1994: 160) observes that in *Tristia* 2 "a eulogistic intent can sometimes hardly be distinguished from a satirical one," without reflecting on the structure that makes that conflation possible.

44. My reading of irony owes much to De Man (1983; 1979).

45. See our earlier discussion of *Ex Ponto* 1.2.28.

46. Fantham (1996: 122) notes that no other poetry from this period survives. Augustus clearly had his reasons to want to get this message out. Claassen's assumption that the poems only circulated privately strains credulity. Likewise her assertion that exile was an attempt to reduce Ovid's hold on the reading public is inexplicable (1999: 210). We know full well that at the time Augustus could have had Ovid's books burned or the man killed. See Fantham (1996: 124); Bartsch (1994: 66); White (1993: 150–52); Syme (1978: 6, 212–13, 220) and their sources.

47. And who would claim irony as a Calvinist virtue?

48. Compare Bartsch (1994: 113) on Tacitus's treatement of Maternus at *Dialogus* 27.3.

49. Thus even as sensitive a reader of the exilic poetry as Claassen (1988) goes to great lengths to find a model that both recognizes the aporias of the exilic poetry and nevertheless redeems a notion of sincerity for the Ovidian persona.

50. See *Tristia* 1.3.73, "Dividor" (I am torn apart), and Videau-Delibes (1988: 27).

51. On the impossibility of proving either the irony or the sincerity of imperial panegyric, see Bartsch (1994: 23, 68–69, 161). What I am arguing is that not only were these two possibilities empirically indistinguishable, but they are structurally identical. The confusion is necessary and functional.

52. On Ovid having access to Augustus's *Commentarii de sua vita*, an earlier and more extensive version of the *Res Gestae*, see Claassen (1999: 220–22).

53. On Augustus's own proclivities toward seduction, see Martial 11.20 and Suetonius.

54. There is debate about the nature of that representation. I incline toward Traill's happy suggestion that the reference is to a fire burning before the temple (Traill 1992: 506).

55. Cf. Propertius 4.6.59–60.

56. This latter day conflation of the *Epistulae ex Ponto* and the *Heroides* represents an interesting problem for Ovidian reception studies.

57. "Ovid, so classical often from the purely ornamental point of view, practices excess with a talent rare among the Latins, especially before the Neronian period. His aesthetic often declares itself to be baroque, as is well known, from the place it makes for ruptures, for irregular movements, etc."

58. On the distinction between utopia, heterotopia, and atopia, see Foucault (1966: 9–10).

59. "For me, an act is simply something that changes the very horizon in which it takes place, and I claim that the present situation closes the space for such acts" (Žižek in Hanlon 2001: 11).

BIBLIOGRAPHY

Adams, J. N. 1982. *The Latin Sexual Vocabulary.* Baltimore: Johns Hopkins University Press.

Adorno, Theodor. 1983. *Negative Dialectics.* Trans. E. B. Ashton. New York: Continuum.

Albrecht, Michael von. 1983. "Properzio poeta augusto." In *Colloquium propertianum (tertium): Atti,* ed. Salvatore Vivona, 59–75. Assisi: Academia del Subasio.

———. 1997. *A History of Roman Literature from Livius Andronicus to Boethius with Special Regard to Its Influence on World Literature.* Vol. 1. Rev. Gareth Schmeling and Michael von Albrecht. Trans. Michael von Albrecht and Gareth Schmeling with the assistance of Frances and Kevin Newman. Leiden: Brill.

Alfonsi, Luigi. 1943. "L'Elegia di Gallo." *Rivista di filologia e di istruzione classica* 21: 46–56.

———. 1979. *L'Elegia di Properzio.* New York: Garland. Originally published 1945.

Althusser, Louis. 1971a. *Lire le Capital.* Vol. 1. Paris: Maspero.

———. 1971b. "Ideology and Ideological State Apparatuses (Notes towards an Investigation) (*January–April 1969*). In *Lenin and Philosophy and Other Essays by Louis Althusser,* 127–86. Trans. Ben Brewster. New York: Monthly Review Press.

———. 1996a. *Writings on Psychoanalysis: Freud and Lacan.* Ed. Olivier Corpet and François Matheron. Trans. Jeffrey Mehlman. New York: Columbia University Press.

———. 1996b. "Letters to D." In Althusser 1996a: 33–77.

———. 1996c. "Freud and Lacan." In Althusser 1996a, 7–32.

Anderson, Perry. 1992. "The Ends of History." In *A Zone of Engagement,* 279–375. London: Verso.

Anderson, R. D., P. J. Parsons, and R.G.M. Nisbet. 1979. "Elegies by Gallus from Qasr Ibrîm." *Journal of Roman Studies* 69: 125–55.

André, Jacques. 1965. *Albius Tibullus: Elegiarum Liber Primus.* Paris: Presses Universitaires de France.

Anna, Giovanni d'. 1983. "Il Rapporto di Properzio con Virgilio: Una sottile polemica col classicismo augusteo." In *Colloquium propertianum (tertium): Atti,* ed. Salvatore Vivana, 45–57. Assisi: Academia Properziana del Subasio.

———. 1986. "Il Quarto libro delle elegie di Properzio." *Cultura e scuola* 25: 68–74.

Arkins, Brian. 1989. "Language in Propertius 4.6." *Philologus* 133: 246–51.

———. 1990. "The Anxiety of Influence: Ovid's Amores as *kenōsis.*" *Latomus* 49: 826–23.

Auerbach, Erich. 1965. *Literary Language and Its Public in Latin Antiquity and in the Middle Ages.* Trans. Ralph Manheim. Bollingen Series. New York: Pantheon.

Avery, William T. 1958. "Iupiter Tonans in Horace and Ovid." *Classical Philology* 52: 247–48.

Badian, Ernst. 1985. "A Phantom Marriage Law." *Philologus* 129: 82–98.

Bakhtin, M. M. 1968. *Rabelais and His World.* Trans. Hélène Iswolsky. Cambridge, Mass.: MIT Press.

———. 1981a. "From the Prehistory of Novelistic Discourse." In *The Dialogic Imagination,* ed. Michael Holquist, 41–83. Trans. Caryl Emerson and Michael Holquist. Austin: University of Texas Press.

———. 1981b. "Forms of Time and of Chronotope in the Novel: Notes toward a Historical Poetics." In *The Dialogic Imagination,* ed. Michael Holquist, 84–258. Trans. Caryl Emerson and Michael Holquist. Austin: University of Texas Press.

———. 1984. *Problems of Dostoevsky's Poetics.* Ed. and trans. Caryl Emerson. Minneapolis: University of Minnesota Press.

———. 1986. *Speech Genres and Other Late Essays.* Ed. C. Emerson and M. Holquist. Trans. V. W. McGee. Austin: University of Texas Press.

Bakhtin, M.M., P. M. Medvedev. 1985. *The Formal Method in Literary Scholarship: A Critical Introduction to Sociological Poetics.* Trans. Albert J. Wehrle. Cambridge, Mass.: Harvard University Press.

Ball, Robert J. 1979. "Tibullus's Structural Strategy: The External Ordering." *Prudentia* 11: 1–6.

———. 1983. *Tibullus the Elegist: A Critical Survey. Hypomnemata* 77. Göttingen: Vandenhoeck & Ruprecht.

Bannet, Eve Tavor. 1989. *Structuralism and the Logic of Dissent: Barthes, Derrida, Foucault, Lacan.* Urbana: University of Illinois Press.

Barber, E. A. 1953. *Sexti Properti Carmina.* Oxford: Oxford University Press.

Barsby, John. 1978. *Ovid.* Greece & Rome: New Surveys in the Classics, no. 12. Oxford: Clarendon Press.

——— ed. and trans. 1979. *Ovid: Amores I.* Bristol: Bristol Classical Press.

Barton, Carlin A. 1993. *"The Sorrows of the Ancient Romans: The Gladiator and the Monster.* Princeton University Press.

Bartsch, Shadi. 1994. *Actors in the Audience: Theatricality and Doublespeak from Nero to Hadrian.* Cambridge, Mass.: Harvard University Press.

Barthes, Roland. 1967. *Elements of Semiology.* Trans. Annette Lavers and Colin Smith. New York: Hill and Wang.

Bataille, Georges. 1957. *L'érotisme.* Paris: Minuit.

Bauer, Dale M., and S. Jaret McKinstry, eds. 1991. *Feminism, Bakhtin and the Dialogic.* Albany: SUNY Press.

Beard, Mary. 1980. "The Sexual Status of the Vestal Virgins." *Journal of Roman Studies* 70 (1980): 12–27.

Bedient, Calvin. 1986. *"He Do the Police in Different Voices":* The Wasteland *and Its Protagonist.* Chicago: University of Chicago Press.

Beer, Gillian. 1993. "Wave Theory and the Rise of Literary Modernism." In Levine 1993a: 193–213.

Bell, Shannon. 1998. "Aphrodite of the Marketplace: Fetishism, Value, and [Sexual] Pragmatism." *Rethinking MARXISM* 10.4: 134–40.

Beltrami, Lucia. 1989. "Properzio 4,4: La colpa della vestale." In *Tredici secoli di elegia latina: Atti del Convegno Internazionale: Assisi, 22–24 aprile 1988*, ed. Giuseppe Catanzaro and Francesco Santucci, 267–72. Assisi: Accademia Properziana de Subasio.

Benediktson, D. Thomas. 1989. *Propertius: Modernist Poet of Antiquity*. Carbondale: Southern Illinois University Press.

Benjamin, Anna S. 1965. "A Note on Propertius 1.10. *O iucunda quies*." *Classical Philology* 60: 178.

Benstock, Sheri. 1991. *Textualizing the Feminine: On the Limits of Genre*. Norman: University of Oklahoma Press.

Besnier, R. 1979. "Properce (Elégies II, VII et VIIa) et le premier échec de la législation démographique d'Auguste." *Revue historique droit français et étranger* 57: 191–203.

Bews, Janet P. 1984. "The Metamorphosis of Vergil in the *Tristia* of Ovid." *Bulletin of the Institute of Classical Studies* 31: 51–60.

Black, Joel. 1991. *The Aesthetics of Murder*. Baltimore: Johns Hopkins University Press.

Bloch, Ernst. 1977. "Nonsynchronism and the Obligation to Its Dialectics." *New German Critique* 11: 22–38.

Bonjour, Madelleine. 1985. "*Roma Interdicta*: Transgression de l'interdit dans les *Tristes* et les *Pontiques* d'Ovide." In *Journées Ovidiennes de Parménie: Actes du Colloque sur Ovide (24–26 juin 1983)*, ed. Jean-Marc Frécaut et Danielle Porte, 9–23. Collection Latomus 189. Brussels: Latomus.

Booth, Joan. 1991. *Ovid: The Second Book of the* Amores. Warminster: Aris & Philips.

Bornecque, Henri, ed. and trans. 1961. *Ovide: Les amours*. Paris: Budé.

Boucher, Jean-Paul. 1980. *Etudes sur Properce: Problèmes d'inspiration et d'art*. 2nd ed. Paris: Boccard.

Bowditch, Phebe Lowell. 2001. *Horace and the Gift Economy of Patronage*. Berkeley: University of California Press.

Boyd, Barbara Weiden. 1984a. "*Parva seges satis est*: The Landscape of Tibullan Elegy in 1.1 and 1.10." *Transactions of the American Philological Association* 114: 273–80.

———. 1984b. "Tarpeia's Tomb: A Note on Propertius 4.4." *American Journal of Philology* 105: 85–86.

———. 1997. *Ovid's Literary Loves: Influence and Innovation in the* Amores. Ann Arbor: University of Michigan Press.

Boyne, Roy. 1990. *Foucault and Derrida: The Other Side of Reason*. London: Unwin Hyman.

Bramble, J. C. 1974. *Persius and the Programmatic Satire: A Study in Form and Imagery*. Cambridge: Cambridge University Press.

Braund, Susanna Morton. 1997. "Personal Plurals." In *Compromising Traditions: The Personal Voice in Classical Scholarship*, ed. Judith P. Hallett and Thomas Van Nortwick, 38–53. New York: Routledge.

Brenk, F. E. 1979. "Tarpeia among the Celts: Watery Romance from Simylos to Propertius." In *Studies in Latin Literature and Roman History*, vol. 1., ed. Carl Deroux, 166–74. Brussels: Collection Latomus.

Briggs, Ward W., Jr. 1983. "Housman and Polar Errors." *American Journal of Philology* 104: 268–77.

Bright, David F. 1976. "*Confectum Carmine Munus*: Catullus 68." *Illinois Classical Studies* 1: 86–112.

———. 1978. *Haec mini Fingebam: Tibullus and His World*. Leiden: E. J. Brill.

Brunt, P. A. 1971a. *Social Conflicts in the Roman Republic*. New York: Norton.

———. 1971b. *Italian Manpower: 225 B.C.–A.D. 14*. Oxford: Clarendon Press.

Buchan, Mark. 1995. "*Ovidius Imperamator*: Beginnings and Endings of Love Poems and Empire in the *Amores*." *Arethusa* 28 (1995): 53–85.

Burch, Erich. 1966. "Zur Komposition des vierten Buches des Properz." *Wiener Studien* 79: 405–27.

Butler, H. E., ed. and trans. 1912. *Propertius*. Cambridge, Mass.: Harvard University Press.

Butler, H. E., and E. A. Barber. 1969. *The Elegies of Propertius*. Hildesheim: Olms. Originally published 1933.

Butler, Judith. 1990. *Gender Trouble: Feminism and the Subversion of Identities*. New York: Routledge.

———. 1999. *Subjects of Desire: Hegelian Reflections in Twentieth-Century France*. 2nd ed. New York: Columbia University Press.

Cairns, Francis. 1979a. *Tibullus: A Hellenistic Poet at Rome*. Cambridge: Cambridge University Press.

———. 1979b. "Propertius on Augustus' Marriage Law (II,7)." *Grazer Beiträge* 8: 185–204.

———. 1983a. "Propertius 1,4 and 1,5 and the 'Gallus' of the Monobiblos." *Papers of the Liverpool Latin Seminar* 4: 61–102.

———. 1983b. "L'Elegia IV, 6 di Properzio: Manierismo Ellenistico e Classicismo Augusteo." In *Colloqium propertianum (tertium): Atti*, ed. Salvatore Vivona, 97–115. Assisi: Academia Properziana del Subasio.

———. 1984. "Propertius and the Battle of Actium (4.6)." In *Poetry and Politics in the Age of Augustus*, ed. Tony Woodman and David West, 129–68. Cambridge: Cambridge University Press.

Calame, Claude. 1977. *Les choeurs de jeunes filles en Grèce archaïque*, vol. 1. Rome: Edizioni dell' Ateneo e Bizzarri.

Cameron, Alan. 1995. *Callimachus and His Critics*. Princeton: Princeton University Press.

Camps, W. A. 1961. *Propertius: Elegies Book I*. Cambridge: Cambridge University Press.

———. 1965. *Propertius: Elegies Book IV*. Cambridge: Cambridge University Press.

———. 1966. *Propertius: Elegies Book III*. Cambridge: Cambridge University Press.

———. 1967. *Propertius: Elegies Book II*. Cambridge: Cambridge University Press.

Carnes, Jeffrey S. 1998. "This Myth Which Is Not One: Construction of Discourse in Plato's *Symposium*." In *Rethinking Sexuality: Foucault and Classical Antiquity*, ed. David H. J. Larmour, Paul Allen Miller, and Charles Platter, 104–21. Princeton: Princeton University Press.

Chomarat, J. 1988. "Les Tristes d'Ovide." *Vita Latina* 109 March: 13–24.

Citti, Francesco. 2000. *Studi Oraziani: Tematica e Intertesualità*. Bologna: Pàtron Editore.

Claassen, Jo-Marie. 1988. "Ovid's Poems from Exile: The Creation of a Myth and the Triumph of Poetry." *Antike und Abendland* 34: 158–69.

———. 1989. "Carmen and Poetics: Poetry as Enemy and Friend." In *Studies in Latin Literature and Roman History*, vol. 5, ed. Carl Deroux, 252–66. Brussels: Collection Latomus.

———. 1990a. "Ovid's Wavering Identity: Personfication and Depersonalization in the Exilic Poems." *Latomus* 49 (1990): 102–16.

———. 1990b. "Ovid's Poetic Pontus." In *Papers of the Leeds International Latin Seminar: Sixth Volume 1990*, ed. Francis Cairns, 65–94. Leeds.

———. 1999. *Displaced Persons: The Literature of Exile from Cicero to Boethius*. Madison: University of Wisconsin Press.

Clément, Cathérine B. 1975. "La coupable." In *La jeune née*, 8–113. Paris: Union Générale d'Edition.

Cohen, Ralph. 1986a. "Reply to Dominick La Capra and Richard Harvey Brown." *New Literary History* 17: 229–32.

———. 1986b. "History and Genre." *New Literary History* 17: 203–18.

Colakis, Marianthe. 1987. "Ovid as *Praeceptor Amoris* in *Epistulae ex Ponto* 3.1." *Classical Journal* 82: 210–15.

Commager, Steele. 1974. *A Prolegomenon to Propertius*. Cincinnati: University of Cincinnati Press.

Connolly, Joy. 2000. "Asymptotes of Pleasure: The Nature of Roman Erotic Elegy." *Arethusa* 33: 71–90.

Connor, P. J. 1974. "His Dupes and Accomplices: A Study of Ovid the Illusionist in the *Amores*." *Ramus* 3: 18–40.

———. 1978. "The Actian Miracle: Propertius 4.6." *Ramus* 7: 1–11.

Conte, Gian Biagio. 1994. *Latin Literature: A History*. Trans. Joseph B. Solodow. Rev. Don Fowler and Glenn W. Most. Baltimore: Johns Hopkins University Press.

Copjec, Joan. 1994. *Read My Desire: Lacan against the Historicists*. Cambridge, Mass.: MIT Press.

Copley, Frank O. 1956. *"Exclusus Amator": A Study in Latin Love Poetry*. Philological Monographs Published by the American Philological Association, 17. Ed. Francis R. Walton. Madison, Wis.: American Philological Association.

Cornish, F. W., ed. and trans. 1962. *The Poems of Gaius Valerius Catullus. Catullus, Tibullus and Pervigilium Veneris*. Loeb Classical Library. Cambridge, Mass.: Harvard University Press.

Courtney, Edward. 1968. "The Structure of Propertius Book I and Some Textual Consequences." *Phoenix* 22: 250–58.

———. 1985. "Three Poems of Catullus." *Bulletin of the Institute for Classical Studies* 32: 85–100.

Courtney, Edward. 1993. *The Fragmentary Latin Poets*. Oxford: Clarendon Press.

Cremona, Virginio. 1987. "Emulazione e polemica: Properzio III, 1–5: Orazio III, 1–6." *Euphrosyne* 15: 247–56.

Crowther, N. B. 1983. "C. Cornelius Gallus: His Importance in the Development of Roman Poetry." In *Aufstieg und Niedergang der Römischen Welt*, II, 30.3, ed. Hildegard Temporini and Wolfgang Haase, 1622–48. Berlin: Walter de Gruyter.

Cutolo, Paolo. 1995. *Politica, poetica, poesia nel II libro dei "Tristia."* Catania: Centro di Studi Sull'Antico Cristianesimo Università di Catania.

Daube, David. 1966. "No Kissing, or Else . . ." In *The Classical Tradition: Literary and Historical Studies in Honor of Harry Caplan*, ed. Luitpold Wallach, 222–31. Ithaca, N.Y.: Cornell University Press.

Davidson, Arnold. 1994. "Ethics as Ascetics, Foucault, the History of Ethics, and Ancient Thought." In *The Cambridge Companion to Foucault*, ed. Gary Gutting, 115–40. Cambridge: Cambridge University Press.

———. 1995. "Introduction: Pierre Hadot and the Spiritual Phenomenon of Ancient Philosophy." In Hadot 1995: 1–45.

Davis, John T. 1971. "Propertius 1.21–22." *Classical Journal* 66: 209–13.

———. 1989. *Fictus Adulter: Poet as Actor in the* Amores. Amsterdam: J. C. Gieben.

———. 1993. "Thou Shalt Not Cuddle: *Amores* 1.4 and the Law." *Syllecta Classica* 4: 64–69.

Davis, P. J. 1999. "Ovid's *Amores*: A Political Reading." *Classical Philology* 94: 431–49.

Dean-Jones, Lesley. 1993. "The Politics of Pleasure: Female Sexual Appetite in the Hippocratic Corpus." *Helios* 19: 72–91.

Degl'Innocenti Pierini, Rita. 1990. *Tra Ovidio e Seneca*. Bologna: Pàtron.

Delpeyroux, Marie-Françoise. 1993. "Ovide: Autobiographie et apologie dans les oeuvres de l'exil." In *L'invention de l'autobiographie d'Hésiode à Saint Augustin: Actes du deuxième colloque de l'Equipe de Recherche sur l'Hellénisme Post-Classique (Paris, Ecole Normale Supérieure, 14–16 juin 1990)*, ed. Marie-Françoise Baslez, Philippe Hoffman, and Laurence Perot, 1810–87. Paris: Presses de l'Ecole Normale Supérieure.

De Man, Paul. 1979. *Allegories of Reading: Figural Language in Rousseau, Nietzsche, Rilke, and Proust*. New Haven: Yale University Press.

———. 1983. "The Rhetoric of Temporality." In *Blindness and Insight: Essays in the Rhetoric of Contemporary Criticism*, 187–228. 2nd ed. rev. Minneapolis: University of Minnesota Press.

Derrida, Jacques. 1976. *Of Grammatology*. Trans. Gayatri Spivak. Baltimore: Johns Hopkins University Press.

———. 1978. "From Restricted to General Economy: A Hegelianism without Reserve." *Writing and Difference*, 251–76. Trans. Alan Bass. Chicago: Chicago University Press.

———. 1993. *Spectres de Marx*. Paris: Galilée.

Dettmer, Helena. 1980. "The Arrangement of Tibullus Books 1 and 2." *Philologus* 124: 68–82.

———. 1983. "The 'Corpus Tibullianum.' " In *Aufstieg und Niedergang der Römischen Welt*, II, 30.3. Hildegard Temporini and ed. Wolfgang Haase, 1962–75. Berlin: Walter de Gruyter.

Dickinson, R. J. 1973. "The *Tristia*: Poetry in Exile." In *Ovid*, ed. J. W. Binns, 154–90. London: Routledge & Kegan Paul.

Dollar, Ben. 1997. "Genre Crossing and Intertextuality in Catullus 68." M.A. thesis, University of Texas at Austin.

Dowling, William C. 1984. *Jameson, Althusser, Marx: An Introduction to the Political Unconscious*. Ithaca: Cornell University Press.

Dreyfus, Hubert L., and Paul Rabinow. 1982. *Michel Foucault: Beyond Structuralism and Hermeneutics*. Chicago: University of Chicago Press.

Dumézil, Georges. 1969. *Idées romaines*. 2nd ed. Paris: Gallimard.

———. 1996. *Archaic Roman Religion*. Trans. Philip Krapp. Baltimore: Johns Hopkins University Press. Originally published 1970.

Dunlop, Philip, trans. 1972. *Tibullus: The Poems*. London: Penguin.

Du Quesnay, I. M. Le M. 1973. "The *Amores*." In *Ovid*, ed. J. W. Binns, 1–48. London: Routledge & Kegan Paul.

Eagleton, Terry. 1976. *Criticism and Ideology: A Study in Marxist Literary Theory*. London: New Left Books.

———. 1983. *Literary Theory: An Introduction*. Minneapolis: University of Minnesota Press.

Eck, Werner. 1984. "Senatorial Self-Representation: Developments in the Augustan Period." In *Caesar Augustus: Seven Apsects*, ed. Fergus Millar and Erich Segal, 129–68. Oxford: Clarendon Press.

Eco, Umberto. 1976. *A Theory of Semiotics*. Bloomington: Indiana University Press.

———. 1985. "How Culture Conditions the Colors We See." In *On Signs*, ed. Marshall Blonsky, 157–75. Baltimore: Johns Hopkins University Press.

Edwards, Catherine. 1993. *The Politics of Immorality in Ancient Rome*. Cambridge: Cambridge University Press.

———. 1996. *Writing Rome: Textual Approaches to the City*. Cambridge: Cambridge University Press.

Edwards, M. J. 1991. "The Theology of Catullus 68b." *Antike und Abendland* 37: 68–81.

Eisenhut, Werner. 1983. *Catulli Veronensis Liber*. Leipzig: Teubner.

Elder, J. P. 1962. "Tibullus: *Tersus Atque Elegans*." In *Critical Essays on Roman Literature: Elegy and Lyric*, ed. J. P. Sullivan, 65–106. Cambridge, Mass.: Harvard University Press.

Elia, Salvatore d'. 1981. "I Presupposti sociologici dell' esperienza elegiaca Properziana." In *Colloquium Propertianum (secundum): Atti*, ed. Francesco Santucci and Salvatore Vivona, 59–80. Assisi: Academia Properziana del Subasio.

Eliot, Vivian, ed. 1971. *T. S. Eliot The Waste Land: A Facsimile of the Original Drafts Including the Annotations of Ezra Pound*. New York: Harcourt Brace and Jovanovich.

Enk, Petrus Johannes. 1946. *Sex. Propertii Elegiarum Liber I (Monobiblos)*. Vol. 2. Leiden: Brill.

Enk, Petrus Johannes. 1962. *Sex. Propertii Elegiarum Liber Secundus.* Vol. 2. Leiden: A. W. Sythoff.

———. 1978. *Ad Propertii Carmina Commentarius Criticus.* New York: Garland. Originally published 1911.

Evans, Harry B. 1983. *Carmina Publica: Ovid's Books from Exile.* Lincoln: University of Nebraska Press.

Fairweather, Janet. 1984. "The 'Gallus Papyrus': A New Interpretation." *Classical Quarterly* 34 (1984): 167–74.

Fantham, Elaine. 1996. *Roman Literary Culture: From Cicero to Apuleius.* Baltimore: Johns Hopkins University Press.

Fear, Trevor. 2000. "The Poet as Pimp: Elegiac Seduction in the Time of Augustus." *Arethusa* 33: 217–39.

Fedeli, Paulo. 1980. *Sesto Properzio: Il Primo libro delle elegie.* Florence: Leo S. Olschki Editore.

———. 1983. "'Properti monobiblos': Struttura e motivi." In *Aufstieg und Niedergang der Römischen Welt,* II, 30.3, ed. Hildegard Temporini and Wolfgang Haase, 1858–1922. Berlin: Walter de Gruyter.

———. 1994. *Sexti Properti Elegiarum Libri IV.* Leipzig: Teubner.

Feeney, D. C. 1992. "'Shall I Compare Thee . . .?': Catullus 68B and the Limits of Analogy." In *Authors and Audience in Latin Literature,* ed. Tony Woodman and Jonathan Powell, 33–44. Cambridge: Cambridge University Press.

Ferguson, John. 1985. *Catullus.* Lawrence, Kans.: Coronado Press.

Fineberg, Brenda. 1991. "Configurations of Desire in the Elegies of Tibullus." Ph.D. diss., University of Chicago.

Fish, Stanley E. 1980. "Interpreting the *Variorum.*" In *Reader Response Criticism: From Formalism to Post-Structuralism,* ed. J. P. Tompkins, 164–84. Baltimore: Johns Hopkins University Press.

Fisher, J. M. 1983. "The Life and Work of Tibullus." In *Aufstieg und Niedergang der Römischen Welt,* II, 30.3, ed. Hildegard Temporini and Wolfgang Haase, 1924–61. Berlin: Walter de Gruyter.

Fitton Brown, A. D. 1985. "The Unreality of Ovid's Tomitan Exile." *Liverpool Classical Monthly* 10.2: 18–22.

Fitzgerald, William. 1995. *Catullan Provocations: Lyric Poetry and the Drama of Position.* Berkeley: University of California Press.

Flynn, Thomas. 1994. "Foucault's Mapping of History." In *The Cambridge Companion to Foucault,* ed. Gary Gutting, 28–46. Cambridge: Cambridge University Press.

Fordyce, C. J. 1978. *Catullus: A Commentary.* Oxford: Clarendon Press.

Foucault, Michel. 1966. *Les mots et les choses.* Paris: Gallimard.

———. 1972. *Histoire de la folie à l'âge classique.* Paris: Gallimard.

———. 1976. *La volonté de savoir.* Vol. 1 of *Histoire de la sexualité.* Paris: Gallimard.

———. 1977a. *Discipline and Punish: The Birth of the Prison.* Trans. Alan Sheridan. New York: Pantheon.

———. 1977b. "A Preface to Transgression." In *Language, Counter-Memory, Practice: Selected Essays and Interviews,* ed. Donald F. Bouchard, 29–52. Trans. Donald F. Bouchard and Sherry Simon. Ithaca: Cornell University Press.

———. 1984. *Le souci de soi*. Vol. 3 of *Histoire de la sexualité*. Paris: Gallimard.

———. 1994a. *Dits et écrits: 1954–1988*. Vol. 4. Ed. Daniel Defert and François Ewalt. Paris: Gallimard.

———. 1994b. "Préface à l' 'Histoire de la sexualité'." In Foucault 1994a: 578–84.

———. 1994c. "A propos de la généalogie de l'éthique: un aperçu du travail en cours." In Foucault 1994a: 609–31.

———. 1994d. "L'écriture de soi." In Foucault 1994a: 415–30.

———. 1994e. "L'herméneutique du sujet." In Foucault 1994a: 353–65.

———. 1994f. "Les techniques de soi." In Foucault 1994a: 783–813.

———. 1994g. "L'éthique du souci de soi comme pratique de la liberté." In Foucault 1994a: 711–12.

———. 1994h. "Subjectivité et vérité." In Foucault 1994a: 213–18.

———. 1994i. "Le Retour de la morale." In Foucault 1994a: 696–703.

Francis, James A. 1995. *Subversive Virtue: Asceticism and Authority in the Second-Century Pagan World*. University Park: Penn State University Press.

Frécaut, Jean-Marc. 1972. *L'esprit et l'humour chez Ovide*. Grenoble: Presse Universitaire de Grenoble.

Fredrick, David. 1997. "Reading Broken Skin: Violence in Roman Elegy." In *Roman Sexualities*, ed. Judith P. Hallett and Marilyn B. Skinner, 172–93. Princeton: Princeton University Press.

Freud, Sigmund. 1952. *On Dreams*. Trans. James Strachey. Standard Edition. New York: Norton.

———. 1955. *An Infantile Neurosis and Other Works*. Trans. James Strachey and Anna Freud. Standard Edition. London: Hogarth Press.

———. 1961a. *Civilization and Its Discontents*. Trans. James Strachey. Standard Edition. New York: Norton.

———. 1961b. *Beyond the Pleasure Principle*. Trans. James Strachey. Standard Edition. New York: Norton.

Frow, John. 1986. *Marxism and Literary History*. Cambridge, Mass.: Harvard University Press.

Fukuyama, Francis. 1992. *The End of History and the Last Man*. New York: Freedom Press.

Gaisser, Julia Haig. 1983. "*Amor, rura* and *militia* in Three Elegies of Tibullus: 1.1, 1.5, 1.10." *Latomus* 42: 58–72.

Galinsky, Karl. 1996. *Augustan Culture: An Interpretive Introduction*. Princeton: Princeton University Press.

Gansiniec, Zofia. 1949. *Tarpeia: The Making of a Myth*. Acta Societatis Archaeologicae Polonorum I. Ed. Kazimierz Majewski. Wrocław.

Gantar, K. 1976. "Einige Beobachtungen zu Catulls C. 68.71–73." *Grazer Beiträge* 5: 117–21.

Garber, Marjorie. 1992. *Vested Interests: Cross-Dressing and Cultural Anxiety*. New York: Routledge.

Gardiner, Michael. 1992. *The Dialogics of Critique: M. M. Bakhtin and The Theory of Ideology*. London: Routledge.

Garrison, Daniel. 1995. *The Student's Catullus*. 2nd ed. Norman: University of Oklahoma Press.

Giardina, G. C. 1977. *Propertius: Elegiarum Liber II*. Torino: Paravia.

Glover, T. R. 1934. "The Literature of the Augustan Age." In *The Cambridge Ancient History*, vol. 10, ed. S. A. Cook, E. A. Adcock, and M. P. Charlesworth, 512–44. Cambridge: Cambridge University Press.

Gold, Barbara K. 1982. "Propertius 3.9: Maecenas as *Eques, Dux, Fautor.*" *Literary and Artistic Patronage in Ancient Rome*, ed. Barbara K. Gold, 103–17. Austin: University of Texas Press.

———. 1987. *Literary Patronage in Greece and Rome*. Chapel Hill: University of North Carolina Press.

———. 1993. "'But Ariadne Was Never There in the First Place': Finding the Female in Roman Poetry." In *Feminist Theory and the Classics*, ed. Nancy Sorkin Rabinowitz and Amy Richlin. 75–101. New York: Routledge.

Goold, G. P., ed. and trans. 1990. *Propertius: Elegies*. Cambridge, Mass.: Harvard University Press.

Goux, Jean Joseph. 1990. *Symbolic Economies after Marx and Freud*. Trans. Jennifer Curtiss Gage. Ithaca: Cornell University Press.

Gowers, Emily. 1993. *The Loaded Table: Representations of Food in Roman Literature*. Oxford: Clarendon Press.

Green, Peter. 1982. *Ovid: The Erotic Poems*. Penguin: London.

———. 1990. *Alexander to Actium: The Historical Evolution of the Hellenistic Age*. Berkeley: University of California Press.

———. 1994. *Ovid: The Poems of Exile*. Penguin: London.

Greene, Ellen. 1994. "Sexual Politics in Ovid's *Amores*: 3.4, 3.8, and 3.12." *Classical Philology* 89: 344–50.

———. 1998. *The Erotics of Domination: Male Desire and the Mistress in Latin Love Poetry*. Baltimore: Johns Hopkins University Press.

———. 1999. "Domination and Deceit as the Way of Love: *Amores* 1.7." *Classical World* 92.5: 409–18.

———. 2000. "Gender Identity and the Hero: Propertius 2.1." *Arethusa* 33: 241–61.

———. Forthcoming. "Gender and Genre in Propertius's Second Book of Elegies."

Greimas, Algirdas Julien. 1987. *On Meaning: Selected Writings on Semiotic Theory*. Trans. Paul J. Perron and Frank H. Collins. Minneapolis: University of Minnesota Press.

Griffin, Jasper. 1977. "Propertius and Antony." *Journal of Roman Studies* 67: 17–26.

———. 1985. *Latin Poets and Roman Life*. London: Duckworth.

Grimal, Pierre. 1951. "Etudes sur Properce, II: César et la légende de Tarpeia." *Revue des études latines* 29: 201–14.

———. 1952. "Les intentions du Properce et la composition du livre IV des 'Elégies.'" *Latomus* 11: 181–97, 315–26, 437–50.

———. 1986. *Love in Ancient Rome*. Trans. Arthur Train Jr. Norman: University of Oklahoma Press.

———. 1987. "Catulle et les origines de l'élégie romaine." *Mélanges d'archéologie et de l'histoire de l'école française de Rome, antiquité* 99: 243–56.

Groag, Edmundus, and Arturus Stein. 1933. *Prosopographia Imperii Romani Saec. I. II. III.* Berlin: De Gruyter.

Gruen, Erich S. 1995. *The Last Generation of the Roman Republic.* 2nd ed. Berkeley: University of California Press. Originally published 1974.

Gunderson, Erik. 1997. "Catullus, Pliny, and Love-Letters." *Transactions of the American Philological Association* 127: 201–29.

Günther, Hans-Christian. 1997. *Quaestiones Propertianae.* Leiden: Brill.

Gurval, Robert Alan. 1995. *Actium and Augustus: The Politics and Emotions of Civil War.* Ann Arbor: University of Michigan Press.

Gutzwiller, Kathryn J., and Ann Norris Michelini. 1991. "Women and Other Strangers: Feminist Perspective in Classical Literature." In *(En)Gendering Knowledge: Feminists in Academe*, ed. Joan E. Hartman and Ellen Messer-Davidow, 66–84. Knoxville: University of Tennnesse Press.

Guyomard, Patrick. 1992. *La jouissance tragique: Antigone, Lacan et le désir de l'analyste.* Paris: Aubier.

Habinek, Thomas. 1997. "The Invention of Sexuality in the World-City of Rome." *The Roman Cultural Revolution*, ed. Thomas Habinek and Alessandro Schiesaro, 23–43. Cambridge: Cambridge University Press.

———. 1998. *The Politics of Latin Literature: Writing, Identity, and Empire in Ancient Rome.* Princeton: Princeton University Press.

Hadot, Pierre. 1987. *Exercices spirituels et philosophie antique.* 2nd ed. Paris: Etudes Augustiniennes.

———. 1992. *La citadelle intérieur: Introduction aux* Pensées *de Marc Aurèle.* Paris: Fayard.

———. 1995. *Philosophy as a Way of Life: Spiritual Exercises from Hadot to Foucault.* Ed. Arnold I. Davidson. Trans. Michael Chase. Oxford: Blackwell.

Hallett, Judith. 1973. "The Role of Women in Roman Elegy: Counter-Cultural Feminism." *Arethusa* 6: 103–23.

———. 1974. "Women in Roman Elegy: A Reply." *Arethusa* 7: 211–17.

———. 1977. "Perusinae Glandes and the Changing Image of Augustus." *American Journal of Ancient History* 2: 151–71.

———. 1993. "Feminist Theory, Historical Periods, Literary Canons, and the Study of Greco-Roman Anitquity." In *Feminist Theory and the Classics.* Ed. Nancy Sorkin Rabinowitz and Amy Richlin, 44–72. New York: Routledge.

Halperin, David M. 1995. *Saint Foucault: Towards a Gay Hagiography.* New York: Oxford University Press.

Hanlon, Christopher. 2001. "Psychoanalysis and the Post-Political: An Interview with Slavoj Žižek." *New Literary History* 32: 1–22.

Hanslik, Rudolf. 1979. *Sex. Propertii Elegiarum Libri IV.* Leipizig: Teubner.

Hardie, Alex. 1983. *Statius and the* Silvae: *Poets, Patrons and Epideixis in the Graeco-Roman World.* Liverpool: Francis Cairns.

Hardt, Michael, and Antonio Negri. 2000. *Empire.* Cambridge, Mass.: Harvard University Press.

Hayles, N. Katherine. 1993. "Constrained Constructivism: Locating Scientific Inquiry in the Theater of Representation." In Levine 1993a: 27–43.

Heiden, Bruce. 1995. "Sic te servato: An Interpretation of Propertius 1.21." *Classical Philology* 90: 161–67.

Hellgouarc'h, Joseph. 1963. *Le vocabulaire latin des relations et des partis politiques sous la république.* Paris: Les Belles Lettres.

Helm, Rudolf. 1963. *Catull Gedichte.* Damrstadt: Wissenschaftliche Buchgesellschaft.

Helzle, Martin. 1988. "Ovid's Poetics of Exile." *Illinois Classical Studies* 13: 73–83.

———. 1989. *Publii Ovidii Nasonis Epistularum ex Ponto liber IV: A Commentary on Poems 1 to 7 and 16.* Hildesheim: Olms.

Henderson, John. 1993. "Persius' Didactic Satire: The Pupil as Teacher." *Ramus* 20: 123–48.

Herndl, Diane Price. 1991. "The Dilemmas of a Feminine Dialogic." In Bauer and McKinstry 1991: 7–24.

Heyne, C. G., and E. C. F. Wunderlich. 1975. *Albius Tibullus: Carmina Libri Tres, cum libro quarto Supliciae et aliorum.* Hildeshiem: Georg Olms. Originally published by Leipzig, 1817.

Higham, T. F. 1934. "Ovid: Some Aspects of His Character and Aim." *Classical Review* 48: 105–16.

Hinds, Stephen. 1998. *Allusion and Intertext: Dynamics of Appropriation in Roman Poetry.* Cambridge: Cambridge University Press.

Hodge, R.I.V., and R. A. Buttimore. 1977. *The "Monobiblos" of Propertius: An Account of the First Book of Propertius Consisting of a Text, Translation, and Critical Essay on Each Poem.* Cambridge: D. S. Brewer.

Holleman, A. W. J. 1969. "Ovidii Metamophoseon liber XV 622–870 (*Carmen et error*)." *Latomus* 28: 42–59.

Holquist, Michael. 1990. *Dialogism: Bakhtin and His World.* London: Routledge.

Hubbard, Margaret. 1974. *Propertius.* Oxford: Oxford University Press.

Hubbard, Thomas K. 1984. "Catullus 68: The Text as Self-Demystification." *Arethusa* 17 (1984): 29–49.

Irigaray, Luce. 1974. *Speculum de l'autre femme.* Paris: Minuit.

———. 1977a. "Le marché des femmes." In *Ce sexe qui n'en est pas un,* 167–85. Paris: Minuit.

———. 1977b. "Des marchandises entre elles." In *Ce sexe qui n'en est pas un,* 189–93. Paris: Minuit.

———. 1977c. "Cosi fan tutti." In *Ce sexe qui n'en est pas un,* 85–101. Paris: Minuit.

———. 1977d. "Quand nos lèvres se parlent." In *Ce sexe qui n'en est pas un,* 205–17. Paris: Minuit.

———. 1977e. "Ce sexe qui n'en est pas un." In *Ce sexe qui n'en est pas un,* 23–32. Paris: Minuit.

———. 1977f. "La 'méchanique' des fluides." In *Ce sexe qui n'en est pas un,* 103–15. Paris: Minuit.

Jacoby, Felix. 1909. "Tibulls erste Elegie." *Rheinische Museum* 64: 601–66.

———. 1910. "Tibulls erste Elegie." *Rheinische Museum* 65: 22–87.

James, Sharon. 2003. *Learned Girls and Male Persuasion: Gender and Reading in Roman Love Elegy.* Berkeley: University of California Press.

Jameson, Fredric. 1972. *Prisonhouse of Language: A Critical Account of Structuralism and Russian Formalism.* Princeton: Princeton University Press.

———. 1981. *The Political Unconscious: Narrative as a Socially Symbolic Act.* Ithaca: Cornell University Press.

———. 1988. "Imaginary and Symbolic in Lacan." In *The Ideologies of Theory*, 1: 75–115. Minneapolis: University of Minnesota Press.

———. 1991. *Postmodernism or the Cultural Logic of Late Capitalism.* London: Verso.

———. 1998. "Marxism and the Historicity of Theory: An Interview with Fredric Jameson." *New Literary History* 29 (1998): 353–84.

Janan, Micaela. 1994. *"When the Lamp Is Shattered": Desire and Narrative in Catullus.* Carbondale: Southern Illinois University Press.

———. 2001. *The Politics of Desire: Propertius IV.* Berkeley: University of California Press.

Jauss, Hans Robert. 1986. "Littérature médiévale et théorie des genres." In *Théorie des genres*, ed. Gerard Genette and Tzvetan Todorov, 37–71. Paris: Seuil.

Johnson, W. R. 1973. "The Emotions of Patriotism: Propertius 4.6." *California Studies in Classical Antiquity* 6: 151–80.

———. 1978–79. "The Desolation of the *Fasti*." *Classical Journal* 74: 7–18.

———. 1982. *The Idea of Lyric: Lyric Modes in Ancient and Modern Poetry.* Berkeley: University of California Press.

———. 1990. "Messalla's Birthday: The Politics of Pastoral." *Arethusa* 23: 93–113.

Jordanova, Ludmilla. 1993. "Museums: Representing the Real?" In Levine 1993a: 255–78.

Joshel, Sandra R. 1992. *Work, Identity and Legal Status at Rome: A Study of the Occupational Inscriptions.* Norman: University of Oklahoma Press.

Julien, Phillipe. 1990. *Pour lire Jacques Lacan.* 2nd ed. Paris: E. P. E. L.

Kang, Liu. 1995. "The Problematics of Mao and Althusser: Alternative Modernity and Cultural Revolution." *Rethinking MARXISM* 8: 1–25.

Kant, Immanuel. 1951. *Critique of Judgement.* Trans. J. H. Bernard. New York: Macmillan.

Kaster, Robert. 1997. "The Shame of the Romans." *Transactions of the American Philological Association* 127: 2–19.

Kennedy, Duncan. 1982. "Gallus and the *Culex*." *Classical Quarterly* 32: 371–89.

———. 1993. *The Arts of Love: Five Essays in the Discourse of Roman Love Elegy.* Cambridge: Cambridge University Press.

Kenney, E. J, ed. 1961. *P. Ovidi Nasonis Amores, Medicamina Faciei Femineae, Ars Amatoria, Remedia Amoris.* Oxford: Oxford University Press.

———. 1969. "Ovid and the Law." *Yale Classical Studies* 21: 241–63.

———. 1983. "Ovid." In *The Cambridge History of Classical Literature*, vol. 2, pt. 3, ed. E. J. Kenney and W. V. Clausen, 124–61. Cambridge: Cambridge University Press.

———. 1990. "Introduction" and "Notes." In Melville 1990: viii–xxxvi and 175–255.

King, Joy K. 1975–76. "Propertius' Programmatic Poetry and the Unity of the *Monobiblos*." *Classical Journal* 71: 108–20.

King, Joy K. 1980a. "Propertius 2.1–12: His Callimachean Second Libellus." *Würzburger Jahrbücher für die Altertumswissenschaft* n.s., 6: 61–84.

———. 1980b. "The Two Galluses of Propertius' Monobiblos." *Philologus* 124: 212–30.

———. 1988. "Catullus' Callimachean Carmina, cc. 65–116." *Classical World* 81: 383–92.

King, Richard. 1990. "Creative Landscaping: Inspiration and Artifice in Propertius 4.4." *Classical Journal* 85: 225–48.

Kittler, Friedrich A. 1999. *Gramophone, Film, Typewriter*. Trans. Geoffrey Winthrop-Young and Michael Wutz. Stanford: Stanford University Press.

Koenen, Ludwig. 1976. "Egyptian Influence in Tibullus." *Illinois Classical Studies* 1: 125–59.

Konstan, David. 1994. *Sexual Symmetry: Love in the Ancient Novel and Related Genres*. Princeton: University Press.

———. 1997. *Friendship in the Classical World*. Cambridge: Cambridge University Press.

Kraffert, Herrmann. 1883. *Beiträge zur Kritik und Erklärung lateinscher Autoren*. Aurich: R. Reents.

Kremer-Marietti, Angèle. 1985. *Michel Foucault: Archéologie et généalogie*. 2nd ed. rev. Paris: Livre de Poche.

Kristeva, Julia. 1977. "D'une identité l'autre." In *Polylogue*, 149–72. Paris: Seuil.

———. 1979. "Le temps des femmes." *Cahiers de rechereche de S. T. D. Paris VII* 5: 5–18.

———. 1982. *Powers of Horror: An Essay on Abjection*. Trans. Léon Roudiez. New York: Columbia University Press.

———. 1983. "Stabat Mater." In *Histoires d'amour*, 223–47. Paris: Edition Denoël.

———. 1989. *Black Sun: Depression and Melancholia*. Trans. Leon S. Roudiez. New York: Columbia University Press.

Kroll, Wilhelm. 1980. *Catull*. Stuttgart: Teubner. Originally published 1922.

Krostenko, Brian A. 2001. *Cicero, Catullus, and the Language of Social Performance*. Chicago: University of Chicago Press.

Kuhn, Thomas. 1962. *The Structure of Scientific Revolutions*. Chicago: University of Chicago Press.

Labate, Mario. 1987. "Elegia triste ed elegia lieta. Un caso di riconversione letteraria." *Materiali e discussioni per l'analisi dei testi classici* 19: 91–129.

Lacan, Jacques. 1966a. "De nos antécédents." In *Ecrits I*, 79–97. Paris: Seuil.

———. 1966b. "Le stade du miroir comme formateur de la fonction du Je." In *Ecrits I*, 89–97. Paris: Seuil.

———. 1966c. "Le séminaire sur 'La Lettre Volée.'" *Ecrits I*, 18–75. Paris: Seuil.

———. 1973. *Le séminaire livre XI: Les quatre concepts fondamentaux de la psychanalyse*. Ed. Jacques-Alain Miller. Paris: Seuil.

———. 1975. *Le séminaire livre XX: Encore*. Ed. Jacques-Alain Miller. Paris: Seuil.

———. 1976. "Le sinthome." Unpublished transcript of the twenty-third seminar in the library of the University of Texas, Arlington.

———. 1982. "Seminar of 21 January 1975." In *Feminine Sexuality: Jacques Lacan and the école freudienne*, ed. Juliet Mitchell and Jacqueline Rose, 162–71. Trans. Jacqueline Rose. New York: Pantheon.

———. 1986. *Le séminaire VII: L'éthique de la psychanalyse*. Ed. Jacques-Alain Miller. Paris: Seuil.

———. 1991. *Le séminaire VIII: Le transfert*. Ed. Jacques-Alain Miller. Paris: Seuil.

Lachmann, Karl. 1873. *Q. Valerii Catulli Veronensis Liber*. 3rd ed. Berlin: Ge. Remeri.

———. 1973. *Sextus Propertius: Carmina*. Olms: Hildesheim. Originally published 1816.

La Penna, Antonio. 1977. *L'integrazione difficile: Un profilo di Properzio*. Turin: Einaudi.

Laqueur, Thomas. 1990. *Making Sex: Body and Gender from the Greeks to Freud*. Cambridge, Mass.: Harvard University Press.

Larmour, David H. J., Paul Allen Miller, and Charles Platter. 1998. "Introduction: Situating the *History of Sexuality*." In *Rethinking Sexuality: Foucault and Classical Antiquity*, ed. David H. J. Larmour, Paul Allen Miller, and Charles Platter, 3–41. Princeton: Princeton University Press.

Last, H. 1934. "The Social Policy of Augustus." In *The Cambridge Ancient History*, vol. 10, ed. S. A. Cook, F. E. Adcock, and M. P. Charlesworth, 423–64. Cambridge: Cambridge University Press.

Leach, Eleanor Winsor. 1978. "Vergil, Horace, Tibullus: Three Collections of Ten." *Ramus* 7: 79–105.

———. 1980a. "Poetics and Poetic Design in Tibullus' First Elegiac Book." *Arethusa* 13: 79–96.

———. 1980b. "Sacral-Idyllic Landscape Painting and the Poems of Tibullus' First Book." *Latomus* 39 (1980): 47–69.

———. 1999. "Ciceronian '*Bi-Marcus*': Correspondence with M. Terentius Varro and L. Papirius Paetus in 46 B.C.E." *Transactions of the American Philological Association* 129: 139–79.

Lee, Guy. 1974. "*Otium cum indignitate*: Tibullus 1.1." In *Quality and Pleasure in Latin Poetry*, ed. Tony Woodman and David West, 94–114. Cambridge: Cambridge University Press.

———. 1982. *Tibullus: Elegies*. Leeds: Francis Cairns.

Lee-Stecum, Parshia. 1998. *Powerplay in Tibullus: Reading Elegies Book One*. Cambridge: Cambridge University Press.

Lefèvre, Eckard. 1991. "Was Hatte Catull in der Kapsel, die er von Rom nach Verona mitnahm? Zu Aufbau und Aussage der Allius- Elegie." *Rheinisches Museum für Philologie* 134: 311–26.

Lefkowitz, Mary. 1981. *Heroines and Hysterics*. New York: St. Martin's Press.

Lemaire, Nicolaus Eligius. 1832. *Sexti Aurelii Propertii Elegiarum Libri Quattuor*. Paris: Julius Didot.

Leo, Friedrich. 1960. "Das Schlussgedicht der ersten Buches des Properz." In *Ausgewählte kleine Schriften*, vol. 2, ed. Eduard Fraenkel, 169–78. Rome: Edizioni di Storia e Letteratura.

Levine, George, ed. 1993a. *Realism and Representation: Essays on the Problem of Realism in Relation to Science, Literature and Culture.* Madison: University of Wisconsin Press.

———. 1993b. "Looking for the Real: Epistemology in Science and Culture." In Levine 1993a: 3–23.

Liberman, Gauthier. 1995. "En Lisant Properce." *Mélanges de l'Ecole française de Rome, Italie et Méditerranée* 107: 315–34.

Lieberg, Godo. 1962. *Puella Divina: Die Gestalt de göttlicher Geliebten bei Catulle im Zusammenhang der antiken Dichtung.* Amsterdam: P. Schippers.

Lilja, Saara. 1965. *The Roman Elegists' Attitude to Women.* Annales Academiae Scientiarum Fennicae, vol. 135, series B. Helsinki: Academia Scientiarum Fennicae.

Little, D. 1990. "Ovid's Last Poems: Cry of Frolic from Exile or Literary Frolic in Rome?" *Prudentia* 22: 23–29.

Littlewood, R. J. 1970. "The Symbolic Structure of Tibullus Book 1." *Latomus* 29: 661–69.

———. 1983. "Humour in Tibullus." In *Aufstieg und Niedergang der Römischen Welt,* II, 30.3, ed. Hildegard Temporini and Wolfgang Hause, 2128–58. Berlin: Walter de Gruyter.

Luck, Georg. 1960. *The Latin Love Elegy.* New York: Barnes & Noble.

———. 1977. *P. Ovidius Naso: Tristia.* Vol. 2. Heidelberg: Carl Winter.

———. 1988. *Tibullus.* Stuttgart: Teubner.

Lyne, R.O.A.M. 1980. *The Latin Love Poets: From Catullus to Ovid.* Oxford: Oxford University Press.

Macey, David. 1993. *The Lives of Michel Foucault.* New York: Pantheon.

Mack, Sara. 1988. *Ovid.* New Haven: Yale University Press.

MacCleod, C. W. 1974. "A Use of Myth in Ancient Poetry." *Classical Quarterly* 24: 82–93.

Maleuvre, Jean-Yves. 1998. *Jeux de masques dans l'élégie latine: Tibulle, Properce, Ovide.* Louvain: Editions Peeters.

Maltby, Robert. 1980. *Latin Love Elegy.* Waucunda, Ill: Bolchazy-Carducci.

Marr, J. L. 1970. "Notes on Propertius 4.1 and 4.4." *Classical Quarterly,* n.s. 21: 160–73.

Martin, Charles. 1992. *Catullus.* New Haven: Yale University Press.

Martyn, John R. C. 1981. "Naso-*Desultor amoris* (Amores I–III)." In *Aufstieg und Niedergang der Römischen Welt,* II.31.4, ed. Wolfgang Haase, 2436–59. Berlin: De Gruyter.

McKeown, J. C. 1987. *Ovid: Amores, Text, Prolegomena and Commentary in Four Volumes.* Vol. 1. Leeds: Francis Cairns.

———. 1989. *Ovid: Amores, Text, Prolegomena and Commentary in Four Volumes.* Vol. 2. Leeds: Francis Cairns.

———. 1998. *Ovid: Amores, Text, Prolegomena and Commentary in Four Volumes.* Vol. 3. Leeds: Francis Cairns.

Melville, A. D., trans. 1990. *Ovid: The Love Poems.* Oxford: Oxford University Press.

Merriam, C. U. 1990. "The New Gallus Revisited." *Latomus* 49: 443–52.

Merrill, Elmer Truesdale. 1893. *Catullus.* Cambridge, Mass.: Harvard University Press.

Miles, Gary B. 1992. "The First Roman Marriage and the Theft of the Sabine Women." In *Innovations of Antiquity*, ed. Ralph Hexter and Daniel Selden, 161–96. New York: Routledge.

Miller, J. Hillis. 1981. "The Ethics of Reading: Vast Gaps and Parting Hours." In *American Criticism in the Poststructuralist Age*, ed. Ira Konigsberg, 19–41. Ann Arbor: University of Michigan Press.

Miller, James. 1993. *The Passion of Michel Foucault*. New York: Simon and Schuster.

Miller, Paul Allen. 1989. "Sive deae seu sint dirae obscenaeque volucres." *Arethusa* 22: 47–79.

———. 1994. *Lyric Texts and Lyric Consciousness: The Birth of a Genre from Archaic Greece to Augustan Rome*. London: Routledge.

———. 1995. "The Minotaur Within: Fire, the Labyrinth, and Strategies of Containment in *Aeneid* 5 and 6." *Classical Philology* 90: 225–40.

———. 1998a. "Catullan Consciousness, the 'Care of the Self,' and the Force of the Negative in History." In Larmour et al., 171–203. Princeton: Princeton University Press.

———. 1998b. "Images of Sterility: The Bodily Grotesque in Roman Satire." *Arethusa* 31: 257–83.

———. 1999. "The Classical Roots of Poststructuralism: Lacan, Derrida, and Foucault." *International Journal of the Classical Tradition* 5: 204–25.

———. 2002. *Latin Erotic Elegy: An Anthology and Reader*. London: Routledge.

Miller, Paul Allen, and Charles Platter. 1999. "Crux as Symptom: Augustan Elegy and Beyond." *Classical World* 92: 445–54.

Minyard, J. D. 1988. "The Source of the Catulli Veronensis Liber." *Classical World* 81: 343–53.

Moi, Toril. 1985. *Sexual/Textual Politics: Feminist Literary Theory*. London: Routledge.

Moore, Timothy J. 1989. "Tibullus 1.7: Reconciliation through Conflict." *Classical World* 82: 423–31.

Morris, Meaghan. 1988. "The Pirate's Fiancée: Feminists and Philosophers, or Maybe Tonight It'll Happen." In *Feminism and Foucault: Reflections on Resistance*, ed. Irene Diamond and Lee Quinby, 21–42. Boston: Northeastern University Press.

Morson, Gary Saul. 1989. "Parody, History, and Metaparody." In *Rethinking Bakhtin: Extensions and Challenges*, ed. Gary Saul Morson and Caryl Emerson, 63–86. Evanston, Ill.: Northwestern University Press.

Morson, Gary Saul, and Caryl Emerson. 1990. *Mikhail Bakhtin: Creation of a Prosaics*. Stanford: Stanford University Press.

Moxey, Keith P. F. 1991. "Semiotics and the Social History of Art." *New Literary History* 22: 985–99.

Munari, Franco, ed. and trans. 1970. *P. Ovidi Nasonis Amores*. Florence: La Nuova Italia.

Murgatroyd, Paul. 1991. *Tibullus 1*. Bristol: Bristol Classical Press. Originally published Natal, 1980.

———. 1994. *Tibullus: Elegies II*. Oxford: Oxford University Press.

Myers, Tony. 2001. "Modernity, Postmodernity, and the Future Perfect." *New Literary History* 32: 33–46.

Mynors, R. A. B. 1958. *Valerii Catulli Carmina*. Oxford: Oxford University Press.

Nagle, Betty Rose. 1980. *The Poetics of Exile: Program and Polemic in the* Tristia *and* Epistulae ex Ponto *of Ovid*. Brussels: Collection Latomus.

Nagy, Gregory. 1974. *Comparative Studies in Greek and Indic Meter*. Cambridge, Mass.: Harvard University Press.

———. 1990. *Pindar's Homer: The Lyric Possession of an Epic Past*. Baltimore: Johns Hopkins University Press.

Nappa, Christopher. 2001. *Aspects of Catullus' Social Fiction*. Frankfurt am Main: Peter Lang.

Nell, Sharon Diane. 2000. "Julie and Anamorphosis: The Spectacle of Death in *La nouvelle Heloise*." Paper presented at the Western Society for Eighteenth Century Studies, Las Vegas.

Nethercut, William Robert. 1963. "Propertius and Augustus." Ph.D. diss. Columbia University.

———. 1971. "The ΣΦΡΑΓΙΣ of the Monobiblos." *American Journal of Philology* 92: 464–72.

———. 1976. Review of Ross's *Backgrounds to Augustan Poetry*. *American Journal of Philology* 97: 412–13.

———. 1983. "Recent Scholarship on Propertius." In *Aufstieg und Niedergang der Römischen Welt*, II, 30.3, ed. Hildegard Temporini and Wolfgang Haase, 1813–57. Berlin: Walter de Gruyter.

Newman, John Kevin. 1997. *Augustan Propertius: The Recapitulation of a Genre*. Hildesheim: Olms.

Newman, Robert J. 1989. "*Cotidie meditare*. Theory and Practice of the *meditatio* in Imperial Stoicism." In *Aufstieg und Niedergang der Römischen Welt*, II, 36.3, ed. Hildegard Temporini and Wolfgang Haase, 1473–517. Berlin: Walter de Gruyter.

Nicholson, Nigel. 1998–99. "Bodies without Names, Names without Bodies: Propertius 1.21–22." *Classical Journal* 94: 143–61.

Nicolet, Claude. 1966. *L'ordre équestre à l'époque républicaine*. vol. 1. Paris: Editions de Boccard.

Nippel, Wilfried. 1995. *Public Order in Ancient Rome*. Cambridge: Cambridge University Press.

Nugent, S. Georgia. 1990. "*Tristia* 2: Ovid and Augustus." In *Between Republic and Empire: Interpretations of Augustus and His Principate*, ed. Kurt A. Raaflaub and Mark Toher, 239–57. Berkeley: University of California Press.

O'Gorman, Ellen. 1997. "Love and the Family: Augustus and Ovidian Elegy." *Arethusa* 30: 103–23.

O'Hara, James J. 1989. "The New Gallus and the Alternae Voces of Propertius 1.10.10." *Classical Quarterly* 39: 561–62.

Oliensis, Ellie. 1997. "The Erotics of *Amicita*: Readings in Tibullus, Propertius, and Horace." In *Roman Sexualities*, ed. Judith P. Hallett and Marilyn B. Skinner, 151–71. Princeton: Princeton University Press.

Ollfors, Anders. 1967. *Textkritische und interpretatorische Beiträge zu Lucan*. Acta Regiae Societatis Scientiarum et Litterarum Gothoburgensis. Humaniora 2. Göteborg.

O'Neill, Kerill. 1995. "Propertius 4.4 and the Burden of Aetiology." *Hermathena* 158: 53–60.

Olstein, Katherin. 1980. "*Amores* 1.9 and the Structure of Book 1." *Studies in Latin Literature and Roman History*, vol. 2, ed. Carl Deroux, 286–300. Brussels: Collection Latomus.

Otis, Brooks. 1966. *Ovid as an Epic Poet*. Cambridge: Cambridge: University Press.

Paganelli, D. 1964. *Properce: Elégies*. Paris: Budé.

Page, D. L. ed., 1975. *Epigrammata Graeca*. Oxford: Oxford University Press.

Paley, Frederick A. 1853. *The Elegies of Propertius with English Notes*. London: John W. Parker and Son.

Parker, Douglass. 1969. "The Ovidian Coda." *Arion* 8: 80–97.

Parker, Holt N. 1997. "The Teratogenic Grid." In *Roman Sexualities*, ed. Judith P. Hallett and Marilyn B. Skinner, 47–65. Princeton: Princeton University Press.

Parkhurst, Michael. 1995. "Adorno and the Practice of Theory." *Rethinking MARXISM* 8: 48–58.

Perrone, Giovanni. 1989. "Alcune note filologiche su Properzio IV 4,1–20." *Civiltà classica e cristiana* 10: 49–69.

———. 1991a. "Un Problema testuale nel monologo di Tarpeia (Prop. IV 4,34)." *Civiltà classica e cristiana* 12: 83–86.

———. 1991b. "Tarpeia Regina: Una crux in Prop. IV 4,55." *Civiltà classica e cristiana* 12: 285–95.

Philips, Charles Robert, III. 1980. "Love's Companions and Ovid, *Amores* 1.2." In *Studies in Latin Literature and Roman History*, vol. 2, ed. Carl Deroux, 269–77. Brussels: Collection Latomus.

Philips, Jane E. 1976. "The Pattern of Images in Catullus 68.51–62." *American Journal of Philology* 97: 340–43.

Pillinger, Hugh E. 1969. "Some Callimachean Influences on Propertius Book 4." *Harvard Studies in Classical Philology* 73: 171–200.

Platter, Charles. 1995. "*Officium* in Catullus and Propertius: A Foucauldian Reading." *Classical Philology* 90: 211–24.

Ponchont, Max, ed. 1967. *Tibulle et les auteurs du corpus tibullianum*. Paris: Société d'édition "Les Belles-Lettres."

Pöschl, Viktor. 1983. *Catull*. Freiburg: Verlag Ploetz.

Postgate, J. P. 1884. *Select Elegies of Propertius*. London: Macmillan.

———. 1910. *Selections from Tibullus and Others*. London: Macmillan.

———. 1915. *Tibulli Aliorumque Carminum Libri Tres*. Oxford: Oxford University Press.

Powell, Barry B. 1974. "The Ordering of Tibullus Book 1." *Classical Philology* 69: 107–12.

Prato, Carlo. 1964. *Gli Epigrammi Attribuiti a L. Anneo Seneca*. Roma: Ateneo.

Pucci, Pietro. 1961. "Il Carme 50 di Catullo." *Maia* 13: 249–56.

Puhvel, Jaan. *Comparative Mythology*. Baltimore: Johns Hopkins University Press, 1987.

Putnam, Michael C. J. 1973. *Tibullus: A Commentary*. Norman: University of Oklahoma Press.

Putnam, Michael C. J. 1974. "Catullus 11: The Ironies of Integrity." *Ramus* 3: 70–86.

———. 1976. "Propertius 1.22: A Poet's Self-Definition." *Quaderni urbinati di cultura classica* 23: 93–123.

———. 1980. "Propertius and the New Gallus Fragment." *Zeitschrift für Papyrologie und Epigraphik* 39: 49–56.

———. 1982. "Simple Tibullus and the Ruse of Style." In *Essays on Latin Lyric, Elegy and Epic*, 163–74. Princeton: Princeton University Press.

Quinn, Kenneth. 1969. *The Catullan Revolution*. Cambridge: Cambridge University Press.

———. 1973. *Catullus: The Poems*. New York: St. Martin's.

Rabasa, José. 2001. "*For* Empire." *Rethinking MARXISM* 13: 8–15.

Rabinowitz, Nancy Sorkin. 1993. *Anxiety Unveiled: Euripides and the Traffic in Women*. Ithaca: Cornell University Press.

Ragland-Sullivan, Ellie. 1986. *Jacques Lacan and the Philosophy of Psychoanalysis*. Urbana: University of Illinois Press.

Richardson, L., Jr. 1977. *Propertius: Elegies I–IV*. Norman: University of Oklahoma Press.

Richter, R. 1873. *De Albii Tibulli tribus primis carminibus disputatio*. Progr. Zwickau.

Riposati, Benedetto. 1945. *Introduzione allo studio di Tibullo*. Como: Carlo Marzorati.

Ross, David O., Jr. 1969. *Style and Tradition in Catullus*. Cambridge, Mass.: Harvard University Press.

———. 1975. *Backgrounds to Augustan Poetry: Gallus, Elegy and Rome*. Cambridge, Mass.: Harvard University Press.

Rothstein, Max. 1979. *Die Elegien des Sextus Propertius*. 2 vols. 2nd ed. New York: Garland. Originally published 1920.

Rothwell, K. S. 1996. "Propertius on the Site of Rome." *Latomus* 55: 829–54.

Roudinesco, Elizabeth. 1997. *Jacques Lacan*. Trans. Barbara Bray. New York: Columbia University Press.

Rouse, Joseph. 1994. "Power/Knowledge." In *The Cambridge Companion to Foucault*, ed. Gary Gutting, 92–114. Cambridge: Cambridge University Press.

Rubino, Carl A. 1975. "The Erotic World of Catullus." *Classical World* 68: 289–98.

Rutledge, Harry C. 1964. "Propertius' *Tarpeia*: The Poem Itself." *Classical Journal* 60: 68–73.

Rykwert, Joseph. 1976. *The Idea of a Town: The Anthropology of Urban Form in Rome, Italy, and the Ancient World*. Princeton: Princeton University Press.

Ste. Croix, G.E.M. de. 1981. *The Class Struggle in the Ancient Greek World: From the Archaic Age to the Arab Conquests*. Ithaca: Cornell University Press.

Saller, Richard P. 1982. *Personal Patronage under the Early Empire*. Cambridge: Cambridge University Press.

Salvatore, Armando. 1965. *Studi Catulliani*. Naples: Libreria Scientifica Editrice.

Santirocco, Matthew S. 1986. *Unity and Design in Horace's Odes*. Chapel Hill: University of North Carolina Press.

———. 1995. "Horace and Augustan Ideology." *Arethusa* 28: 225–43.

Sarkissian, John. 1983. *Catullus 68: An Interpretation*. Mnemosyne Supplement 76. Leiden: E. J. Brill.

Schneiderman, Stuart. 1983. *Jacques Lacan: The Death of an Intellectual Hero*. Cambridge, Mass.: Harvard University Press.

Schoonhoven, Henk. 1983. "The 'Panegyricus Messallae': Date and Relation with Catalepton 9." In *Aufstieg und Niedergang der Römischen Welt*, II, 30.3, ed. Hildegard Temporini and Wolfgang Haase, 1681–1707. Berlin: Walter de Gruyter.

Schwab, Gail M. 1991. "Irigarayan Dialogism: Play and Powerplay." In Bauer and McKinstry 1991: 57–72.

Scullard, H. H. 1963. *From the Gracchi to Nero: A History of Rome from 133 BC to AD 68*. London: Methuen.

Sedgwick, Eve Kosofsky. 1990. *Epistemology of the Closet*. Berkeley: University of California Press.

Shackleton Bailey, D. R. 1967. *Propertiana*. Amsterdam: Hakkert. Originally published 1956.

———, ed. and trans. 1999. *Cicero: Letters to Atticus*. Vol. 4. Cambridge, Mass.: Harvard University Press.

Sharrock, A. R. 1990. "Alternae Voces—Again." *Classical Quarterly* 40: 570–71.

———. 1995. "The Drooping Rose: Elegiac Failure in *Amores* 3.7." *Ramus* 24: 152–80.

———. 2000. "Constructing Characters in Propertius." *Arethusa* 33: 263–84.

Shelton, Jo-Ann. 1998. *As the Romans Did: A Sourcebook in Roman Social History*. 2nd ed. Oxford: Oxford University Press.

Shipton, K.M.W. 1983. "A House in the City: Catullus 68,68." *Latomus* 42: 869–76.

———. 1985. "Catullus 68 and the Myth of Agememnon." *Latomus* 44: 55–71.

———. 1987. "No Alternative to Ceremonial Negligence (Catullus 68.73ff.)." *Symbolae Osloenses* 62: 51–68.

Showerman, Grant, ed. and trans. 1977. *Heroides and Amores*. 2nd ed. Rev. G. P. Goold. Cambridge, Mass.: Harvard University Press.

Skinner, Marilyn. 1981. *Catullus' Passer: The Arrangement of the Book of Polymetric Poems*. New York: Arno Press.

———. 1988. "Aesthetic Patterning in Catullus: Textual Structures, Systems of Imagery and Book Arrangements. Introduction." *Classical World* 81: 337–40.

Skutsch, Franz. 1906. *Aus Virgil's Fruehzeit: Gallus und Vergil*. Leipzig: Teubner.

Smith, K. F. 1964. *The Elegies of Albius Tibullus*. Darmstadt: Wissenschaftliche Buchgesellschaft. Originally published 1913.

Spivak, Gayatri Chakravorty. 1976. "Translator's Preface." In *Of Grammatology*, by Jacques Derrida, ix–lxxxvii. Baltimore: Johns Hopkins University Press.

Stahl, Hans Peter. 1985. *Propertius: "Love" and "War": Individual and State Under Augustus*. Berkeley: University of California Press.

Staples, Ariadne. 1998. *From Good Goddess to Vestal Virgins: Sex and Category in Roman Religion*. London: Routledge.

Stapleton, M. L. 1996. *Harmful Eloquence: Ovid's* Amores *from Antiquity to Shakespeare*. Ann Arbor: University of Michigan Press.

Steele, Cassie Premo. 2000. *We Heal from Memory: Sexton, Lorde, Anzaldúa and the Poetry of Witness*. New York: Palgrave.

Steele, Meili. 1997. *Theorizing Textual Subjects: Agency and Oppression.* Cambridge: Cambridge University Press.

Stoekl, Allan. 1992. *Agonies of the Intellectual: Commitment, Subjectivity, and the Performative in the Twentieth-Century French Tradition.* Lincoln: University of Nebraska Press.

Stroh, Wilfried. 1979. "Ovids Liebkunst und die Ehegesetze des Augustus." *Gymnasium* 86: 323–52.

Suits, Thomas A. 1976. "The Iambic Character of Propertius 1.4." *Philologus* 120: 86–91.

Sullivan, J. P. 1964. *Ezra Pound and Sextus Propertius: A Study in Creative Translation.* Austin: University of Texas Press.

———. 1972. "The Politics of Elegy." *Arethusa* 5: 17–34.

———. 1976. *Propertius: A Critical Introduction.* Cambridge: Cambridge University Press.

———. 1984. "Propertius Book IV: Themes and Structures." *Illinois Classical Studies* 9: 30–34.

Sweet, Fredrick. 1972. "Propertius and Political Panegyric." *Arethusa* 5: 169–75.

Syme, Ronald. 1960. *The Roman Revolution.* Oxford: Oxford University Press.

———. 1978. *History in Ovid.* Oxford: Clarendon Press.

Tatum, W. Jeffrey. 1997. "Friendship, Politics, and Literature in Catullus: Poems 1, 65 and 66, 116." *Classical Quarterly* 47: 482–500.

Taylor, Lilly Ross. 1925. "Horace's Equestrian Career." *American Journal of Philology* 46: 161–70.

———. 1968. "Republican and Augustan Writers Enrolled in the Equestrian Centuries." *Transactions of the American Philological Association* 99: 469–86.

Thibault, John C. 1964. *The Mystery of Ovid's Exile.* Berkeley: University of California Press.

Thomas, Richard F. 1979. "New Comedy, Callimachus, and Roman Poetry." *Harvard Studies in Classical Philology* 83 (1979): 179–206.

Thompson, D.F.S. 1997. *Catullus: Edited with a Textual and Interpretive Commentary.* Toronto: University of Toronto Press.

Todorov, Tzvetan. 1984. *Mikhail Bakhtin: The Dialogical Principle.* Trans. Wlad Godzich. Minneapolis: University of Minnesota Press.

Tracy, Valerie A. 1978–79. "Ovid's Self-Portrait in the *Amores.*" *Helios* 6: 57–62.

———. 1979. "One Aspect of *nequitia* in Ovid's *Amores.*" *Latomus* 164: 343–48.

Traill, David A. 1992. "Ovid, *Tristia* 2.8, 296, and 507: Happier Solutions." *Hermes* 120: 504–7.

———. 1994. "Propertius 1.21: The Sister, the Bones, and the Wayfarer." *American Journal of Philology* 115: 89–96.

Tränkle, Hermann. 1960. *Die Sprachkust des Properz und die Tradition der lateinischen Dichtersprache.* Wiesbaden: Franz Steiner.

———. 1983. "Properzio poeta dell' opposizione politica?" In *Colloquium Propertianum (tertium): Atti,* ed. Salvatore Vivona, 149–62. Assisi: Academia Properziana del Subasio.

Trypanis, C. A., ed. and trans. 1978. *Callimachus: Aetia, Iambi, Hecale, and other Fragments.* Cambridge, Mass.: Harvard University Press.

Valvo, Alfredo. 1983. "M. Valerio Messalla Corvino negil studi più recenti." In *Aufstieg und Niedergang der Römischen Welt*, II, 30.3, ed. Wolfgang Haase, 1663–80. Berlin: Walter de Gruyter.

Van der Stockt, Luc. 1999a. "A Plutarchan Hypomnema on Self-Love." *American Journal of Philology* 120: 575–99.

———. 1999b. "Three Aristotles Equal but One Plato: On a Cluster of Quotations in Plutarch." In *Plutarco, Platón y Aristóteles. Actas del V Congresso de la I. P. S. (Madrid-Cuenca, 4–7 de mayo de 1999)*, 127–40. Madrid: Ediciones Clásicas.

Van Nortwick, Thomas. 1990. "*Huc Veniet Messalla Meus*: Commentary on Johnson." *Arethusa* 23: 115–23.

Verducci, Florence. 1984. "On the Sequence of Gallus' Epigrams: *Molles Elegi, Vasta Triumphi Pondera*." *Quaderni urbinati du cultura classica* 45: 119–36.

Vernant, Jean-Pierre. 1990. "Greek Religion, Ancient Religion." Trans. H. Piat. *Mortals and Immortals: Collected Essays*, ed. Froma I. Zeitlin, 269–89. Princeton: Princeton University Press.

Veyne, Paul. 1987. "The Roman Empire." In *A History of Private Life*, vol. 1, *From Pagan Rome to Byzantium*, ed. Philippe Ariès and Georges Duby, 5–234. Trans. Arthur Goldhammer. Cambridge, Mass.: Harvard University Press.

———. 1988. *Roman Erotic Elegy: Love Poetry and the West*. Trans. David Pellauer. Chicago: University of Chicago Press.

Viarre, Simone. 1988. "Les aspects mythiques du pays d'exil dans les *Tristes* et les *Pontiques* d'Ovide." In *Peuples et pays mythiques: Actes de Ve Colloque du Centre de Recherches Mythologiques de l'Université de Paris X, Chantilly, 18–20 septembre 1986*, ed. François Jouan and Bernard Deforge, 149–58. Paris: Les Belles Lettres.

Videau-Delibes, Anne. 1988. "Parole de l'interruption, interruption de la parole (sur les "Tristes" d'Ovide)." *Bulletin de l'association Guillaume Budé*, no. 1 (March): 26–37.

———. 1991. *Les* Tristes *d'Ovide et l'élégie romaine: Une poétique de la rupture*. Paris: Klincksieck.

Villalobos-Ruminott, Sergio. 2001. "*Empire*, a Picture of the World." Trans. Isis Sadek. *Rethinking MARXISM* 13: 31–42.

Voloshinov, V. N. 1986. *Marxism and the Philosophy of Language*. Trans. Ladislav Matejka and I. R. Titunik. Cambridge, Mass.: Harvard University Press.

Wallace-Hadrill, Andrew. 1985. "Propaganda and Dissent? Augustan Moral Legislation and the Love-Poets." *Klio* 67: 180–84.

———. 1997. "*Mutatio morum*: The Idea of a Cultural Revolution." In *The Roman Cultural Revolution*, ed. Thomas Habinek and Alessandro Schiesaro, 3–22. Cambridge: Cambridge University Press.

Walter, Hermann. 1999. "Zum Gedichtschluss von Ovid, *Am.* 1,2." In *Ovid: Werk und Wirkung, Festgabe für Michael von Albrecht zum 65 Geburtstag*, vol. 1, ed. Werner Schubert, 87–98. Frankfurt: Peter Lang.

Walters, Jonathan. 1997. "Invading the Roman Body: Manliness and Impenetrability in Roman Thought." In *Roman Sexualities*, ed. Judith P. Hallett and Marilyn B. Skinner, 29–43. Princeton: Princeton University Press.

Warden, John. 1978. "Another Would-Be Amazon: Propertius 4.4.71–72." *Hermes* 106: 177–87.

Weed, Elizabeth. 1994. "The Question of Style." In *Engaging with Irigaray*, ed. Carolyne Burke, Naomi Schor, and Margaret Whitford, 79–109. New York: Columbia University Press.

Wellesley, Kenneth. 1969. "Propertius' Tarpeia Poem (IV 4)." *Acta classica universitatis scientiarum Debreceniensis* 5: 93–103.

Whitaker, Richard. 1983. *Myth and Personal Experience in Roman Love-Elegy: A Study in Poetic Technique*. Göttingen: Vanderhoek & Ruprecht.

White, Peter. 1993. *Promised Verse: Poets in the Society of Augustan Rome*. Cambridge, Mass.: Harvard University Press.

Wiedemann, Thomas. 1975. "The Political Background to Ovid's *Tristia* 2." *Classical Quarterly* 25: 264–71.

Wiggers, Nancy. 1977. "Reconsideration of Propertius 2.1." *Classical Journal* 72 (1977): 334–41.

Wilamowitz-Moellendorf, Ulrich von. 1924. *Hellenistische Dichtung*. Vol. 2. Berlin: Weidmann.

Wilkinson, L. P. 1974. *The Roman Experience*. New York: University Press of America.

Wille, Günther. 1984. "Zum künstlerischen Aufbau von Ovids *Amores*." In *Navicula Tubingensis—Studia in honorem Antonii Tovar*, ed. Franzisco J. Oroz Rizcuren, 389–423. Tübingen: Günther Narr Verlag.

Williams, Gareth D. 1994. *Banished Voices: Readings in Ovid's Exile Poetry*. Cambridge: Cambridge University Press.

Williams, Gordon. 1968. *Tradition and Originality in Roman Poetry*. Oxford: Clarendon Press.

———. 1980. *Figures of Thought in Roman Poetry*. New Haven: Yale University Press.

Wimmel, Walter. 1976. *Tibull und Delia: Erster Teil, Tibulls Elegie 1,1*. Hermes: Zeitschrift für klassiche Philologie: Einzelschriften, Heft 37. Wiesbaden: Franz Steiner Verlag.

Wiseman, T. P. 1969. *Catullan Questions*. Leicester: Leicester University Press.

———. 1982. "*Pete nobiles amicos*: Poets and Patrons in Late Republican Rome." In *Literary and Artistic Patronage in Ancient Rome*, ed. Barbara K. Gold, 28–49. Austin: University of Texas Press.

———. 1985. *Catullus and His World: A Reappraisal*. Cambridge: Cambridge University Press.

Wray, David. 2001. *Catullus and the Poetics of Roman Manhood*. Cambridge: Cambridge University Press.

———. Forthcoming. "What Poets Do: Tibullus on 'Easy' Hands." *Classical Philology*.

Wyke, Maria. 1987. "The Elegiac Woman at Rome." *Proceedings of the Cambridge Philological Society*, n.s., 33: 153–78.

———. 1989. "Mistress and Metaphor in Augustan Elegy." *Helios* 16: 25–47.

———. 1995. "Taking the Woman's Part: Engendering Roman Love Elegy." In *Roman Literature and Ideology: Ramus Essays for J. P. Sullivan*, ed. A. J. Boyle, 110–28. Bendigo, Australia: Aureal.

Zajko, Vanda. 1997. "False Things Which Seem Like the Truth." In *Compromising Traditions: The Personal Voice in Classical Scholarship*, ed. Judith P. Hallett and Thomas Van Nortwick, 54–72. New York: Routledge.

Zizek, S. 1989. *The Sublime Object of Ideology.* London: Verso.

———. 1991. *Looking Awry: An Introduction to Jacques Lacan through Popular Culture.* Cambridge, Mass.: MIT Press.

———. 1993. *Tarrying with the Negative: Kant, Hegel, and the Critique of Ideology.* Durham, N.C.: Duke University Press.

INDEX LOCORUM

GENERAL INDEX